The Artist's Guide to SKETCHING

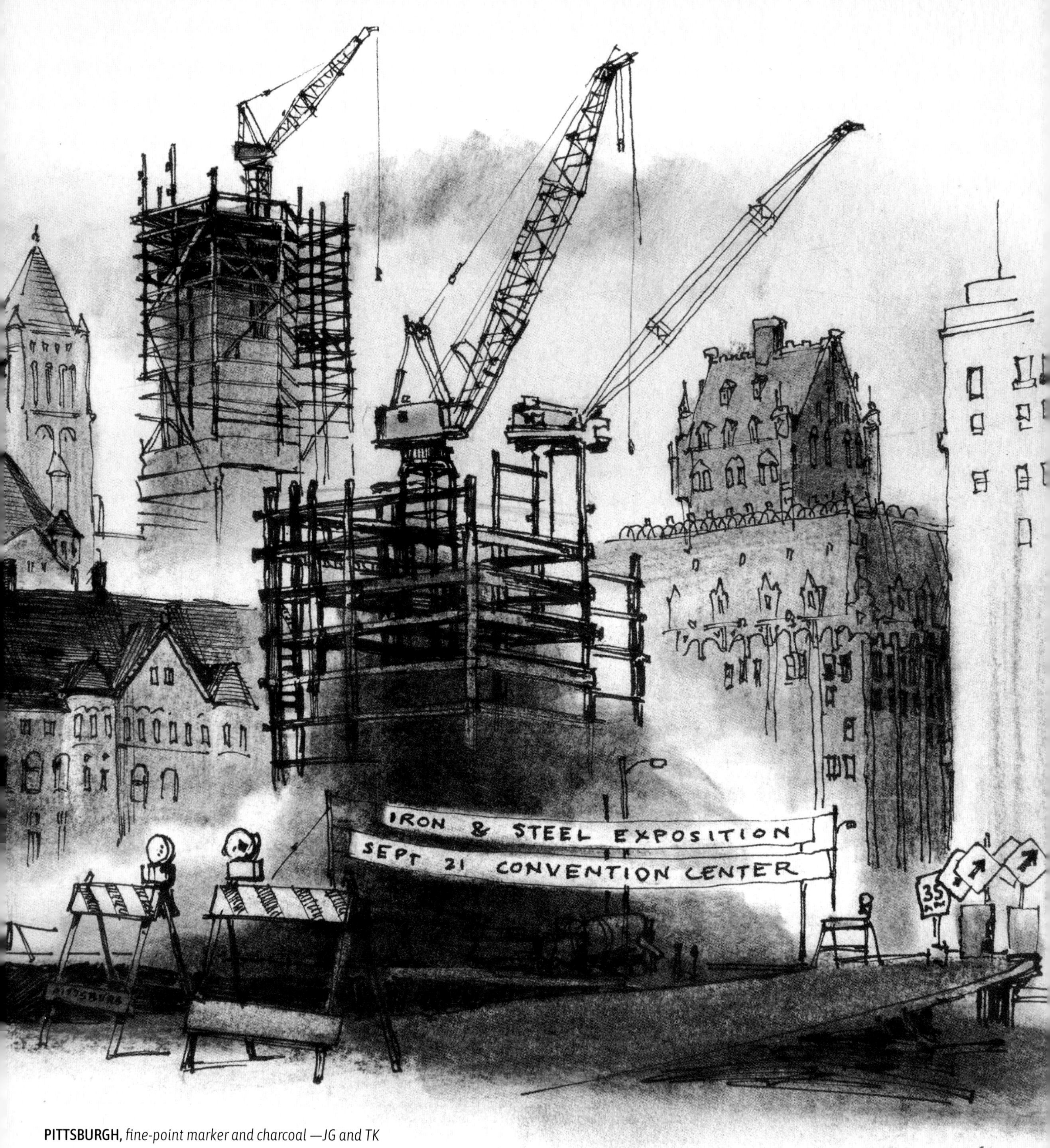

PITTSBURGH, *fine-point marker and charcoal —JG and TK*

The Artist's Guide to SKETCHING

The Classic Book about Making Art on Location

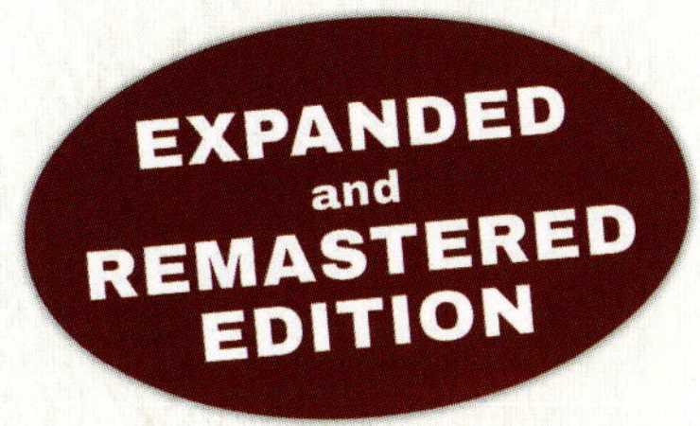

James Gurney and Thomas Kinkade

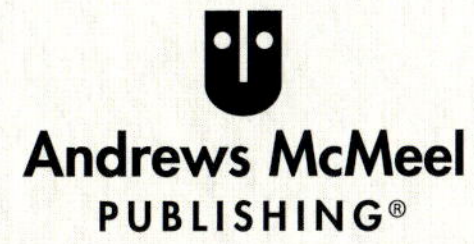

Andrews McMeel Publishing
a division of Andrews McMeel Universal
1130 Walnut Street, Kansas City, Missouri 64106

www.andrewsmcmeel.com

Originally published as *The Artist's Guide to Sketching: A Handbook for Drawing On-the-Spot* by Watson-Guptill Publications, 1982

A special thank you to Jeanette Gurney, Nanette Kinkade, Chandler Kinkade, and Merritt Kinkade for their artistic and editorial guidance in the expanded and remastered edition of *The Artist's Guide to Sketching.*

25 26 27 28 29 TEN 10 9 8 7 6 5 4 3 2 1

ISBN: 978-1-5248-9293-7

Library of Congress Control Number: 2024944267

Editor: Lucas Wetzel
Art Director: Holly Swayne
Production Editor: Brianna Westervelt
Production Manager: Tamara Haus

Contents

CHAPTER 9: EXPLORING THE MAN-MADE WORLD 149

CHAPTER 10: SKETCHING IN YOUR LIFE 160

How We Wrote This Book on Sketching

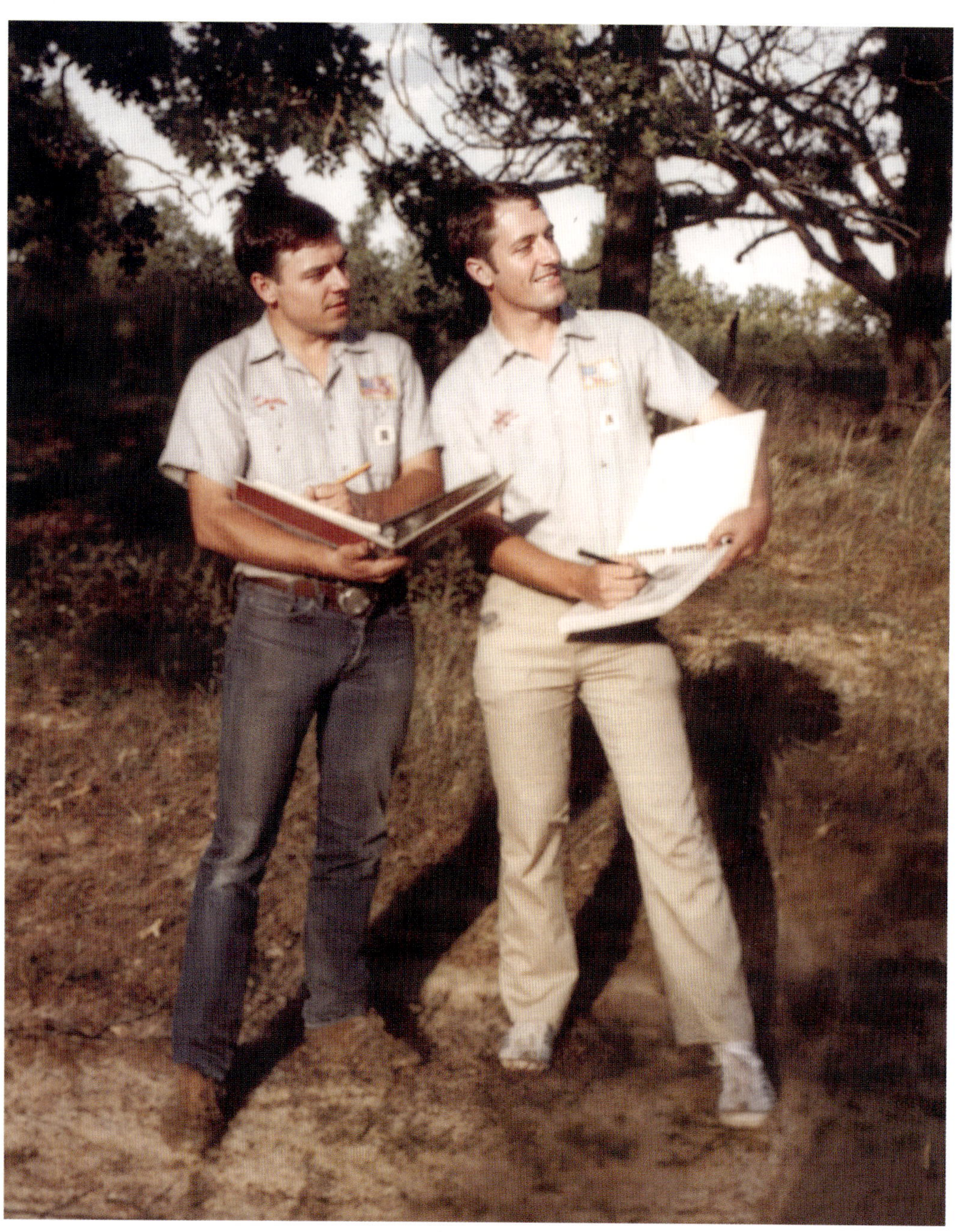

by James Gurney

BEFORE HE WAS the Painter of Light, and before I was the creator of *Dinotopia,* Tom Kinkade and I were two unknown and penniless art students. We had grown weary of sitting in windowless classrooms enduring lectures about art theory. We hatched an audacious plan to drop out of school for a while, hop on a freight train, and discover America, documenting everything in our sketchbooks. Our heroes were Lewis and Clark, John Steinbeck, and Jack Kerouac. My mother was so terrified of the fate that might befall me (her brother was killed by a freight train) that she took out a life insurance policy on me.

On September 16, 1980, a friend dropped us off at the Los Angeles freight yard. We spotted a boxcar with an open door, threw our backpacks into it, climbed aboard, and sat in the shadows waiting for the train to start rolling east.

I first met Tom Kinkade four years earlier, when he was assigned as my freshman-year roommate at UC Berkeley. During the time I knew him, he was painting gritty urban scenes and "street people." The print business, with its glowing cottages, came later. We saw ourselves as rootless bohemians, called each other "Jackson," and invented a secret language that only we understood so we could comment freely in public. We concocted the train riding idea after we

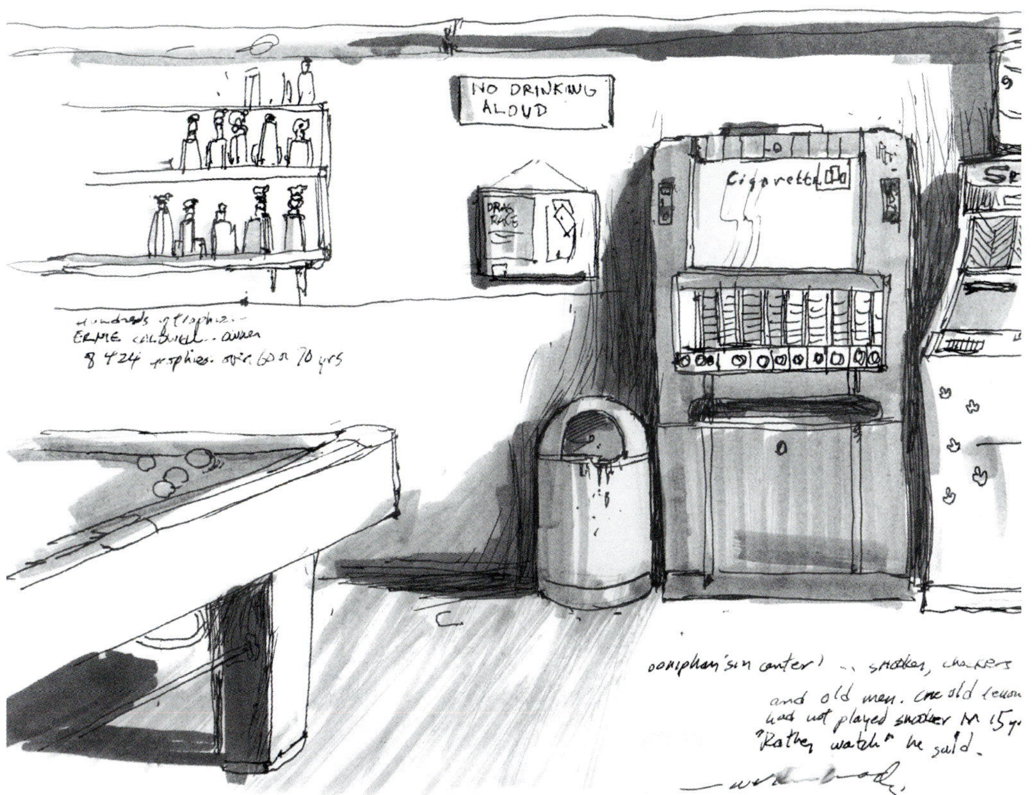

▲ **SIN CENTER, DONIPHAN, MISSOURI,** *fine-line and gray markers on smooth paper* —TK

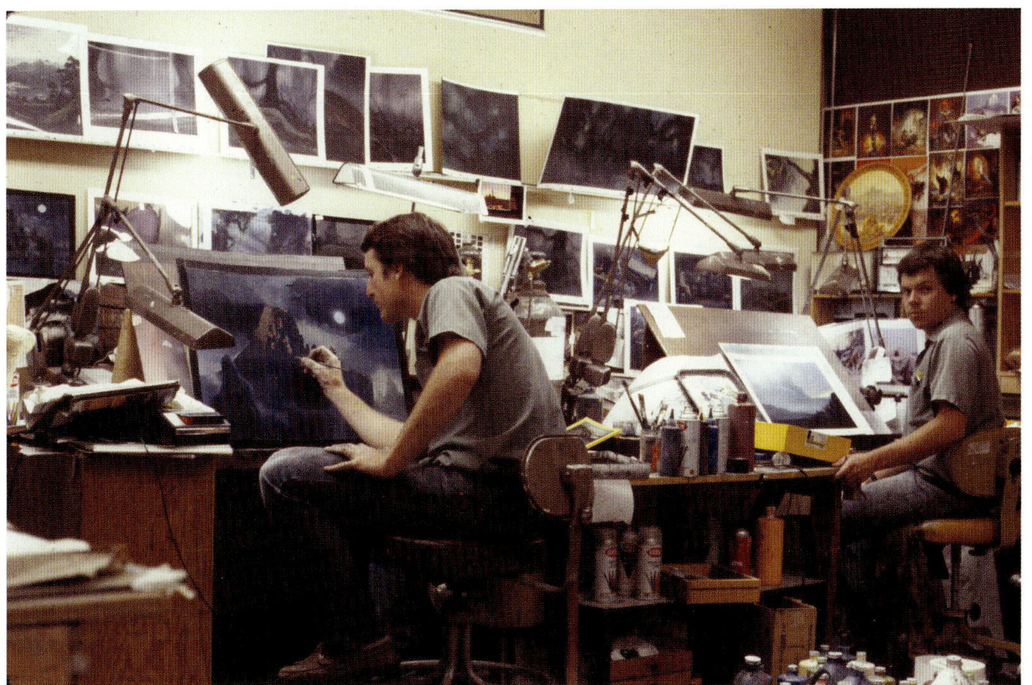

met a guy named Bud at a freight yard in Los Angeles. He told us which train cars to ride and where to catch them.

We got short haircuts and matching gas-station uniform shirts that said "Jim" and "Tom." We packed our backpacks with sketchbooks, pens, gray markers, corncob pipes, felt hats, a cheap camera, tape recorders, and harmonicas. We slept in graveyards and on rooftops and sketched portraits of lumberjacks and coal miners. To make money we drew two-dollar portraits in bars by the light of cigarette machines. One night we slept in the bicycle parking room of a college dorm. Another night we slept on top of a load of hay bales stacked on a parked truck. The truck started rolling at dawn, and we had to jump onto the cab to get the driver to stop. We spent some time in the little town of Doniphan, Missouri, where Tom's mom lived.

We boarded the freights again and rode all the way to Willard, Ohio, where we were kicked off at gunpoint by police officers, who had received reports that we were trying to fly a kite off the top of the train. By the time we got to New York City, we had concocted another crazy idea: to write a how-to book on sketching. We figured out the basic plan for the book on paper placemats from a Burger King on the Upper West Side. We made the rounds of the publishers without much luck.

After returning to Los Angeles, we still had no money, so we got a job painting backgrounds for an animated film called *Fire and Ice*. We eventually got the book contract from Watson-Guptill, but we had to break the news to the film's producer that we would have to write our book on sketching during long weekends while still keeping up our production quotas. *The Artist's Guide to Sketching* was published in 1982. It is as much about the adventure of sketching on the road as it is about technique.

We never returned to art school. My friend Jeanette and I stayed in touch, and we did some sketching trips together. She eventually graduated from art school, and I learned what I could from her class notes. After the book was published, Tom returned to his hometown and married Nanette, his childhood sweetheart, and I married Jeanette. Tom and I were Best Man for each other's weddings.

I was always friendly with Tom in later years, but we were both busy and lived on opposite ends of the USA. Our families got together for a few painting excursions during the subsequent decades, to Ireland, to Colorado, and to the Catskills of New York State. Tom and I didn't keep in close contact with each other during the years he was building up his print company, and I was only dimly aware of the personal issues that eventually led to his death in 2012. Our friendship was partly fueled by a good-natured, high-spirited friendly competition and a spirit of daring and discovery that still drives me today. The Kinkade I knew was a puckish prankster, fearless and exuberant. He was a good foil to my personality, a Huck Finn to my Tom Sawyer.

In the more than four decades since *The Artist's Guide to Sketching* was first published, sketching from life has grown more and more popular. I've been pleased to witness the emergence of the movements that have come to be known as "plein-air painting" and "urban sketching." Today aspiring artists can find friends in almost any region of the world and share their sketches and stories with online communities.

Writing this book was my art education. It set the personal compass for my career afterward. It's no accident that I conceived *Dinotopia* as an explorer's sketchbook. Sketching in black and white was a helpful training ground for me to learn painting in full color. But the greatest benefit of sketching has been connecting with new places and new people. It taught me to be not just an eyewitness but also an engaged participant in the ever-changing world around us.

In compiling this new edition, we've kept everything as it was as much as possible, except for the "Materials" chapter, where we've updated the art supplies to include what's available now. We've also added the following pages of artwork, which were not included in the original edition.

—James Gurney
Rhinebeck, New York, 2023

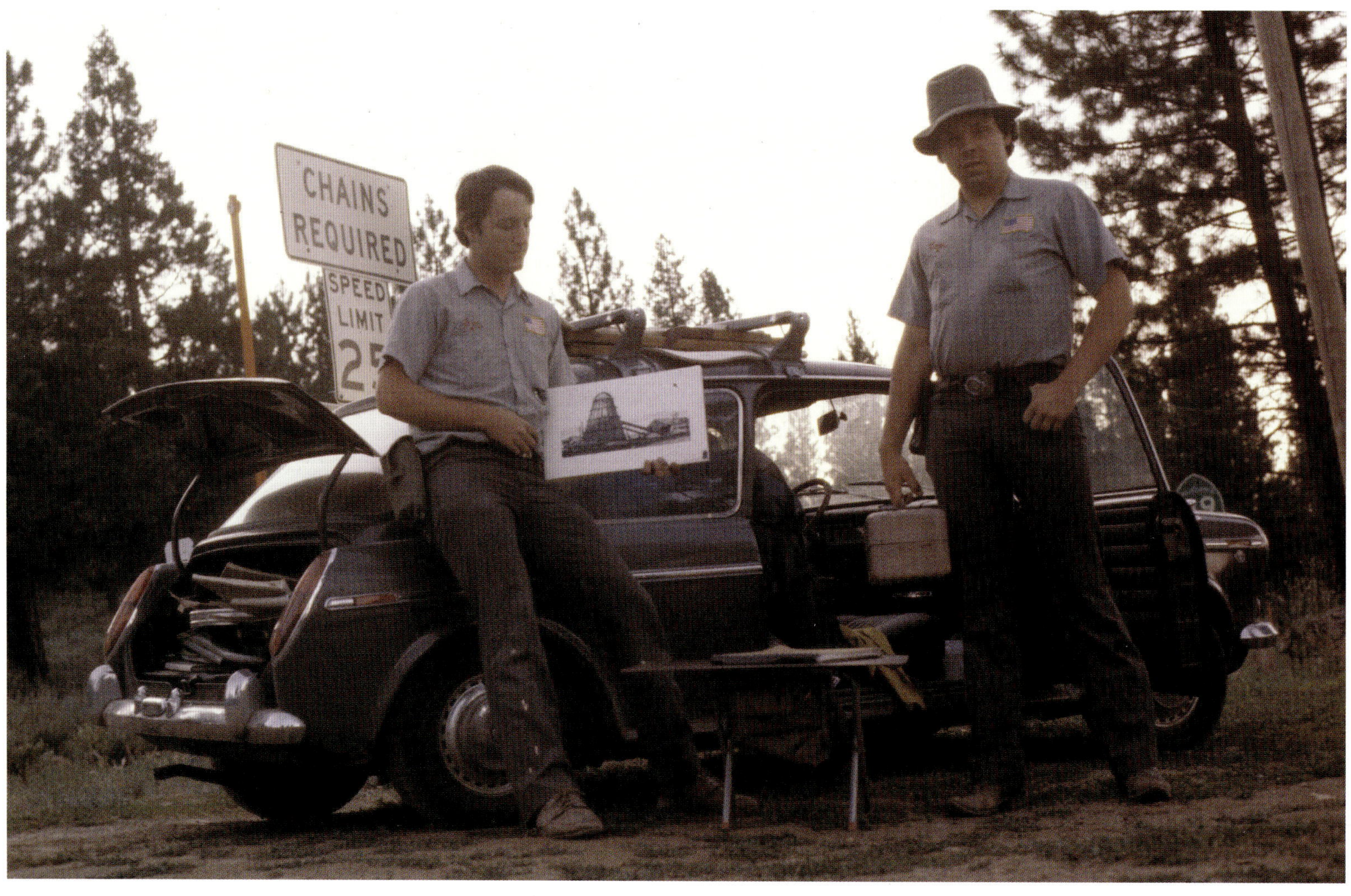

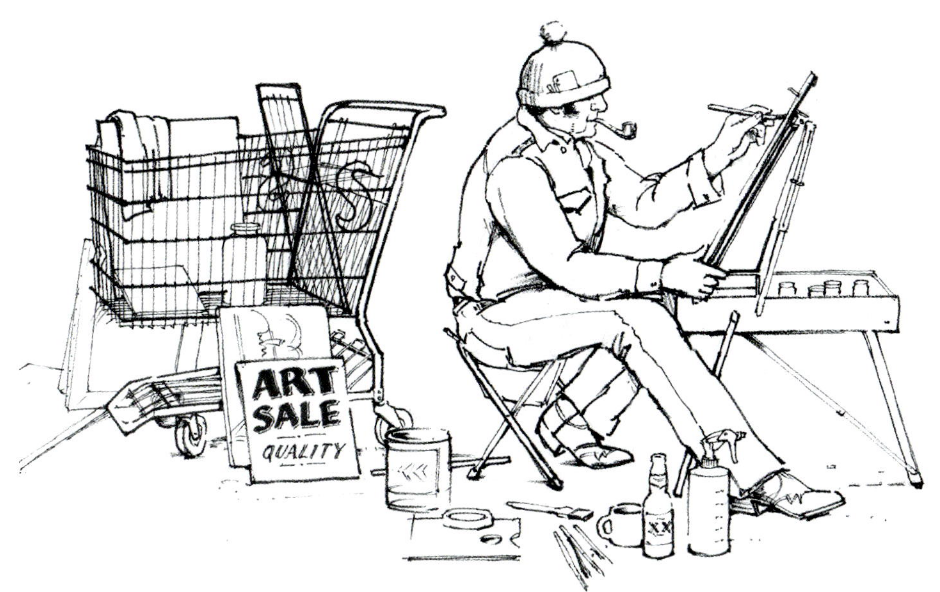

▲ **TOM KINKADE AS A STARVING ARTIST,** *dip pen on smooth paper —JG*

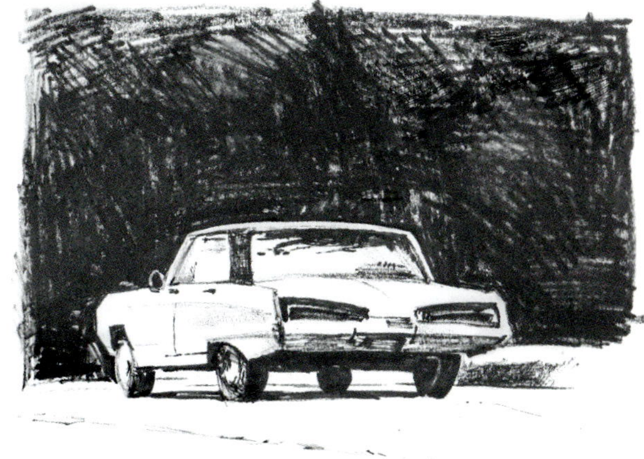

▲ **PARKED CAR,** *calligraphy marker on drawing paper —TK*

▼ **BARBERSHOP,** *brush and ink on smooth paper —JG*

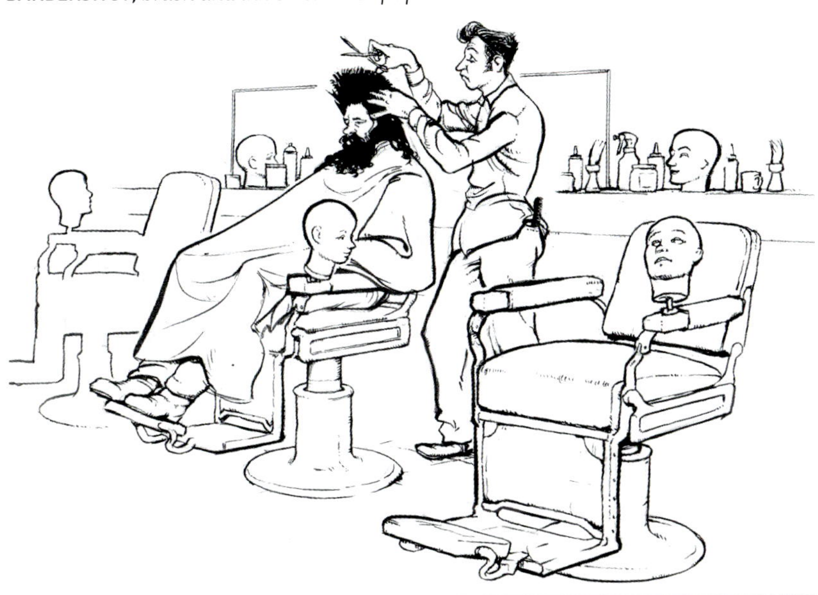

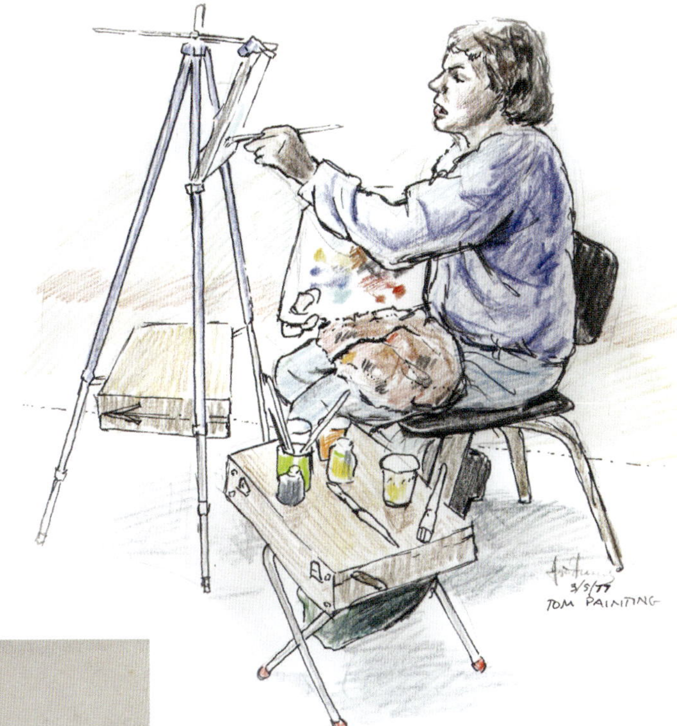

▲ **TOM PAINTING IN OUR DORM ROOM,** *fine-line marker and colored pencils —JG*

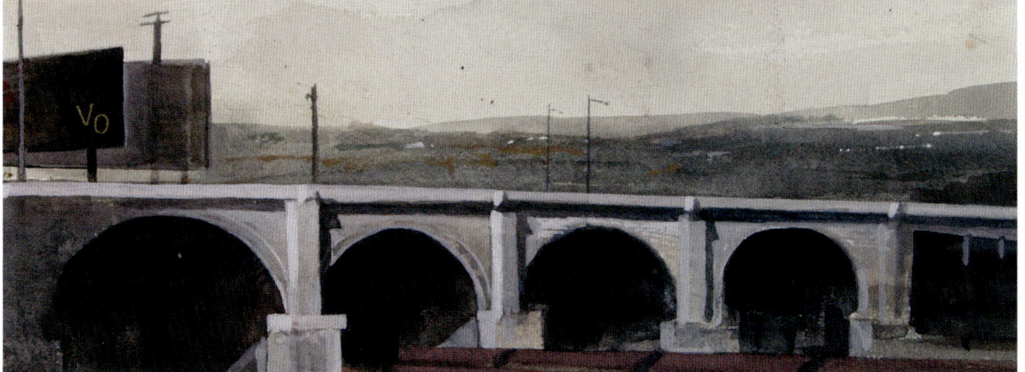

◀ **SIXTH STREET VIADUCT,** *watercolor and gouache —TK*

▶ **CARD SHOP, NIAGARA FALLS,** *fine-line and gray markers on smooth paper —TK*

▼ **CHEVROLET TRUCK,** *oil on panel —JG*

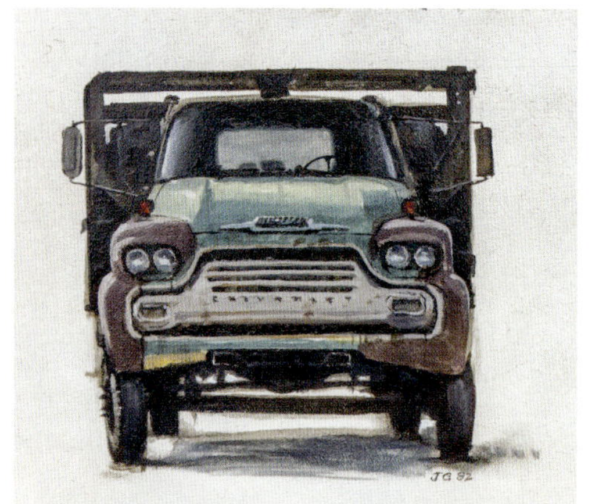

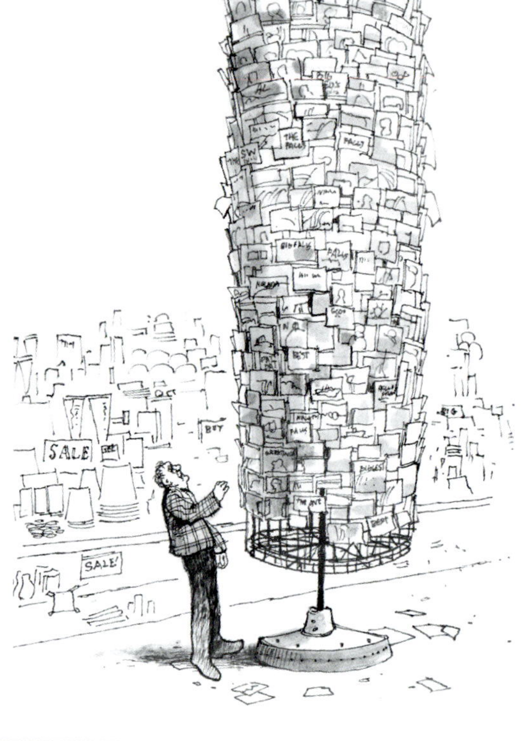

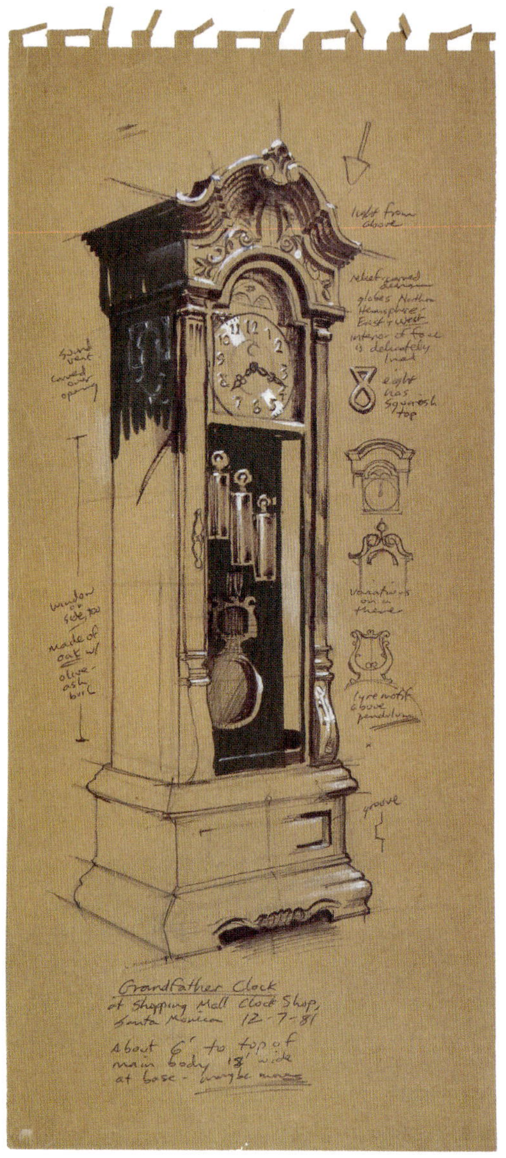

▲ **GRANDFATHER CLOCK,** *calligraphy marker and white gel pen —JG*

◀ **BILLBOARD,** *markers, pen, and gouache —TK*

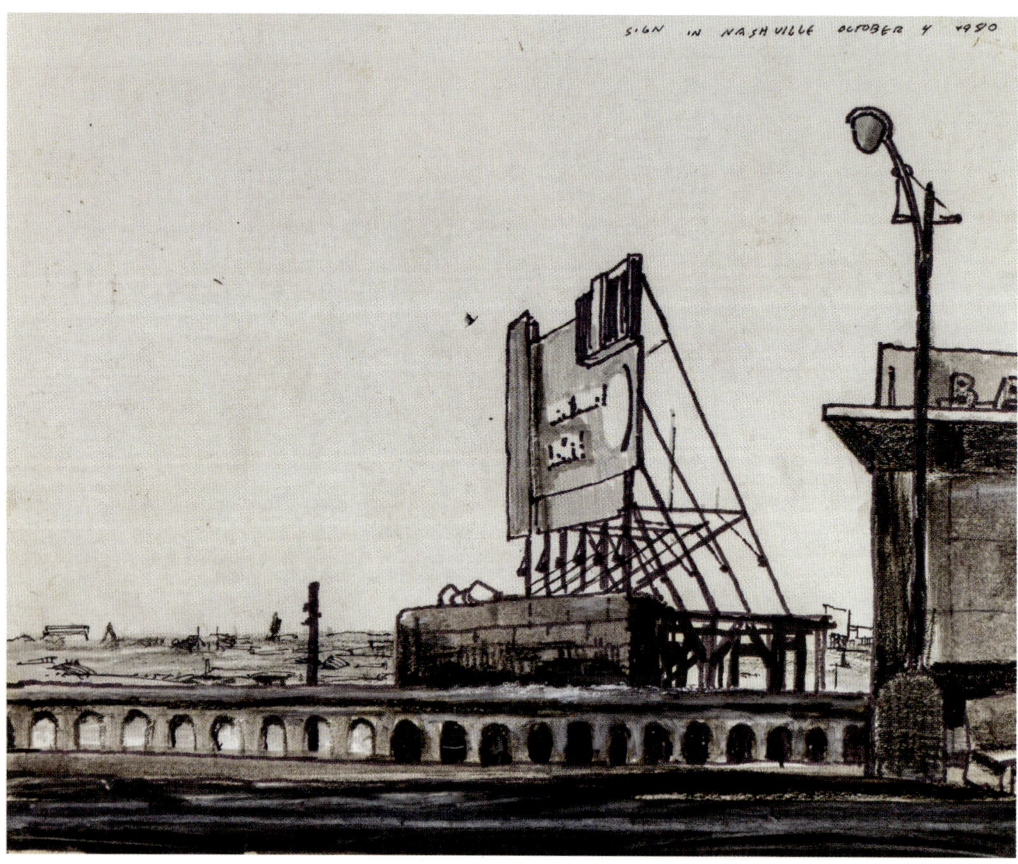

▼ **FARM NEAR JULIAN,** *oil on panel —JG*

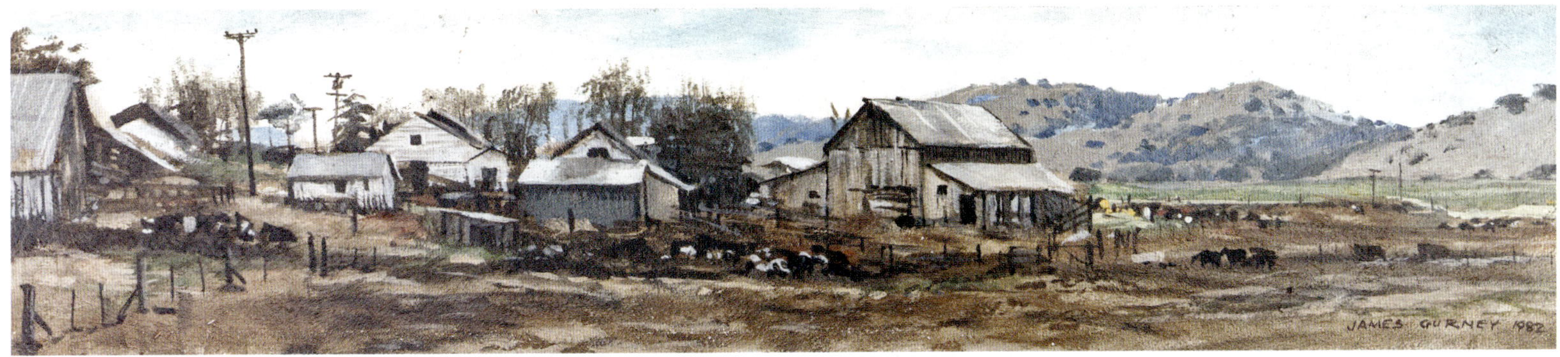

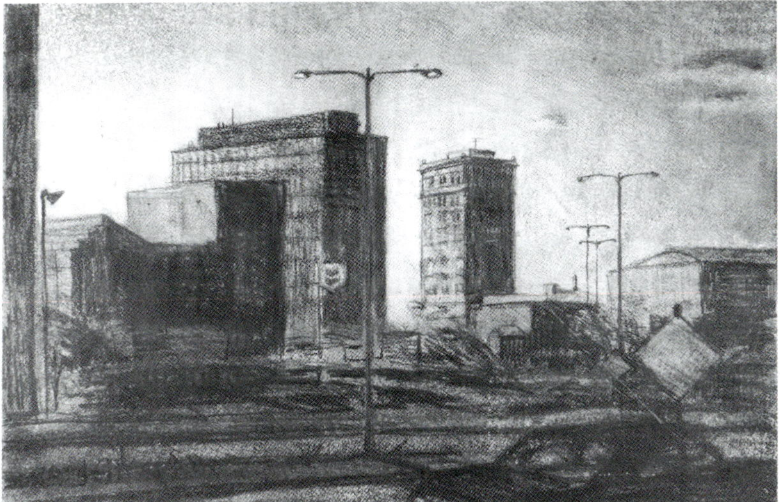

▲ **DOWNTOWN,** *charcoal and marker —TK*

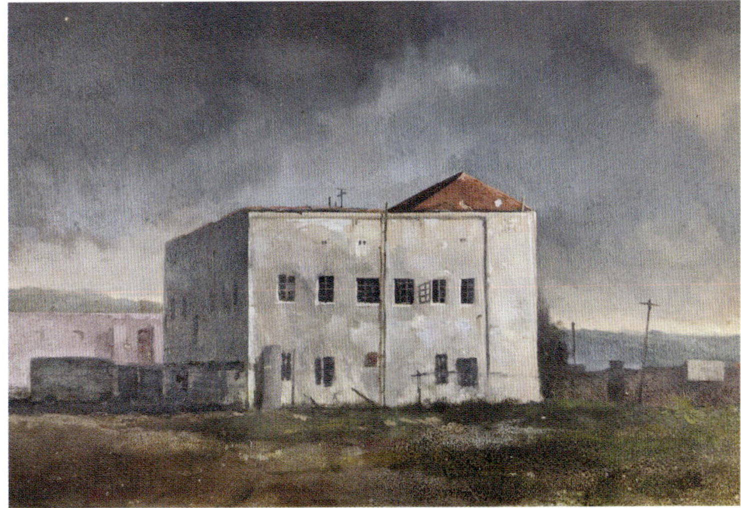

▲ **WAREHOUSE,** *oil on panel —TK*

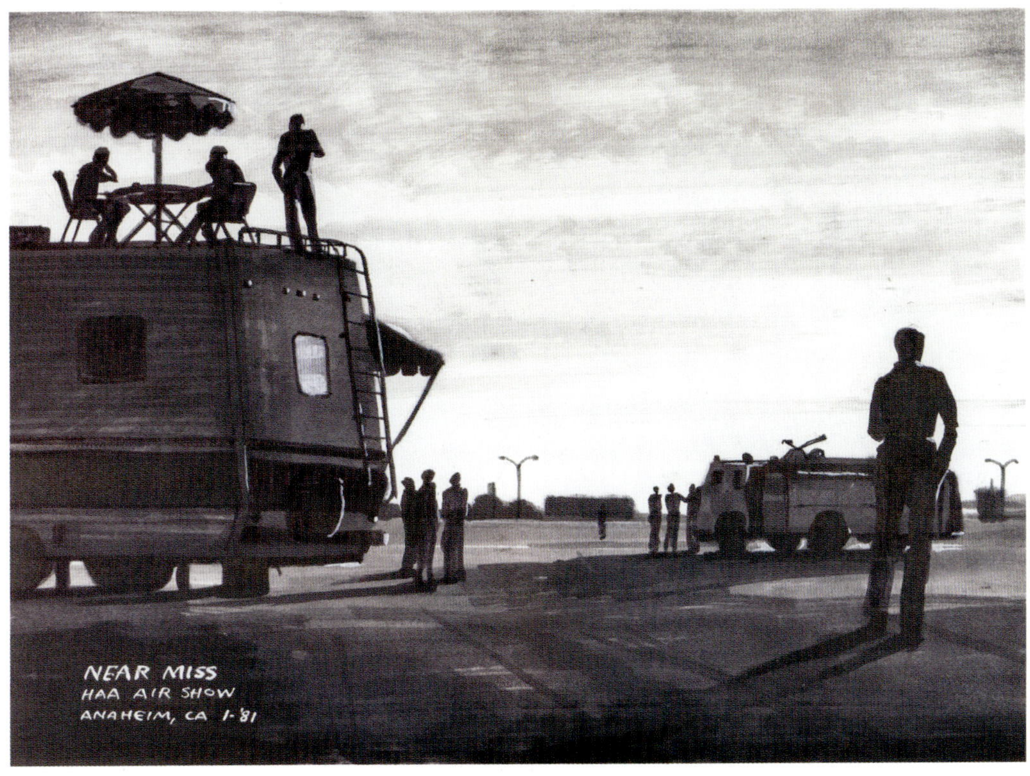

◀ **NEAR MISS,** *gray markers and white gouache —JG*

Introduction

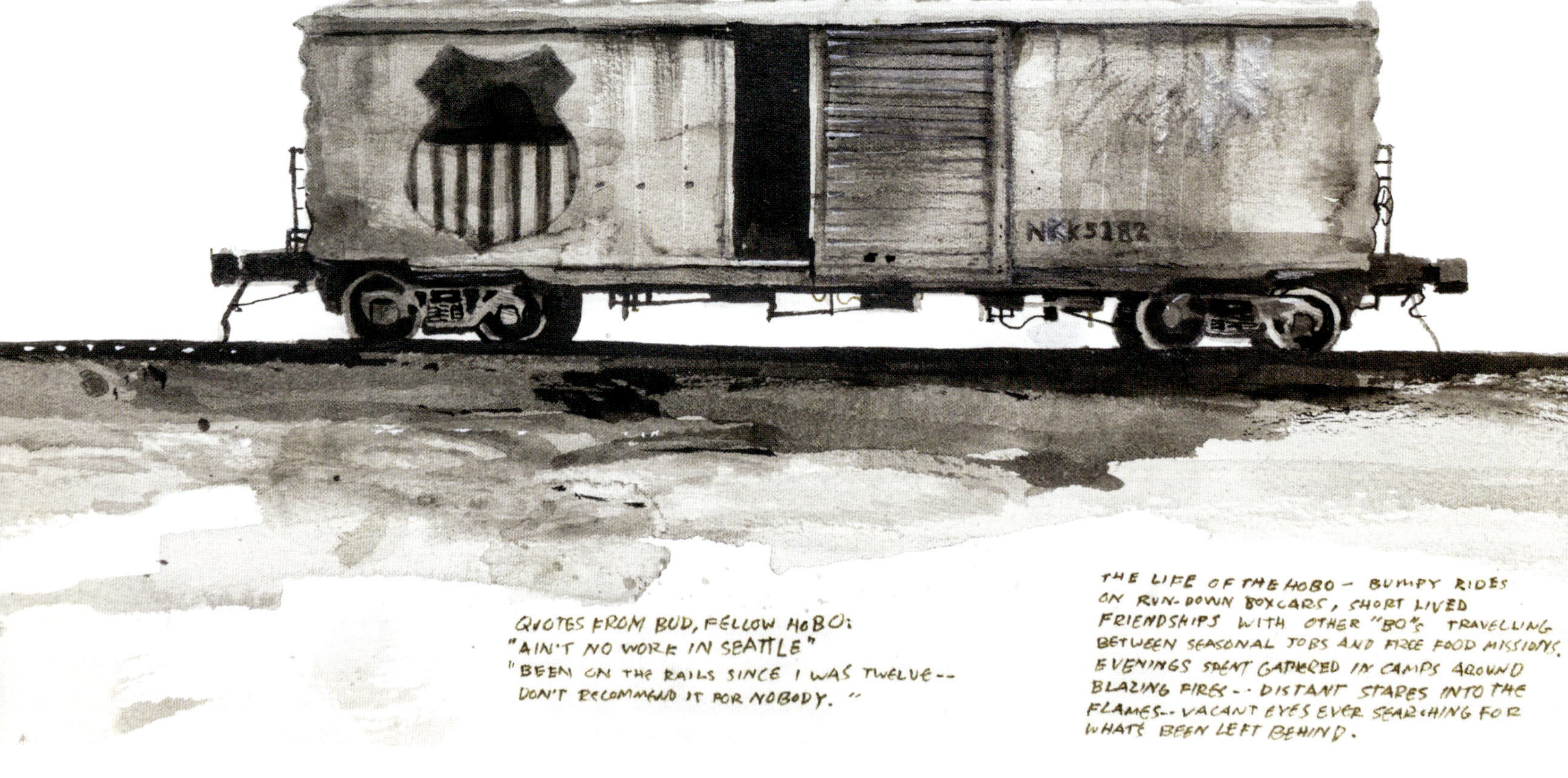

◀ **THE EXPERIENCE OF SKETCHING.** *Sketching opens the door to adventure. Sun, wind, rain, and even curious spectators pose unique challenges that you would never face in any other kind of art. To maintain your concentration despite these distractions requires a little ingenuity and a lot of practice. But once you get used to the idea of making the outdoor world your studio, you're ready for adventure. The two of us hopped on a boxcar just like the one in this sketch just for the sake of exploring America with a sketchbook. —TK*

When you think of sketching, what comes to mind? You might think of loose, quick, unfinished drawings done on location for pure enjoyment. Well, you are totally right—almost. Sketches *are* quick, and they use techniques that are more direct and spontaneous than the kind of work that is done in the studio. And certainly you are right when you think that sketching should be enjoyable.

Then why did we say "almost"? If you are like most people, you may not be fully aware of how much *more* is possible with sketching. Sketches don't have to be the kind of undeveloped scribbles that you may be used to seeing. In an afternoon, you can make a sketch that is packed full of closely observed details. Also, you can sketch in any medium, from a ballpoint pen to a full set of oils. You can sketch any subject—kangaroos, tow trucks, cirrus clouds, or clock repairmen at work. And no one says you have to copy what you see; you can let your imagination transform any subject into a creative exaggeration of the real world.

Many artists tell us: "I guess I should sketch more often, but I never really get the chance." We know the feeling. There just doesn't seem to be enough time in the day, and when the opportunity does come up, the sketchbook is never handy. On a vacation it seems much easier to use a camera than a sketchbook to record your experiences.

And yet almost every artist deep down wants to do more sketching. The reason that not everyone does has nothing to do with motivation or self-discipline. In fact, the very reason many of us don't get around to sketching is that we consider it a kind of obligation, something that artists have always done through the generations, a mandatory habit for the profession. But no one ever tells us *why* sketching is so important, or how it should function in our creative lives.

Take a handful of old and nineteenth-century masters—let's say da Vinci, Rembrandt, Breugel, Dürer, Van Gogh, and Degas. Everyone knows that they were all avid sketchers. But consider how central their sketching was to their work. Almost invariably the sketchbooks cover a far broader range of subject matter than the final paintings do. Many of the original seeds of ideas for the great masterpieces are found there. In general, we feel in old master sketches a free play of fancy, an absolutely honest technique, a keen discerning eye observing the world. And most of all we feel a lively, joyful, exuberant spirit in their sketches, which in turn enriched everything else they created. For these masters, sketching served as the vehicle through which they made contact with the real world.

Unfortunately, this attitude has been overlooked by many contemporary painters who have become overdependent on the habits and theories of the studio. When this happens, art loses its relationship to life and grows inbred with mannerisms. Could you imagine a novelist writing about life in the desert without ever feeling the dust on his shoes or the sun on his back? Of course not, and the same is true for artists. Art is born of an artist's contact with the world around him, and the best vehicle for that contact is sketching.

If you are an illustrator, easel painter, architect, cartoonist, or devoted amateur, your work will thrive on sketching. Through your sketchbook you will fill your mental storehouse of images. You will be able to recreate from memory anything that you have observed once, whether it's a streetlight, cowboy boot, or willow tree. The sketches themselves, as they begin to accumulate, will become a prized collection for future reference. Your sketches will serve as a testing ground for new techniques. There is no risk of failure and you are your own judge of any sketch that you do.

Suppose you do not consider yourself an artist, but rather a person for whom drawing is only a hobby. How

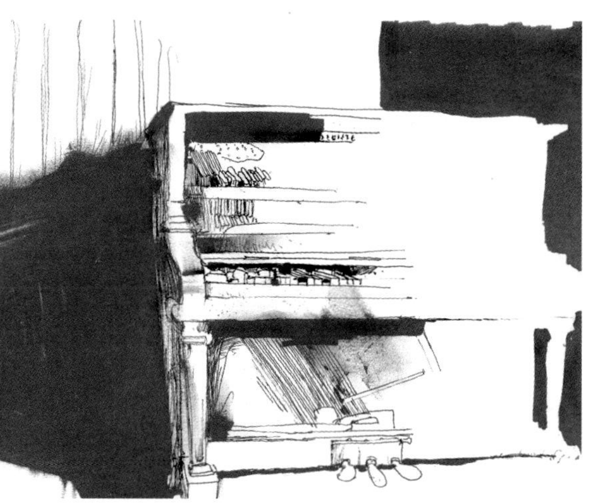

▲ **MATERIALS.** *There are four requirements for sketching materials: simplicity, economy, portability, and speed. Over the years we've narrowed down our materials to a handful of favorite tools that can be used to quickly capture any subject on paper. We've found that it is possible to achieve a variety of effects with a minimum of tools. For example, this sketch of a dilapidated piano was executed with just a fine-line pen and a broad-tip black marker. The fine-line pen was used for the thin outlines and cross-hatching, while the black marker was used for the rich dark areas and was smudged with a wet finger to achieve the grainy textural areas. —TK*

can sketching fit into your life? With your limited time schedule, you may well decide to allow only an hour a week to your hobby. That's enough time to fill several pages of a sketchbook. You can take some time on the way home from work or errands to stop and sketch a tree or a building that has caught your imagination. Or during those occasional waiting periods—waiting for an appointment, or for a bus, or for food at a restaurant—you can easily take advantage of the time to practice your hobby and pass the time in a relaxing, enjoyable manner. Your average week will be enriched by the texture of small details that you have observed along the way through sketching. For you, sketching may be the only kind of art that you pursue regularly.

Whether you are a full-time artist or not, you'll find that the big rewards of sketching go far beyond the simple satisfaction of putting lines on paper. Think of the act of drawing as a doorway that leads you into a far richer world of experience and discovery. It provides the excuse to leave home for an afternoon in order to meet new people, or poke around on the far side of town. It gives you an opportunity to sit on a stream bank for two hours looking at nothing but a six-inch-high plant. It gets you out there in the wonderful carnival of the human race, as you go people-watching with a pencil. That act of drawing also opens the door into your inner self: your sensitivity to mood, your creative imagination, and your personal memory of experience.

For us, it was those fringe benefits that drew us into sketching. Soon after we left art school, we traveled across the country on freight trains, with nothing but backpacks stuffed full of peanut butter, a few clothes, and a single 9" x 12" sketchbook each. On board the boxcars, living the life of the hobo, we journeyed from one small town to another. A lot of little glimpses of America found their way into our sketchbooks—pictures of abandoned tractors and motel signs and jukeboxes. The more we sketched, the more we began to realize that sketching is both the motivation and the reward for experiencing new things. That is, we made a special point to travel to unusual places in order to sketch there, and afterward our sketches became the living documents of the experience which we could share with others. Had it not been for sketching, we would never even have considered knocking on the doors of a lumberjack in northern California, a lighthouse keeper in Rhode Island, or a jazz pianist in New Orleans. All welcomed us in for hour after hour of warm conversation as we drew their portraits, and we repaid their kindness with a nice sketch of their homes.

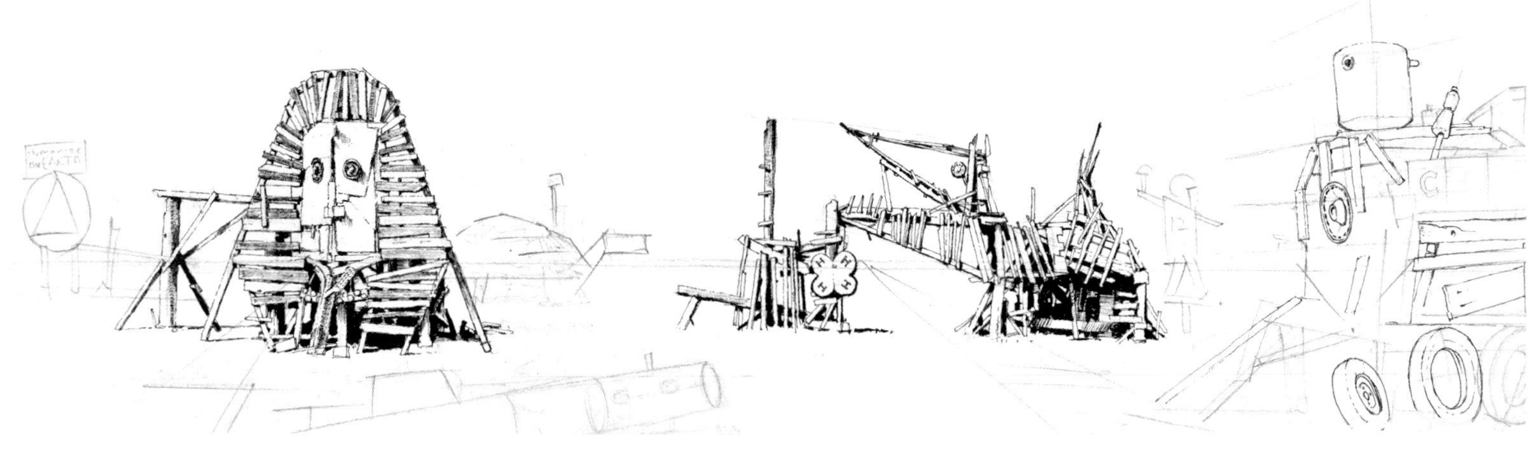

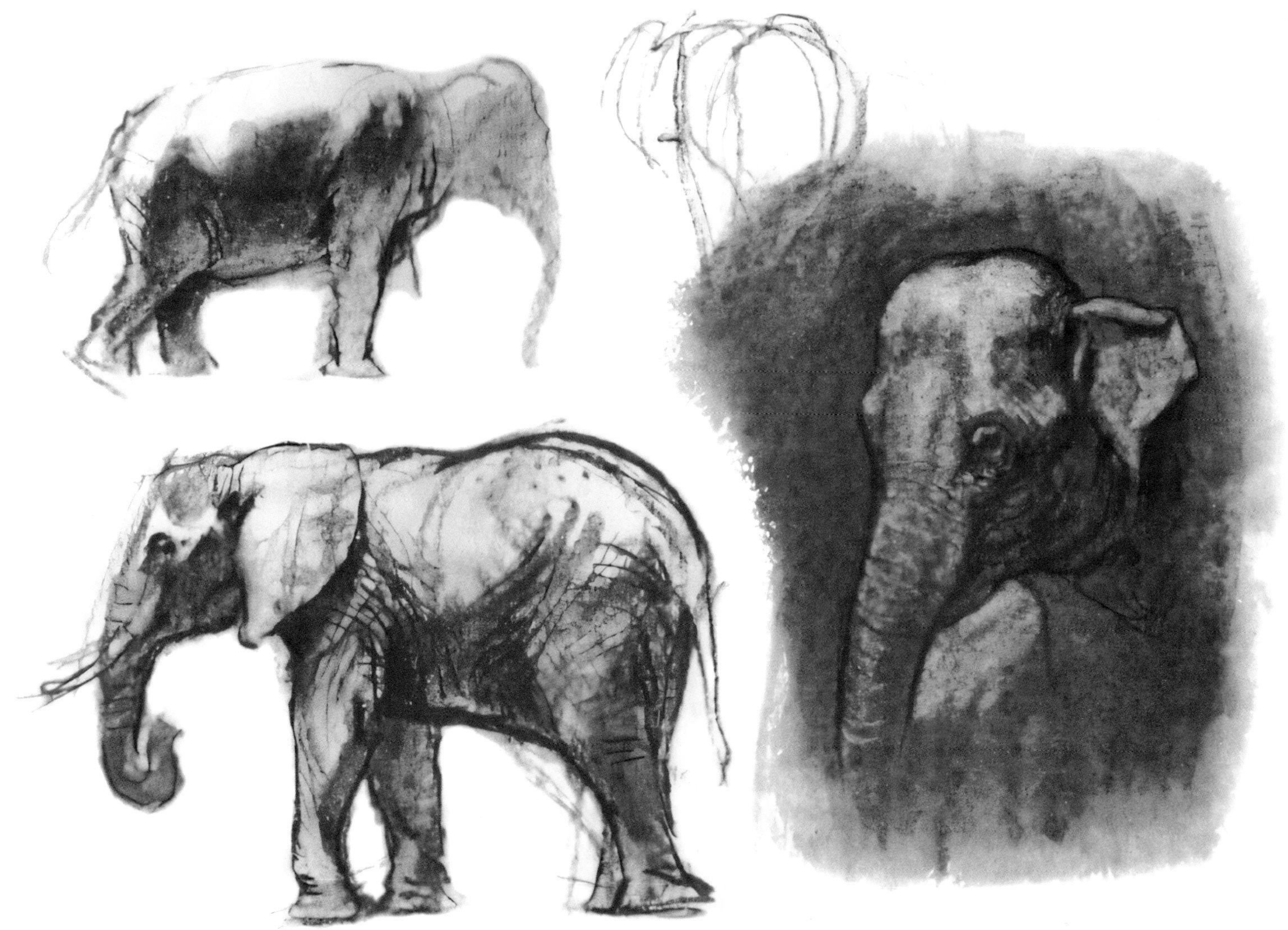

▲ **CAPTURING MOTION.** *An entirely different approach to drawing is needed for subjects that move—which includes just about every person or animal. For fast motion, the secret is to isolate a single pose by shutting your eyes at a peak of the action, and then to quickly translate your impression onto paper. The sketch of the walking elephant at the upper left was made by quickly smudging a tone that represented the gesture of the pose, and then refining the smudge with rhythmic lines. —JG*

◀ **ACHIEVING ACCURACY.** *No matter how complex your subject, you can be assured of accuracy if you spend a few minutes on a pencil underdrawing. Our procedure involves a series of measurements and comparisons that can eliminate errors before you begin the final rendering. At the same time, it keeps the sketch in a state of flux long enough to allow you to make changes in the composition before it's too late. The resulting confidence releases your ability to be spontaneous. —JG*

Meanwhile, on the road or on the rails, we sketched anything we could find. We never sketched two subjects in quite the same way. A moving figure seemed to call for a totally different frame of mind than did a storefront scene. For one, we were interested only in capturing a quick notation of a fleeting observation, and for the other we were concerned with making a finished, detailed drawing on-the-spot. Sometimes we wanted to record exactly what we saw; other times we wanted to add a twist of imagination or to enhance the mood. And always there were the little notations, the personal scribbles that made sense to no one but ourselves.

After we returned from our sketching adventure, we showed our sketchbooks to both artist and non-artist friends who were very curious about how we worked, telling us they wanted to try some sketching themselves. When we began to think carefully about how we work on-the-spot, we realized that there is no single approach that can work in all instances. The traditional books on drawing that we were familiar with usually show a single approach to drawing, using stationary still lifes and posed models. You are probably quite familiar with these books. They are very useful for helping you draw in the classroom or studio, but they cannot prepare you for the specific demands of on-the-spot sketching. Drawing something that is moving is a completely different experience from drawing a stationary object, and it's different still from drawing from the imagination. And yet all of these skills are necessary for sketching.

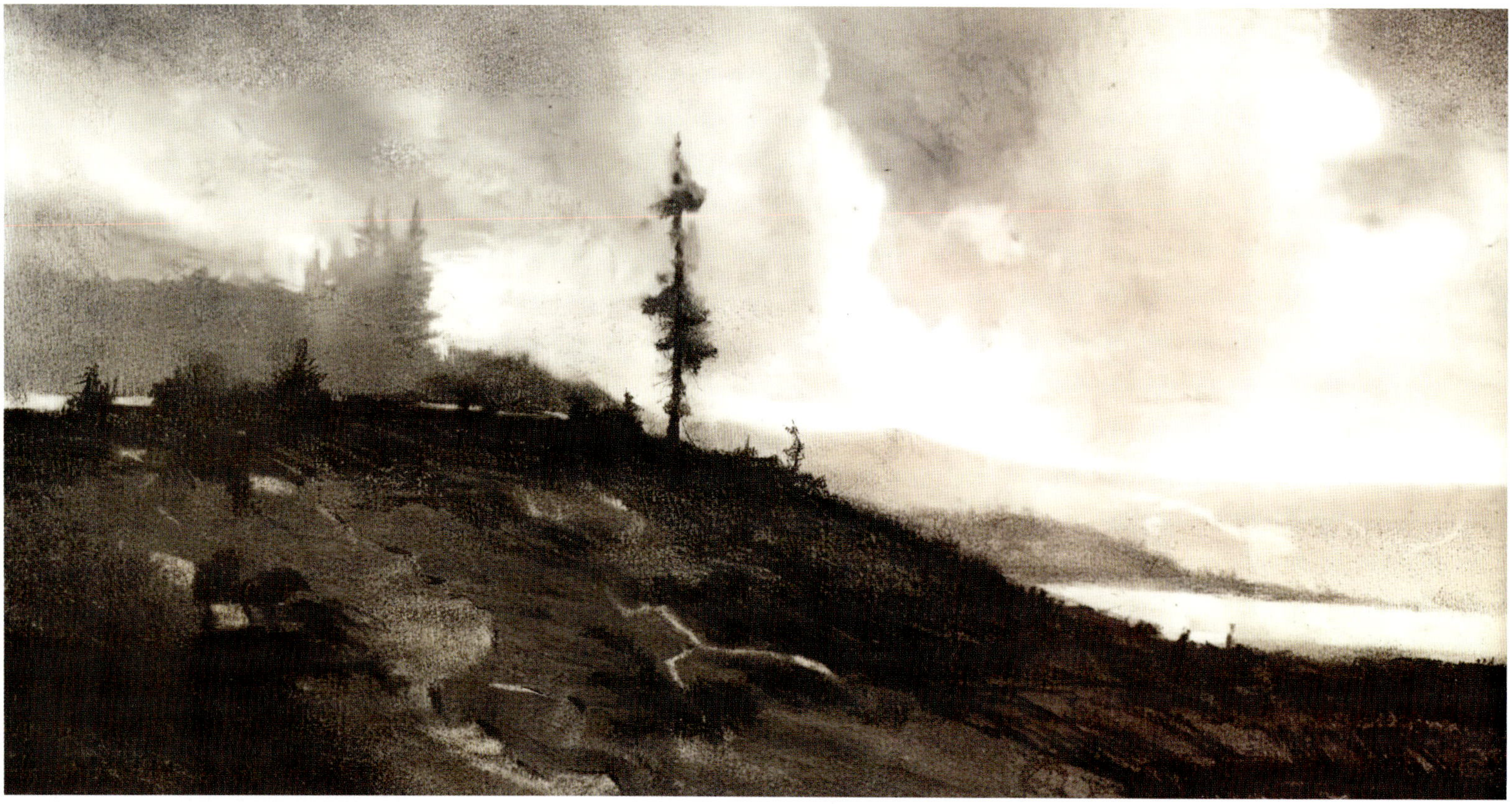

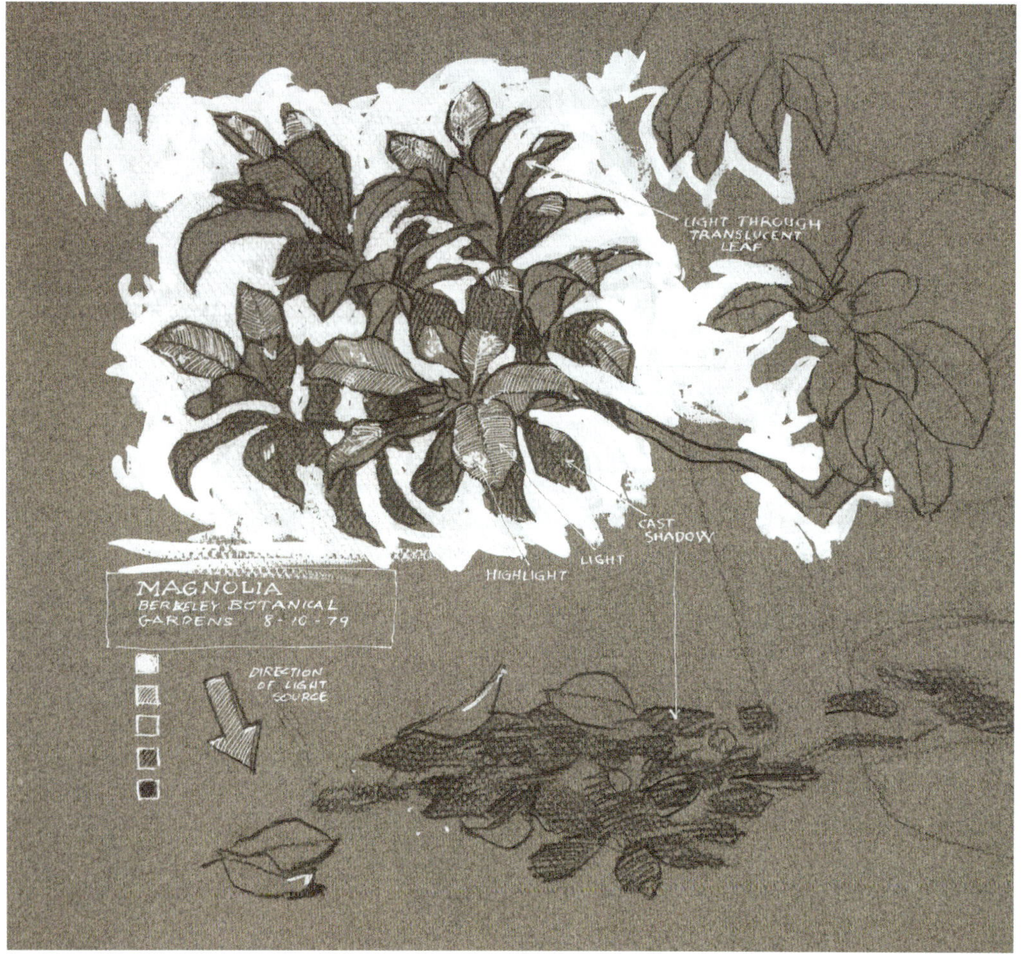

▲ **CREATING MOOD.** *The setting sun behind an unfinished building, the stillness of a forest, the gloom of an empty room—these are moods that you are already very sensitive to, but want to express better in a sketch. To do this requires that you plan exactly what effect you want to achieve and organize your picture so that every line, tone, and shape works to support that effect. Changes will be made from the subject, but they will be changes with a clear purpose. In this sketch, the foreboding mood was achieved by darkening the tones of the sky and placing strategic white accents throughout the composition. —TK*

◀ **STUDYING NATURE.** *Nature yields her secrets to the patient observer. All you need is a simple sketch set-up that you can carry into the wilds in a small knapsack. But even for the city-bred artist, nature is fully accessible for sketching in botanical gardens, natural history museums, zoos, and even your backyard. —JG*

▶ **USING IMAGINATION.** *To experience a childlike joy in drawing doesn't mean you have to draw like a child. But it does mean that you must be willing to break all the rules and playfully transform what you see into something that could only exist on paper. The actual building facades in Philadelphia were only half as tall, half as detailed as this exaggerated version. —JG*

And aside from the purely technical skill of drawing, there are other factors that make sketching deserve special consideration. Nowhere else do you contend with bright sunlight, the dim light of night, the challenges of a strong wind. Subjective human factors also enter in—curious spectators watching you work, and people looking up to notice that you are keenly staring at them with a sketchbook in your hands.

We designed this book for anyone who wants to make sketching as fulfilling as it can possibly be. The first four chapters are intended to fully prepare you for going out to sketch. The chapter on materials offers suggestions for simple, portable, and inexpensive sketchbooks and drawing materials that will allow you to create a wide range of effects with a minimum of bother. With an equipment set-up similar to the one we suggest, and with the instruction that we offer for achieving accuracy and capturing motion, you are ready to head out in search of adventure-filled picture making.

The next two chapters, "Creating Mood" and "Using Imagination," deal with ways of going beyond the dry facts of what you see. This is where the fun really begins. Even if you are a beginner just becoming acquainted with observational drawing, these chapters will help you to become more actively involved with your picture, so that you become the master of what you are sketching, not vice versa. The simplest subjects that you might want to sketch—a tree trunk, an old car, or a row of houses—can become exciting pictures when they are transformed by a sensitive, moody treatment or by an imaginative fantasy approach. The principles that we use when we do this sort of sketching are not new—artists have used them for centuries to add interest to their work. But by applying them to sketching, you will discover a new excitement in the process of drawing from life.

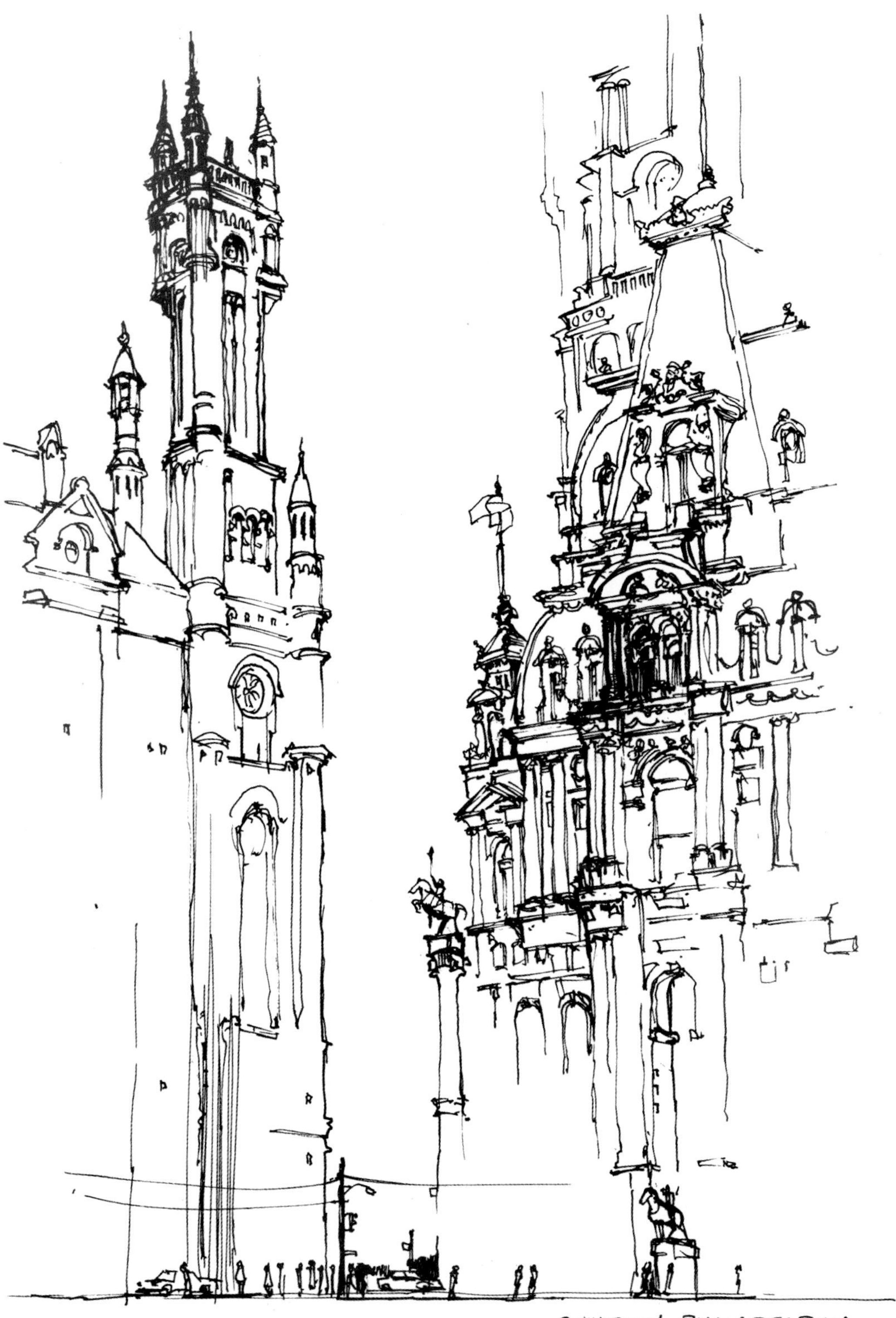

DOWNTOWN PHILADELPHIA

▶ **SKETCHING PEOPLE.** *What makes one portrait or figure drawing stand out from another is a feeling of character. That's something you find in abundance when you're on-the-spot—people of all shapes and sizes, no two alike. Most of the time the people you sketch will be strangers you never talk to, but it's surprisingly easy to make friends with potential subjects and have them pose for you. This lady, whom we met near the ocean in southern California, told us that she is really an Inca princess, "born in thunder and lightning." —TK*

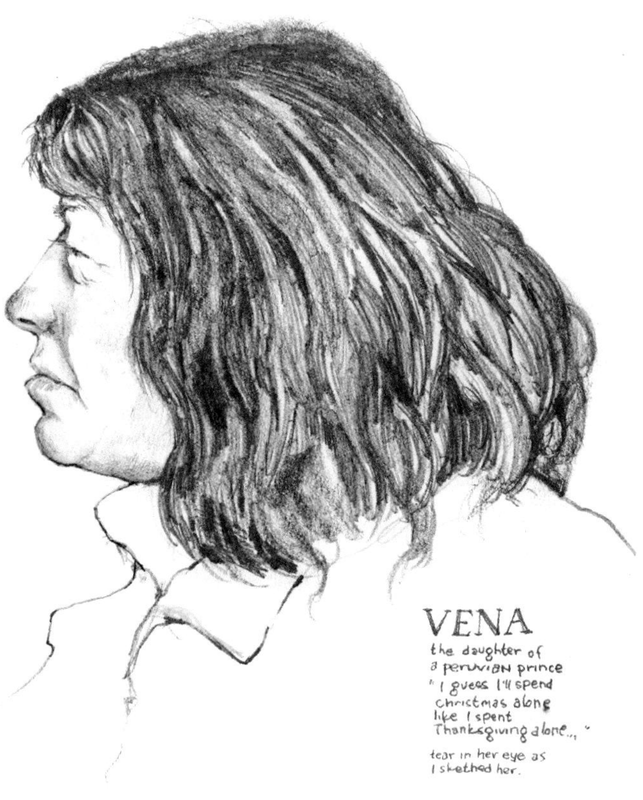

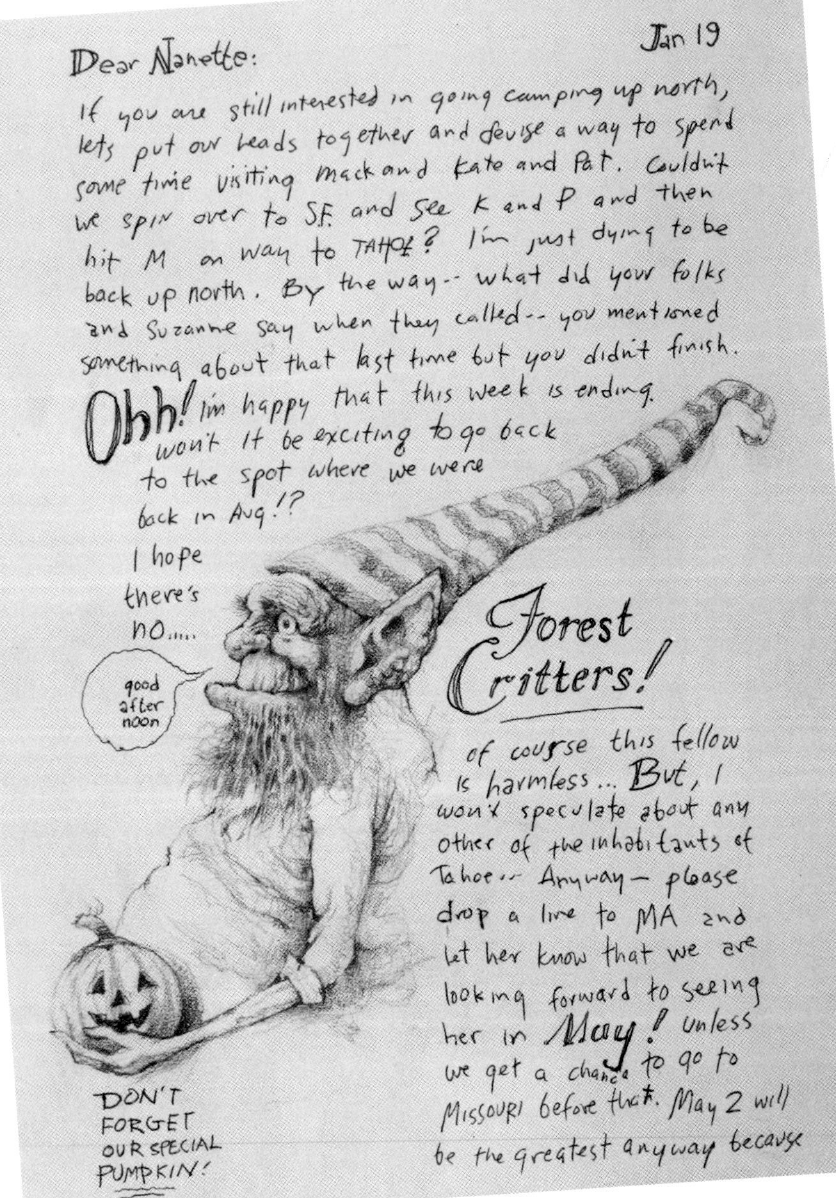

Jan 19

Dear Nanette:

If you are still interested in going camping up north, lets put our heads together and devise a way to spend some time visiting Mack and Kate and Pat. Couldn't we spin over to S.F. and see K and P and then hit M on way to TAHOE? I'm just dying to be back up north. By the way -- what did your folks and Suzanne say when they called -- you mentioned something about that last time but you didn't finish.

Ohh! I'm happy that this week is ending. won't it be exciting to go back to the spot where we were back in Aug.!? I hope there's no.....

good after noon

Forest Critters!

of course this fellow is harmless... But, I won't speculate about any other of the inhabitants of Tahoe -- Anyway – please drop a line to MA and let her know that we are looking forward to seeing her in May! unless we get a chance to go to Missouri before that. May 2 will be the greatest anyway because

DON'T FORGET OUR SPECIAL PUMPKIN!

◀ **SKETCHING IN YOUR LIFE.** *As you become more familiar with sketching, you will realize that it is much more than an isolated pastime. Sketching can be a vital part of your entire life. It is a motivation for traveling, a means of documenting ideas of every sort, a tool for developing paintings and illustrations, and a very personal way to share with others. One good way of sharing your sketching ability with others is by including small sketches in your personal letters. This letter is illustrated with a sketch of a fellow not uncommon around campfires in the woods and on dark nights. I find that adding a quick sketch to every letter I send increases the interest of the letter immensely. —TK*

The following three chapters, "Studying Nature," "Sketching People," and "Exploring the Man-Made World," offer in-depth treatments of the three big categories of subject matter for sketching. You might have a favorite kind of thing to sketch—trees, for instance. The chapter on nature sketching is designed to make your experience more rewarding and to improve the quality of your results. If you've always loved to sketch people, you might want to try some of the more specialized approaches to people-sketching, like the on-the-spot portrait or the extended group character study. "Exploring the Man-Made World" offers a variety of sketching experience, from rendering a rusted latch on a barn door to crouching in the engine room of a tugboat. We hope these chapters will not only fulfill your potential in the areas that interest you, but also excite you to try new kinds of sketching experiences.

And how does all this sketching relate to your life as an artist in person? That's the topic of the last chapter, "Sketching in Your Life." Sketching doesn't stop with the row of sketchbooks on your shelf. It can be the seedbed of ideas for studio pictures; it can be the testing ground for new techniques; it can be the record book of your personal experiences; and it can be the doorway through which you share those experiences with others.

In short, we've made it our goal to make this book a complete guide for all kinds of sketching, offering you more than just systems for how to draw a tree or a person or a house. We want to give you the more substantial tools that give you the power not only to draw what you see, but also to take absolutely any subject, no matter how unpromising it may seem at first, and see beyond the surface to the wonderful sketch it can yield. We want you to be a confident sketcher, able to turn any subject or experience into a beautiful memory on paper. When you reach this point, you will no longer wonder why artists are supposed to sketch. You will instead wonder how you got by so long without making sketching an active part of your life.

EXPLORING THE MAN-MADE WORLD. *From a city skyline to an ordinary saltshaker, the world of objects and buildings awaits your discovery through sketching. The infinite variety of non-moving forms can train your eye to observe detail, and, at the same time, increase your awareness of the material world as it reflects human society. —TK*

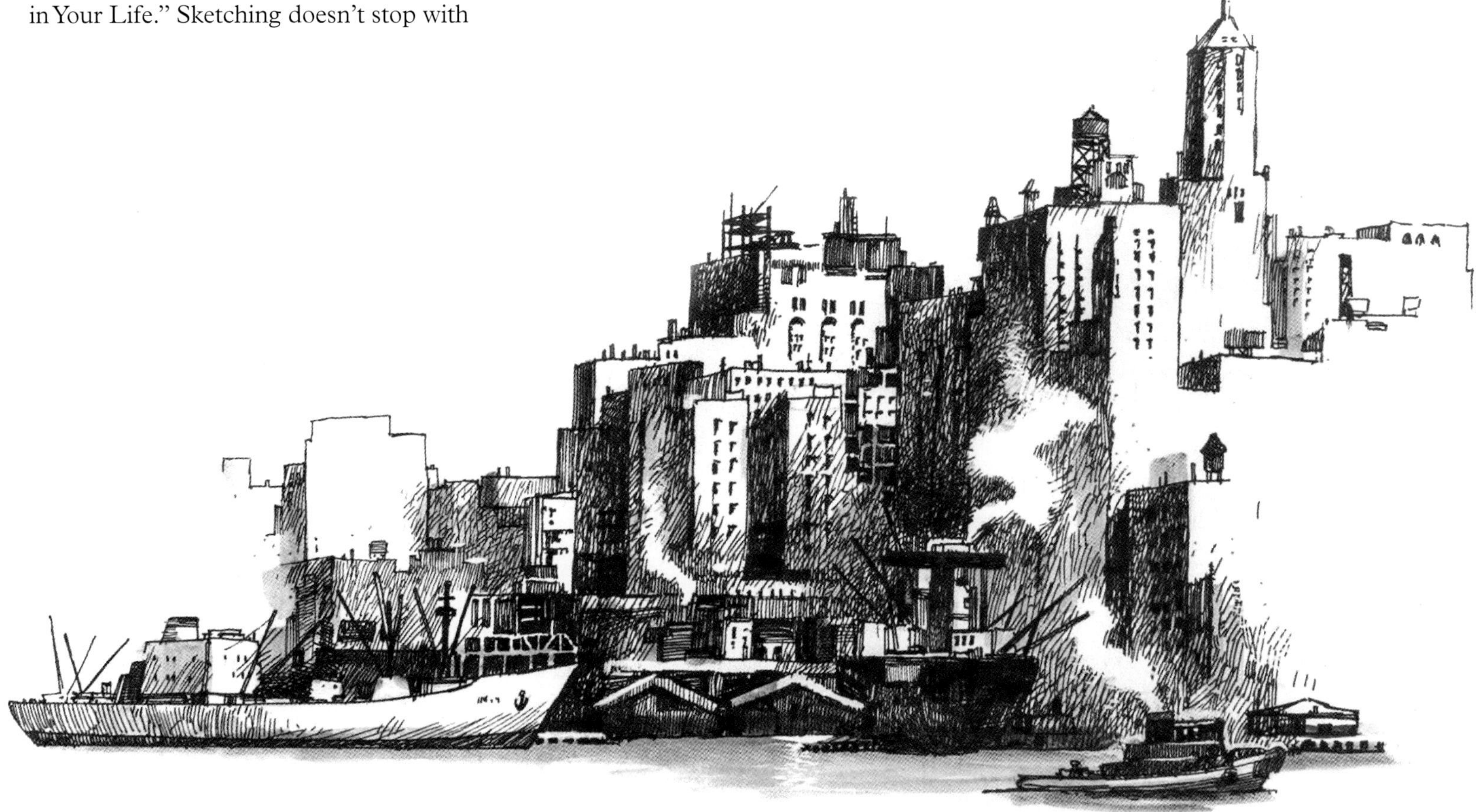

The Experience of Sketching

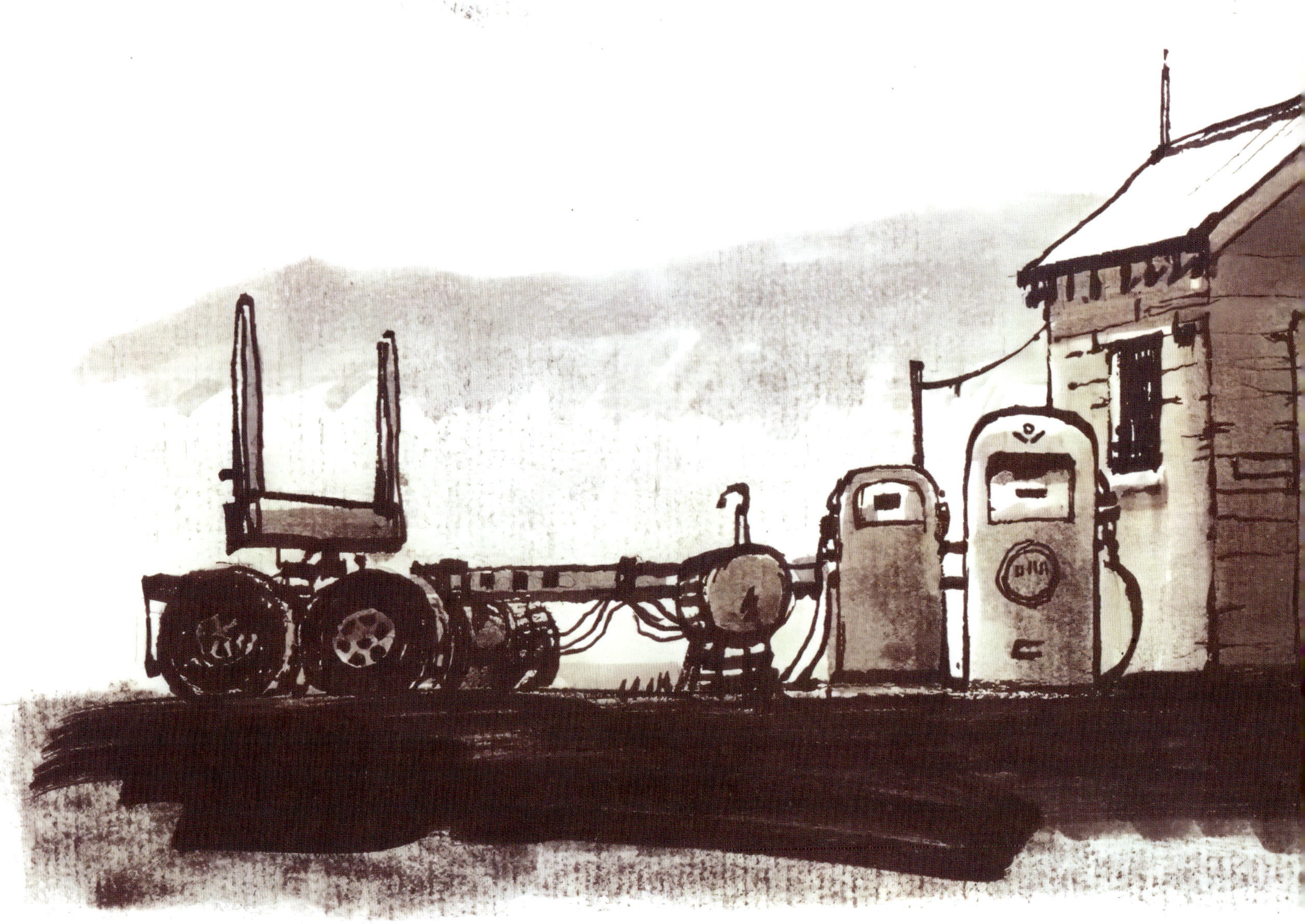

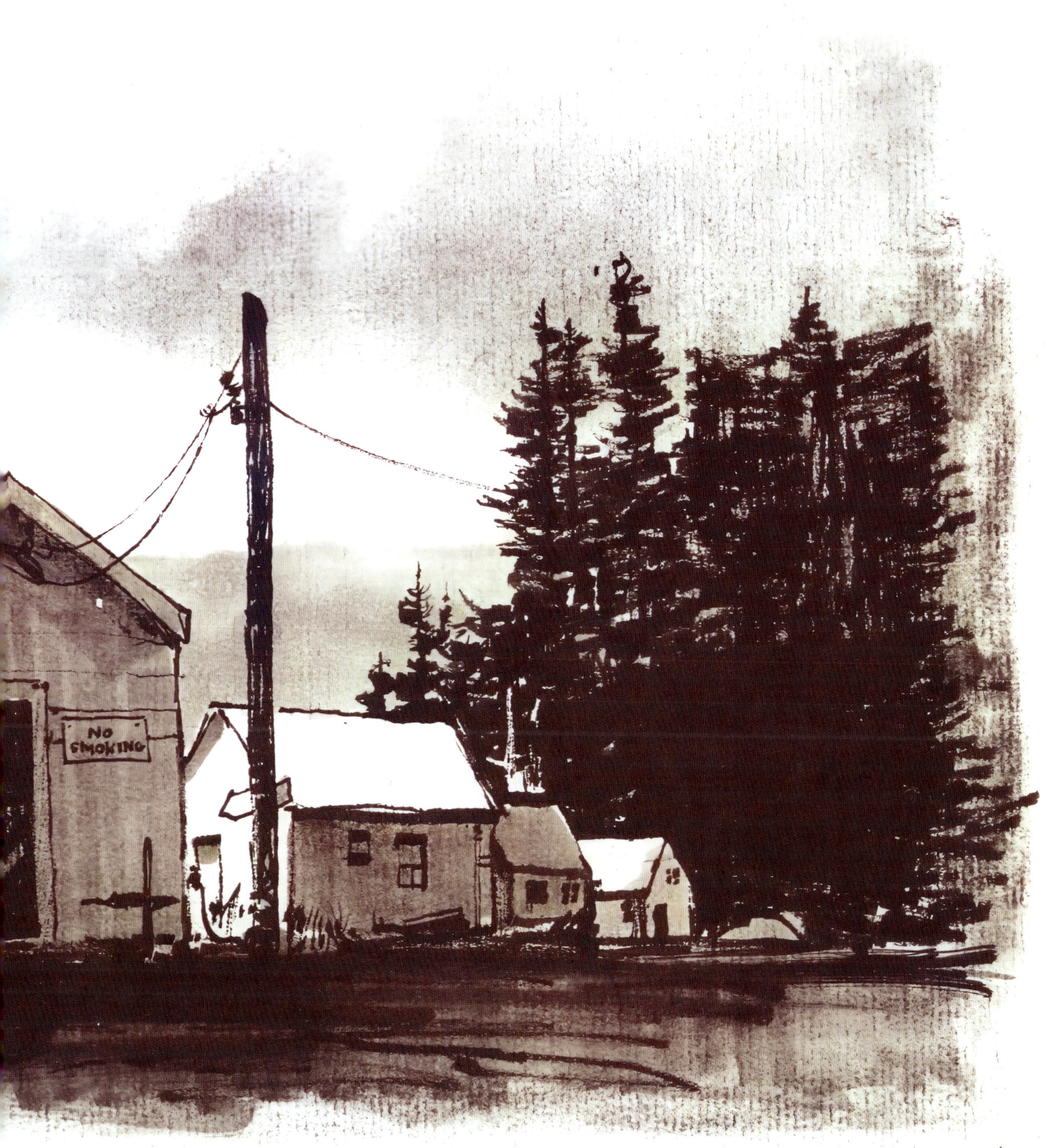

LOGGING CAMP, N. CALIFORNIA

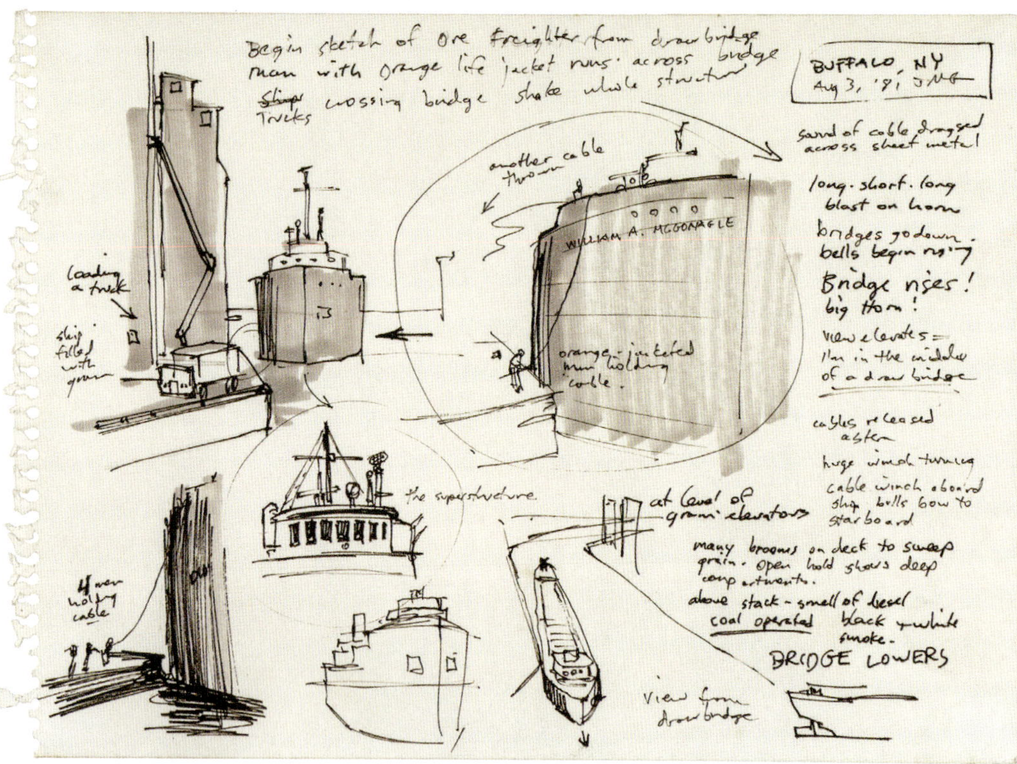

▲ **VIEWS FROM A RISING DRAWBRIDGE,** *fountain pen and gray marker on drawing paper, 9" x 12". I never know what to expect when I begin a sketch. Had I known that the vertical-lift drawbridge was about to raise, I would have thought twice about sitting up there. Nevertheless, once the bells and horns and sirens sounded, and the huge cables and chains were set into motion, I made the most of the experience by recording everything I saw and felt. From my vantage point, high above all the grain silos, I could see the whole industrial section of Buffalo, New York, in a magnificent panorama. Far below, on the decks of the ship, workmen were busy sweeping up the grain that had spilled beside the hatches and operating the winches that helped pull the big ship around the turns in the waterway. After the bridge gently lowered back down, I had in my possession a drawing that was far more than a technical exercise—it was a record of an experience. —JG*

◀◀ **LOGGING CAMP,** *calligraphy pen and gray marker on charcoal paper, 11" x 17". Loggers know about trees, but they also know about the cold. This sketch was done in the frozen morning stillness of a logging camp near Truckee in northern California. My fingers were losing their strength as I sketched in the morning chill, but I found that occasionally thrusting my hands under my arms warmed them enough to continue sketching. Halfway through the sketch I was approached by a logger who offered a cup of coffee as further refuge from the cold. After finishing the sketch, I joined him in the small cabin that he called home. Though a rather timid fellow, he permitted me to sketch him. (My sketch of the logger appears in Chapter 8, "Sketching People.") —TK*

When you sketch, you make the world your studio. You will find yourself bringing out your sketchbook at the most unlikely times and places and getting to work on a drawing. We've made sketches while goats nibbled on our paper, while being jostled by an angry crowd of demonstrators, and even while perched on a rising drawbridge. This outdoor studio, with all its distractions, is what all sketchers thrive on, because it makes the act of drawing more than just a technical exercise—it makes it an experience. But as invigorating as these circumstances are, they do present challenges to you, especially if you are accustomed to working only in the quiet of your studio at home. Being able to concentrate on-the-spot is one of the most important skills you will develop in sketching. In this chapter we will prepare you to concentrate on-the-spot by giving you some of the insights we've gained about the unique circumstances of sketching. By limiting the amount of distraction, you can improve the quality of your sketches.

COPING WITH THE WEATHER

Whenever you sketch out-of-doors, you are vulnerable to the weather. Wind, rain, and fog will beset you at times, but the most common weather obstacle is the sunshine on your sketchbook page. A piece of white paper in direct sunlight gives off many times as much light as the same piece of paper in normal indoor light. Your eyes can adjust to some extent, but you still may find yourself squinting while you draw. If your subject is in shadow, it may take several seconds for your eye to adjust as it alternates from the glaring page to the subdued subject.

To solve this problem, you should strive to keep the light on your page and the light on your subject more or less equal so that you can comfortably glance back and forth from one to the other without having to adjust. Polarized sunglasses help immensely in bright light

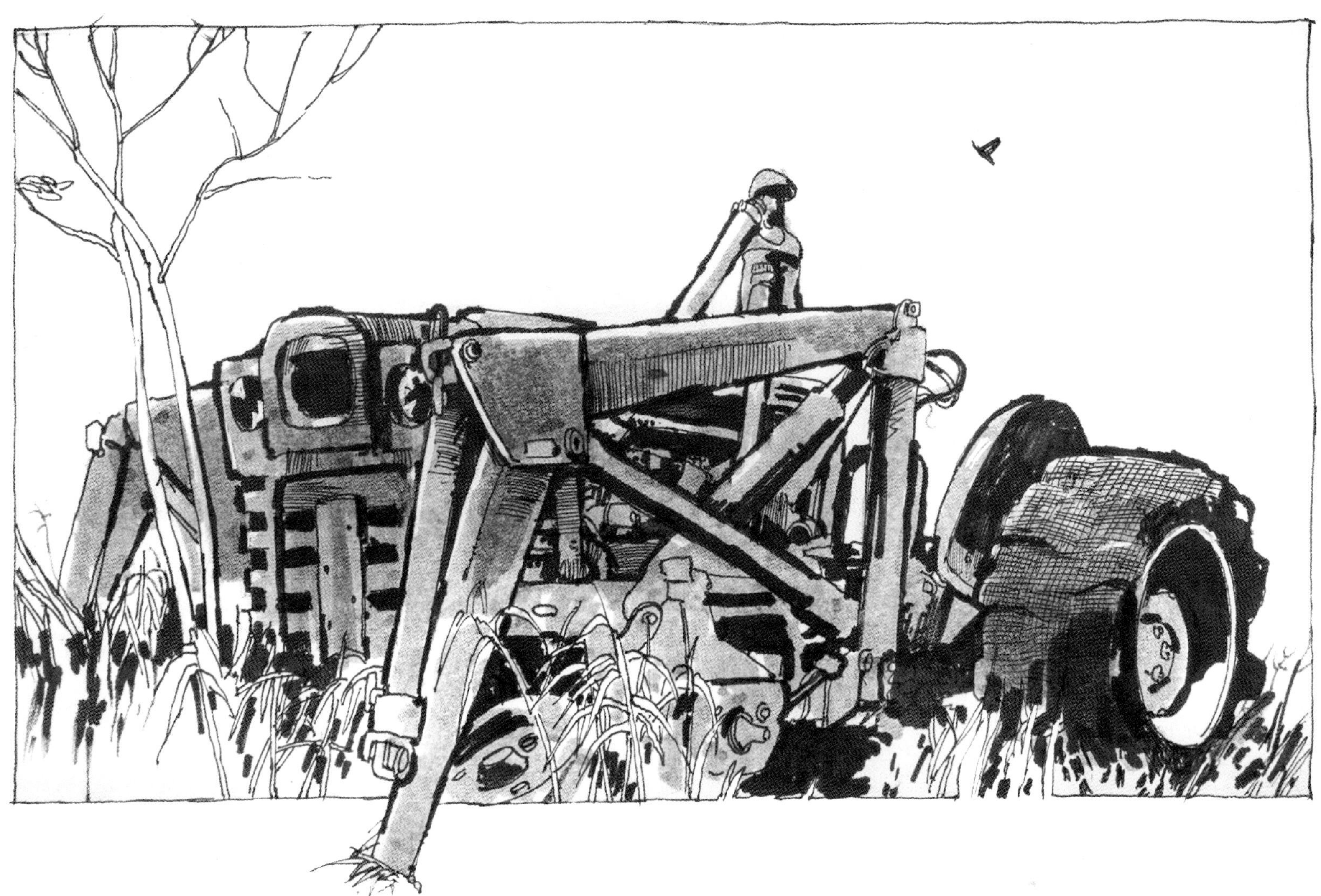

situations. Carry a pair with you when you go sketching on bright days. Another solution, when possible, is simply to find a shady spot. There is almost always a tree or building somewhere that can serve to cast a shadow on your work. Being able to find such a spot often plays a big part in our choice of subject matter, even if it means passing up a good viewpoint in the sun for the sake of comfort. If you have no other choice but to sit in the sun, another option is to cast a shadow from your own body as you work, which means that you have to be sitting so that your back is to the sun. Wearing a large-brimmed hat makes it easier to cover your entire paper and shadow. Some artists even use a parasol in conjunction with a painting easel setup for this purpose.

On a partly cloudy day, your subject will go in and out of sunlight as the clouds move overhead and intermittently block the sun. Naturally, the pattern of light and shade that you had been representing will be obliterated. But you can still keep working if you have indicated in your pencil underdrawing (a technique discussed in Chapter 3, "Achieving Accuracy") where the shadows begin and end on the forms. Each time the sun comes out, recheck the indication of shadows on your drawings. As you get more experienced, you can take advantage of the light situation on partly cloudy days by throwing some areas into light and others into shadow as a dramatic device. Further, you can even invent a light source, or change the available light

ABANDONED TRACTOR, *markers on smooth paper, 9" x 11". Like a sunbathing robot, this abandoned tractor lay in the middle of a brightly lit Tennessee meadow. I wanted to record the unusual interplay of form and void that characterizes heavy machinery. Yet there was a problem. The sun, which so beautifully illuminated the gadgetry of the rusting machine, also created a glare on my sketchbook page which made it impossible to sketch. The nearest shelter was quite a way off, so I needed to improvise my own shade. I found that if I sat with the sun behind me and leaned forward a bit, my own body cast enough of a shadow over my sketchbook so that it was possible to work without squinting. —TK*

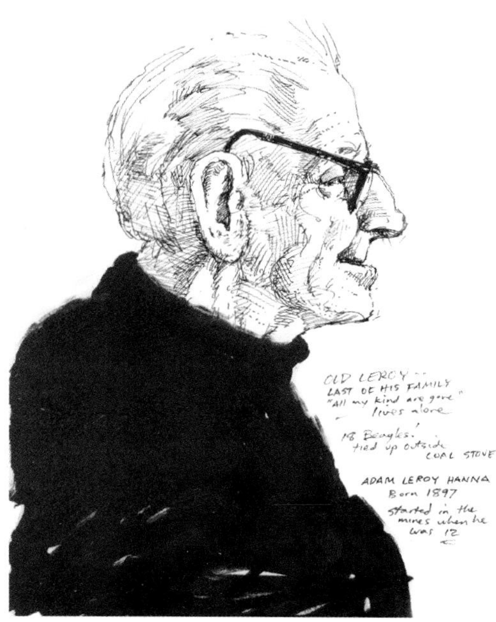

PENNSYLVANIA COAL MINER, *fine-tip felt pen and black marker on smooth paper, 9" x 12". Having good lighting is an important consideration in any sketch. In this case, I had made friends with an eighty-five-year-old retired coal miner and had gotten his permission to sketch a quick portrait. However, with no electricity inside his tiny shack, the light was too dim to see the details of his face. Outside the light was soft and cool, but clouds overhead threatened rain. I had no choice but to have him sit in the doorway facing outside, while I pulled up an old metal kerosene can as a makeshift chair for myself. As I sketched, the cloudburst broke, spattering mud on his boots. Seemingly oblivious to everything, he peered out the door and recalled his boyhood adventures in the mines. —JG*

to heighten mood (we'll discuss more about how and why to use these effects in Chapter 5, "Creating Mood").

The sun's movement through the sky requires a similar ability to control shadows if you are planning to work for more than a couple of hours. At sunset and twilight, some of the light effects will change in as little as fifteen minutes. You can handle this by indicating the boundaries and directions of all the shadows in pencil while on the spot, and then completing your drawing in the studio using this indication as a guide. It also helps to use media such as markers and charcoal which allow you to capture an impression of light and dark in a very short time.

Can you sketch when it's raining? Of course, as long as you are safely beneath an overhanging awning. On a misty or drizzly day, avoid using gouache or water-based markers, which will run and discolor when even the tiniest drop touches your paper. On the other hand, deserts will dry water-based paint in a matter of seconds, especially if there is some wind. Squeeze your paints onto a wet piece of paper towel and use a spray bottle to renew the moisture on your palette whenever it begins to dry. If you are sketching with markers, keep those that you are not using at the moment tightly capped.

Wind poses another challenge to sketching on the spot, as we accidentally discovered. Once, when we were sketching a helicopter landing field, the hurricane-force wind from the rotors of passing helicopters instantly dried the paints on the palette and blew all the loose pieces of paper across the airfield. Under normal conditions, however, wind doesn't present a problem as long as you are prepared for it. Use three-inch bulldog clips, available at any stationery or department store, to hold together the loose pages of your sketchbook.

It is even possible to sketch in snow and subfreezing temperatures with a bit of preparation. In fact, many of the die-hard sketch artists who accompanied expeditions such as that of Lewis and Clark favored oil paints simply because they have a lower freezing point than do watercolors! No one needs to tell you to work fast—the cold will encourage you to do that. We usually make quick thumbnails in pencil and take down some written notations about color while we're on the spot. The sketch can then be developed in the warmth of the studio.

SKETCHING AT NIGHT

Sketching outdoors at night is easy enough as long as you have proper lighting. Make sure that your paper is lit by a light that is bright enough to allow you to see your drawing, but not so glaring that you have to readjust to see into the darkness again. The overhead light from a streetlight is ideal. A small flashlight hung around your neck will also serve to illuminate your work when you cannot use available light.

The soft glow of moonlight is a beautiful effect to sketch, though you can usually convey only the most broad statements unless your paper is lit by something other than the moonlight alone. Since details in moonlit scenes tend to diffuse, use charcoal and strive for an overall softness in your sketch, particularly in the treatment of trees.

Typical outdoor night scenes such as street scenes or riverfront scenes usually consist of a range of dark values with a few crisp light accents. It's usually helpful to ignore the white accents until the very end of your sketch. After you have concentrated on the forms of the buildings and trees against the sky using pencil, marker, or charcoal, then you can add the white accents to suggest the streetlights and interiors by erasing back to the white paper or by adding touches of white gouache over your original medium.

Indoor night scenes often present you with similar circumstances—heavy, dark areas with occasional light accents. Whether you sketch in tone or line, you will find that low-lit taverns and restaurants are wonderful sketching opportunities because people are relaxed and natural. You can usually situate yourself near enough to a lit sign of some sort to allow you to see clearly what you are sketching while still allowing a view of the rich shadows and glowing lights of the central areas. We did a lot of portraits in midwestern honky-tonks by the light of flashing neon beer signs and cigarette machines.

SITTING OR STANDING?

As a rule, you can sketch much more comfortably and for longer periods of time when you are sitting than when you are standing. Whether you decide to sit or stand depends on two factors: how long you intend to spend on a sketch and how cumbersome your materials are. Standing is possible only with fairly quick, simple sketches, while sitting allows you to take your time and set the materials you are not using on a convenient surface near you.

The chair we recommend for most sketching needs is a lightweight aluminum fishing stool with a canvas seat. It folds down to about 12" x 17" flat, so that you can carry it quite easily with your other sketching supplies. If you prefer a chair with a back, and don't mind carrying a little more equipment, we recommend the larger aluminum folding lawn chairs.

If you have no chair and don't wish to sit on the ground, you can always look for a rock, stairway, fence rail, or fire hydrant to sit upon. If none is available, lean against a building or tree. This makes it easier to keep your balance and remain steady while you sketch. Squatting, with one knee on the ground and the other knee supporting the sketchbook, is another alternative. Try it and see if it is comfortable for you.

In museums or zoos you often have no choice but to stand up while you sketch. For this you will want a spiral-bound sketchbook with some rigidity because it is the easiest to hold. Sketchbooks over about 11" x 14" can be

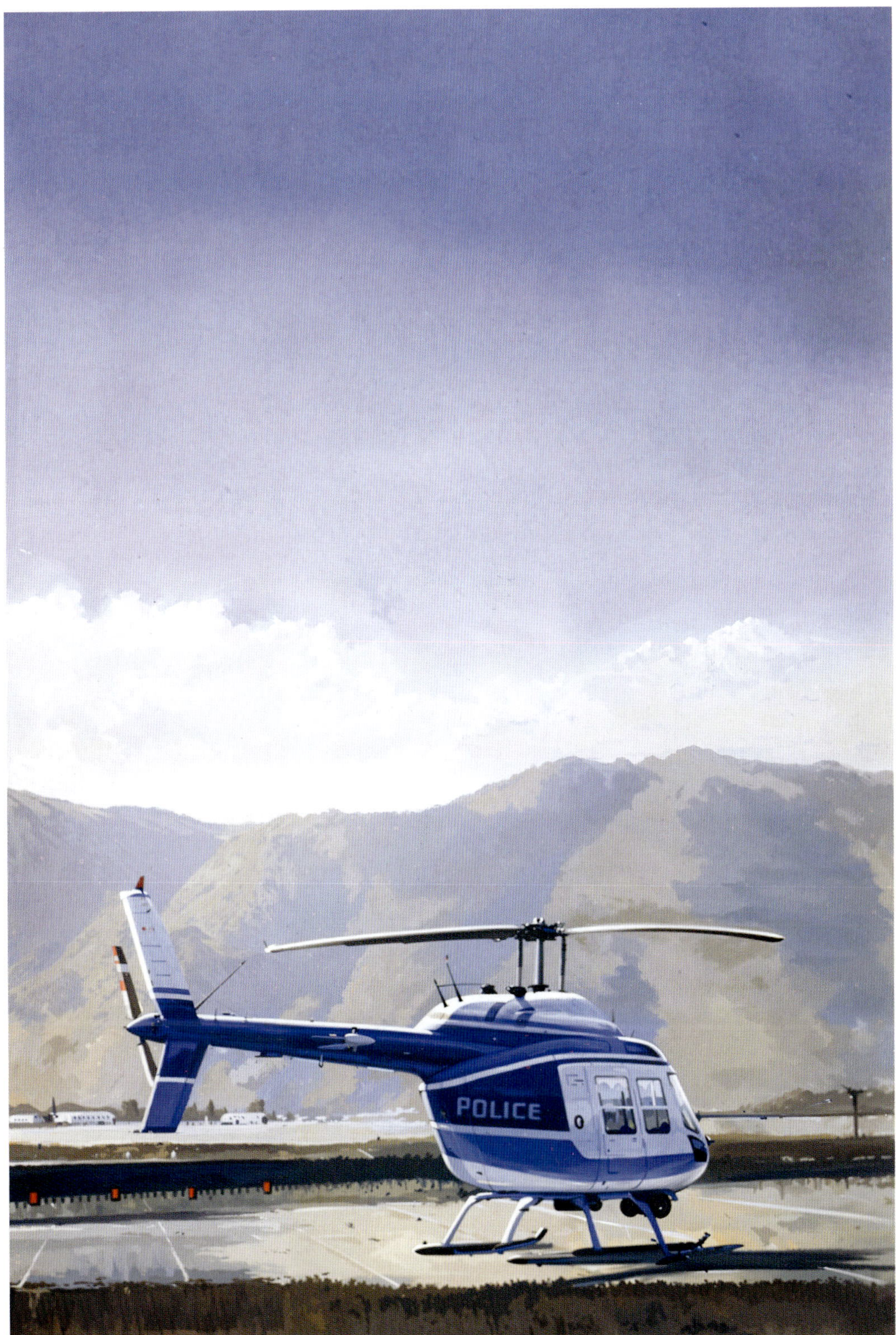

PATROL HELICOPTER, *gouache on illustration board, 9½" x 13". A field in Glendale, California, contains what I'm told is the world's largest collection of police helicopters. In order to sketch this one, I got permission to sit right next to the landing area. Each time another helicopter passed by the area, I was met with a blast of air from the rotors. The wind blew dust and gravel into the paints, dried them, and blew all of my loose equipment around the airfield. At the same time, the sun was so bright that even with sunglasses, I had to squint to see the painting as I worked. Despite all that, I was able to concentrate fully on the sketch and enjoyed the whole experience far more than if I had worked in the controlled environment of my studio. —JG*

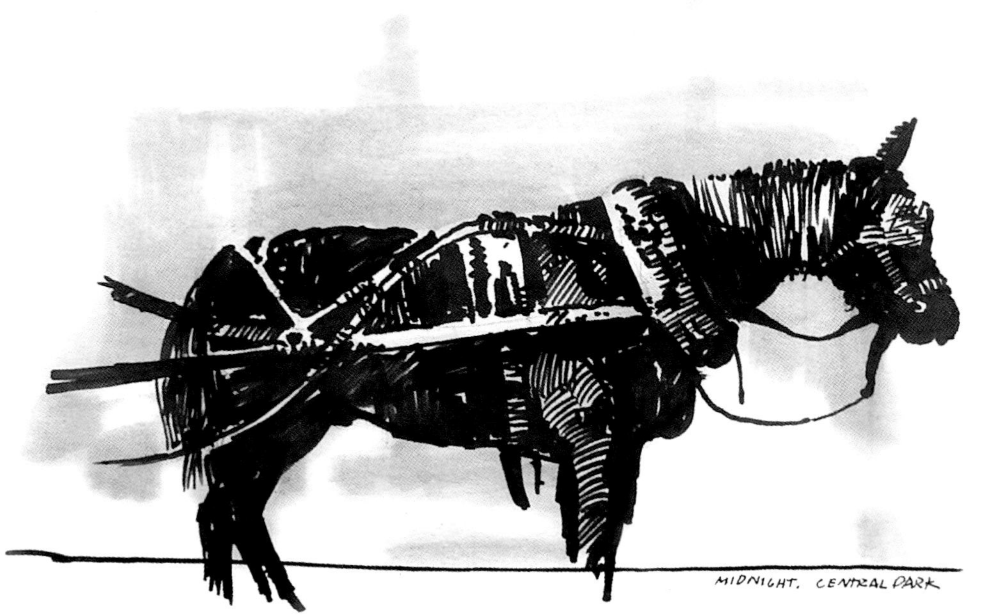

◀ **CENTRAL PARK HORSE,** *calligraphy pen on smooth paper, 9" x 11". Certain sketches can recall for you very distinct nonvisual sensations. Every time I see this sketch, the first thing that comes to mind is my memory of the stinging cold of that November evening in New York. To combat the cold I pulled my overcoat down over my hand so that only the marker was extending through the opening at the end of the sleeve. This prevented any delicate techniques, but at least my hand kept warm enough so that I could draw. A small pocket hand warmer, the kind that duck hunters use, is a big help if you plan to sketch very often in extreme cold. An occasional dip into the pool of warmth in your pocket will revive your hands long enough for a few more minutes of working. —TK*

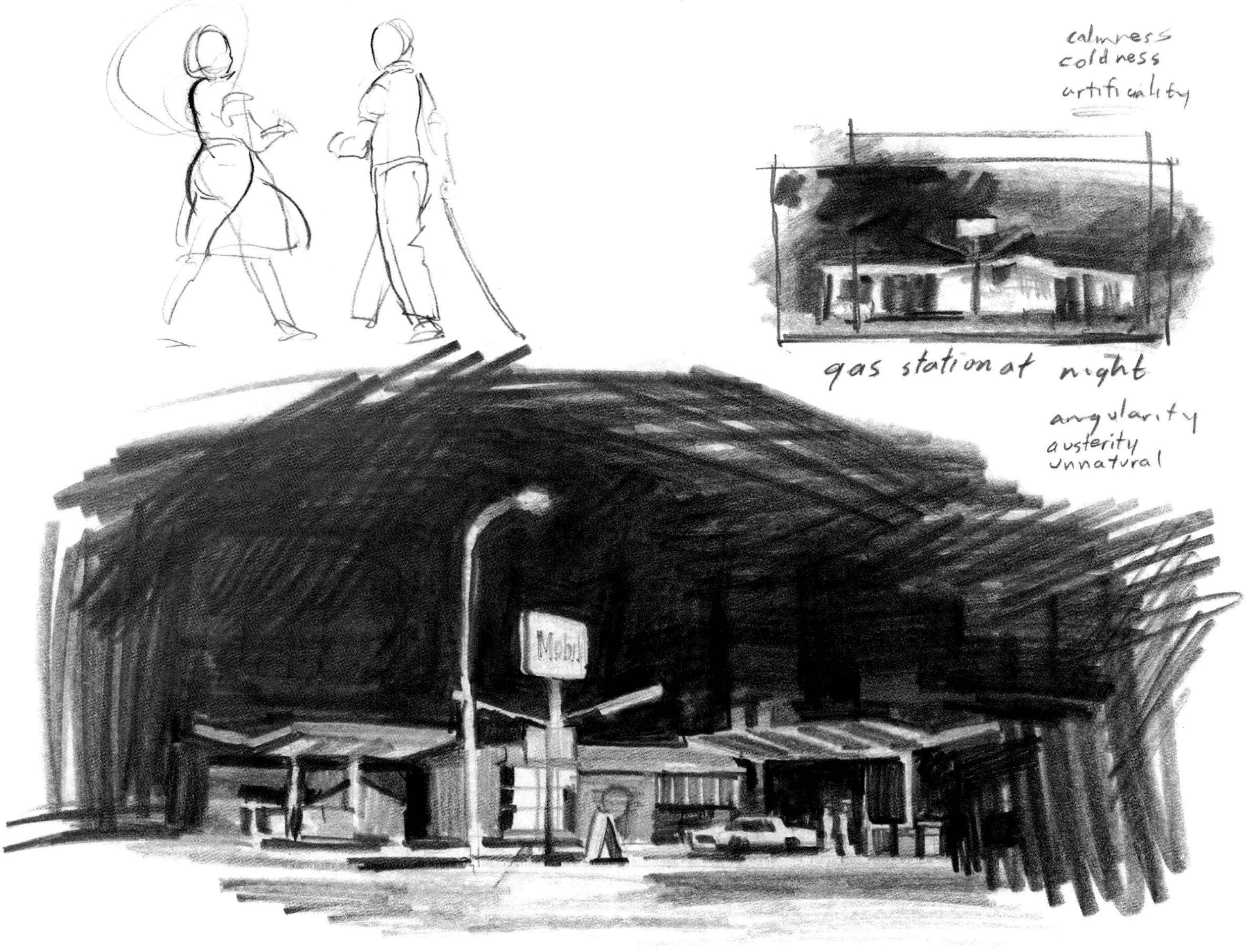

calmness
coldness
artificiality

gas station at night

angularity
austerity
unnatural

▼ **FIGURES IN A VIDEO ARCADE,** *calligraphy pen and charcoal with touches of white Conté on brown paper, 8½" x 11". Is it best to stand or sit for a sketch? Sometimes there is no choice but to stand, as when I was faced with drawing the people in this video arcade. To set up my folding chair would have made me conspicuous and obtrusive, so I leaned against a pillar in the middle of the room. Even so, I made a point of using only simple materials that I could hold in my left hand while I sketched with my right. —JG*

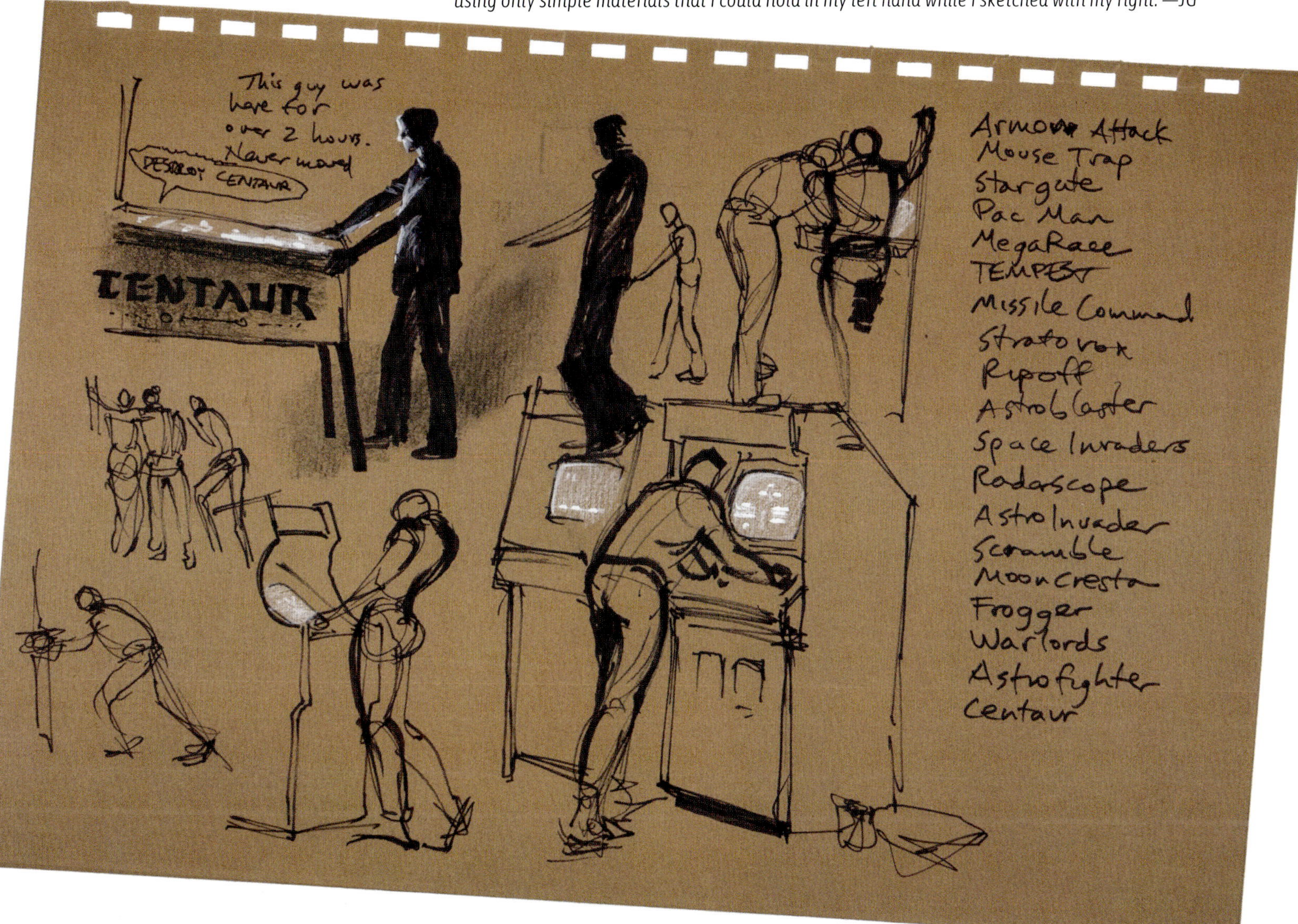

◀ **GAS STATION AT NIGHT,** *soft pencil on smooth paper, 11" x 14". The major challenge in working outdoors at night is adjusting where you sit so that the light on your subject equals the light on your page. If one or the other were too bright, you would have to waste time waiting for your eyes to adjust between extreme brightness and extreme darkness. For this sketch I found a place on the curb underneath a buzzing streetlight, which gave me just enough light to see by. However, the air was so cold that my hand began to shake when I was blackening in the sky, and I was forced to hurry the drawing so that I could get back into the warmth of the car and continue driving down the highway. —JG*

FOXHOUNDS—GREENVILLE, MISSOURI, *ballpoint pen on drawing paper, 6" x 12". We have happened upon many unique experiences as a result of being friendly with onlookers. One time we were sketching a wall of trophies in a tiny Ozark mountain town when we chanced to meet its owner, a congenial man who had been watching us sketch. "My dog Checkers won most of them trophies," he told us, "but I reckon old Hi-Boy and Hi-Girl won't do too bad either this year." By coincidence, the Annual State Foxhunt was to take place that week. He invited us to sit in the back of his pickup along with the dogs as he drove out to Greenville. More than two hundred other dogs arrived from all over the state and were kept in a long row of pens at the edge of the park while their owners swapped dog stories. While I sketched the dogs resting in their pens, another spectator asked me if he could pay me to do a portrait of his dog. Before long I had a regular business going, and in addition to making a little money, I had a chance to learn a great deal about all the different types of sporting dogs and how they are run in regional contests. —JG*

supported by holding the far edge with your hand and propping the near edge on your waist.

DEALING WITH CURIOUS SPECTATORS

Do you remember when you were a child how fascinating it was to see an artist making a picture? Even the simplest line drawing seemed like magic. Shapes and forms appeared from nowhere right before your eyes. More than likely you were transfixed. Perhaps your curiosity prompted a few questions: "Are you an artist?" "How long does it take to learn to draw like that?" Now the tables are turned, and when you sit in public to sketch, you are the artist, subject to the same attention that you once gave as a spectator. Keep in mind that most people have never seen a drawing being made and are completely enchanted by the process of making forms appear on paper. Even though you might think your drawing looks awkward, chances are the people around you deeply admire what you are doing and would like to be sketching also. You might even receive open admiration from spectators wishing they were in your place. If so, encourage them; after all, sketching is for everyone.

If you are so inclined and can maintain your concentration, open up a conversation with one of the onlookers. We have met many interesting people by conversing with them while they watched us sketch. One stock car owner at an auto race watched us sketch for a bit, agreed to pose for us, and also invited us to dinner. A Missouri dog trainer invited us as special guests to the state foxhunt, where we had an opportunity to draw commissioned portraits of the winning dogs. Drawing and talking at the same time is a special skill that takes practice, primarily because the two skills require very different brain functions—drawing uses the right hemisphere while speaking uses the left. Portrait artists often become experts at conversing while they draw and paint because of the special circumstances under which they work.

Depending on your personality you may even want to become something of a

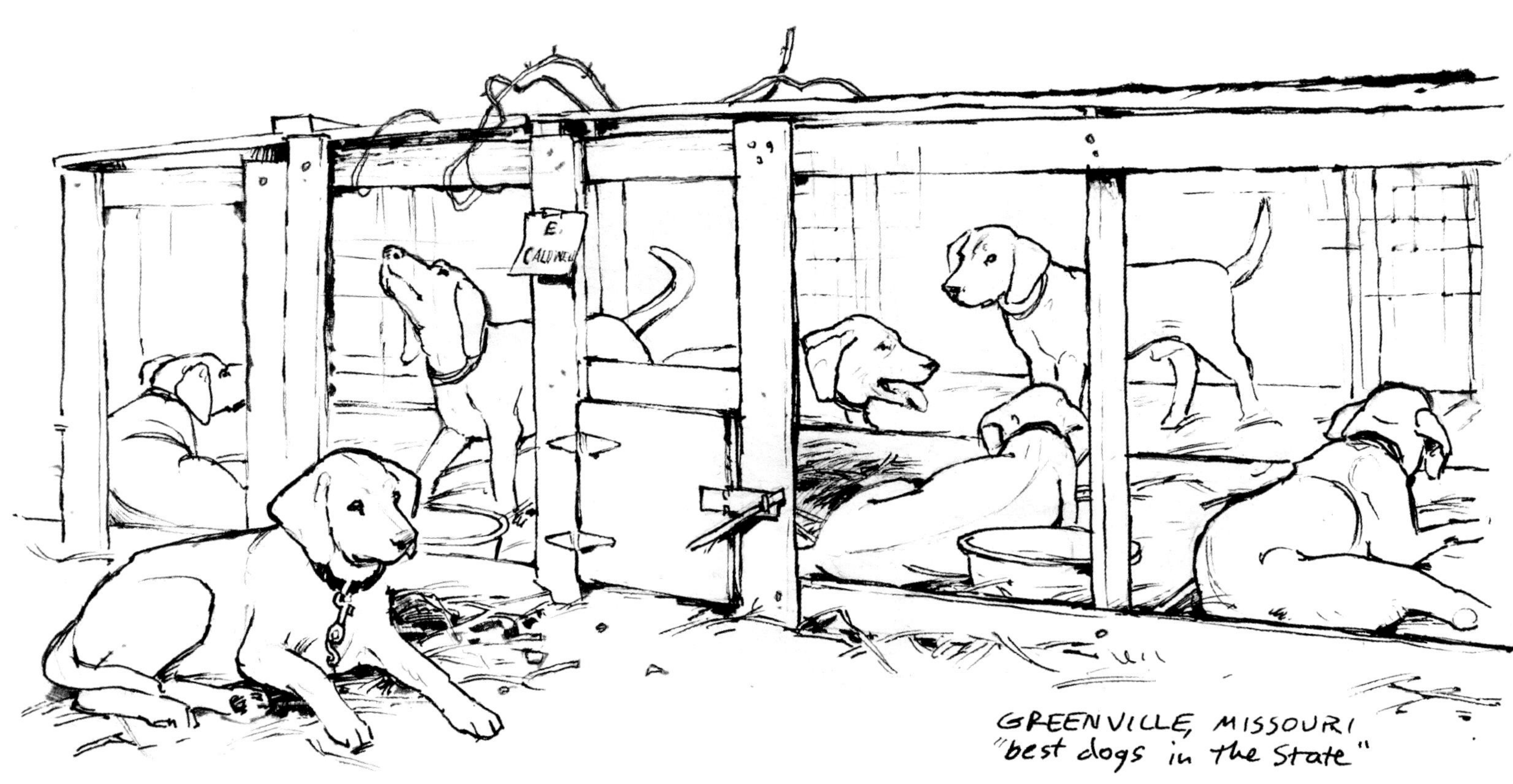

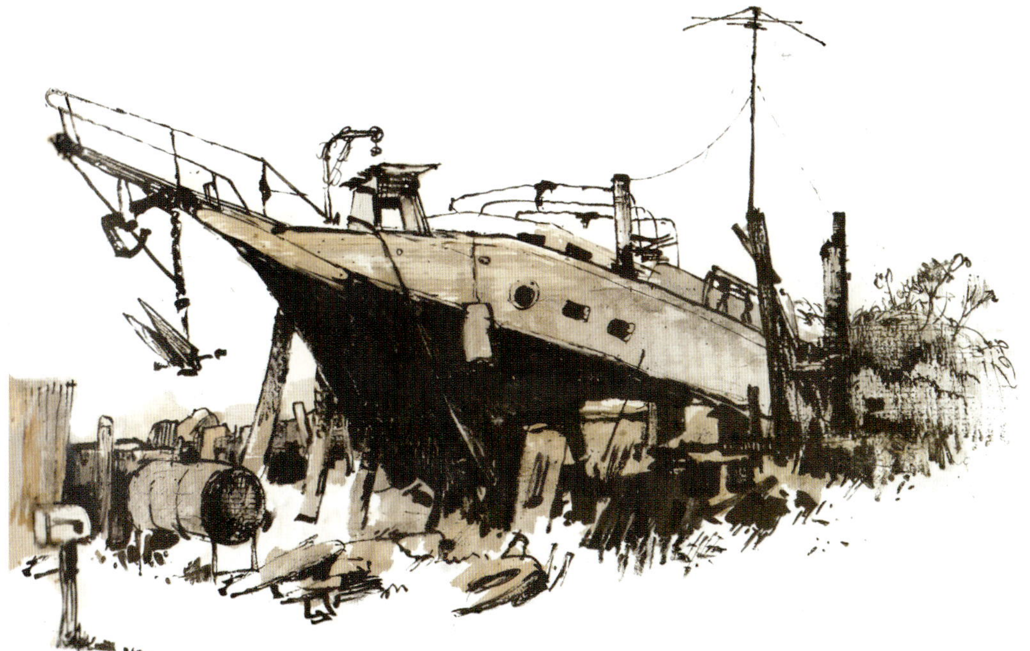

◀ **BOAT HOME,** *calligraphy pen and gray marker on charcoal paper, 9" x 12". If I were a newspaper reporter instead of an artist, I would enjoy filling the newspapers with unusual stories of people and their lives. This boat, for example, is inhabited by a German family that had fled from Germany during World War II. The mother of the family came out of the boat as I was sketching and engaged me in a conversation about her youth in Germany. She confessed that it was her desire to return to Germany in the boat she was living in. Yet as I gazed about at the grounded boat, I realized that her goal was probably an idle dream. In a situation like this, a sketch artist must maintain rapport and at the same time concentrate on drawing. In this instance, it was easy because the conviction with which the woman spoke left little room for my input. —TK*

showman as you sketch, especially when there are kids watching. You can draw a monster in the scene as a final touch, or let them draw their own version. (In Chapter 6, "Using Imagination," you will find ideas for this kind of on-the-spot creativity.) When we do portraits in taverns we have even gone so far as to do a little juggling with our markers in order to hold the interest of bystanders and develop a relaxed rapport with our sitter.

Sketching can be a very personal form of escape, but don't feel you have to be a recluse when you sketch. There are times when getting away from people and being unnoticed is worthwhile. But once you allow yourself to be open with the public about your sketching, you may find that the warm response and support melts away any desire for privacy.

BEING INCONSPICUOUS

There are certain times when you most definitely do *not* want to attract attention, such as when you are sketching a person on the subway, at a wedding, or in a gambling casino. The main reason to be discreet in these instances is to avoid embarrassing the person you are drawing.

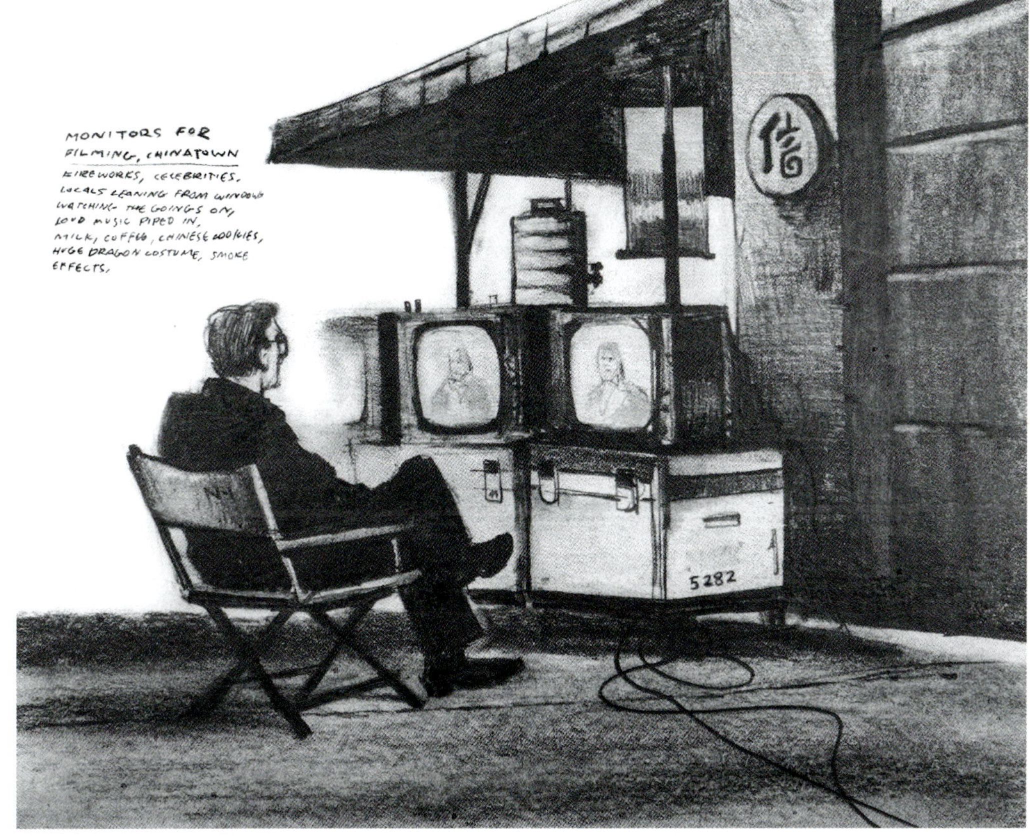

▲ **SECURITY MAN WATCHING TELEVISION MONITORS,** *pencil on illustration board, 8" x 10". I was looking around behind the scenes during the filming of a television commercial when I spotted this security guard seated in front of some video monitors. I realized that sketching the scene meant remaining absolutely inconspicuous since the very person I was sketching would not hesitate to ask me to leave if he realized I wasn't with the crew. I sat down on a bench near my subject and pretended to be watching the monitors instead of sketching. I tried not to let my head bob up and down too much by moving only my eyes from subject to sketch. I also avoided any large sweeping motions of my arm so as not to attract attention. Luckily for me, the guard didn't move so much as a muscle during the twenty minutes or so that I was sketching, and I was able to leave without ever being noticed. —TK*

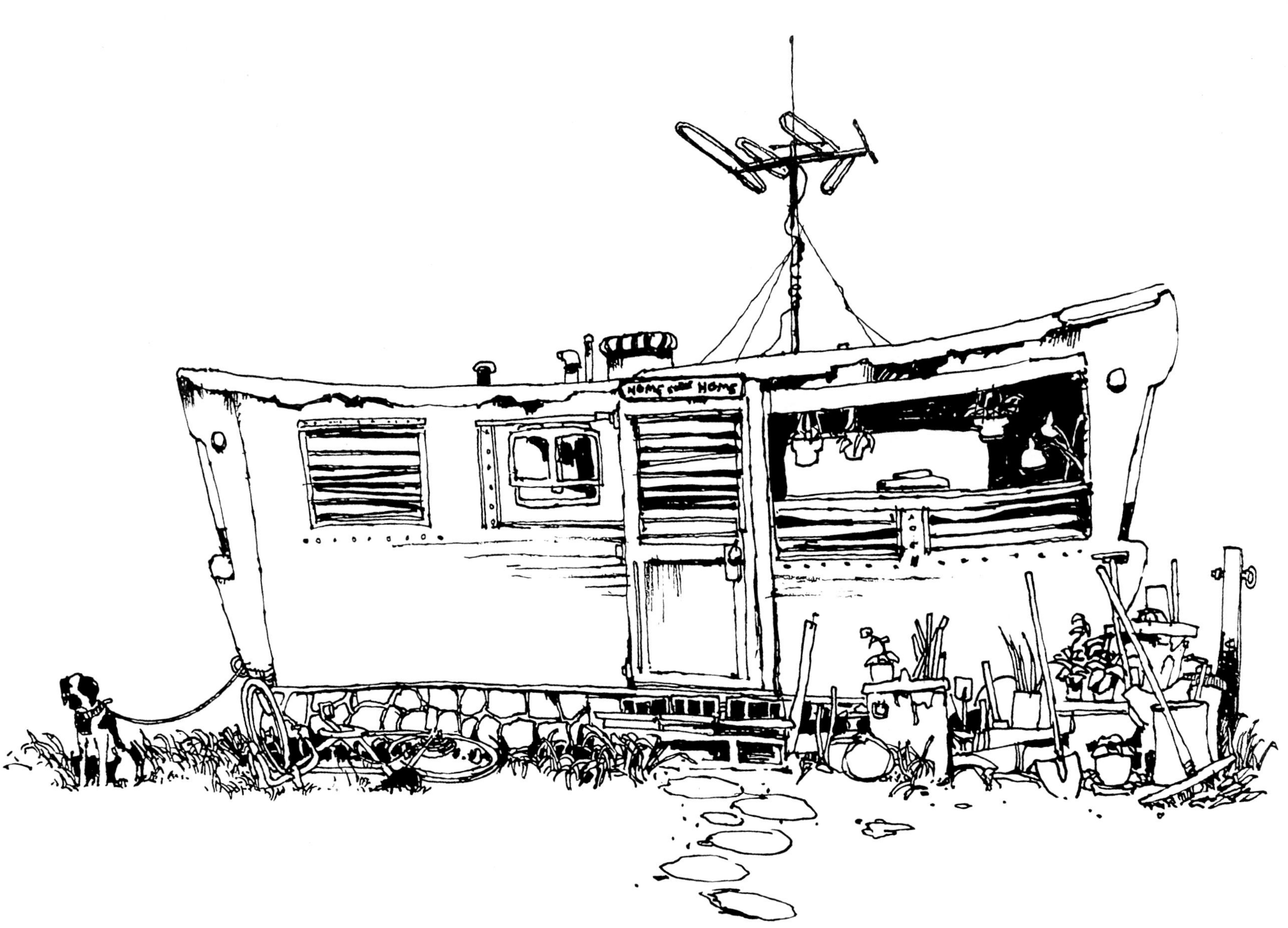

RUN-DOWN TRAILER, *pen and ink, 11" x 14". Sometimes the curious spectator turns out to be the owner of what you are sketching. That was the situation I encountered when I sketched this seemingly abandoned trailer in rural upstate New York. I had found a subject that had just the things I was looking for—a combination of clutter and dilapidation. As I began sketching, I was approached from behind by a young woman with a rather scraggly dog at her side. I was about to comment on the interesting arrangement of rubbish surrounding the trailer, when the woman timidly whispered, "Are you sketching my home?" The woman and I developed an interesting rapport, and, surprisingly enough, as I sketched, she could point out any detail of the clutter that I had overlooked. As a final touch, she even volunteered her dog as a model by tying him to the trailer. The dilapidated dog was the perfect companion for the dilapidated trailer. —TK*

First of all, don't look suspicious. Leave your sunglasses and hat at home. Make sure that the sketchbook you take is small and that your tools are simple—a pencil or a ballpoint pen is all you need. If you have a magazine or book with you, you can hide your sketchbook inside, so that people think you are just taking notes. Toulouse-Lautrec, an avid sketcher, would use the pocket of his overcoat as a place to sketch, but we have never found a need to be so clandestine.

The best technique for being inconspicuous is to avoid eye contact with your subject. When you look up from your drawing, for example, look somewhere else first, and then casually glance at your subject to see if he or she has noticed you. If you look right up and catch the person's eye, he or she will become self-conscious and most likely change the pose. As soon as someone suspects that you are drawing him or her, start a sketch of someone else. Keep a few sketches going at the same time.

It also helps to wear an absent-minded expression. Try to master the ability to look bored. Glance around the scene, and when you look at your subject, act as though you are daydreaming about your sweetheart or stock prices, and then try to hold firmly in your memory the observations you have made. In this way you have to glance back only once or twice more. And when you do look up, avoid moving your head too much or you'll be very conspicuous in people's peripheral vision.

Occasionally, you may be lucky enough to discover a person who decides, as if in unspoken consent, to strike or maintain a pose for you. We've found that big cities are full of people like this who enjoy being the center of your artistic attention. If you happen to be sketching a "free" model, you don't have to be secretive about your observations, and chances are you'll have pretty good luck deriving a worthwhile sketch from a situation.

AT HOME AMID THE ELEMENTS

If you are fairly new to sketching, the best way to develop your confidence in working on the spot is to take your first outings to places where you can sit and draw completely free from distractions. At first you will want to concern yourself only with the mechanics of seeing and drawing. Find a place away from people, in the shade of a good tree, where you can set up your stool and rest your sketchbook comfortably in your lap. In these conditions you may find that your concentration on drawing is even deeper than it is at home, because of the fresh air and abundant light. Whatever level of skill you happen to be at, you will probably surprise yourself with how fast you improve during these peaceful outings.

As you feel more at ease with your sketchbook, bring it out in a totally new environment—a coffee shop, for example, or a street corner, or a museum. This time, don't worry too much about the drawing. Use a small book and spend only about five minutes on each sketch. If you get a good sketch going, spend extra time finishing it; if not, move on to a new page. Above all, make an effort to get involved with the entire scene, including the noises and the people. Let your sketch be a document of that involvement, and you are likely to have much more success than if you had the attitude of trying to tune out distractions.

As you continue to advance, you will become daring enough to sketch in more extreme conditions such as crowded buses, moonlit nights, and rainy afternoons. Don't hesitate to undertake the challenge of these working conditions, because the bigger the challenge, the bigger the reward. Sketches made in less than perfect conditions aren't always successful, but those that are will be prized possessions.

A robust attitude toward working on the spot will ensure your enjoyment of sketching far more than does your drawing ability. You will find that much of the reason that you go sketching will be for the fun of the outing itself, of being outside, discovering new things, and meeting new people. Wind, rain, darkness, the cluster of gaping spectators, and the screech and lurch of the subway will all serve to invigorate you and in turn enliven your artwork.

MUD FLATS, *watercolor on illustration board, 8½" x 18¼". Birds in flight and still pools of water characterize this remote mud flat near San Francisco. There's a calmness to this location that attracts me to it again and again. For some reason, the noise and confusion of daily life seem far removed while I'm sketching there. Perhaps it's due to the ever-present crying of the sea gulls. Perhaps it's the gentleness of the breeze that occasionally ripples across the shallow pools. Locations like this are a paradise for the sketcher who enjoys the peacefulness of being alone. Sketching on buses and streetcorners has a definite appeal for me, but the freedom from spectators and distractions is a welcome alternative. —TK*

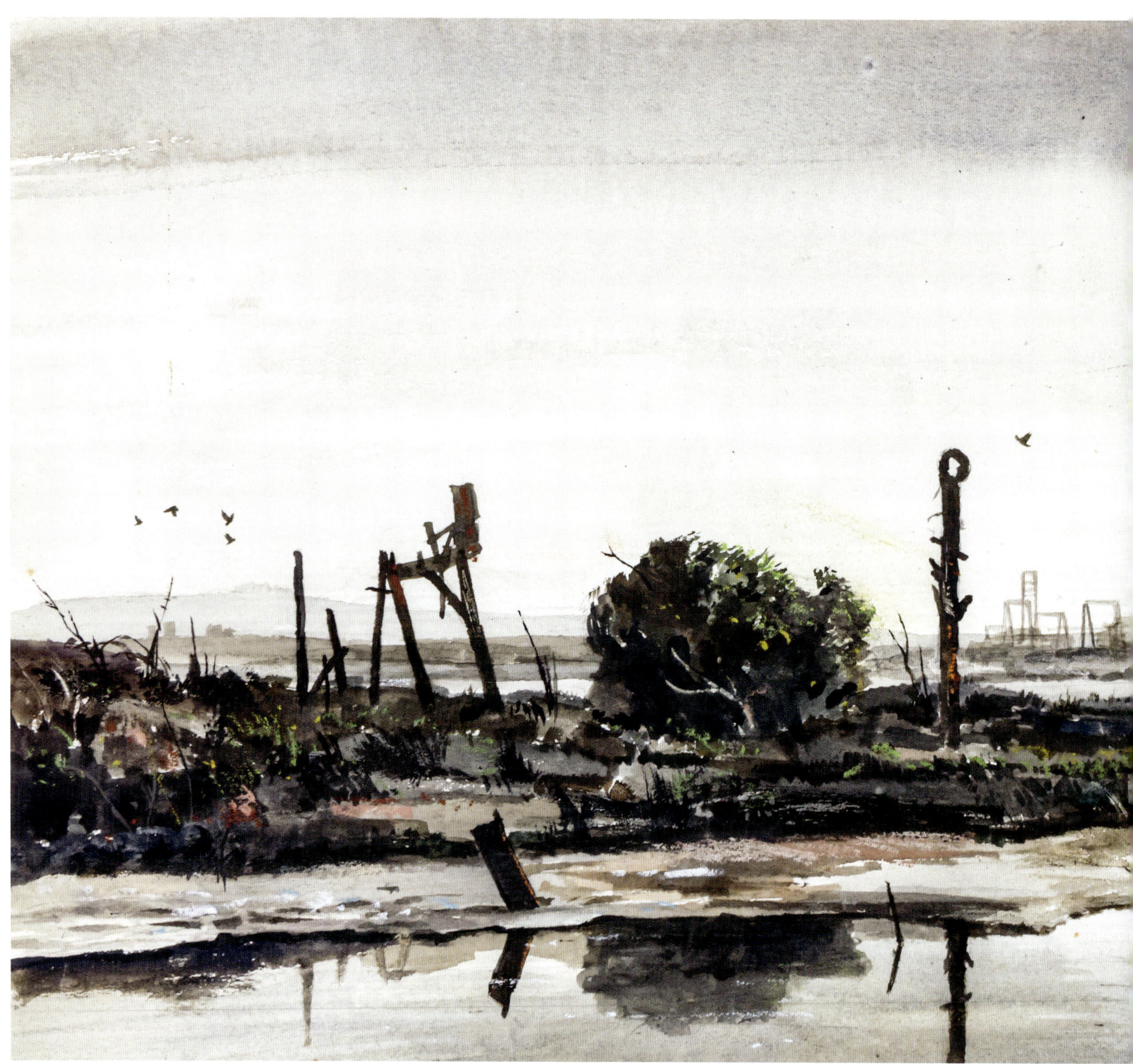

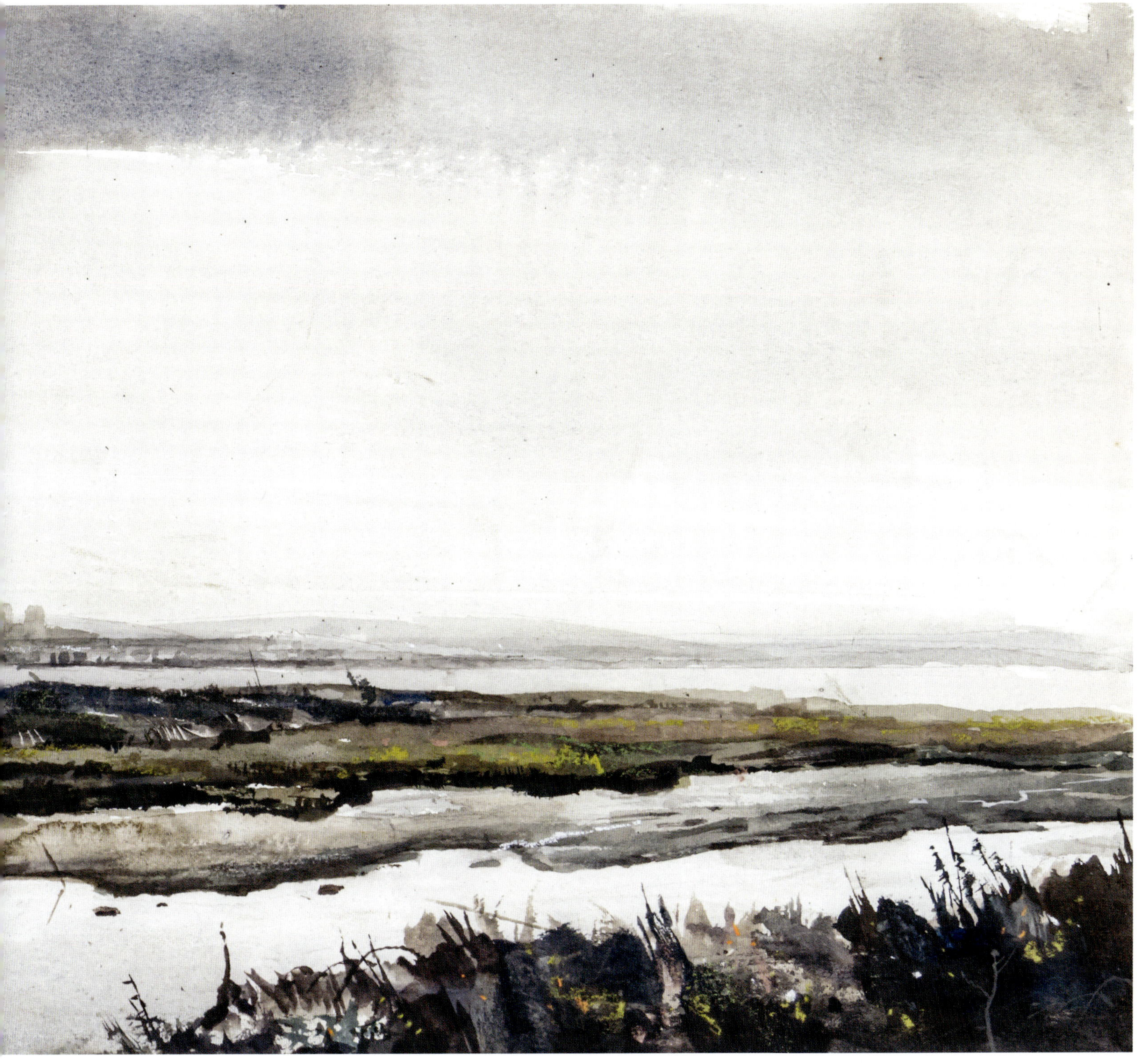

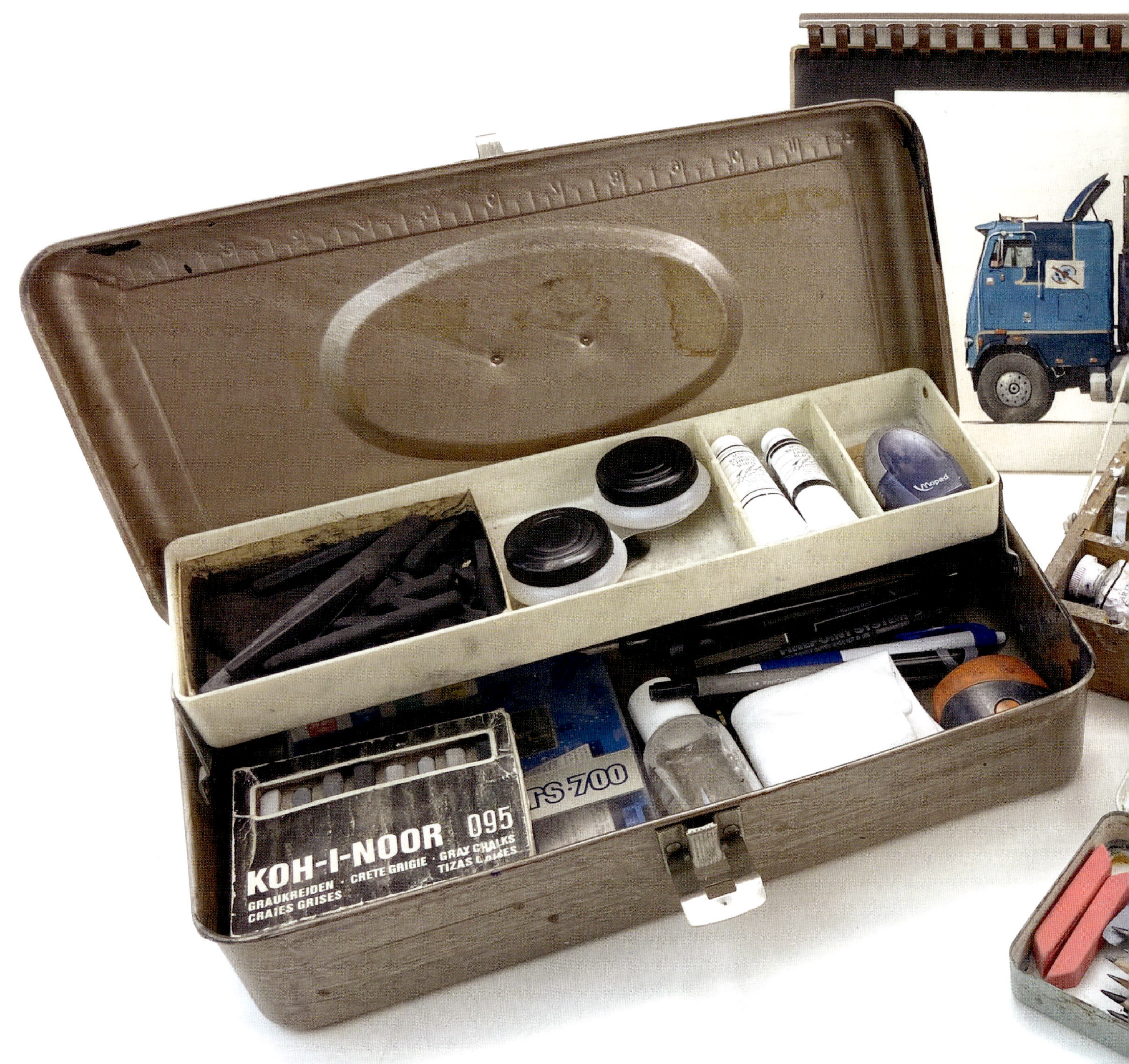

PORTABLE SKETCHBOXES. *Filled with an assortment of drawing tools, these sketchboxes range from a small metal gouache box to a wooden art box with space to store sketchbooks and paper. The box on the left is an old metal fishing tackle box. Before you go on a sketching outing, try to anticipate what materials you will need, and take only the minimum. And in between outings, keep a handful of pens and pencils in your purse, glove compartment, or lunchbox.*

Materials

1980
MARKS-A-LOT
FOUNT INDIA
PRINCETON
AQUA ELITE
Talens
MADE IN HOLLAND
REMBRANDT SKETCHING 6B
BLACKSTONIAN
LYRA
REMBRANDT SKETCHING 4B
GRUMBACHER Charcoal SOFT
A.W.FABER BLACK MAGIC U.S.A. 850
THICK DEEP BLACK LEAD
STAEDTLER Mars Lumograph
STAEDTLER Mars Lumograph
4B
3H
HB

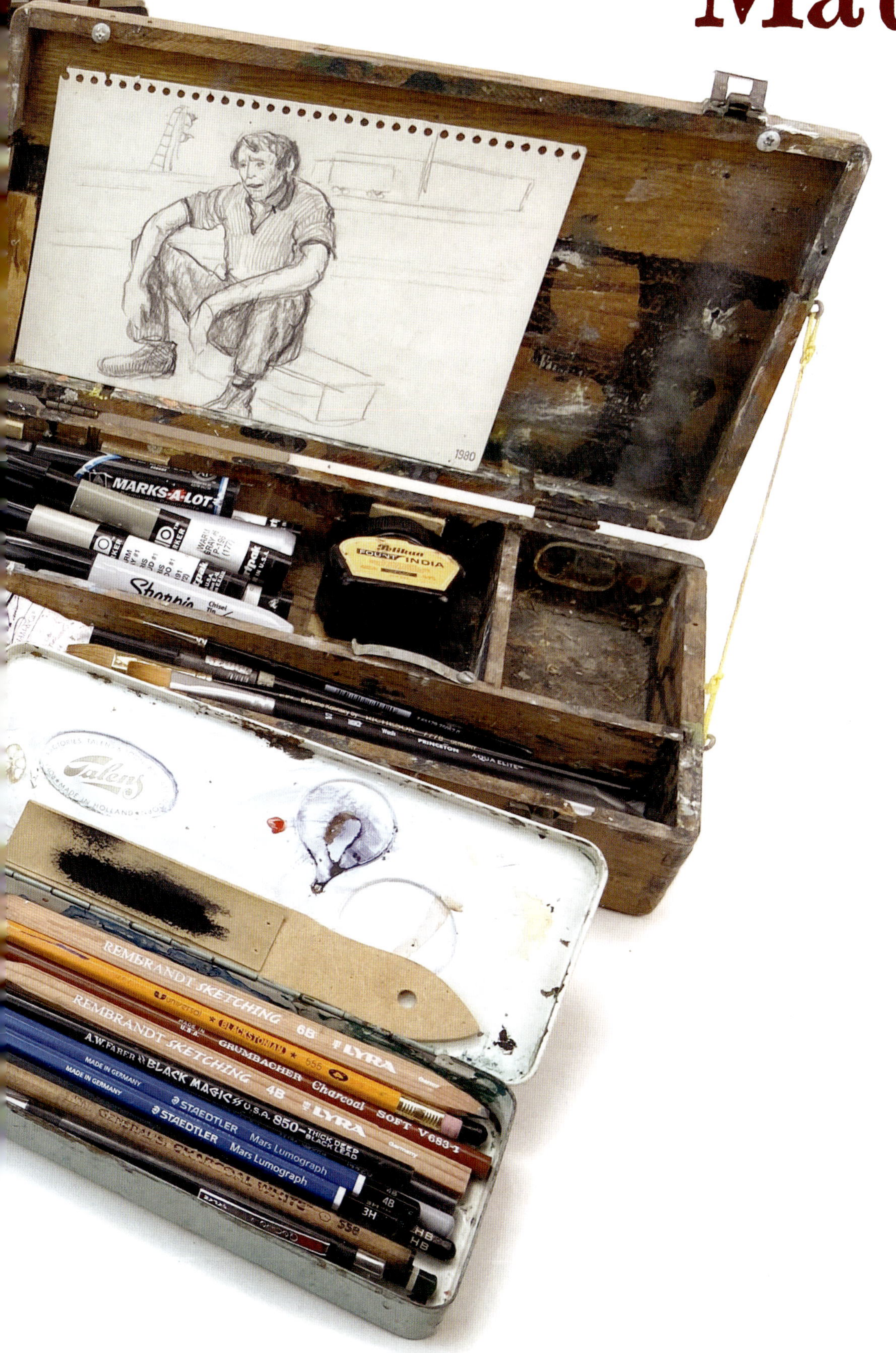

YOUR CHOICE of sketching materials is as individual as you are. Virtually anything you enjoy drawing with can be used for sketching. For this reason, you needn't buy a lot of expensive sketching materials to begin with. A ballpoint pen and some scratch paper are enough to sketch any subject in any of the approaches we describe. As your interest in sketching develops, you will want to purchase more materials to expand your range of effects, but always keep simplicity and economy in mind. We have found through experience that the simplest materials usually yield the best results. Elaborate materials such as paints require an on-the-spot preparation period before the sketching can begin. Taking the time to set up everything can dampen the enthusiasm for the subject. Simple drawing materials are the most satisfactory.

Portability is another important consideration. We rarely carry anything that cannot fit into a small (11" x 14") knapsack. Before leaving the studio, we consider not only what we expect to sketch, but also how long we plan to be on the spot and how much walking we expect to do. The most common mistake we make is to carry too much. Sometimes being limited to just one sketchbook and one drawing tool inspires us to concentrate deeply on the subject rather than getting distracted by elaborate techniques.

SKETCHBOOKS

You will eventually want to own several different sketchbooks to suit the different kinds of sketching you do. As you know, there are dozens to choose from at most art supply stores, varying in size, binding, and paper quality.

Size. The smallest sketchbook we regularly use is a 4" x 6" hardbound blank book, which is convenient enough to be carried all the time for the very quick notations in pencil or ballpoint pen. (See Chapter 10, "Sketching in Your Life," for a description of our use of these books.) At that size you can also find pads with good quality paper that allow you to work a little more on each drawing without wearing through your page. The miniature sketchbooks are ideal for sketching in situations where you wish to remain unobtrusive, as in a theater or on a bus.

If you carry a backpack, briefcase, or purse with you daily, you can comfortably manage the 5½" x 8½" or 9" x 12" format. This scale will probably fill most of your sketching needs. We brought 9" x 12" sketchbooks on our first trip across America, and used them in a variety of settings. This size has the advantage of being easy to hold and carry as well as fitting conveniently on a bookshelf when you are at home.

By the time you move up to the 11" x 14" format, you will want to spend a little more effort on each sketch. This is the perfect size to take when you leave home on a Saturday morning to go nature sketching, for example. Remember that you don't have to do just one drawing per page—you can also fill a page with small studies. The 11" x 14" size is still not unmanageable for sketching in museums or on street corners, but you will definitely be more conspicuous.

The largest sketchbook we find practical is 14" x 17"; beyond that we usually have a definite purpose in mind that calls for individual sheets of paper clipped to a drawing board. Some artists like to use extremely large pads—up to 18" x 24"—for bold, gestural charcoal or crayon sketches, because the large size allows free arm movement from the shoulder. If you feel your work is getting too cramped, try this large size for a change. Then when you return to smaller sizes, you will notice much more boldness in your technique.

Binding. The three most common types of binding available for sketchbooks are hardcover, spiral, and adhesive. The binding that you choose depends on the amount of abuse you expect to give the sketchbook and whether you wish to remove pages from the book. Hardcover sketchbooks are the sturdiest and most permanent, but also the most expensive. However, for a sketchbook that serves as a journal of your vacation experiences or personal inspirations, the investment is well worthwhile. With hardcover binding you never have the problem of pages coming loose. Instead, the pages are all in order and well protected.

Spiral binding holds pages fairly secure, yet allows the book to be folded back so that you have a single flat surface to work on. This feature allows you to easily draw on the entire page of your sketchbook as well as making the sketchbook easier to hold. The spiral binding allows pages to be easily removed, which is handy when a sketch fails and you wish to discard it, or when a sketch goes so well that you wish to frame it or give it to a friend. But beware—rough use can also cause the pages of a spiral-bound sketchbook to fall out or become damaged.

Adhesive-bound sketchbooks are bound in a manner similar to scratchpads. They are usually the least expensive type of sketchbook, and unfortunately the least durable. Folding the front pages back usually causes the book to fall apart, so it is advisable to remove each sketch after you do it and file it in a safe place. In general, these sketchbooks are most useful for quicker sketches. When you intend to spend a great deal of time and effort on a sketch you will probably be better off with a more durable type of sketchbook.

Another option, especially if you prefer working with special paper, is custom binding. It's easier than it sounds—in fact, you can have your sketchbooks bound for much less cost than for commercial sketchbooks. Most print shops can bind any stack of paper in a plastic clasp in just a few minutes. We often buy special papers at low cost at a paper supply warehouse or office supply shop, cut them down to 9" x 12" or 11" x 14" bundles, and have several of them bound at a time. You can also make a sketchbook containing several different kinds of paper, so that you can allow yourself the option of using various techniques while packing only one sketchbook on your outing.

Sometimes you may want to use a special size or type of paper that is not available in commercial sketchbooks. Instead of custom binding, another option is to work with loose sheets held to a drawing board with big metal clips on two or more edges. We have a variety of Masonite panels in sizes up to 22" x 28" which we use for this purpose. Many art supply stores carry large boards with the clips built in and a handle cut into one side for portability. We often use these for sketching in drybrush or wash techniques because the oversize clips work well to hold the illustration board, but they are equally useful for other sketching media.

Paper. The type of paper you choose makes a big difference in how a sketch will turn out. A wash drawing would destroy cheap paper; markers would bleed right through it. On the other hand, the expensive papers should be saved for techniques that call for them.

There are a variety of lightweight and inexpensive bond paper pads that often bear the name "sketch" paper. These really are the bread and butter of sketching. We use them mostly for the fifteen-minute waiting-for-the-bus kind of sketch. The "tooth," or texture, of the surface is smooth enough to allow for fairly delicate shading and cross-hatching as well as the broader, more gestural kind of sketching. This is the kind of paper to use for motion studies and any fairly quick sketches of nature, people, or man-made objects. Be aware of the limitations, however. Bond paper does not hold up to the wet media—brush and ink, wash drawing, watercolor—nor to the blending media such as charcoal or pastel. The best materials to use with bond paper are pencil, ballpoint pen, and fine line markers.

A good versatile paper can be found in the so-called "drawing" pads. The paper generally has a slightly coarser tooth than sketch paper and is of a heavy enough weight that it adapts well to techniques involving extensive working. The surface of "drawing" paper is favorable to pencil, charcoal, pen and ink, and dry brush. However, wash should be used sparingly on "drawing" paper, as the surface tends to buckle with too much moisture.

Watercolor paper and charcoal paper are both high-quality specialized papers with a very coarse tooth, available in various pads as well as individual sheets. In addition to their use with watercolor and charcoal, they also both work very compatibly with such other techniques as brush and ink because of their interesting texture.

Markers have a temperamental personality that demands a particular consideration of the surfaces they're used on. In most papers, the fibers are loosely bound together into a porous

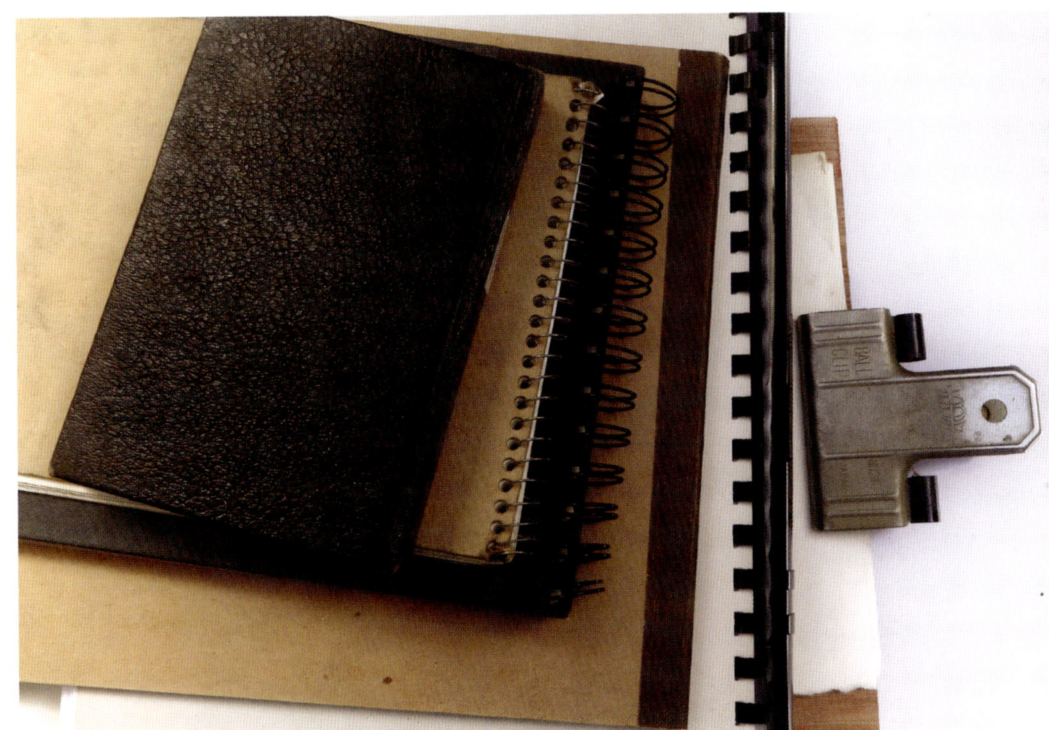

SKETCHBOOK BINDINGS. *Before you choose a sketchbook, consider the advantages and disadvantages of each type of binding. The hardcover binding gives the strongest protection to the pages, but it's also the most expensive and makes removal of pages difficult. The two types of wire spiral binding serve most sketching needs, and they allow you to fold the cover around to the back for a flat working surface. Paste binding permits you to remove pages, but they often fall out by themselves inadvertently. The black plastic binding is a simple custom-binding process that allows you to make your own sketchbooks out of any type of paper. For large individual sheets, use a wood or Masonite backing board and some large artist's clips.*

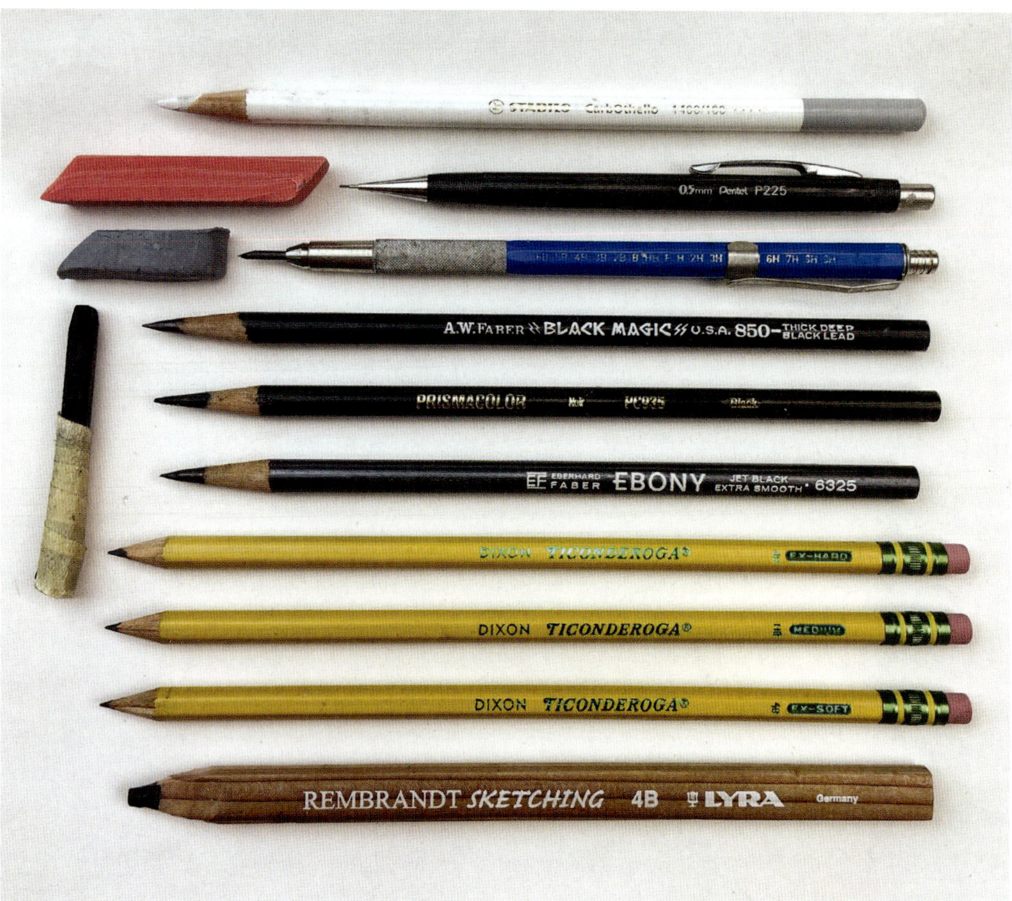

PENCILS. *The flat sketching pencil at the bottom has a rectangular graphite lead. The three pencils are standard yellow office pencils of varying degrees of hardness. They can be used for a wide array of effects in both line and tone. We use these instead of expensive artist's pencils. Continuing on up, the Eberhard Faber Ebony, Berol Prismacolor, and A. W. Faber Black Magic have thicker leads and give rich blacks. The Prismacolor also has a waxy base that makes smudging or erasing difficult. A draftsman's lead-holder pencil takes individual leads that can be bought in any degree from the hard 6H to the soft 6B. Mechanical pencils feature ultrathin leads for delicate lines. On tone paper, we often use the chalky white CarbOthello. A red or pink eraser and a gray kneaded eraser help both with fixing mistakes and adding light accents. Finally, charcoal and Conté are available in both pencils and compressed sticks, shown here partially wrapped in masking tape.*

structure that absorbs the marker solvent, causing the dye to bleed through to the next page as well as creating a fuzzy effect. The commercial marker papers are nonporous, yet they're often too lightweight for most sketching uses. In addition, some are so nonabsorbent that the marker ink never really settles into the paper, and as a result every layer of color that you add to the original tone creates a smear. Certainly all of these effects can be used to advantage, but because of these variables, it's difficult to find a good marker paper for general sketching use.

Surprisingly enough, we've found that Strathmore 300 Series charcoal paper pads come the closest of all sketchpad papers to providing a good surface for marker techniques. But by far our favorite paper for use with markers is a satin-finish white printer's bristol stock, which we refer to as "smooth paper" in the captions. We buy it from a paper warehouse in stacks of 100 sheets, 23" x 29". We then cut it up and bind it into our own sketchbooks. The surface handles pencil very well and tolerates much cross-hatching in pen-and-ink techniques. If you can find some in your area, we recommend giving it a try.

Another favorite paper of ours is the ordinary brown wrapping paper also available at printing paper warehouses. This usually comes in the form of large rolls which we trim ourselves and have bound into convenient sketchbook sizes. Not only does this paper have a smoother tooth than charcoal paper, it's also much cheaper. The color of the paper is grocery-bag brown, which provides a very pleasant middle tone on which to work light and dark, such as with pencil and white gouache. Ballpoint pen also works very well on this paper, as do white pastel pencils, which we sometimes substitute for the gouache.

If you want to sketch on something sturdy and don't mind a bit of extra expense, we recommend illustration board or bristol board. Both of these products are available at most art supply stores and come in two different surfaces—hot pressed and cold pressed. Hot pressed is a smooth surface, while cold pressed is a bit rougher. Both surfaces can be used with any medium, though, generally speaking, hot pressed favors pen and ink while cold pressed favors wash and charcoal. The durability of these papers makes them worthwhile to use for sketches that you plan to spend some time on and that you know you'll want to keep for a while.

PENCILS

The ordinary graphite pencil is a versatile, reliable tool for sketching because it can deliver both a smooth line and a controllable tone. It can be easily erased and it's available in a range of leads from the very scratchy 6H to the butter-smooth 6B. Somewhere in the middle lies the regular #2 office pencil. This is perhaps the most generally useful of all pencils, and it's what we refer to simply as "pencil" in the captions. We use office pencils for the underdrawing stage of almost every sketch we do, as you will see in the next chapter. You can do an entire tonal drawing with a #2, but in general it is useful to have at least one softer and one harder pencil also.

We usually carry a number of pencils with us in order to avoid having to sharpen them constantly. When one pencil gets dull, we simply pull out another one.

Soft Graphite Pencils. There are several brands of soft graphite pencils available. Of these, Eagle's Draughting and Eberhard Faber's Ebony are perhaps the most common. Since these pencils have a thicker lead than most pencils, they can be sharpened into a longer point which facilitates broad, crisp stroking. These are a favorite of ours for quicker, gestural sketching as well as for indicating landscapes. Also available are the flat-lead specialty pencils, usually in 6B leads and often called simply "sketching" pencils. Though handy for some effects, we have found them to be somewhat awkward to use as well as providing no real working advantage over the Draughting and Ebony types. Sketching pencils are fun to use, however, because the flat leads can be used to shade an area very rapidly. Pure graphite sticks also cover large areas quickly and allow for a fluid stroke. The only problem with graphite sticks is their messiness. If you wish to work with these, take the precaution of covering part of the stick with masking tape to avoid getting the soft graphite all over your clothing, hands, and unintended areas of your sketch.

Charcoal Pencils. Graphite pencils aren't the only kind of pencils available, of course. We often use a 6B charcoal pencil or the velvety Conté, both of which provide rich blacks and a less shiny, finished look to the sketch. Charcoal, also available in compressed sticks, has the advantage of being easy to model by smudging and erasing, but you must carry along some fixative if you expect your sketchbook to get a lot of handling on the way home. We like to combine the crispness of pen and ink and markers with the softness of charcoal in a variety of mixed techniques.

Mechanical Pencils. Mechanical pencils allow you to advance the lead as it wears down, rather than continually re-sharpening it. Ultra-thin mechanical pencils feature plastic leads in thickness of .3 mm, .5 mm, and up. These leads are very delicate and will break with exuberant handling; however, there is no comparison for the subtlety of shading and fineness of detail the ultra-thin leads allow. A draftsman's lead holder makes use of much thicker leads, which can be extended far enough from the handle to allow for a broad-stroke technique using the side of the lead.

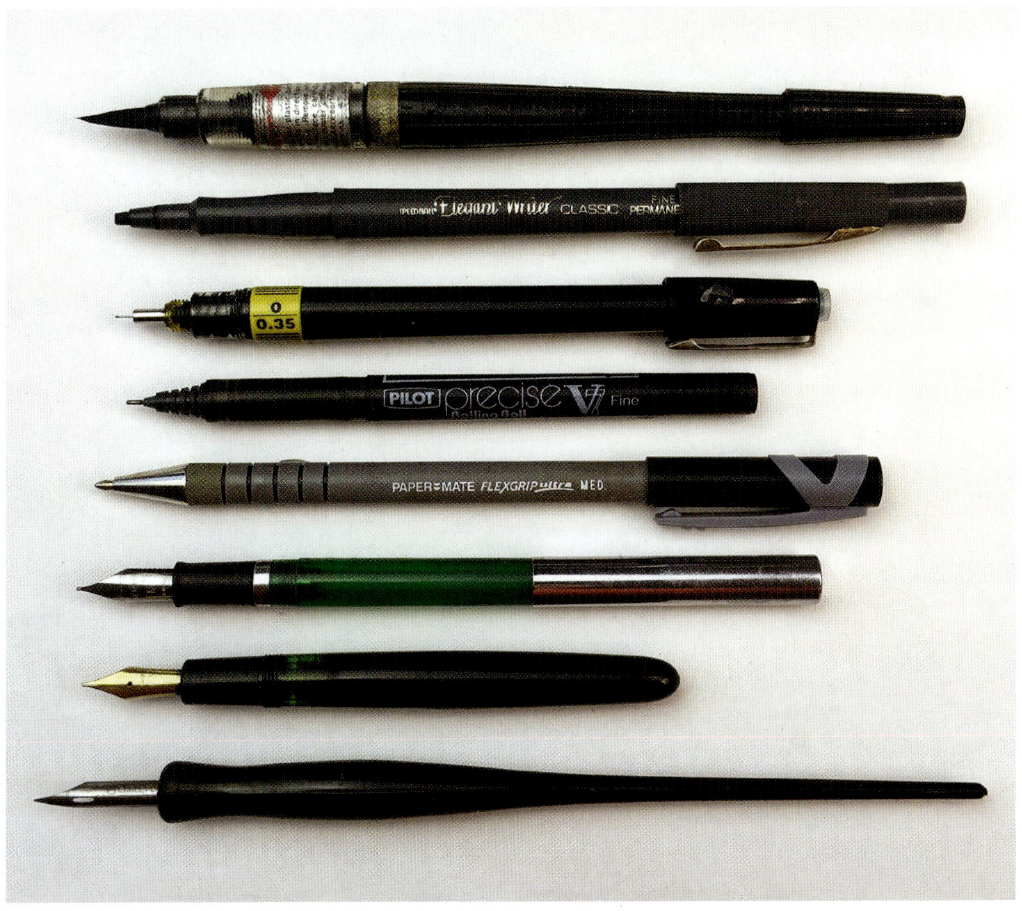

PENS. *The old-fashioned dip pen at bottom has given way to a family of modern specialized pens that require no bottle of ink to be carried on location. Artist's fountain pens, such as the Pelikan 120 and the less expensive Schaeffer cartridge pen, have a refillable ink supply and a rounded nib. Ordinary ballpoint pens have the same feel as a pencil and are useful for quick sketching. The fine-tip felt pen and its more precise cousin, the technical pen, yield a black line of uniform thickness. We use the chisel-tip calligraphy pen for any kind of sketching that combines line and black areas. The brush pen has replaceable ink cartridges and a sturdy nylon-brush tip.*

Erasers. For pencil and charcoal, erasers are essential, not only for fixing errors, but also for lifting out light accents from toned areas. Buy two erasers: a kneaded eraser for correcting lines and modeling toned areas, and a red eraser, which can be cut in half longitudinally and sharpened with a razor blade for creating crisp highlights.

PENS

Pen and ink has long been a favored medium among sketchers because of the spontaneity possible. The rapid flow of ink and the smooth gliding of the pen over paper allow for immediate expression. To capture form with a few quick pen lines is a thrilling experience, and the joy that an artist feels in so doing comes through in the sketches. The work of masters such as Heinrich Kley and Charles Dana Gibson attests to the exhilaration of the pen-and-ink experience.

Dip Pens. The traditional crow quill and other flexible nib pens, which are dipped repeatedly in the ink, provide one of the most satisfying ink lines. Since the nibs are interchangeable, they offer you a wide range of options. The major drawback, of course, is the open bottle of ink, which can easily spill in crowded places or interiors. Because of this, you might be better off to save your dip pens for use only in places where a spill wouldn't be a problem.

Fountain Pens. Fountain pens feature a steady flow of permanent ink to the nib because of a built-in inkwell. These pens have many of the virtues of dip pens without the inconvenience of open ink bottles and constant dipping. Most manufacturers offer three points—fine, medium, and broad—each of which has a slightly flexible nib with a rounded point that won't catch and spatter on an upstroke. Pelikan and Koh-I-Noor manufacture very good refillable fountain pens, but we've found that the Sheaffer cartridge fountain pens, which cost a fraction as much, perform as well or better. These are usually available at office supply stores.

Ballpoint Pens. Dependable, durable, and versatile, the ballpoint pen is the sketcher's most convenient tool. We all need to break down our preconceptions and realize the ballpoint is useful for more than writing.

By controlling the pressure, you can use it as you would a pencil, combining delicate shading with strong fluid lines. Most people find ballpoint pens a bit slippery at first, but that characteristic makes them well suited to quick sketching—especially of moving subjects.

Fine-Tip Felt Pens. For a black line of uniform thickness, try the inexpensive nylon-tipped felt pens, now available from a variety of manufacturers. Unlike technical pens, they have the virtue of being able to move very fast and still maintain an even line. Remember that the ink is water soluble, so they can't be used underneath watercolor or ink washes.

Technical Pens. Technical pens, such as the Rapidograph and the Castell TG, are precise pens intended primarily for drafting uses. Since the ink flows through the center of the point, there is no way to vary the thickness of the line. This is an advantage for making contour lines with an absolutely even character. They also are available with points much finer than any other pen. But like most finely tuned machines, they tend to be somewhat temperamental unless they are used regularly or else cleaned and cared for in between uses. Despite the care they require, technical pens are a delight to work with. The line flows steadily and dries instantly, and the amount of detail possible is amazing. A #2 and a #0 are sufficient for most types of sketching. A #2 produces a quick and fluid line which is useful for spontaneous pen techniques, while the #0 is slower and useful for delicate cross-hatchings and patient contour drawing.

Felt-Tipped Calligraphy Pens. One of our favorite sketching tools is the water-based calligraphy felt pen, with a flat tip about two or three millimeters wide. By turning the tool in your hand, you can instantly switch from fine line to broad black areas. It's hard to beat for quick, painterly indications of complex subjects. Using calligraphy markers on charcoal paper creates an interesting textural effect. Lightly stroking on this surface produces a grainy drybrush look which works well in combination with fine lines and black areas also possible with the calligraphy marker.

Brush Pens. Brush pens resemble regular pens except that they have a nylon brush where the pen point would normally be. We began using these as an alternative to the mess and bother of brush and ink. The tip is very durable and allows both fluid lines and drybrush effects with ease. Of the brush pens we've tried, the Pentel Color Brush seems the most satisfactory. It features a flexible cartridge filled with ink which can release a flow of ink to the brush tip with just a squeeze of the fingers. The cartridge can be replaced when the ink supply has gone dry. We highly recommend that you experiment with brush pens—the ease of handling and versatility of these tools is remarkable.

MARKERS

Markers differ from pens in several ways. Instead of using ink, they generally use a transparent dye dissolved in a fast-drying nonaqueous solvent. The porous tip feeds this dye evenly onto the paper surface, where it instantly absorbs into the fibers of the paper. The chisel-tip style is available in a vast assortment of colors. We do most of our marker sketching with the cool gray chisel-tip markers, which are sold in a value range from #1 (very light) to pure black. We like to limit ourselves to six values: #1, #2, #4, #6, #8, and black, in order to simplify and organize the picture.

Gray markers are best suited to spontaneous tonal techniques in conjunction with a pen line. A typical procedure would be to make a brief pencil underdrawing, then do a line drawing of the subject with a fine-tip felt pen, and finally add a few touches of marker to suggest the local tones of the subject.

Furthermore, markers can be used for very realistic, detailed renderings that resemble wash drawings. The key to rendering in markers is to work from light values to dark. After you have established a fairly tight underdrawing in pencil on illustration board or bristol board, begin laying in the lighter values of your subject. If an area is too light, you can glaze it down with another application. Save the darker values and black for last, and try to avoid outlines altogether. Don't throw away your old, semi-dry markers; you can use them for drybrush effects, a technique in which a semi-dry marker is lightly scrubbed across the paper so that an uneven tone is created. Large black areas can be achieved quickly through the use of the ultra-large black markers commonly sold in stationery stores. The ink in these markers is a rich black, making them ideal for single-coat coverage.

WASH AND DRYBRUSH

Both wash and drybrush are somewhat cumbersome sketching techniques because you must carry a bottle of water and a bottle of ink besides the brush and sketch pad. However, despite the awkwardness of the materials themselves, the effects you can get make both wash and drybrush among the most effective techniques for realistic rendering.

We have simplified the necessary materials to the bare essentials. For brushes we use a #2 and a #8 red-sable or sabeline round watercolor brush as well as a ½-inch flat watercolor brush of red sable or white nylon. If you don't

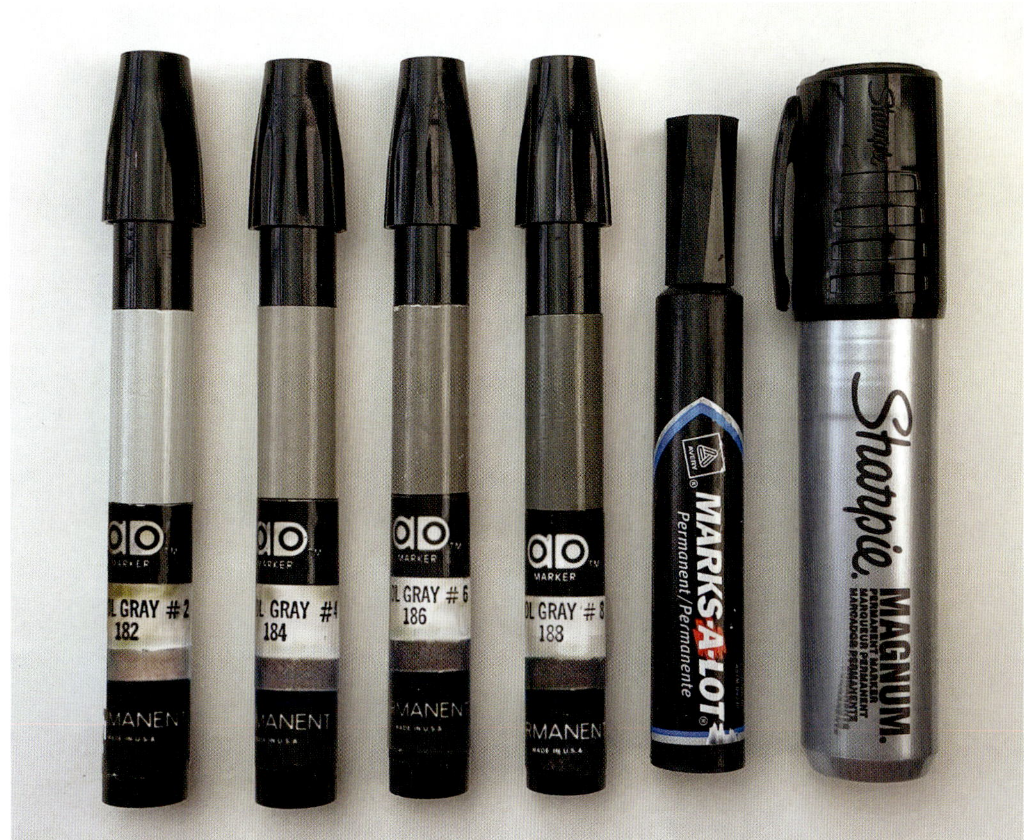

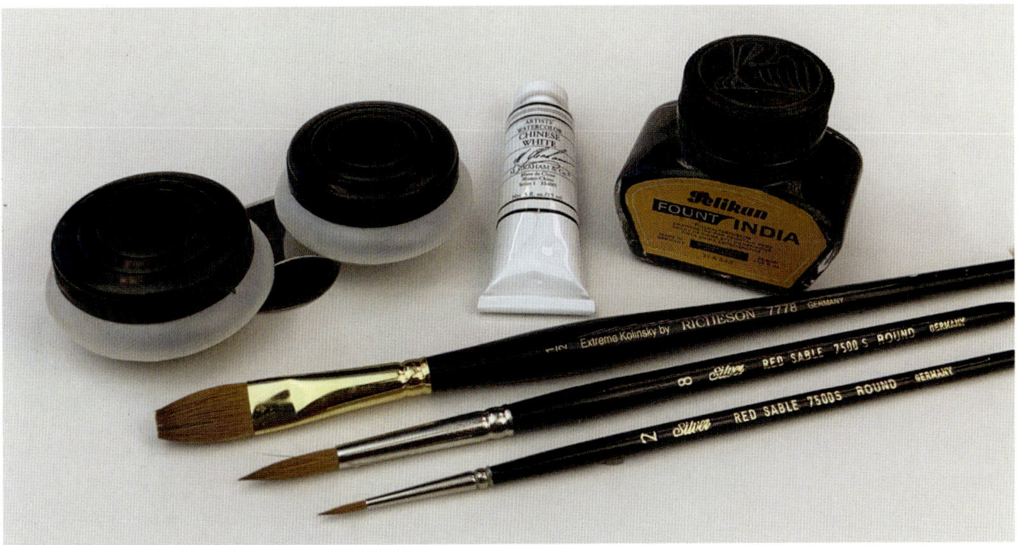

▲▲ **MARKERS.** *For uniform gray tones, we use the cool gray chisel-tip AD markers, which come in a controlled range of values from light to dark. We use #2, #4, #6, and #8. You can buy black markers in a variety of inexpensive brands. We generally use a standard Marks-A-Lot for average-sized sketches and a broad-tip marker for covering large black areas.*

▲ **BRUSH MATERIALS.** *A simple assortment of pure red-sable watercolor brushes—#2, #8, and ½" flat—are worth the investment because they can be used in many different sketching techniques, including wash, drybrush, brush-and-ink line drawing, and white gouache on tone paper. The clip-on covered palette cups can be filled with white gouache or ink on one side and water on the other, and the caps can be used as miniature palettes for diluting the paint. Pelikan Fount India ink is our favorite, because it can be used with the brush directly as well as it can with refillable pens.*

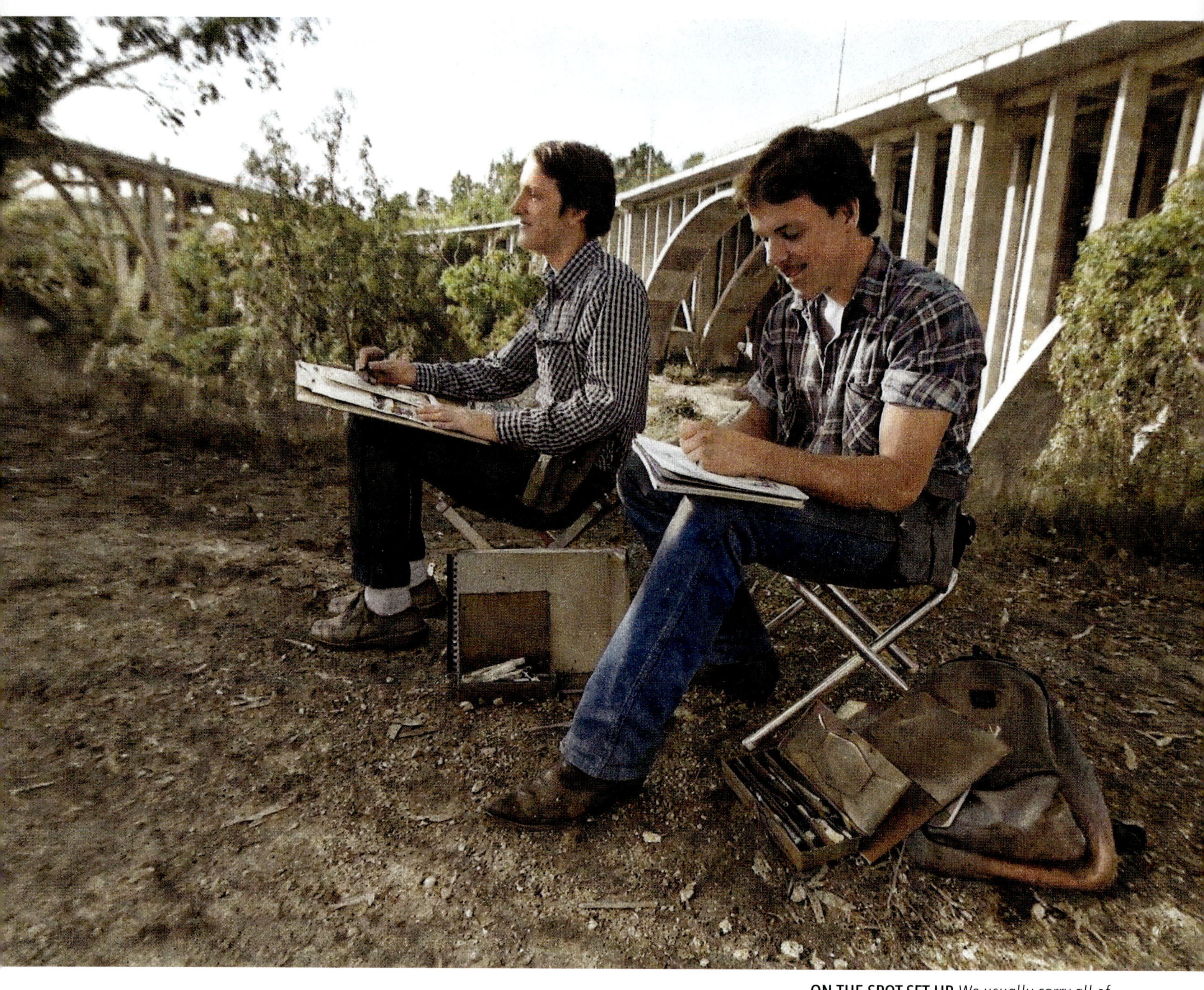

ON-THE-SPOT SET-UP. *We usually carry all of our tools and sketchbooks inside a medium-size knapsack, which can be carried anywhere indoors or out. Even the fishing stool, when folded, fits through a loop on the top of the knapsack. When we don't happen to have the complete set-up with us, we always make sure we have a small belt pouch, containing a 4" x 6" hardbound sketchbook and our most common drawing tools: a #2 pencil, a fountain pen, a calligraphy pen, and a ballpoint pen.*

wish to purchase that many brushes, #2 red sable or sabeline round will do for most sketching needs. The #8 round and the ½-inch flat are useful for large tonal areas such as skies, but they are optional depending on your subject matter. We also use a clip-on palette cup identical to those used by oil painters to hold turpentine and linseed oil. The palette cup features two containers with lids, and we fill these with ink on one side and water on the other. Two small baby food jars or empty 35 mm film containers also work fine for this purpose, though neither is as convenient as the palette cups.

By simplifying the materials, transport becomes easy. The brush and a pencil for the underdrawing as well as a folded paper towel can all fit in a shirt pocket; and the ink and water containers can be carried in a small purse or day pack along with a piece of illustration board or a sketchbook.

After sitting down near your subject, remove the lids from your water and ink containers and set the lids and the containers beside you within easy reach. Dip your brush into the water and bring out a drop of water. By using your two lids as miniature palettes, you can more than adequately get all of the gray mixtures that you will need as you work. Following your sketch, wash your brush as thoroughly as possible in the remaining water, and put the lids back on the containers.

For drybrush, follow the same procedure but use only the ink. Your paper towel comes in handy for drying the tip and spreading the hairs of your brush for the drybrush effect. With practice, drybrush can have an effect not unlike lithographic pencil on rough paper—yet drybrush has the advantage of allowing greater control of detail. You can also use the brush and ink alone for a graceful line drawing. Drawing with a brush allows for much fluctuation between thick and thin lines and has a smoother feel than any kind of pen.

SKETCHBOXES AND CARRYING CASES

A sketchbox is anything used to transport the tools for sketching. It is not necessary to purchase an "artist's" sketchbox. Instead, be creative and fashion one from another container. Over the years, we've used toolboxes, fishing tackle boxes, briefcases, lunchboxes, and even an old violin case. There are times when you are not sure what type of sketch you will be doing and you wish to bring along enough materials to be prepared for any technique you might want to try. In such instances, a medium-sized container such as a fishing tackle box can easily carry all the sketching tools you could need. At other times you will have a specific technique you are interested in using and you'll want to carry only the materials necessary. For these occasions you might be interested in organizing your drawing tools into a few separate containers—one for each technique. Then when you plan to sketch with markers, you simply bring along the marker box; when you feel like sketching with pencils, you bring along the pencil box. With this system, you are always sure you have with you all the materials you need for the technique you are using. The disadvantage is that it doesn't allow you to experiment with combined media such as marker and charcoal.

For the most part, you may find that the sketching set-up you reach for most is simply a pencil and a fountain pen or marker in your shirt pocket and a 9" x 12" spiral-bound sketchbook under your arm. A small knapsack is another simple option for carrying sketching tools. Keep one constantly loaded with a few sketchbooks and drawing tools, and when you want to go sketching, simply grab your knapsack and you're off.

EXPERIENCING YOUR MATERIALS

Perhaps the final word on sketching materials is that they need to be convenient enough for on-the-spot use. For example, you may greatly enjoy painting in gouache while at home, but if you find it such a chore to set up your paints on the spot that you never bother to sketch, you would be better off using pencil or some other simple tool. The enjoyment of sketching derives from the experience of recording the world around you, and your materials shouldn't hinder that enjoyment. Remember: materials are not an end in themselves—they are only a means by which you can produce sketches.

Another important consideration is that your materials be accessible when needed. There is nothing more frustrating than unexpectedly having a moment to sketch a fascinating subject and discovering you have no materials with you. To make it easy to sketch when you want, you may find it helpful to keep materials in the various places you spend your day. If you drive a car often, you could keep a few sketchbooks and some pencils and pens under the front seat or in the trunk. A sketchbook kept at the place you work would allow you to sketch your fellow employees or the surrounding neighborhood during your lunchbreak. If you spend a lot of time during the day on your feet or running errands, you may want to keep a sketchbook with you in a purse or backpack, or even in a shirt pocket or a small belt pouch. No matter what system you prefer, have your sketching tools available when you need them. After all, your materials have no value unless they are used.

Achieving Accuracy

Broken Neon tells the story of Old Long Beach. A whole section of town, including the Panama room, Dine-Fine restaurant, and Gilson's Malt shop are getting torn down to make way for the new big hotels

Marmion + Co
3rd Street - Book of Long Beach -

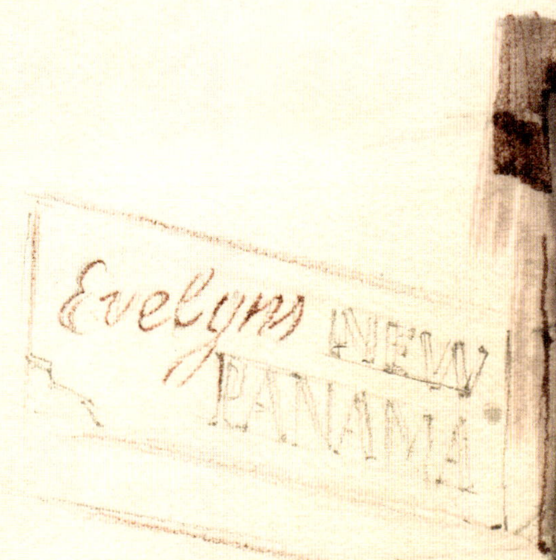

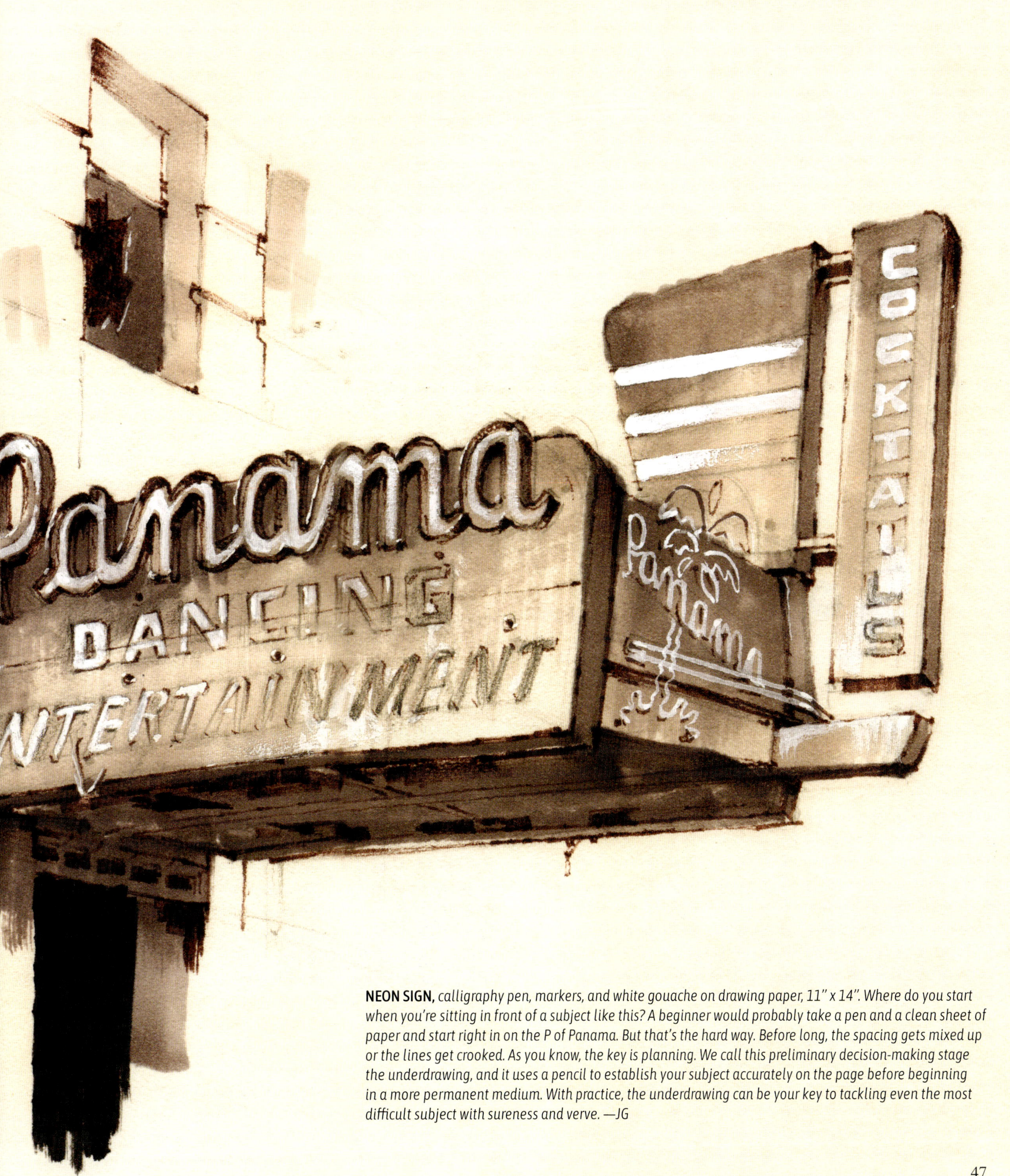

NEON SIGN, *calligraphy pen, markers, and white gouache on drawing paper, 11" x 14". Where do you start when you're sitting in front of a subject like this? A beginner would probably take a pen and a clean sheet of paper and start right in on the P of Panama. But that's the hard way. Before long, the spacing gets mixed up or the lines get crooked. As you know, the key is planning. We call this preliminary decision-making stage the underdrawing, and it uses a pencil to establish your subject accurately on the page before beginning in a more permanent medium. With practice, the underdrawing can be your key to tackling even the most difficult subject with sureness and verve. —JG*

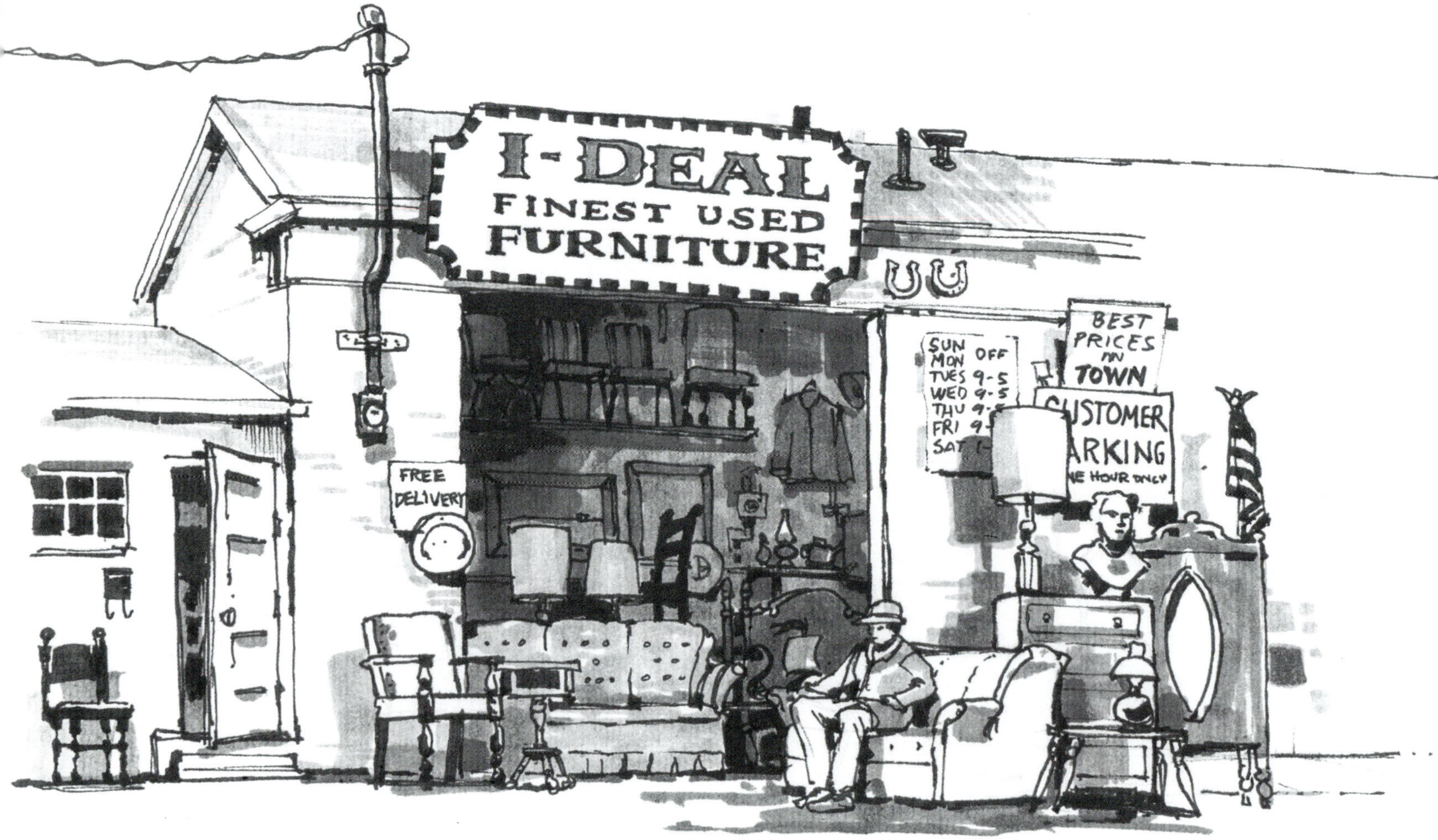

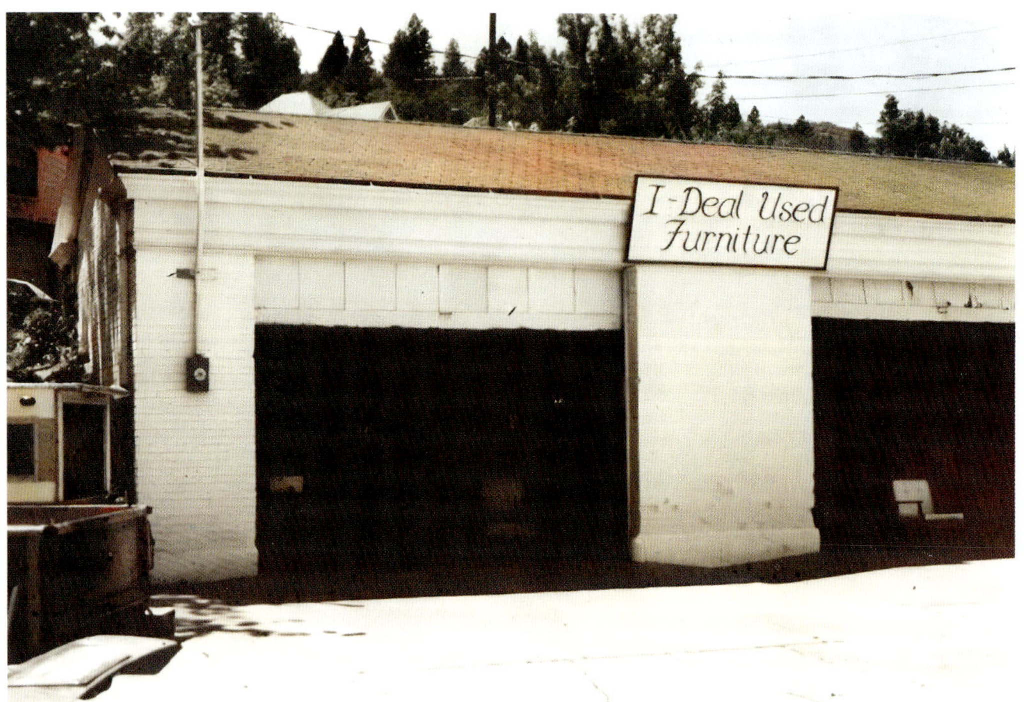

FURNITURE STORE, *calligraphy pen and markers on charcoal paper, 11" x 14". Being accurate doesn't mean being slavish to your subject, as you can see by comparing my sketch to the photograph of the same subject. In addition to the cluttered arrangement of furniture outside the building, the sketched version has a different sign, with more interesting and varied letter forms. The left-hand garage door has been narrowed, and the right-hand door eliminated. The little office on the left side of the sketch doesn't appear in the photo at all—it was borrowed from a building across the street behind me. These changes are typical of the kind of decision-making that lies behind many of the sketches in this book. But the changes are not haphazard or arbitrary. No matter how things are moved around, everything stays in perspective.*
—JG

THE KEY to achieving accuracy is to use a little forethought before beginning your sketch. We almost always plan our sketches a bit by using a lightly drawn pencil indication of the subject as a guide to the final sketch. This indication is called an underdrawing.

In this chapter we will look at the subject of underdrawing. We will begin by examining a few hows and whys, and then introduce you to the specific methods of seeing and measuring your subject that we use when creating an underdrawing. The methods are simple, but they will help you draw any subject, no matter how complex.

With experience, you will adapt the pencil underdrawing procedure to your own personal needs. You won't go through every step every time. Instead you will use each of these methods only as needed for a particular drawing problem. Keep in mind that these methods are in no way meant to affect the enjoyment or freedom of sketching for you, but in fact are meant to give you the control and confidence you need to be able to accurately draw what you see. The concept is simple: begin your sketch with lightly drawn pencil lines to establish what you want before using a more unalterable medium.

WHEN TO USE AN UNDERDRAWING

When is it appropriate to begin a sketch with an underdrawing? We used an underdrawing on virtually every sketch in this book, with the exceptions of the very quick personal sketches and motion studies. For a two-hour sketch, we'll spend ten minutes on the underdrawing; for a half-hour sketch, we may spend five; for a ten-minute sketch we may spend thirty seconds. You will probably discover that once you get in the habit of using an underdrawing, it will seem awkward not using one. Drawing all over a fresh sketchbook page with marker or heavy pencil lines will seem clumsy by comparison to warming up with a few lightly drawn pencil lines.

By using an underdrawing you keep the image in a state of flux while you decide the direction you want to go with it. For instance, if you were doing a sketch inside a cafeteria, you might decide once you've begun that the coffee machine would look good next to the salad counter instead of behind the refrigerator. With a touch of the kneaded eraser and a few new pencil lines, the change has been made. Then, after you have laid out the entire interior the way you want it, a burly cook comes out and begins wiping the counter. You decide to include him in front of the salad area and quickly indicate his broad contours in pencil and erase any excess lines. To improve interest you also invent a sign saying NO ORDERS TO GO and hang it from the coffee machine. You now get out your marking pens and start making final lines, satisfied that your underdrawing has captured all of the aspects of the cafeteria that interested you.

This freedom to change and improve upon what you see is what using an underdrawing gives you. Your drawing will be well thought out and have an interesting sense of organization. Furthermore, the accuracy of your drawing is greatly improved because you can make all the mistakes you need to, and easily correct them by erasing the lightly drawn lines.

HOW MUCH UNDERDRAWING IS NECESSARY?

How much underdrawing you use for a sketch will vary according to the complexity of the subject and the amount of time you intend to spend on the sketch. If a subject is complex, such as a city street scene complete with cars and buildings in perspective, you will need to spend as much as half of your sketching time making an underdrawing. On the other hand, a sketch of a pumpkin in a field may involve a ten-second underdrawing.

In the remaining sections of the chapter we will discuss specific methods for establishing your subject accurately on the page; however, keep in mind that there's no reason to carry the underdrawing to a stage of high polish. As soon as you have the important forms of your subject pinned down, go ahead with the actual sketch. The underdrawing is meant as a timesaver, and it *will* be if you use it as a guide. If you feel your final drawing is nothing but a cold, lifeless execution, obviously you've gone too far. If you feel lost and anxious as you grope to understand your subject, you have not gone far enough in your underdrawing. The right degree of development will give you a definite sense of confidence, and as a result, your sketch will look spontaneous.

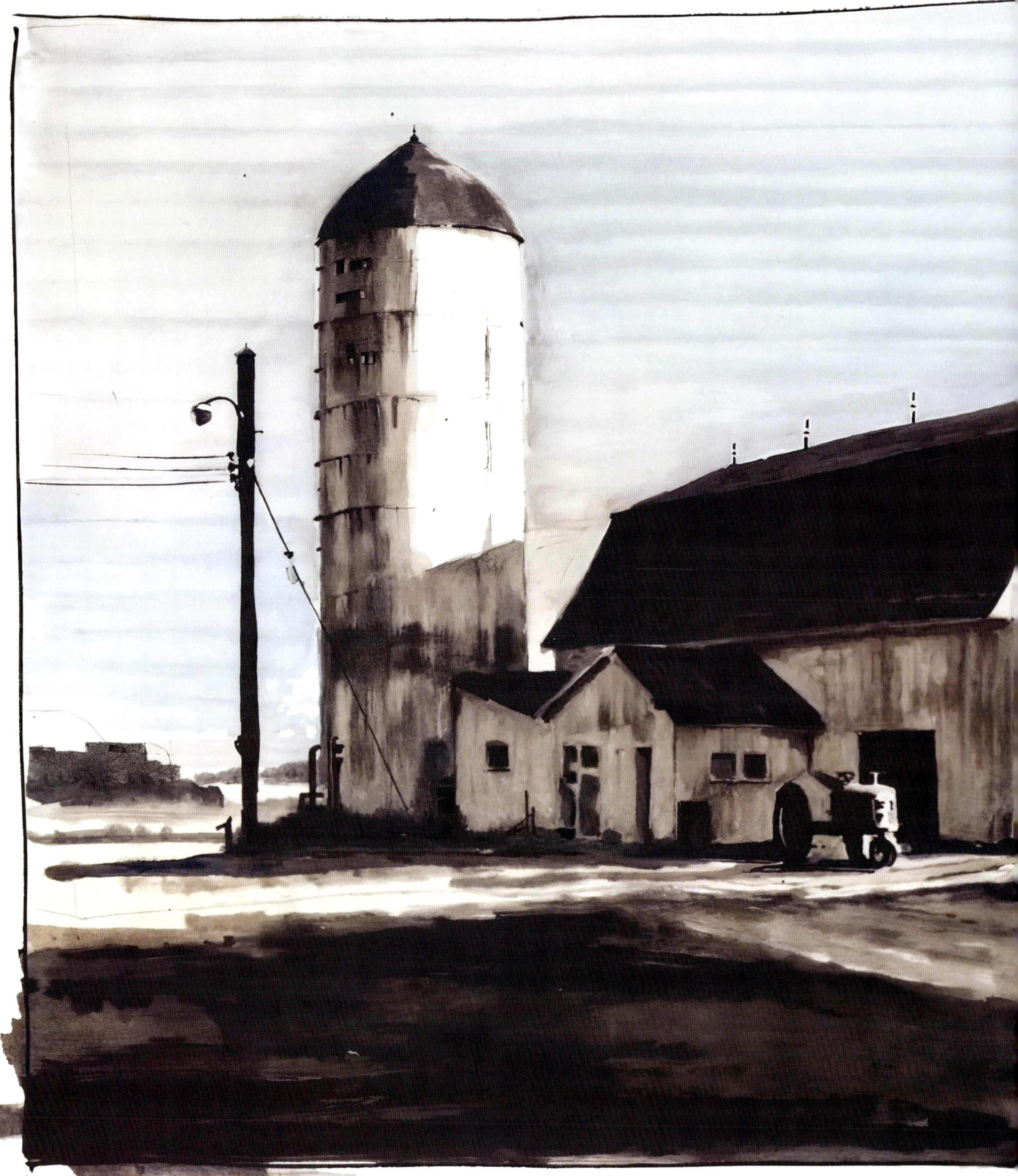

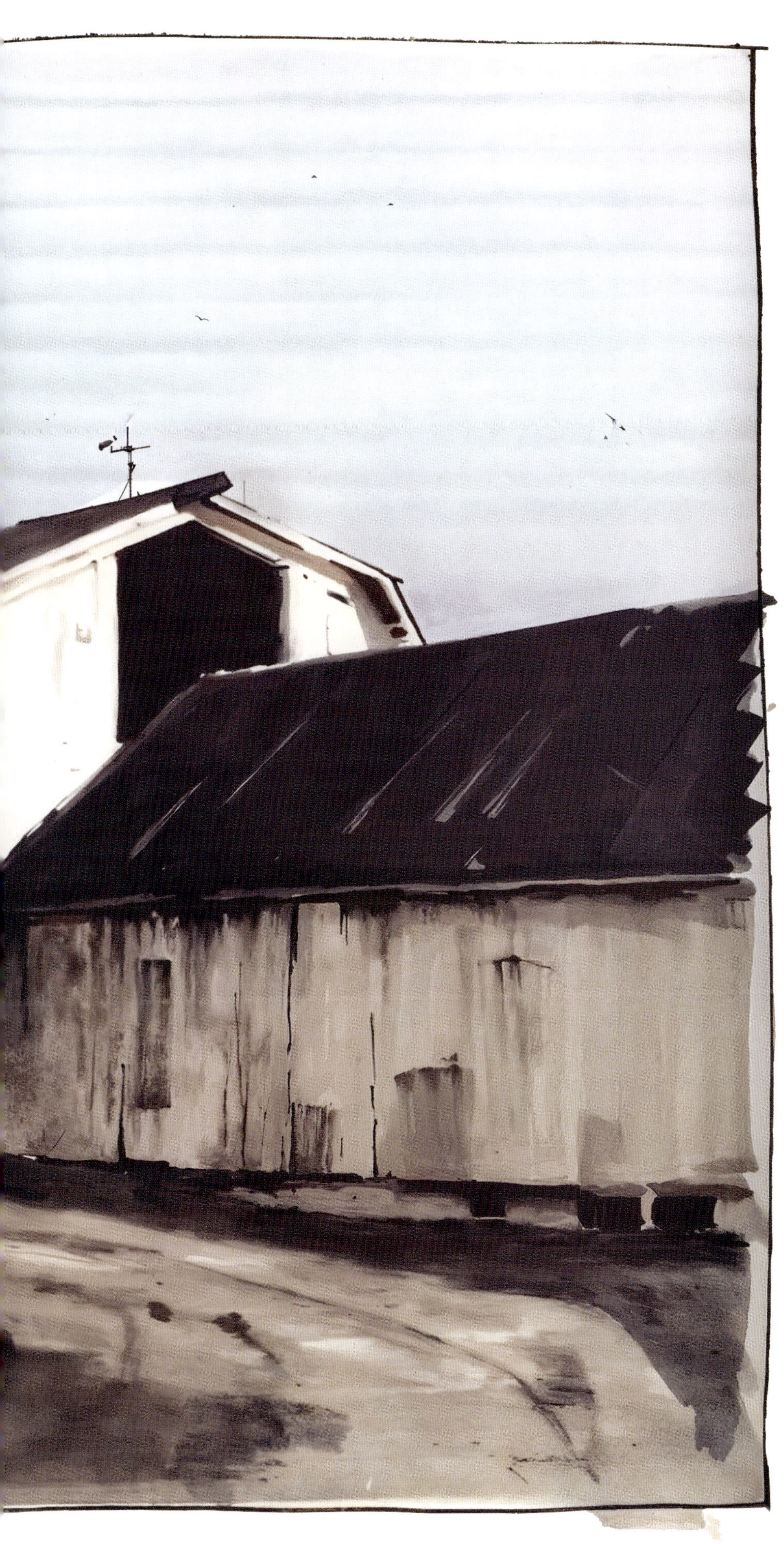

FARM BUILDINGS, NEW YORK STATE, *markers and fountain pen on smooth paper, 8" x 11". This sketch, along with the following diagrams, will demonstrate the various stages of the underdrawing. These are the first steps we take when we begin drawing just about any subject. Although these underdrawings are intended as diagrams, in actual sketches these steps are done very lightly with a #2 office pencil on the sketchbook page before any of the final rendering is undertaken. What you see here is the end result of our demonstrations. This is what the sketch looks like after the marker tones are applied. For this marker rendering I used the even-numbered values of cool gray chisel-tip AD markers: #2 for the sky, #4 for the shadow side of the buildings and ground, #6 for the rooftops, and #8 for the open hayloft and foreground darks. After all these gray tones were established, I added a few crisp accents in black with the fountain pen to complete the value range. The whole procedure, from the first pencil lines to the final accents, took about an hour and forty-five minutes. —JG*

STEP ONE: ESTABLISHING THE LARGE SHAPES

The first thing to consider in making your underdrawing is the arrangement of the large two-dimensional shapes. These are what first attracted your eye to the subject, and in your drawing, they are what will first attract the eye of the viewer. Squint your eyes and look for the broad statement, the silhouette of a tree against the sky, for example, or the walls and floor of an interior. The accuracy of your final sketch will depend on a strong arrangement of simple shapes more than anything else. As an aid in sketching the large shapes, look for imaginary triangles, squares, and rectangles in your subject. For example, an ordinary pickup truck seen from the side could be considered as fitting within a large rectangle, while the smaller shapes that comprise it, such as the bed and the cab, can be seen as smaller rectangles within the large one.

When you are looking for the large shapes, try to ignore the smaller details of your subject, which can distract you from the overall form. Blurring your eyes helps to do this, because it eliminates textures and highlights. It also helps to imagine that you have a piece of glass like a window in front of you and to pretend that you are tracing the shapes onto the glass with a grease pencil. Ignore the interior lines of a silhouette, and establish only the big basic shapes.

The purpose of this step is to see roughly how the composition will sit on your page. It shouldn't take more than a minute at most. Accuracy is not important yet; you will refine that later. But placement is important, because the first ten seconds you spend placing the subject on the page will determine more than anything else the final look of the sketch. If your quick indication of the basic shapes seems too small or too crowded, this is the time to reconsider. Is there another approach to the composition that is more creative? Once you're satisfied with the overall placement of the large shapes, you can begin the process of refinement and measurement.

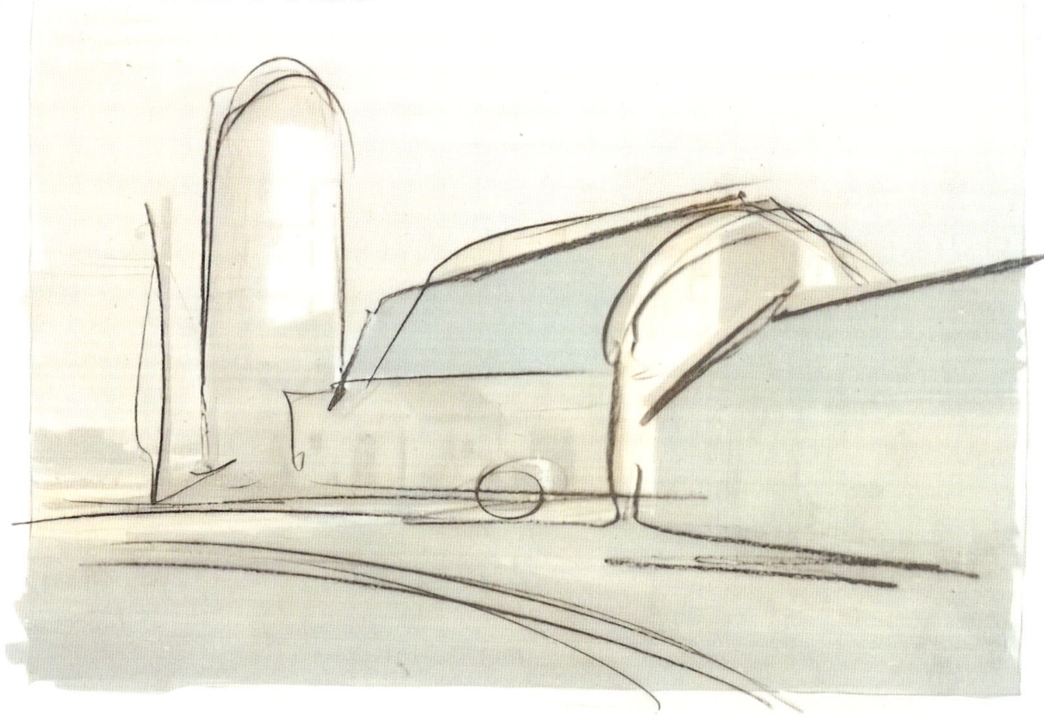

STEP ONE: *The first thing you do when you begin the pencil underdrawing is to suggest a rough approximation of the whole subject. The purpose is just to get an idea of how your subject sits on the page. Don't worry too much about accuracy at this stage. What's more important is placement. If it seems too high or too low on the page, simply erase the scribble and redraw it quickly. This step shouldn't take more than about one minute. What you are trying to convey is a broad statement of the two-dimensional shapes; the details are not important. In this diagram, the scribble follows the main shapes of the farm buildings and the grain silo. I paid more attention to the outer silhouette edge of the buildings than to the details, like the small toolsheds on the side of the barn. The underdrawing is now ready for the process of refinement and measurement.*

STEP TWO: MEASURING LENGTHS

The method we use for measuring lengths guarantees that the proportions of the drawing will be absolutely accurate. This method has been around since the time of the Renaissance, and it works. The goal is to use your pencil held in front of you to compare the apparent lengths of some of the key lines in the subject. The word "apparent" is important to keep in mind because you will not be interested in measuring the *actual* length of what you see, but rather the length that is *apparent* from where you are sitting. In other words, we know the length of a car's wheelbase is actually longer than the distance between the headlights, but from a frontal view, you will actually perceive the wheelbase to be much shorter. The error of elongating these foreshortened lengths is so compelling that any artist, regardless of experience, is likely to make this mistake, unless he or she checks with a measurement.

The procedure for measuring lengths involves holding your pencil vertically in a closed grip with your thumb resting on the shaft of the pencil. Straighten your arm all the way out until your elbow locks. With the tip of the eraser corresponding to one endpoint of the line you wish to measure, move your thumb along the pencil shaft until you find the place that marks the apparent length of the line you are measuring. This measured segment becomes a standard of comparison for any other line you wish to check. For example, after measuring the distance between the headlights of a car, you can then compare that length with other important lengths. Perhaps the distance from the ground to the hood is two-thirds of the headlight measurement and the distance from the hood to the roof is one-half of the headlight measurement. Make a mental note of these proportions and make them similar in your drawing. Measuring and comparing will often reveal errors in your judgment. For example, you may be surprised to find that a sailboat's mast, which seemed so tall at first, turns out to be shorter than the hull. When you discover a mistake, don't hesitate to use your eraser—after all, you are still at the underdrawing stage of your sketch, and making corrections is a part of underdrawing.

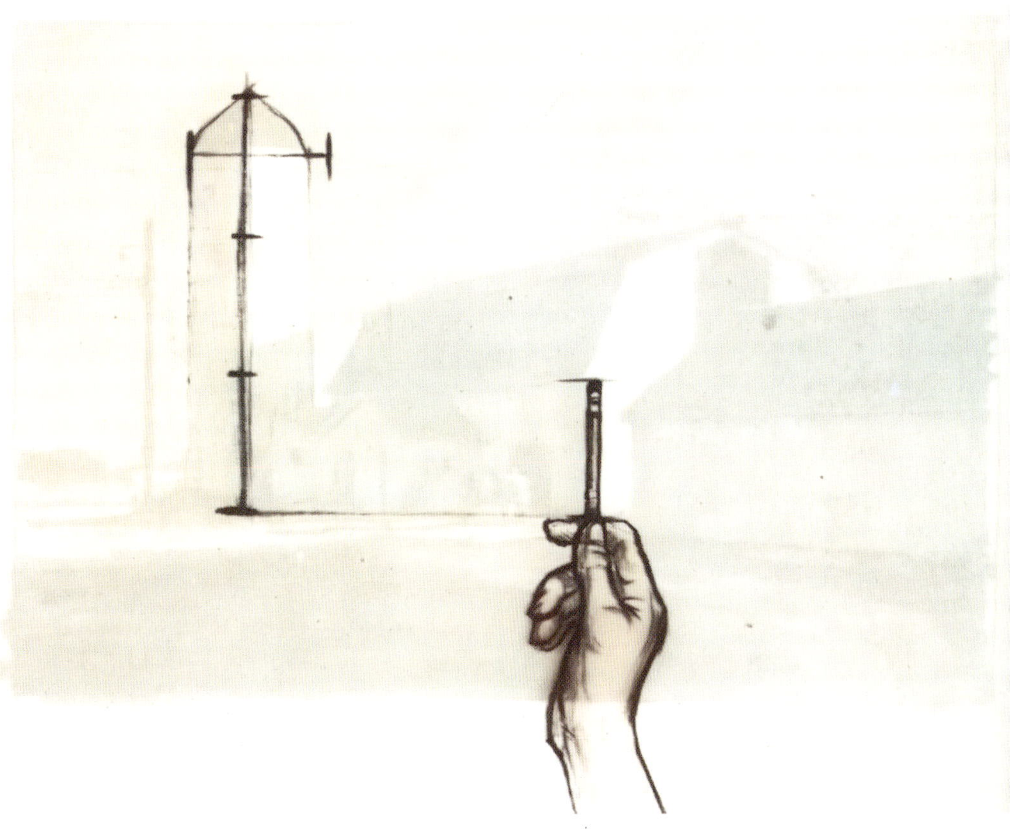

STEP TWO: *As you begin to refine your initial statement of the subject, it helps to check proportions by comparing the lengths of various key lines in the composition relative to a fixed reference segment. This reference segment is chosen from the subject itself—in this case I decided to use the segment along the corner of the barn between the eaves and the ground. When I looked at the actual barn, I squinted an eye and held out my hand at full length, as far as my arm could reach. I positioned a pencil in my hand so that the tip of the eraser corresponded with the eaves of the barn. Then I moved my thumb up and down along the pencil until the thumb position corresponded exactly with the foot of the wall. As long as I held my arm in the fully extended position, I had an unchanging standard of the length of that segment. All I had to do was move the hand and pencil over to the grain silo to see that it was exactly three units tall and slightly less than one unit wide. Similar measurements were made elsewhere in the picture. With each new measurement, I adjusted the initial statement of the large shapes, until I was satisfied that the overall proportions of the indication were accurate.*

STEP THREE: MEASURING SLOPES

Have you ever had a hard time estimating how steeply to draw a roofline or the edge of a sidewalk seen from an oblique angle? There's a method that will make you absolutely sure that you've got it right, just as you see it in the subject. The method resembles the one you used for measuring lengths in that you are again holding the pencil in front of you at arm's length. But this time you hold it in your fingertips with your arm facing the subject.

Here's the procedure: first, choose a line in the subject that you want to measure, then hold your pencil at arm's length with the overhand grip, as shown in the illustration. Make sure that the pencil is at right angles to your line of vision. In other words, don't let the pencil point either toward you or away from you. Now match the slope of the pencil to the slope that you see in the subject. Looking at the pencil, estimate the slope by comparing it to surrounding horizontals and verticals. Is it just a gentle tilt, or a very steep angle? Whatever it is, record it just as you see it on your sketchbook page. You can actually hold your pencil firmly in its sloping position and move it down from your line of vision to your drawing to check the slope.

It's a good idea to start by measuring the slopes of the larger, more important lines at first, such as the roofline of a building, rather than smaller line segments, such as window frames. Not only are the longer lines easier to measure, but also, once established, they function as a reference from which to compare related lines.

The procedure for measuring slopes also helps you to cross-check the placement of any two points in a scene, even if there is no actual line between them. For example, the most accurate and the easiest way to draw the masts of a schooner in proper position is to judge the slope of the imaginary line running from the top of one mast to the top of the other. Even the untrained eye is very sensitive to slopes. Proof of this is that when a picture on a wall hangs as little as two degrees askew, it looks noticeably wrong. This sensitivity to slopes can help you check the accuracy of your drawings by using the slope-measuring method.

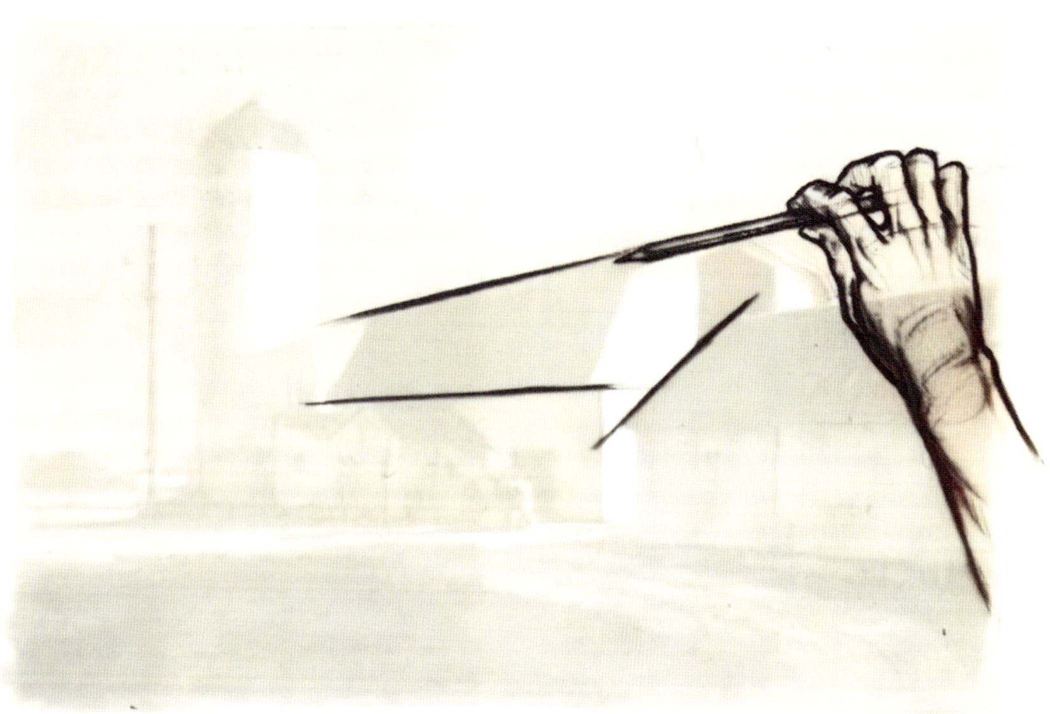

STEP THREE: *Here's the method for troublesome lines that seem to be slanting off at the wrong angle. Hold your hand in front of yourself again, this time with the pencil held in the fingertips with your palm facing directly toward the subject. The pencil should be at right angles to the direction you are looking, not sloping back in space. In the diagram, the hand is holding the pencil at the same angle as the ridge of the roof and the barn. Similar measurements could be made along the eaves of the barn or along the gable of the building in the foreground. Now look at the slope of the pencil. How much is it tilting away from the horizontal? The ridgeline is a gentle slope; the eaves are almost flat, and the gable is about forty-five degrees. With your pencil held fixed at this angle and your sketchbook held vertically in front of you, make a direct transfer of the sloping line from your subject to your sketch. Which lines should you measure? Only the long, major lines of the composition, especially the extreme lines bordering the outsides of the composition and the extreme lines bordering the outsides of major shapes. You don't need to bother with the small, short lines, like the one along the top edge of the doorway behind the tractor. In the next step we'll set up some perspective guidelines that will put these minor lines in place.*

STEP FOUR: USING PERSPECTIVE GUIDELINES

Many artists are intimidated by the idea of perspective when it comes to sketching, but there's really no reason to be. The method that we use on the spot is really very simple; it doesn't involve rulers or T-squares or triangles, and you don't even have to worry about vanishing points or complex construction lines. But if you take the time to set up these guidelines, you can be confident that all the lines in your subject are in proper perspective.

The first step is to find eye level, the most important line of all. Eye level is a term often used interchangeably with horizon line. The two mean basically the same thing, but it is less confusing to use the label eye level in circumstances where the actual horizon is blocked by buildings or mountains. What is eye level? Eye level is the imaginary horizontal line that runs through the subject at the same height as the viewer's eye. Thus, when you are sitting down at a booth in a diner, for example, your eye level will intersect everything at about four feet off the ground. Perhaps the line would run along the top of a jukebox, across the scoreboard of a pinball machine, through the door about a foot above the knob, and right through the heads of other seated figures. However, if you were to stand up, the eye level would raise up about a foot and a half, running along the top edge of the pinball machine, above the heads of the seated customers, etc. An infallible way to find the eye level in your scene is to point directly in front of you, as if you were pointing at an imaginary ship far away at sea. Whatever you actually point at is on the eye level. After having discovered where eye level is, you can then present it as a horizontal line extending across the page wherever you want eye level in your sketch. For most subjects, an eye-level line about one-third up the page is convenient.

How do you go about actually drawing a horizontal line so that it is straight and level? If you are using a sketchbook or a piece of illustration board, there's a fast, reliable method to get a straight horizontal line every time. Here's how you do it: hook the little finger of your drawing hand under the bottom edge of your sketchbook and, with pencil in hand, slide down the length of the page, using your little finger as a guide. The line you make will be parallel to the horizontal edge of the book. Try it. With a little practice you can draw horizontal lines all the way to the center of an 11" x 14" sketchbook page, even from the spiral-bound edge. The same idea also works for vertical lines, which are made parallel to the sides of your sketchbook. This technique is handy to know because most subjects, especially buildings, include numerous horizontal and vertical lines. Using this method, your lines will be parallel and accurate.

Go ahead and draw the eye-level line lightly in pencil, and do the same for the important vertical lines. What you now have are the roughed-in basic shapes with a single horizontal and several verticals running through them. Because you have measured some of the lengths and slopes, you know that your proportions are accurate, and also that the slopes of some of the key lines are also accurate.

Choose the highest-sloping perspective line in your subject—perhaps the rooftop of a building or the top edge of a billboard—and double-check the slope measurement. Extend this line all the way across the page. Do the same for the lowest line of your subject, the line farthest below eye level. That might be the bottom edge of a fence or a wall. Your attention should now be focused on three lines: the one above eye level, the one below, and eye level itself. Pretend that these three lines are the ribs of an incomplete hand-held fan. To fill out the fan, you need to draw the rest of the ribs in an array of evenly increasing slopes. With all of these radiating lines in place, you can easily add any new line and be sure it's in perspective, just by comparing it to a nearby guideline.

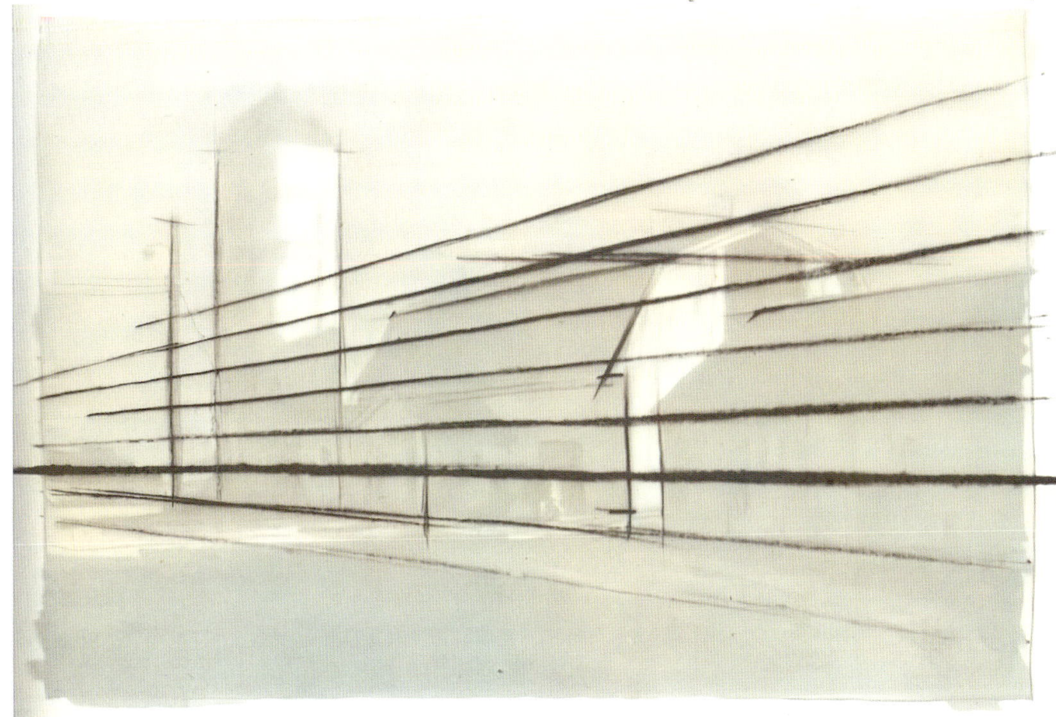

STEP FOUR: *The next procedure is to set up an array of perspective guidelines to put every line into its proper slope relationship. It starts with the eye level, an imaginary horizontal line running through the subject at the same height as the viewer's eye. In the diagram, eye level is the heavy line that coincides with the horizon line in the finished sketch, running along the top edge of the tractor and through the middle of the foreground building. It's important to draw the eye-level line all the way across the picture, even where you can't see the horizon. You don't need to use a ruler—instead hook your little finger over the bottom edge of the sketchbook and slide your hand along the page, holding the pencil as you normally would. A line parallel to the bottom edge of the sketchbook will always be horizontal. This technique is useful for vertical lines if you guide your little finger along the side of the sketchbook. Any lines parallel to that will be vertical. Now you can put your slope-measuring skills to work. Double-check that top roofline of the barn and extend it all the way across the page. Between this line and eye level, construct a series of evenly sloping lines. I added three lines between the roofline and eye level, plus another above the top of the roof, and a couple more down below eye level. The key is to make them slope evenly—it doesn't matter if they correspond with actual lines in the subject. I never use a ruler for these lines when I'm sketching, because I've found that it's possible with just a little practice to draw a freehand line that is, for all practical purposes, absolutely straight. The result of this stage is a perspective grid, a set of lines that you know are accurate and with which you can compare any other small line. The slope of the roof of the door behind the tractor is easy to see now—it's almost always level.*

STEP FIVE: CONSTRUCTING WITH GEOMETRIC FORMS

You have gone about as far as you can with pure observational accuracy. The next step is to *construct* using simple geometric forms. Using the measurements and guidelines you have established, you are now expressing the lines in terms of cones, spheres, cubes, and cylinders. You've probably seen many drawing books with diagrams of simplified form analysis. Why is this method useful? Two reasons: first, simple forms are much easier to keep in perspective, since they are made up of geometric shapes; and second, once you have mastered form construction, you can invent any form and make it appear convincing.

For example, have you ever tried to draw the wheel of an ordinary car and noticed how tricky it is to get it to look correct? It's only difficult if you are relying solely on observation and not knowledgeable construction. If you can draw a cylinder in perspective, you can draw any wheel that you see, since the wheel is nothing more than a set of related cylinders. If you want to do an imaginative sketch of that same car rearing back in the air like a wild animal, you would still have to draw those wheels convincingly, but you couldn't rely *at all* on ordinary observation. You'd have to *construct* them, based on your understanding of the basic forms that comprise them. Suddenly your powers as an artist are greatly increased, and you can take a more active role in your sketch.

The best way to practice form construction is to spend an hour or two drawing cylinders, cubes, box shapes, and cones from all angles. Once you feel comfortable with that step, try drawing these same shapes as if they were lit from different light sources. Then, combine them into more complex clusters of forms—such as a mailbox, which is a rectangular box with a half-cylinder on top, or an old-fashioned watertower, which is a cylinder capped with a cone. When you are on-the-spot, working from actual objects, try to translate what you see into the language of basic forms. This will give your underdrawing solidity and power.

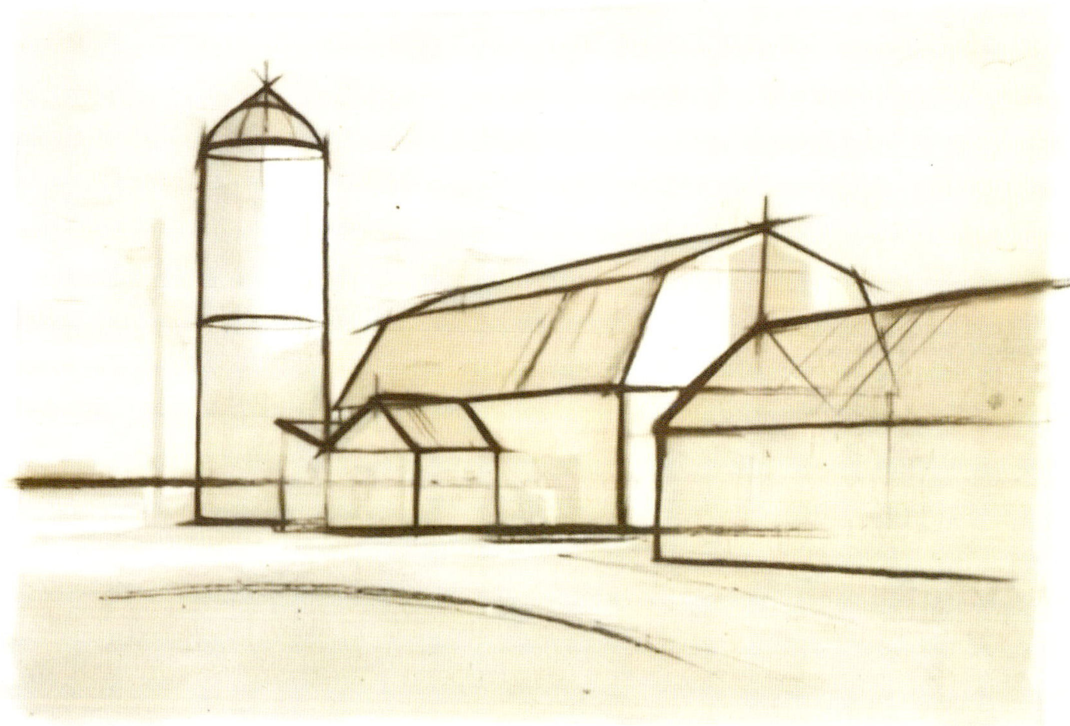

STEP FIVE: *Before going any further with details or individual measurements, the next step is to look at the overall picture again to make sure that all the forms look three dimensional and that they are arranged in an interesting way. To do this, every form is simplified to its geometric equivalent. The grain silo, for example, is a cylinder capped with a rounded cone. The tool sheds are simple boxes with triangular shapes mounted on the top. The barn is a box shape with a four-paneled roof structure. Now would be the time to add or to change the structures, because this can be done easily in simple geometric terms. Also, this is the time to begin thinking about light and shade. In this sketch, the light source is completely invented—it was overcast and dark that day in New York State; in fact, I remember sitting under a tree hoping it wouldn't rain. However, in the geometric-form step of the pencil underdrawing, I decided to bring a light source in from the low right, which would draw attention to the partially obscured front plane of the barn and cast an interesting shadow across the silo. Since I have practiced rendering light and shade many times before on simple cylinders and boxes, it was easy to imagine how these architectural shapes would behave under an invented light source. With these issues settled, I was ready to continue into the detailed line drawing.*

STEP SIX: COMPLETED UNDERDRAWING

Now that the basic foundation has been established, checked, and rechecked, you can finish developing the underdrawing, indicating any of the details that still might confuse you. This stage should be easy, because you have established all the absolutes already. As you work out the plan of the picture, consider what final medium you want to use for the sketch—markers, brush pen, charcoal, fountain pen, or even soft pencil. Start thinking about where the shadows should go and how you want to suggest the variety of textures.

FINAL EXECUTION

When you can't wait any longer, get out your final medium and start rendering. If you want, you can work very spontaneously over your underdrawing, and the spontaneity will look beautiful because it has a strong skeleton of accuracy. If you have the time and the inclination, you may want to spend an hour or more on the final execution. Regardless of how long you spend, you are free to explore the character of line, use of tone, and treatment of edges. You can confidently use your final medium to create a sketch that looks spontaneous and vital. And best of all, after your sketch is done, a few quick wipes with a kneaded eraser and all trace of the underdrawing is removed, giving your sketch the illusion of having been drawn directly in your final medium.

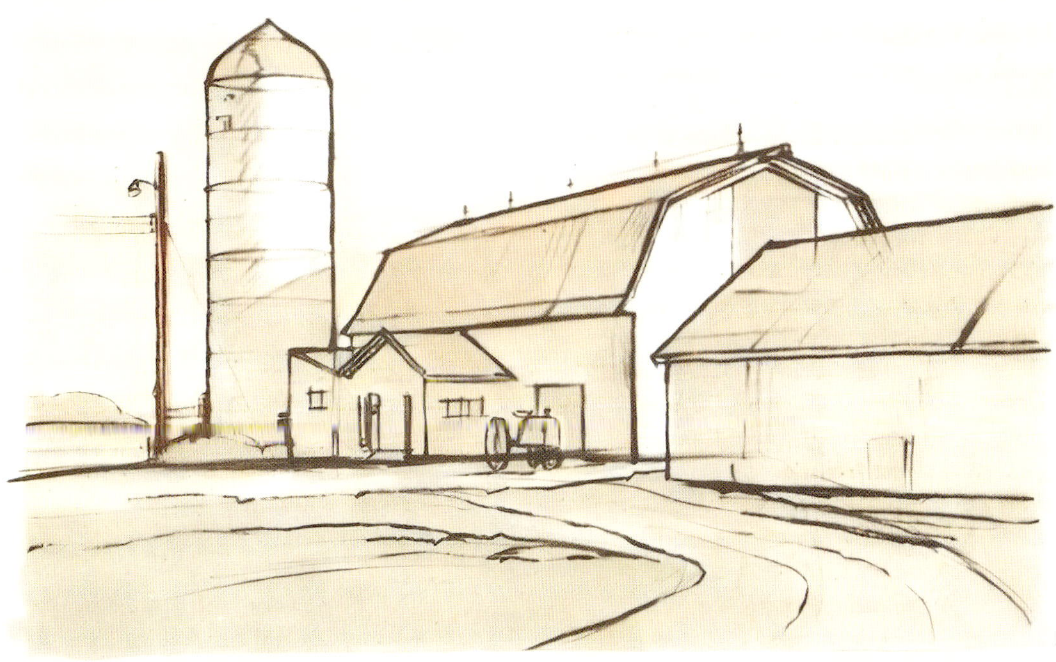

STEP SIX: *The final step is the easiest. All the details fall into place very quickly. The tractor, the windows, the streetlight, and the weather vane are all quickly indicated with the pencil, to be used as a guide for the marker rendering. No more measurement is needed, because every judgment can be easily made in comparison with the absolutes that have already been established. The little windows on the toolshed behind the tractor are quite clearly placed just a little way above the center of the wall. As I make this line drawing, which takes as little as four or five minutes, I'm anticipating how I want to render the final picture. In many cases, I'll leave the decision-making about the details for the pen itself, without making an extensive line drawing. The best way to know when you're finished with the underdrawing and ready to move on is to ask yourself: Am I still finding out anything new, or am I just going over old ground? Are there any major mistakes that couldn't be corrected when I start the final? If not, you are ready to dive in with the final rendering. You'll sketch with confidence and spontaneity, now that you know you're on target. —JG*

▶ **UNFINISHED ANIMAL STUDY,** *wash and pencil on illustration board, 7½" x 10". Underdrawing is just as useful for natural subjects as it is for buildings. After setting up inside the natural history museum, I began this sketch by roughing in the general proportions using a 2H pencil. From these lines I began delineating specific forms, using the length of the head as a measuring standard for the lengths of the other segments of the body. The distance from the tip of the nose to the base of the ear turned out to be the same as from the knee to the elbow, for example, and this kind of specific measurement helped me keep the proportions accurate. When I was satisfied with my underdrawing, I began laying-in tones in wash. Since I'm left handed, I usually work from right to left so as not to rest my hand on finished areas of the sketch. In this case, the museum closed before I had a chance to finish my sketch, leaving the left side of the sketch in the underdrawing stage. —TK*

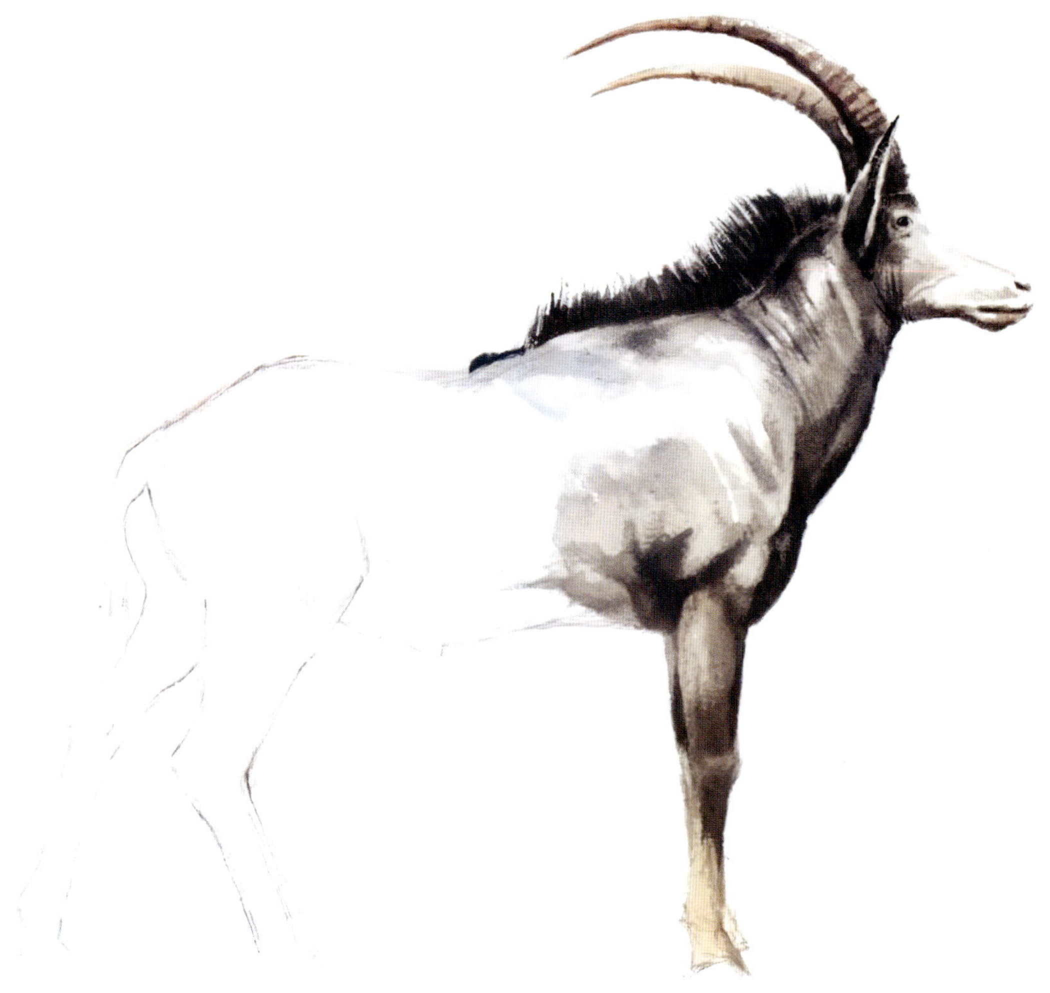

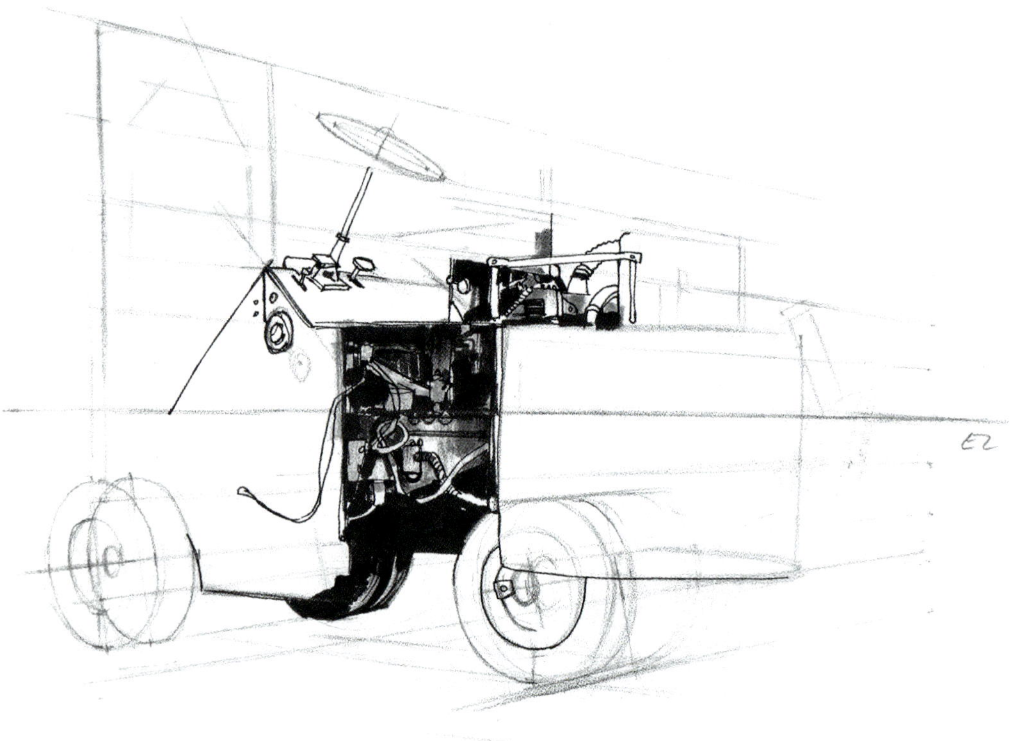

◀ **FORKLIFT,** *calligraphy pens and markers on coquille board, 12" x 14". This half-finished sketch shows how complex details can be rendered over a pencil underdrawing. I began the underdrawing using the normal procedure of establishing shapes and forms. As you can see, the rear half of the forklift is still indicated with a simple rectangle, and the wheels appear like transparent cylinders. Eye level is marked by the horizontal line running through the center. I then measured the slope of the top of the lift and constructed a perspective grid to hold together any details that might be rendered there. All this took only about five minutes, but it is enough underdrawing to make me feel confident jumping in with the smallest details of the exposed engine. I started in the middle and worked outward using first line and then tone and black. —JG*

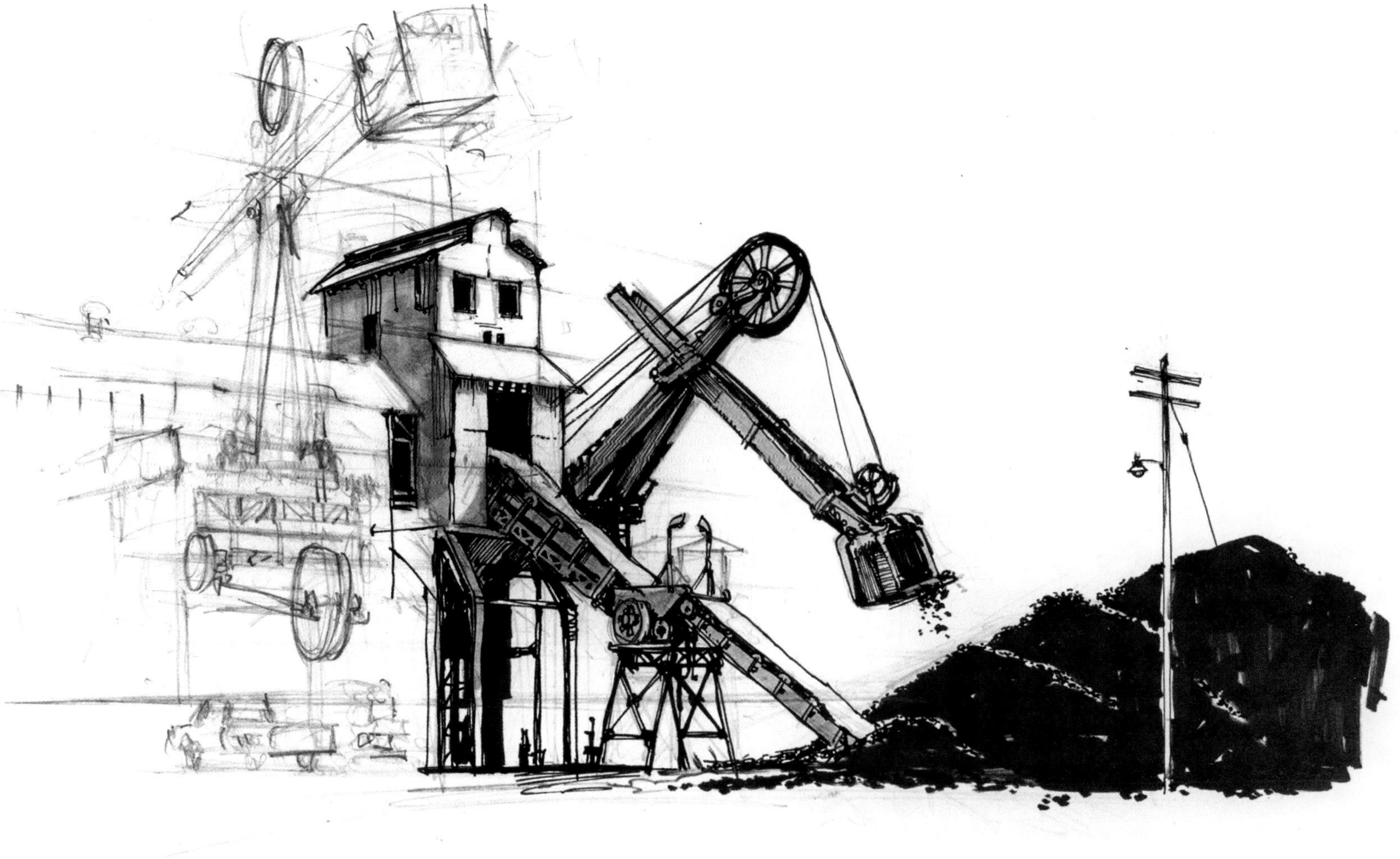

▲ **COAL MINE MONSTER,** *fountain pen and marker over pencil underdrawing, 11" x 14", This sketch was left half-finished by an unexpected Pennsylvania cloudburst. The area remaining in pencil, on the left, shows how the sketch grew out of a hazy, searching underdrawing. As I was exploring ways to make the crane booms into arms for the monster, I made sure to relate everything to the perspective grid. Eye level is even with the roof of the pickup truck. The shapes of the open-mouthed shed do not correspond to the actual subject, of course, so I constructed them from basic geometric shapes. If I had finished this sketch, I would have erased what remained of the pencil lines, leaving the pen and marker rendering alone. —JG*

▼ **PILE OF CHAINS,** *pencil on smooth paper, 11" x 14". Here's an example of a complex subject that didn't require much underdrawing. Though this pile of chains was very intricate, most of the suggestion of detail was done as I worked directly in the darker tones of the pencil. The only underdrawing necessary was a patiently drawn outline of the entire pile to establish its placement on the page. To unify the tones of the subject, I rubbed pencil over the entire scrap pile area and used this light gray value as a base onto which I added darks with my pencil and lights with my eraser. To delineate the individual details, I began with the forms that were in front of the rest and drew them in carefully; then I went on to the forms that were partially obstructed. I was shading as I went, rather than developing a linear underdrawing first and then putting in shading. The shade-as-you-go technique works well on subjects that have an overall evenness of detail. By rendering each section as you go, you can invent any unfinished portions of the sketch from the information recorded in the finished parts. —TK*

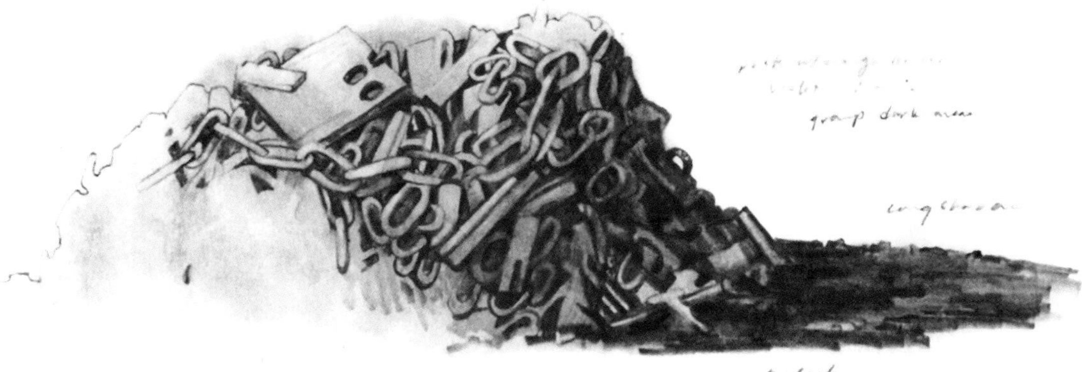

LAS VEGAS STREET SCENE, *gouache on watercolor paper, 8" x 18". Complex architectural subjects are easy to sketch accurately by using a few simple drawing methods. To do this gouache sketch, I began by drawing a horizontal line a few inches from the bottom of the paper to establish the eye level for my subject. Eye level runs along the top edge of the low fence in front of the bushes. Following this, I used the slope-measuring method to find the angle of the uppermost line of the building on the far left. I transferred this angle to my sketch by drawing a diagonal line across the length of my paper to serve as a perspective line for drawing the building. Then, using the horizontal eye-level line and the diagonal perspective line, I subdivided the space between them in progressively steepening angles. At that point my white page had five evenly spaced lines on it, starting at horizontal and getting gradually steeper. Step four gives you an idea how this stage of a sketch looks. After that was established I drew in the specific details, using the perspective grid as a guide. —TK*

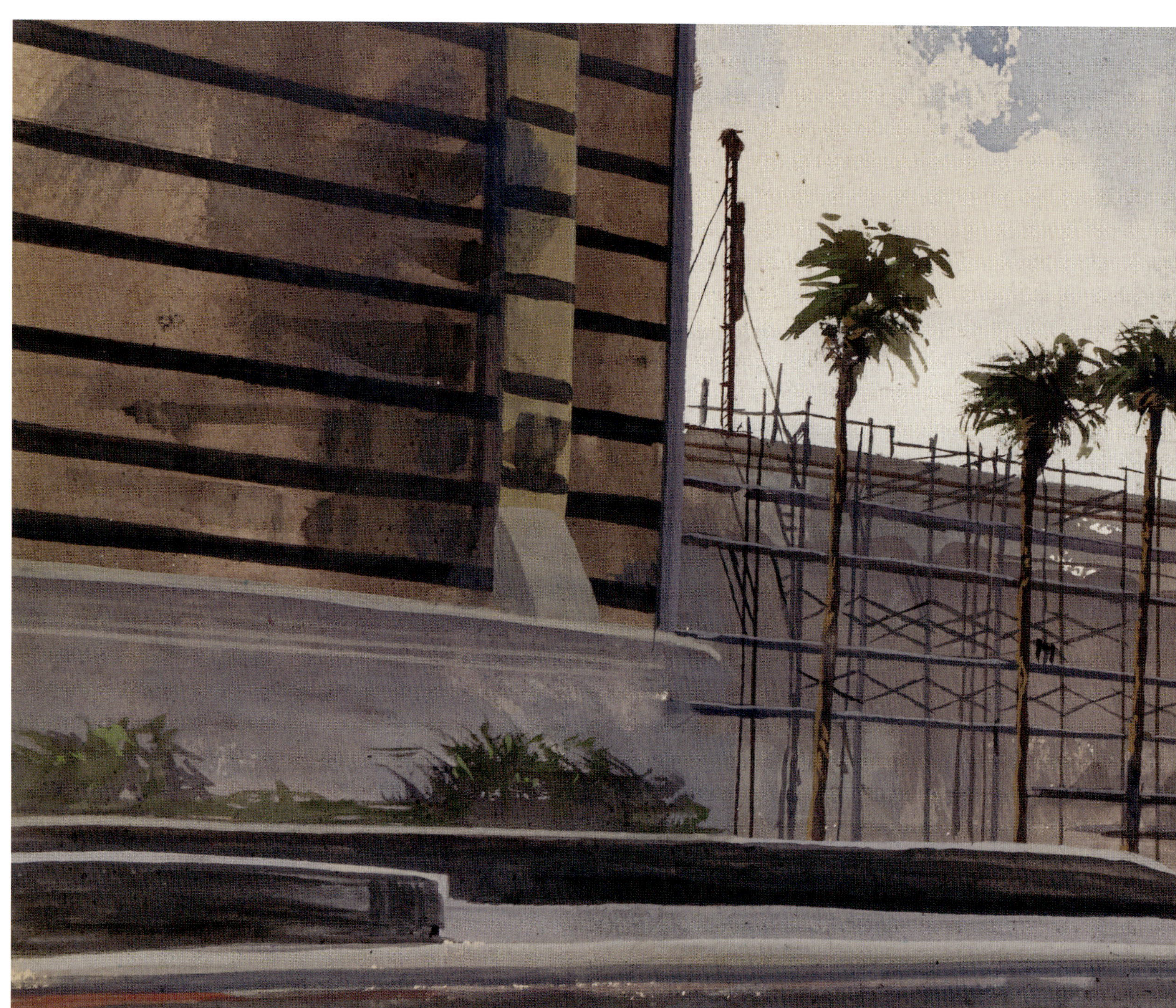

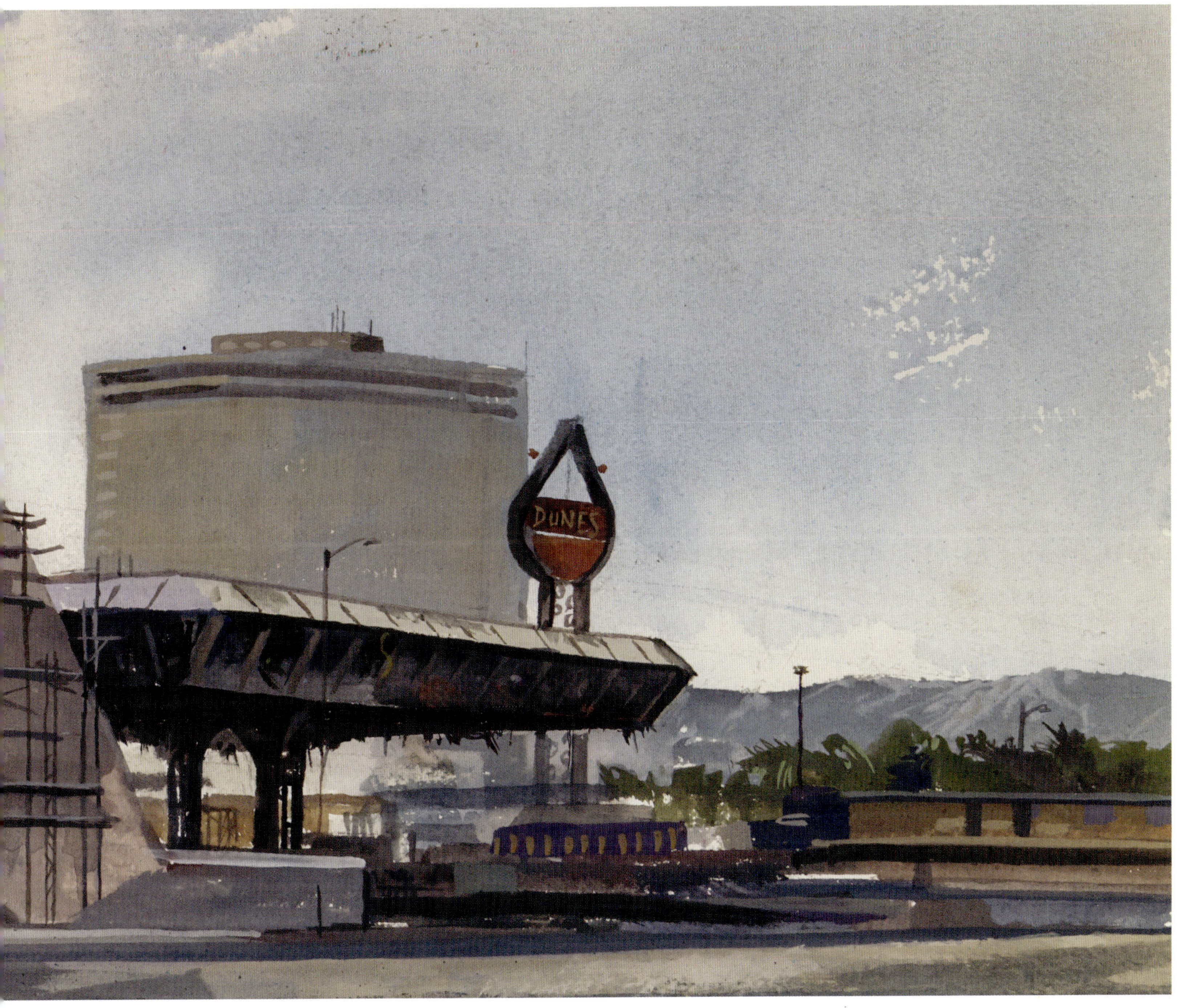
DUNES

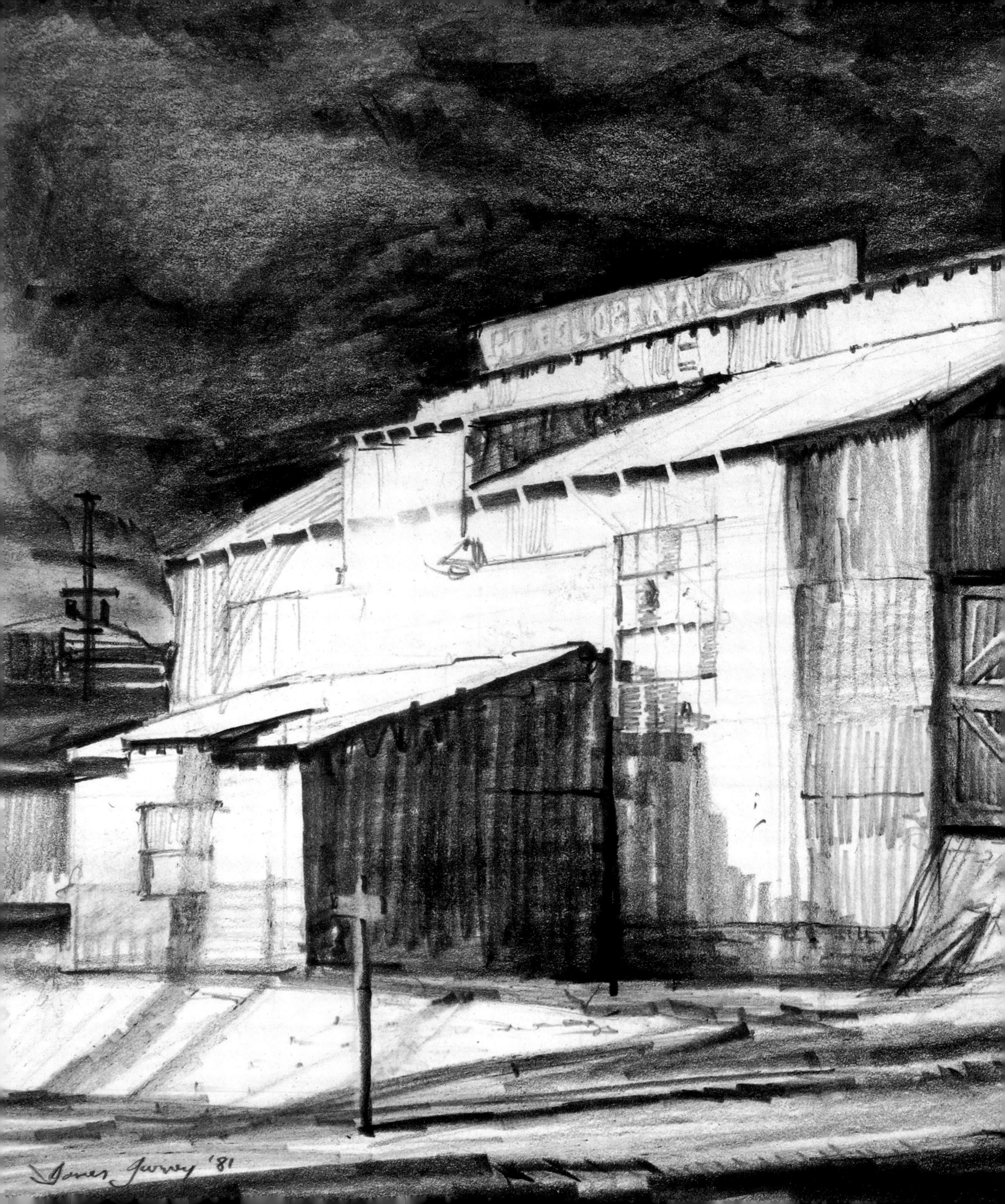

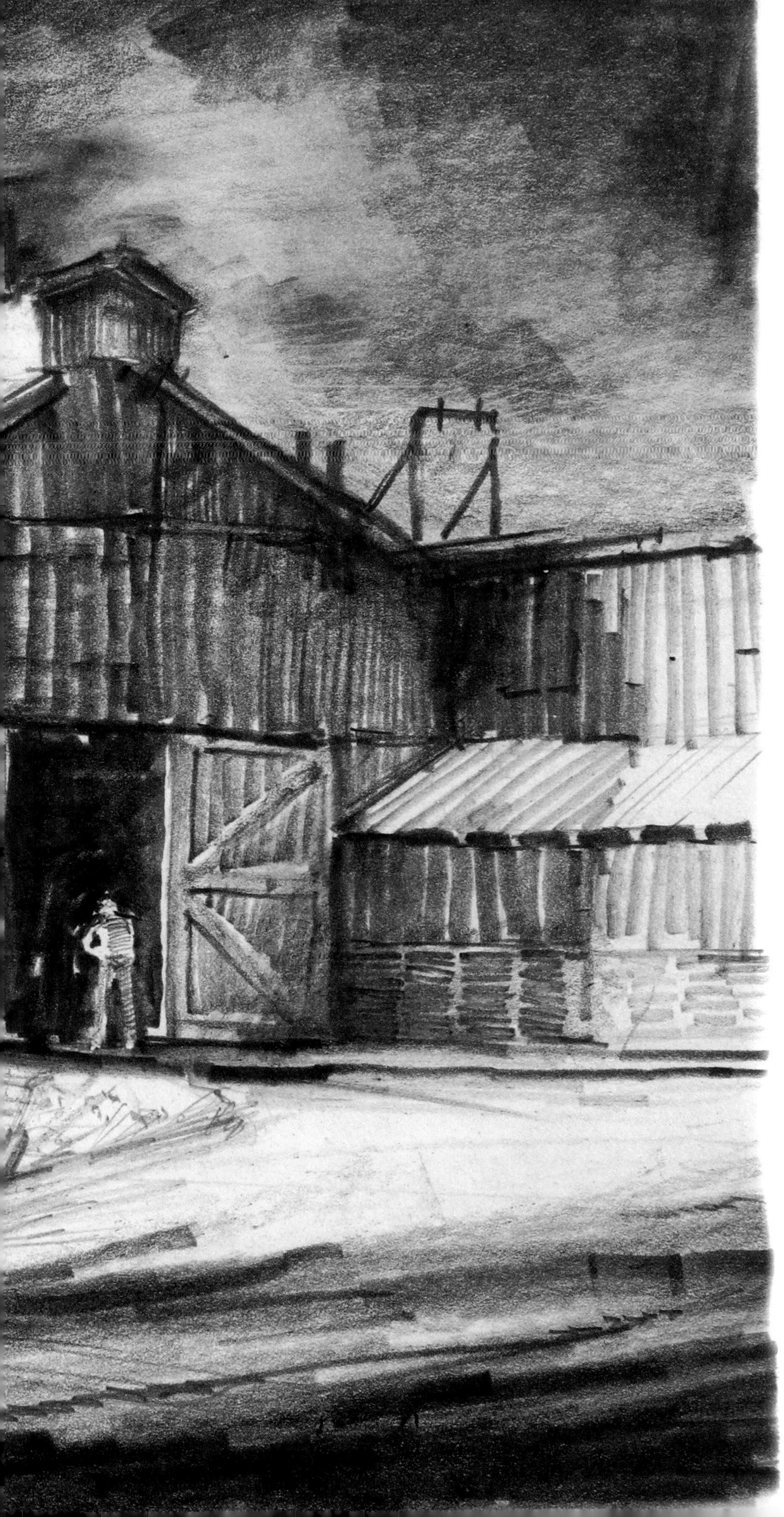

ABANDONED WAREHOUSE, *soft pencil on smooth paper, 8" x 11". Once the pencil underdrawing is carried far enough for you to feel confident that the details will be in proper perspective, you can go ahead with the final execution. You can do the rendering with just about any medium. In this case, I chose to use a soft graphite pencil because it allowed me to suggest both the smooth tones of the dark, stormy sky and the weather-beaten boards of the building. Many of the details, such as the windows on the left side of the warehouse, were sketched in relation to the perspective guidelines that I had established earlier. Note that even though the ground plane is uneven, the eye level remains consistent throughout the picture. In this case the eye level is just a little below the feet of the figure standing in the doorway. —JG*

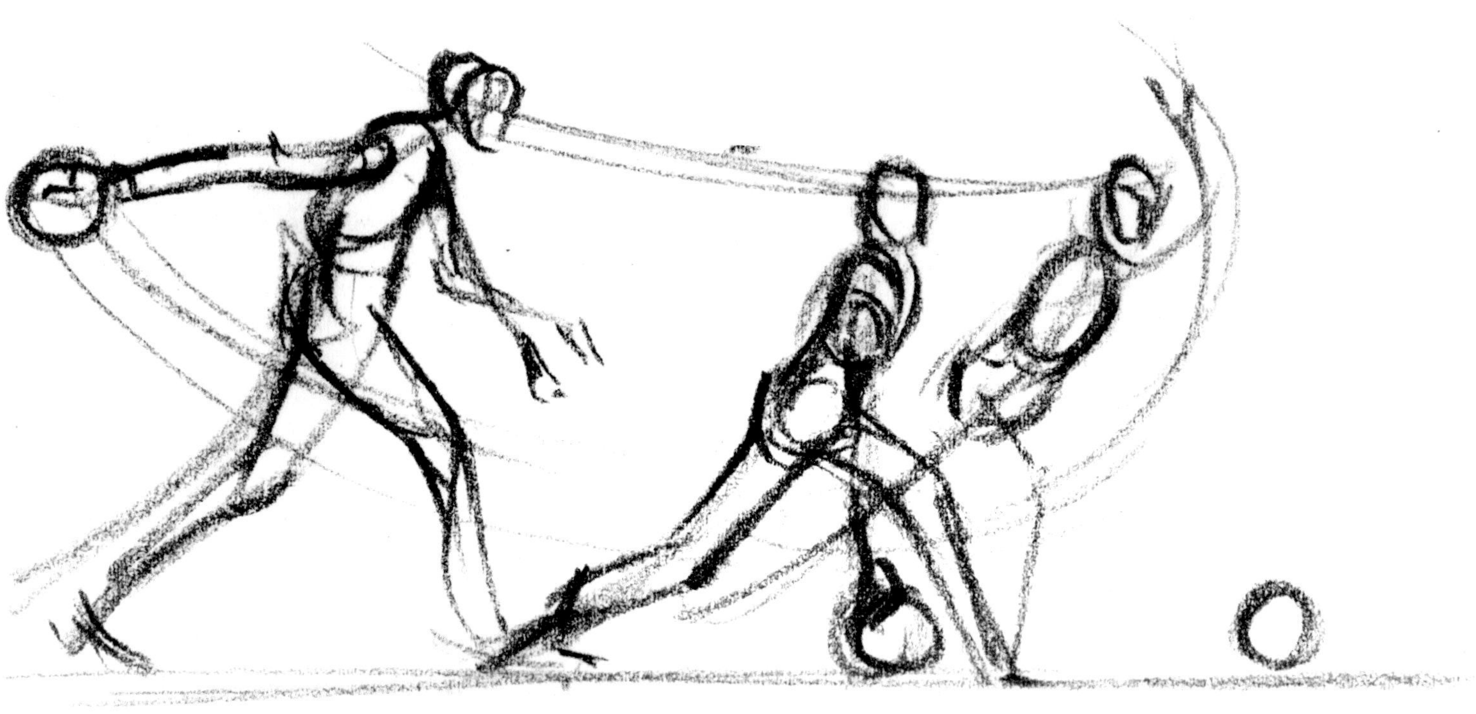

Capturing Motion

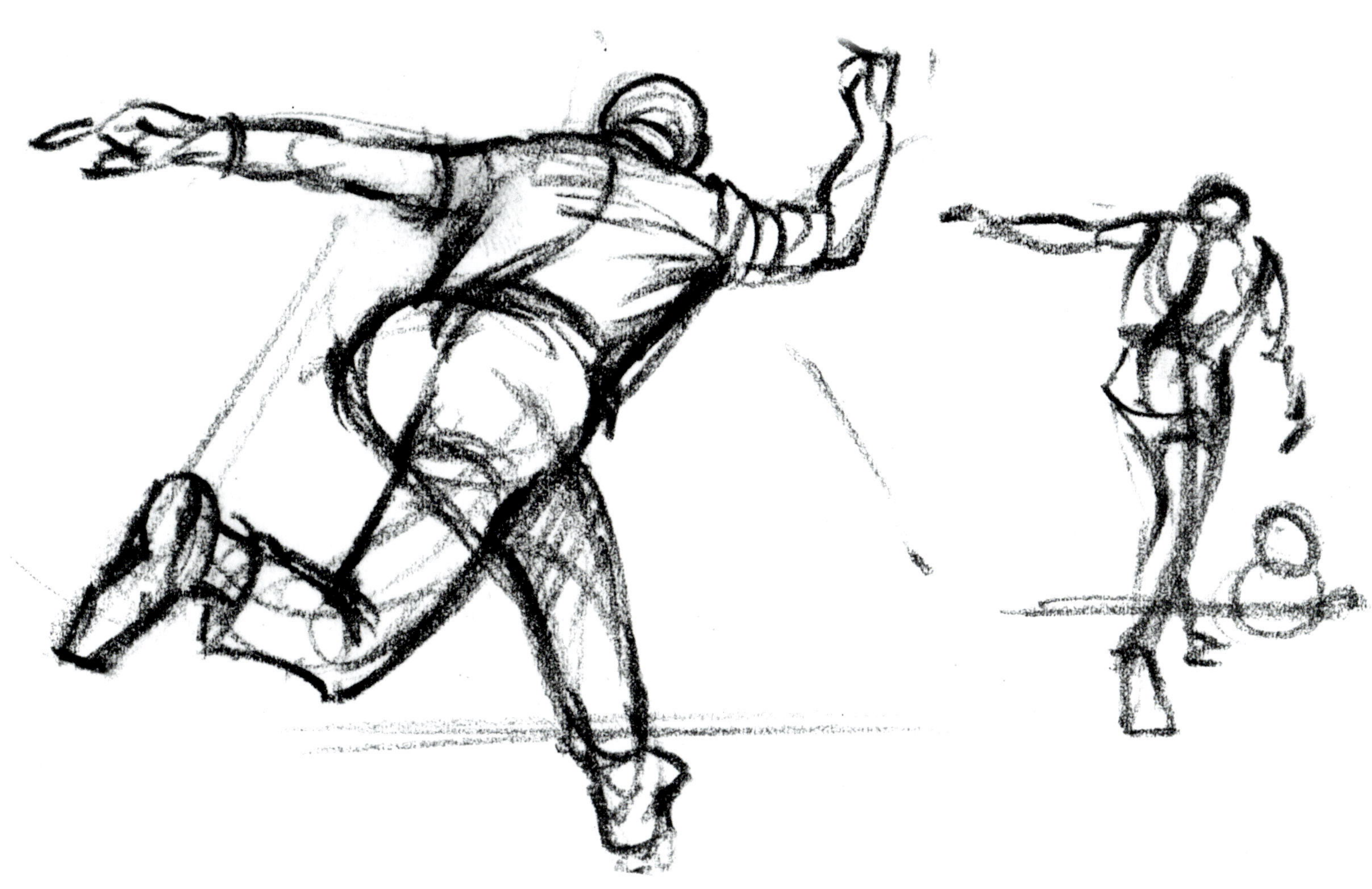

A member of our sketching group recently returned from a visit to the circus. She showed us her sketches in hopes of getting some advice. She had done beautiful fine-line ink drawings of the trapeze pole complete with all the wires and ropes as well as a detailed pencil study of a bank of lights with a sign saying "Refreshments" below it. Her sketches were appealing, yet somehow they failed to capture the essence of a circus. We asked her what impressed her most about the experience. She began to describe in detail the clown acts and the high-wire performance. Why hadn't she sketched these things? She shrugged her shoulders. "It all moved too quickly," she said. "Nothing would hold still long enough to be drawn."

How often we have heard this complaint! Have you ever experienced a similar kind of frustration, trying desperately to capture with static lines the complex motion of people and animals? If so, don't feel alone—everyone discovers at some point the difficulty of drawing motion.

Though motion sketching is inevitably one of the most challenging types of drawing, it can be made easier by using a few simple methods. In this chapter we will look at the methods for sketching motion so that you will have the ability to capture any subject, no matter how fast it moves. With a bit of practice, even circus high-wire acts can be recorded skillfully in your sketchbook.

FREEZING MOTION: A NEW WAY OF DRAWING

You are familiar with the traditional method of drawing, where the model holds absolutely still for you. All you have to do is glance back and forth from your paper to the model, checking and rechecking the stationary drawing against the stationary subject. This is the basic method you may have learned in a drawing class or from books, or by trial and error. And this is the same basic method that we discuss in the previous chapter, "Achieving Accuracy," from the standpoint of creating an accurate pencil underdrawing. It's a method that works well for things that hold still: a tree, a building, a landscape, or a sleeping bulldog. But our standard method of

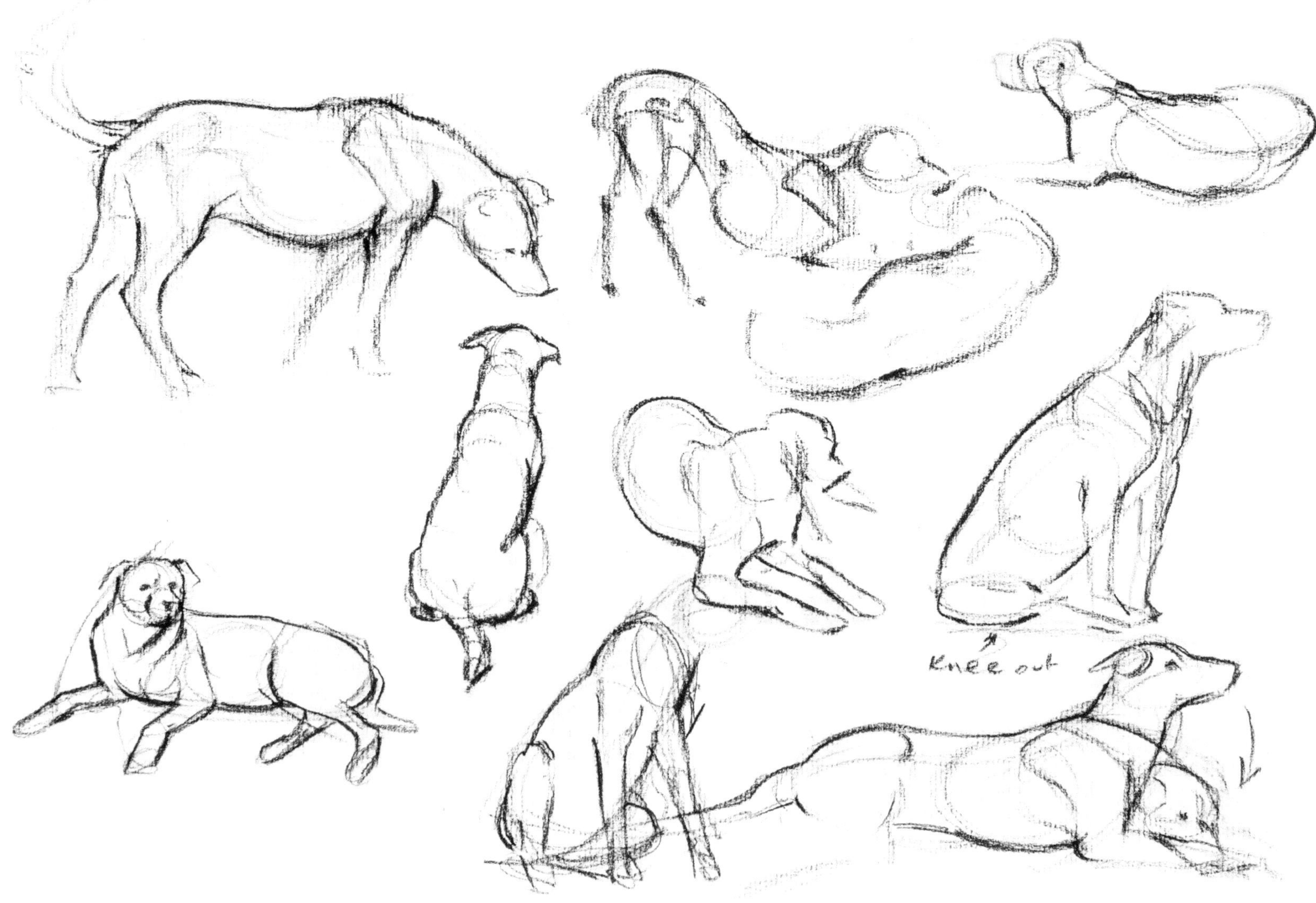

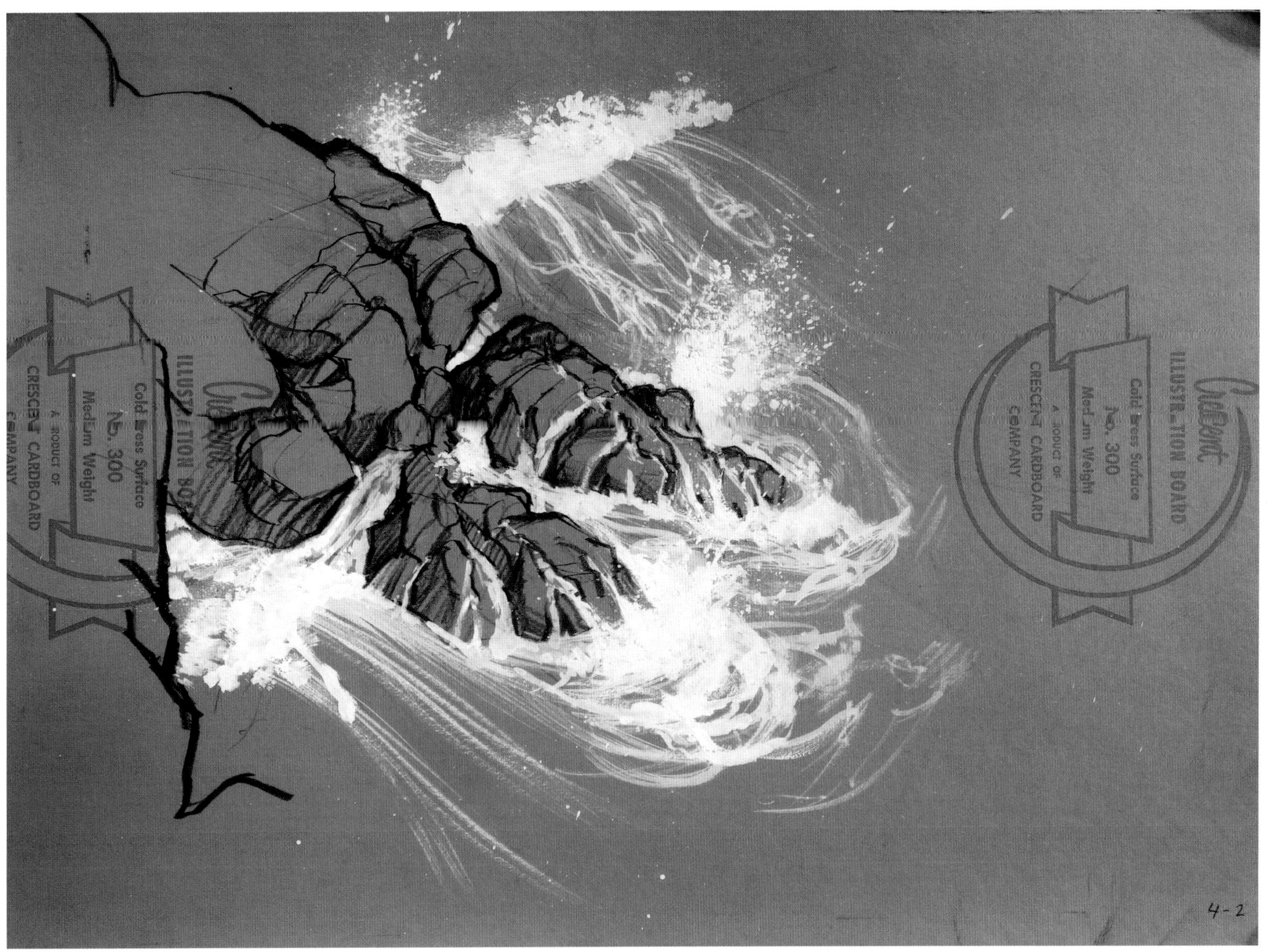

◀ **DOGS IN ACTION,** *6B charcoal pencil on charcoal paper, 11" x 17". I made this page of studies along the row of pens at the dog pound, where the nervous animals were moving constantly. Even when a dog would sit or lie down, I knew that I couldn't count on it to stay still for more than a few seconds. Therefore, I had to rely on a special kind of observation that allows me to take in as much information as possible from a single glance and then transfer that information directly onto the page. To avoid getting bogged down in the detail of the fur and the claws, I recorded only the essential shapes of the dogs' anatomy. —JG*

▲ **BREAKERS ON SEACOAST,** *soft pencil and gouache on backside of illustration board, 15" x 20". The methods for freezing motion that we discuss in this chapter are used mostly for figures and animals, but they can be transferred to other kinds of motions that you find in the nonliving world. Waves have incredibly dynamic and variable motions, with distinct phases occurring in a cycle as the wave forms a crest, breaks, and washes back out. The first step of this sketch was to watch the wave cycle for five minutes or so without drawing at all, in order to choose the single phase of the action that best conveyed the entire feeling of motion. I decided to record the moment after the wave has broken and has passed the leading edge of the rocks, with the spray flying into the air and the remaining water rushing back down in the crevices of rock. Although the technique looks free and expressive, it is really very tightly controlled. The rocks are treated in a simple planar shorthand to show their structure as simply as possible. The gouache was applied with a #8 round sable watercolor brush, using dry gestural strokes along the back of the waves and a generous stippled texture along the foamy leading edge. The spray was made by loading the brush with paint and snapping it downward. —JG*

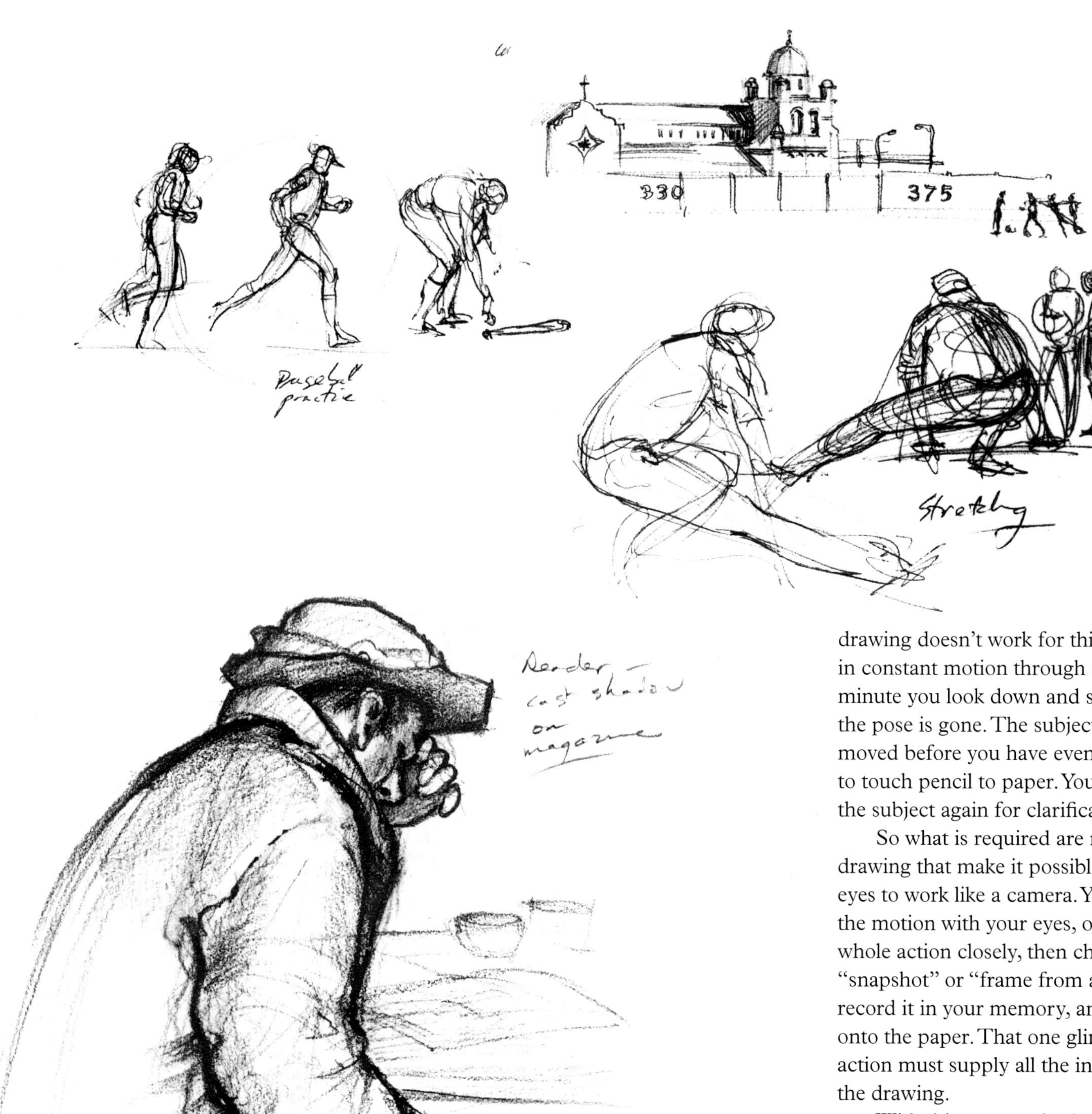

BASEBALL PLAYERS AND SEATED FIGURE, *ballpoint pen and soft pencil on drawing paper, 9" x 12". The sketches on this page represent vastly different methods of seeing and drawing. The seated figure and the building were drawn from subjects that held absolutely still. I was free to use the traditional method of drawing, using a light underdrawing and continually checking and rechecking the drawing against the subject. The baseball players at their afternoon practice, however, required a completely different approach, because as soon as I looked down from the subject to the page, the pose was gone. One glimpse had to supply all of the information for the sketch. This method for drawing depends on memory as well as on observation. —JG*

drawing doesn't work for things that are in constant motion through space. The minute you look down and start drawing, the pose is gone. The subject will have moved before you have even had a chance to touch pencil to paper. You can't refer to the subject again for clarification.

So what is required are methods of drawing that make it possible for your eyes to work like a camera. You follow the motion with your eyes, observing the whole action closely, then choose a single "snapshot" or "frame from a movie," record it in your memory, and transfer it onto the paper. That one glimpse of the action must supply all the information for the drawing.

With this new method, you'll be able to sketch a little girl skipping rope, a horse jumping over a hurdle, or a man playing Ping-Pong. Even though the method is specifically intended to help you capture the motion of figures and animals, it can be transferred to other kinds of sketching. A waving flag, or a crashing wave, for instance, each go through specific motions that can be isolated and recorded in your sketchbook.

But you'll find that the skill of motion sketching is most useful to your other

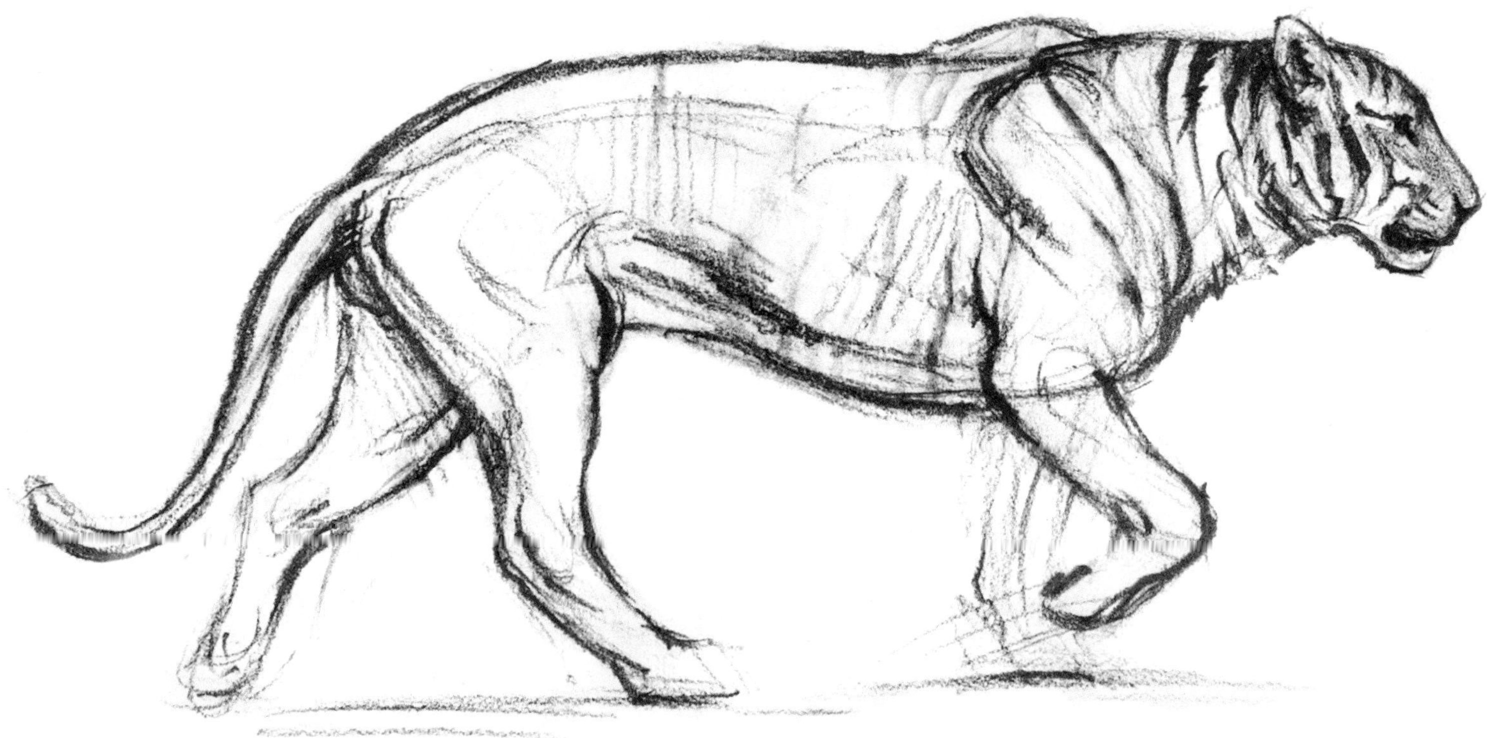

kinds of sketching in the way that it forces you to make judgments about what you see, and to record those judgments immediately. In the future, when you are sketching a nonmoving object, this ability will make it possible for you to render the details in a fraction of the time without any loss in accuracy.

LEARNING TO OBSERVE MOTION

Essentially, the key to sketching motion lies in the ability to *see* motion. No matter what art training you may have had, you have probably discovered that the skills of the eye and the mind, not those of the hand, are the keys to drawing well. This is especially true when sketching motion. Your eye and mind must condense all the information you need for a given drawing into a single impression, from a single glance that may take place in only a tenth of a second.

At first, observe without trying to draw at all. Concentrate all your attention on the motion itself, without letting yourself be distracted by the details. If you're watching a man ride by on a bicycle, for example, concentrate on the curve of the spine and the general position of the legs, not on the individual

▲ **SIBERIAN TIGER,** *pencil on drawing paper, 9" x 12". Anything that goes through repeated, cyclic motion is easier to sketch, because any given pose is struck again and again. This tiger, hungrily awaiting dinner, went through the exact same motion time after time as he paced around his cage in a slow figure-eight pattern. I concentrated on just one fragmentary moment as he passed by—the instant that the left front leg swung ahead of the right, with the right hind leg on the verge of being lifted. Since the zookeeper brought dinner before I had time to finish adding all of the stripes, the sketch remains half-finished. The tail and hind legs remain in the form of preliminary construction lines, while the head and neck are fully rendered with stripes and shadow tones. —JG*

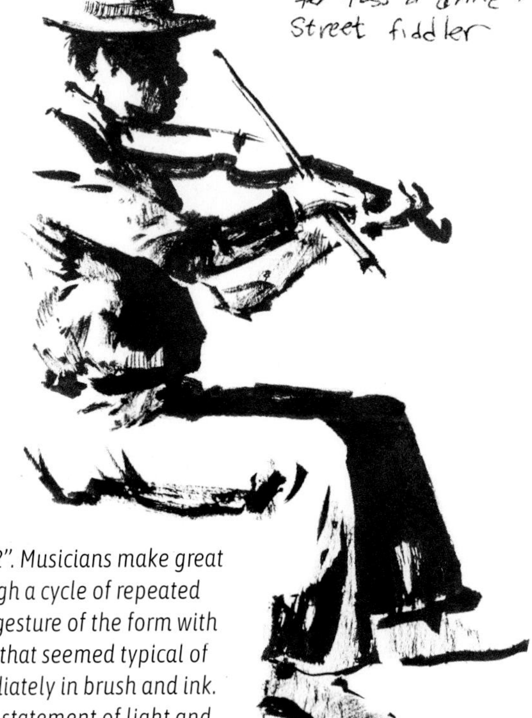

▶ **FIDDLER,** *brush and ink on sketch paper, 9" x 12". Musicians make great subjects for motion studies because they go through a cycle of repeated poses. I began this study by exploring the overall gesture of the form with delicate pencil lines. After I had suggested a pose that seemed typical of the fiddle player's motion, I began working immediately in brush and ink. The boldness of the black ink allowed for a strong statement of light and dark, suggesting the strong light that illuminated my subject from behind. —TK*

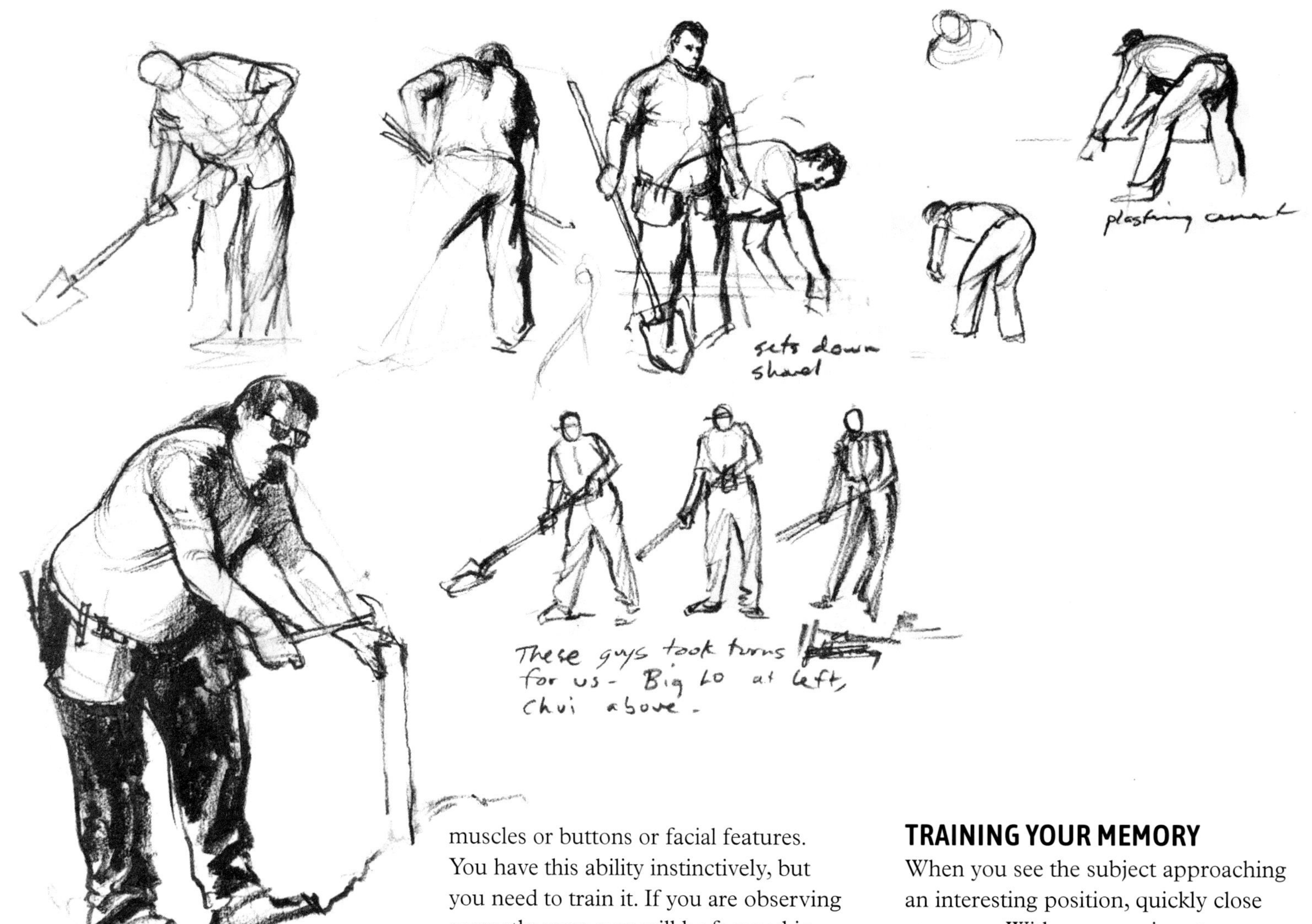

CONSTRUCTION WORKERS, *soft pencil on drawing paper, 11" x 14". Since these workers were constantly on the move, I had to depend on my instantaneous memory to recall the details of the pose. As soon as a given figure reached a pose that interested me, I closed my eyes. Since the last image to reach the retina leaves a brief afterimage, I was able to concentrate fully on just one "snapshot" of movement without being distracted by what followed. On some of the figures I added a dark shadow along the right edge to suggest the fading afternoon sunlight, which was coming from behind and to the left. Seeing that I was sketching him, the heavyset fellow with the little goatee came over and started a friendly conversation with me about his job as a construction worker. —JG*

muscles or buttons or facial features. You have this ability instinctively, but you need to train it. If you are observing correctly, your eyes will be focused in a general region near the center of the moving form, much as a juggler fixes his eyes at an imaginary point in front of him without watching the individual balls.

As you watch a given motion, you will notice that there are certain phases or positions within a motion that are more interesting than others. Animators call these phases "extremes"—most notably the "wind-up" and the "follow-through" in a motion like a ball player swinging a bat. If someone is gesturing as they speak, the extreme would be the point at which the hand briefly pauses before moving to a new position. In a walking cycle the extreme occurs at the moment the leading foot contacts the ground. These are the positions that you will find translate best in drawing. Look for these moments and then freeze these positions in your mind's eye long enough to be able to draw them.

TRAINING YOUR MEMORY

When you see the subject approaching an interesting position, quickly close your eyes. With no more input, you can concentrate all your attention on the single last pose you saw. Try this a few times without actually drawing. You will find that the afterimage is *more* stable on moving objects than on stationary ones. Demonstrate this effect for yourself on joggers, children playing, walking dogs, or any other moving object.

The next step is to reinforce the retinal afterimage so that it's accessible to you for a long enough period of time that you can study its details. Immediately after you shut your eyes, review the details of the afterimage. Where are the feet, for instance? Is the body twisted? Where are the arm positions? After asking yourself all these questions, you can use a variety of techniques to record the retinal afterimage in line, tone, scribbles, etc.

GETTING IT DOWN FAST

At this point, you've observed the motion, closed your eyes, and reviewed the entire gesture, so you are ready to sketch. Your goal is to put on paper the overall sense of the gesture that you have reviewed in the afterimage. It's a race against time. No matter what you do, the memory of the position will fade, and you will reach a point in your sketch when you realize that you are not actually working from what you've seen, but instead are improvising, using your own knowledge about figure drawing to fill in the gaps. After a little practice you will know exactly when you've reached that threshold. For now, stop drawing when you reach that point, even if you can only sketch from memory just a small part of the entire pose. With experience, more and more of the pose will be recalled to your memory, and you will have no trouble getting down the main action of the figure in as little as five or ten seconds.

Every artist has his own favorite method for actually translating the remembered image—for "getting it down fast." But most methods will fall into one of four categories, which we call the "scribble approach," "gestural approach," "mannikin approach," and "tonal mass approach." These are discussed here. Try them all to see which suits your personality best.

THE SCRIBBLE APPROACH

For this method, use an ordinary black ballpoint pen on inexpensive sketch paper. The ballpoint tip delivers a fluid line in all directions without needing to be refilled. Since it cannot be erased, it forces you to be more bold. Don't be afraid to make mistakes.

FIGURE SCRIBBLES, *ballpoint pen on sketch paper, 5½" x 8½". Once an instantaneous pose has been observed, the next step is to get it down fast on paper. This method, the scribble approach, is done with a ballpoint pen on inexpensive paper. Each of the figures is about two inches high, requiring only about ten seconds of very fast pen motions. This kind of drawing is a lot like writing your signature, because all the pen motions are controlled by the muscles of the fingers, not the arm, and the pen does not stop or lift up during the course of each sketch. The line itself is allowed to wander in and out of forms; it does not always have to follow the contour. Lines that would be normally overlapped can be shown as if everything were transparent. The lady with the coat over her arm, for example, second from the right on the bottom row, has been sketched with the back edge of her dress visible right through the coat she is carrying. Try to reach a balance between freedom and control, so that you are neither aimlessly meandering with your line nor rigidly starting and stopping. —JG*

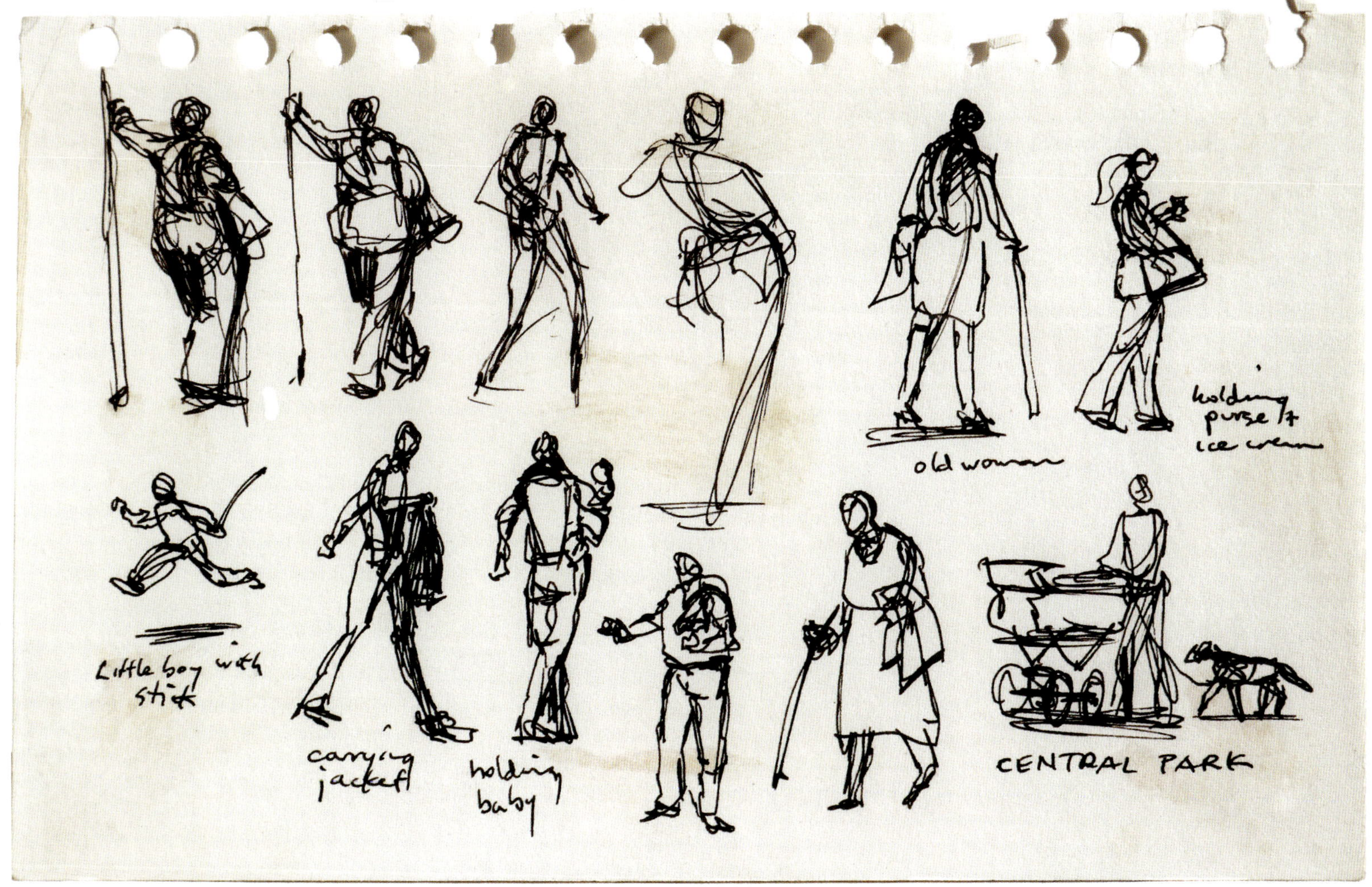

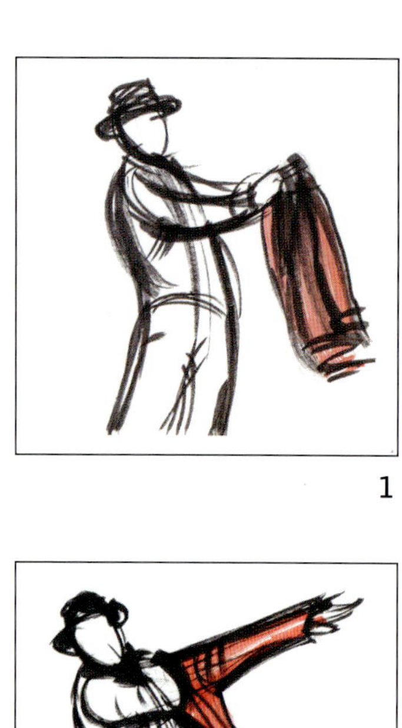

1

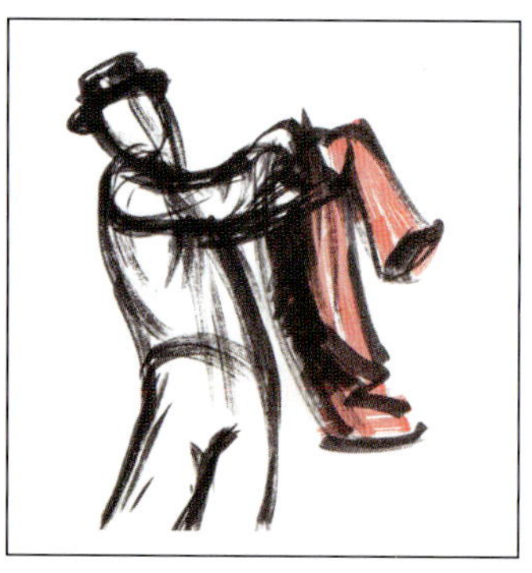

2

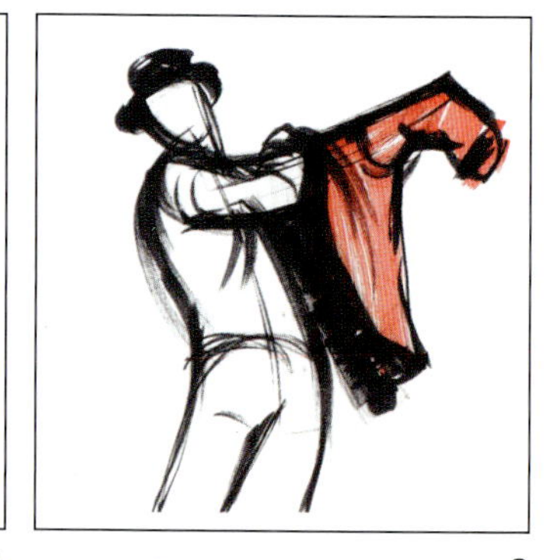

3

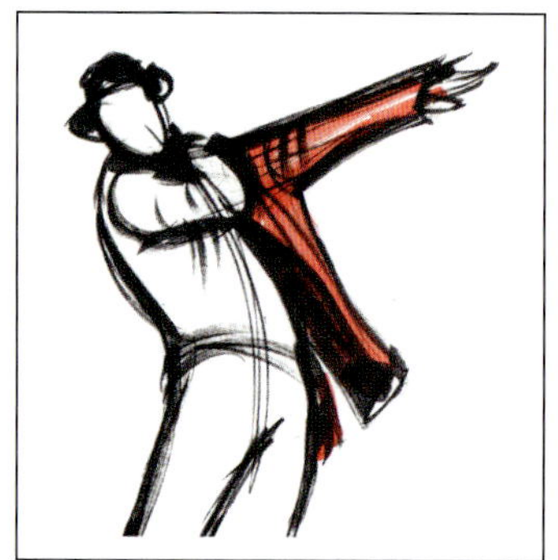

4

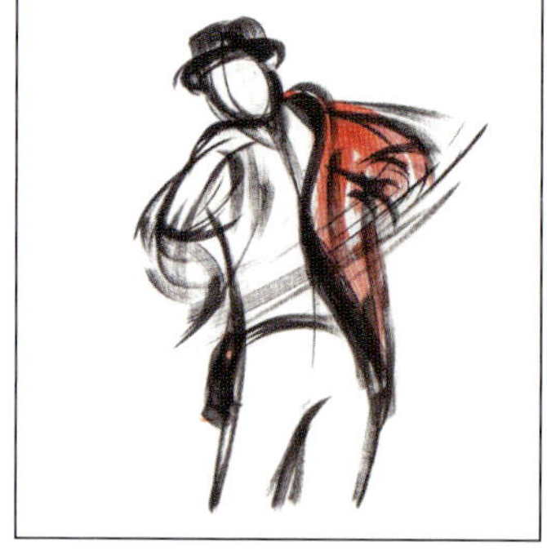

5

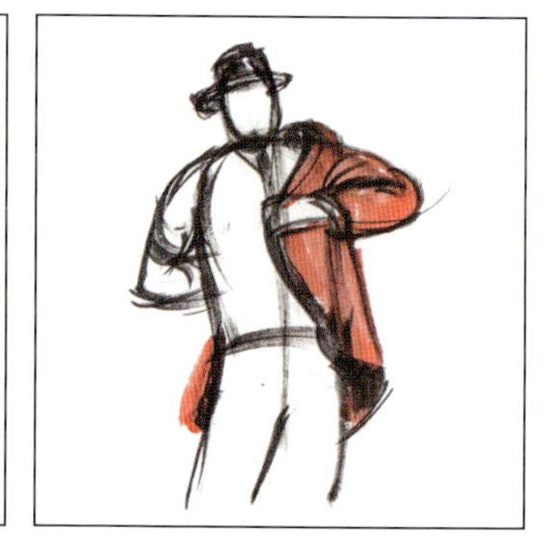

6

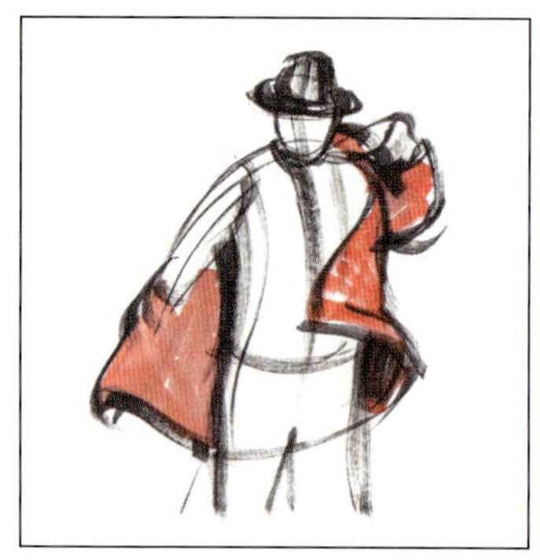

7

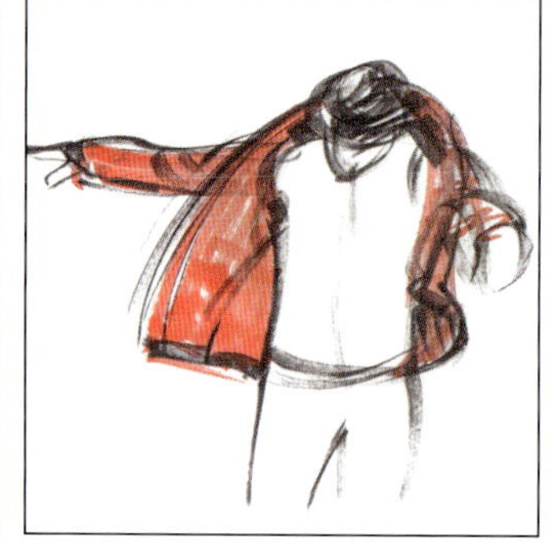

8

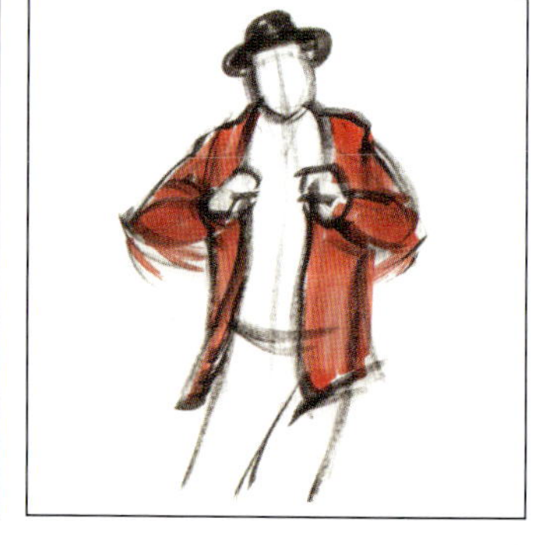

9

PUTTING ON A COAT, *brush and ink with marker tone on bond paper, 8" x 8" each. This little action study, used in an experimental animation sequence, was sketched pose by pose from a friend who went through the simple action of putting on a coat dozens of times. Pose #4 is called an extreme, because it represents the outermost extended portion of the arm, briefly pausing before moving to a new position. Pose #5, halfway between extremes, is difficult to see when you watch the real motion. In fact, the pathway that the arms follow can be sensed more definitely than the position of the arms themselves. I used a gestural approach to record each pose as simply and gracefully as possible. The large #8 round red-sable watercolor brush was discharged of ink on a paper towel before each stroke to keep the lines from getting too black. I made sure every stroke of the brush was controlled by the smooth motions of my shoulder and upper arm rather than by the jerky motions of the figures. —JG*

These sketches should be small—about two inches high per sketch. They should also be very fast. Spend only about ten seconds each, and then move on to the next one. You should have an entire page covered in five minutes.

Hold the pen in your hand as if you were about to write your signature. When you sketch, use only wrist and finger motions, which are fast and fluid. A good way to proceed is to draw a small circle for the head, drop down through the body to the foot, establishing the ground plane right away. Then move your line in and out of forms, letting your hand move freely.

There are only two rules. Keep the pen in constant motion, and never lift the pen from the paper. Your instincts may rebel against these rules at first, but you will discover that these restrictions will liberate your pen line.

Your goal is to achieve rhythm. Rhythm is the graceful, pleasing flow of one contour into another. Since the movement of the hand is graceful, so too is the movement of the viewer's eye. A few preliminary exercises will help you get warmed up. Start out with repeat circles in both directions, then make spirals and continuous figure eights. Your hand should be alert and well trained, ready to follow the command of your memory. If you feel as though you are doodling aimlessly, then your hand is out of control. If it stops every second or so, and moves in a jerky manner, you need to *relax* control. Somewhere between those extremes is an ideal balance that yields rhythmic sketches.

THE GESTURAL APPROACH

Instead of using the small-scale action of the wrist and fingers, you can make use of the action of your shoulder and upper arm for recording the fleeting impression of motion. These sketches are done on a much larger scale. Some people like to do gestural sketches on 18" x 24" sketch-paper pads, with just one or two individual sketches per page. We find this size to be too cumbersome and conspicuous for most typical motion sketching opportunities. Instead we recommend you use an 11" x 14" or 14" x 17" pad with paper that's cheap enough to permit you to use up ten or twenty pages in one sitting. Use either a brushpen held normally or a 6B charcoal pencil held in the fingertips of your hand in an overhand grip, facing palm down.

Using your shoulder makes you draw much more slowly than you would in the scribble approach. Just as if you were throwing a baseball or conducting a symphony, the motions of your hand are simpler and more flowing, because they are weighed down by the bulk of the lower arm. The resultant effect in the sketch will be more a feeling of smoothness, but without the immediacy of a scribble.

In the first lines you draw, look for the long C-shaped or S-shaped lines running through the center of the forms of the person or animal you are drawing, especially the line running along the spine. Draw these with simple, graceful strokes, lifting the pencil between each stroke. Nothing but the tip of the pencil should touch the paper; your hand should move completely freely.

Try this method at home first, sketching other members of your family or recording the action from the TV. Whenever you practice it, consider the first three or four pages to be simply warm-up. It takes a while for your arm to limber up. Don't expect every gesture sketch to be a winner—just try to reach the same balance between freedom and control that we talked about in the section on the scribble approach.

THE MANNIKIN APPROACH

The human form is so complex and features so many movable parts that drawing it in motion inevitably requires some intelligent simplification. Artists throughout history have devised endless systems for indicating the human form with a minimum of lines. Most of these systems boil down to variations of the stick figures that most of us drew as children.

The mannikin formula that we use most often consists of a stick figure with three basic body blocks: an egg shape for the head, a large rectangular block for the ribs and shoulders, and a smaller block for the pelvis. These simplified forms correspond to the basic immovable units of the actual human body. When connected by a single flexible line representing the spine, they can be made to bend or twist into practically any imaginable position. The arms and legs are represented by nothing more than line

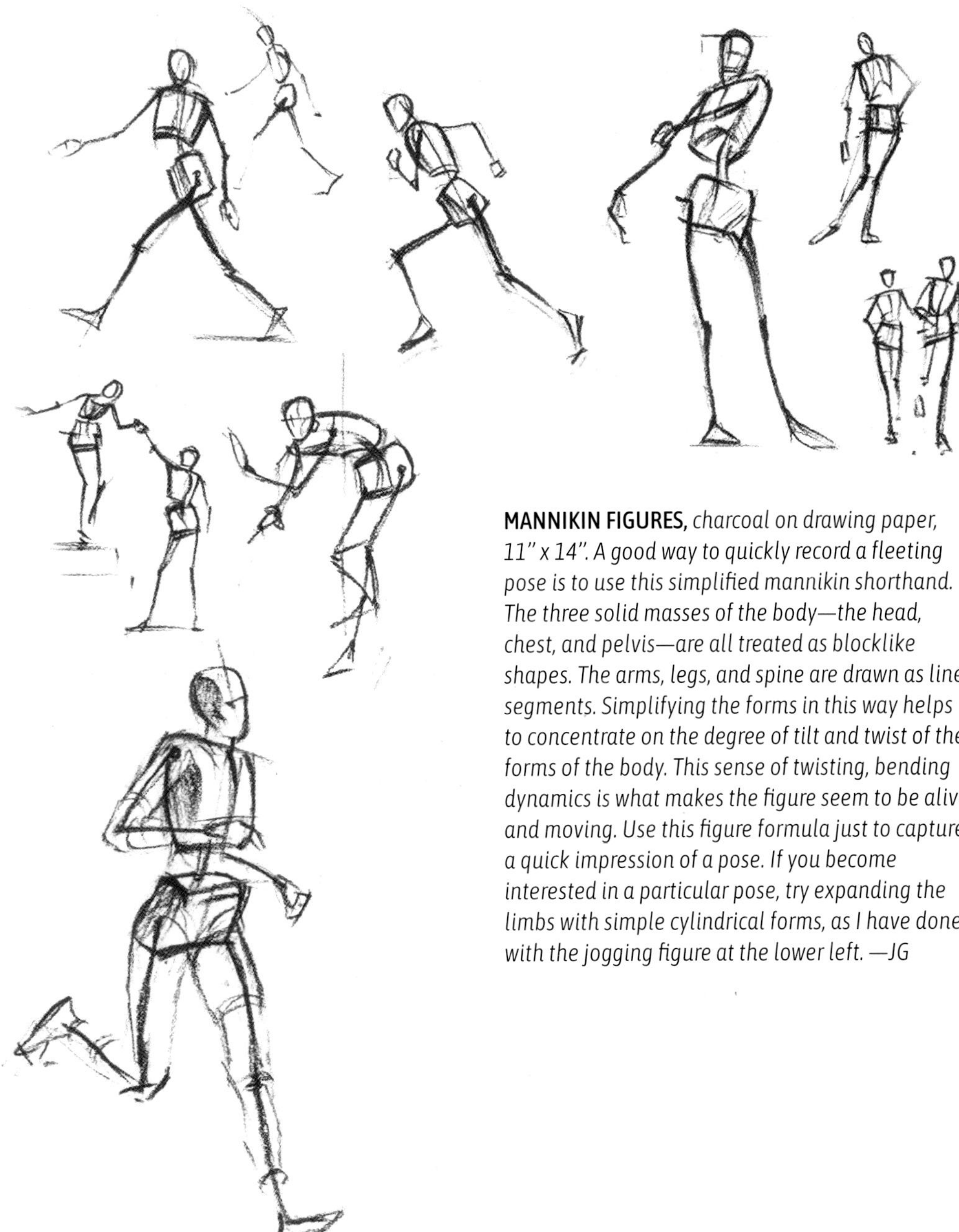

MANNIKIN FIGURES, *charcoal on drawing paper, 11" x 14". A good way to quickly record a fleeting pose is to use this simplified mannikin shorthand. The three solid masses of the body—the head, chest, and pelvis—are all treated as blocklike shapes. The arms, legs, and spine are drawn as line segments. Simplifying the forms in this way helps to concentrate on the degree of tilt and twist of the forms of the body. This sense of twisting, bending dynamics is what makes the figure seem to be alive and moving. Use this figure formula just to capture a quick impression of a pose. If you become interested in a particular pose, try expanding the limbs with simple cylindrical forms, as I have done with the jogging figure at the lower left. —JG*

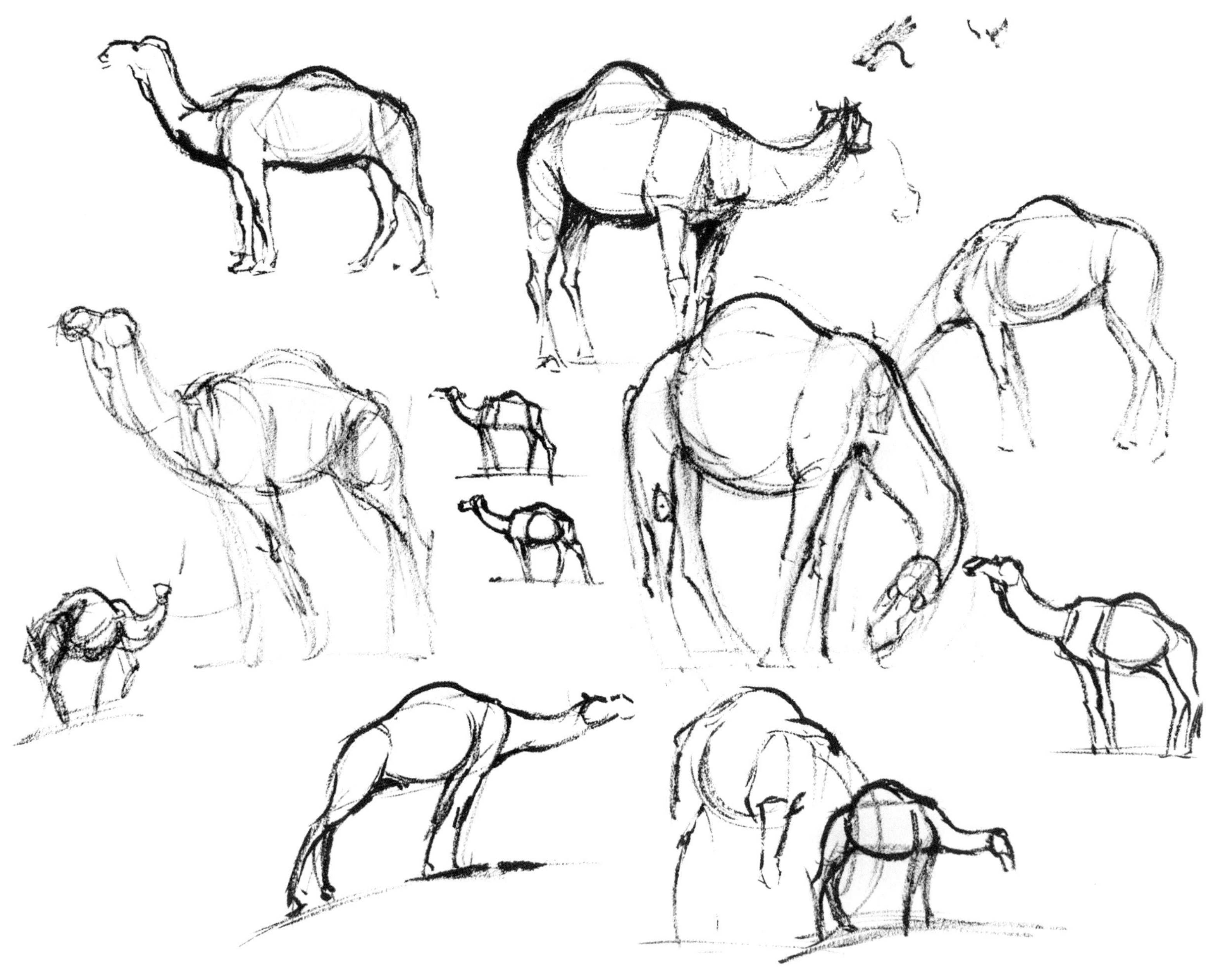

CAMELS, *brush pen on drawing paper, 11" x 14". All of these camels are sketched in terms of a simplified mannikin. The body is divided into three basic units: shoulders, ribs (including the hump), and pelvis area. The tiny sketches in the center of the page show how I was experimenting with showing these units as squarish forms (above) or rounded forms (below). When I sketched the legs on all of these poses, all I was concerned with was placement and direction, not bones, muscles, or fur. In fact, it's perfectly all right to show nothing but a simple line segment below the knee. Over a simple shorthand like this, it would be easy to develop the details and textures of a realistic-looking camel. —JG*

segments representing only the general direction and proportion.

To use a mannikin to capture the gesture of a moving figure, simply catch a single impression in the manner we described earlier and then look at your paper and reconstruct the pose by translating it into the simple terms of a mannikin.

With the legs and arms represented only by line segments, all you have to remember is the *direction* they took in the original pose. You can ignore the outer contours, the muscles, and the folds of clothes.

After indicating a gesture with a simple mannikin, the figure sketch can be elaborated to any degree you like. We generally use tapered cylinder forms to indicate the full volume of arms and legs. Any additional drawing you do over your initial mannikin will be done from your knowledge of form combined with whatever observation you can do that relates to the pose. In other words, after you sketch a simple mannikin, you can construct the basic forms of the body using what you know about how arms, legs, and torsos look. Adding clothes comes last, after you have established the underlying forms. The clothes that you draw can be a pure invention or borrowed from other figures. Glance around and adapt one person's pants, another's jacket, and still another's hair.

The mannikin approach can be modified for use with animals. Like humans, animals can be simplified into three basic rigid body forms—the head, rib cage, and pelvis, which are constructed around the spinal cord. The limbs and tail can be indicated simply as line segments.

THE TONAL MASS APPROACH

Another effective way to capture the fleeting poses of moving people and animals is the tonal mass approach. This method involves scrubbing in a general silhouette of your subject using either a cotton ball rubbed with charcoal or a broad-tip gray marker. As in other methods, the first step is to capture a quick impression of the motion by closing your eyes and retaining the afterimage. Now look immediately to your paper and make a confident stroke with your scrubbing tool. Make your shapes represent the cores of the forms, building from the inside out. Continue working until you have captured a crude suggestion of the pose you saw. Then bring out a more precise tool such as a pencil or pen and begin outlining a more accurate version of the pose on top of your tonal lay-in. Having first established the general forms of your figure with the scrubbed tone, you can now concentrate on the specific forms—clothing, hands, legs—with much more authority. In fact, you may even discover that the tonal underlay actually *suggests* forms to you! For example, you may have done a quick tonal mass lay-in based on a walking businessman, and as you refined the sketch, you discovered that the forms of his briefcase suggested the flare of an open raincoat. Feel free to draw it in that way.

You may find it advantageous to make several preliminary tonal mass lay-ins before beginning any overdrawing. Using pure tone is a good way to loosen up before doing more careful drawing. The secret is to be as loose as possible and not give too much thought to technique.

By the way, this approach to motion sketching can also be used with landscapes, trees, and man-made forms. You can work the same way, beginning with a gestural application of tone, and building up the forms from that basis. Treating a static subject in this way will give it a feeling of motion and mystery. Some forms will seem to emerge from the page; others will be only suggested.

WHEN YOUR SUBJECT MOVES UNEXPECTEDLY

You have just settled down to sketch your pet cat, which is lying below your feet in a posture of utter relaxation. After carefully blocking in the pose with a pencil, you begin the process of refining the sketch with a felt pen only to notice in utter horror that your cat is refusing to cooperate with the sketching experience and has chosen to roll over and assume a totally different pose. Subjects that move infrequently or sporadically present a special kind of challenge to the sketcher. Like continuous motion, occasional motion can be sketched easily after you have mastered a few simple methods.

The first thing to realize is that you cannot control how long a person or an animal will hold a pose. It could be ten seconds or it could be twenty minutes. But you can control your attitude toward your drawing. The key is to try to get down as much information about the pose as you can, knowing that your subject may move at any moment. You may feel a sense of urgency, but that's part of the experience. In fact, it is the pressure that will keep you alert, direct, and brave. Many figure-drawing instructors will use the trick of an unpredictable time limit for posing the model in classroom situations. If you expect someone to hold a pose for twenty minutes, and the instructor unexpectedly calls for a change after only five minutes, chances are you'll be caught off guard. Once you have experienced this surprise change, whether it's a model in a classroom or a cat on the living room floor, you will learn to be more resourceful. The next time you begin to sketch what appears to be a stationary object, you will immediately try to convey the most significant overall aspects of the pose. If the subject happens to move at any point, at least you will have something down on paper.

Take this positive attitude with you when you sketch people or animals. Assume that you only have a few seconds to work with. Make every line count right from the start. As long as your subject holds the pose, do your best to capture all you can in the available time. And when

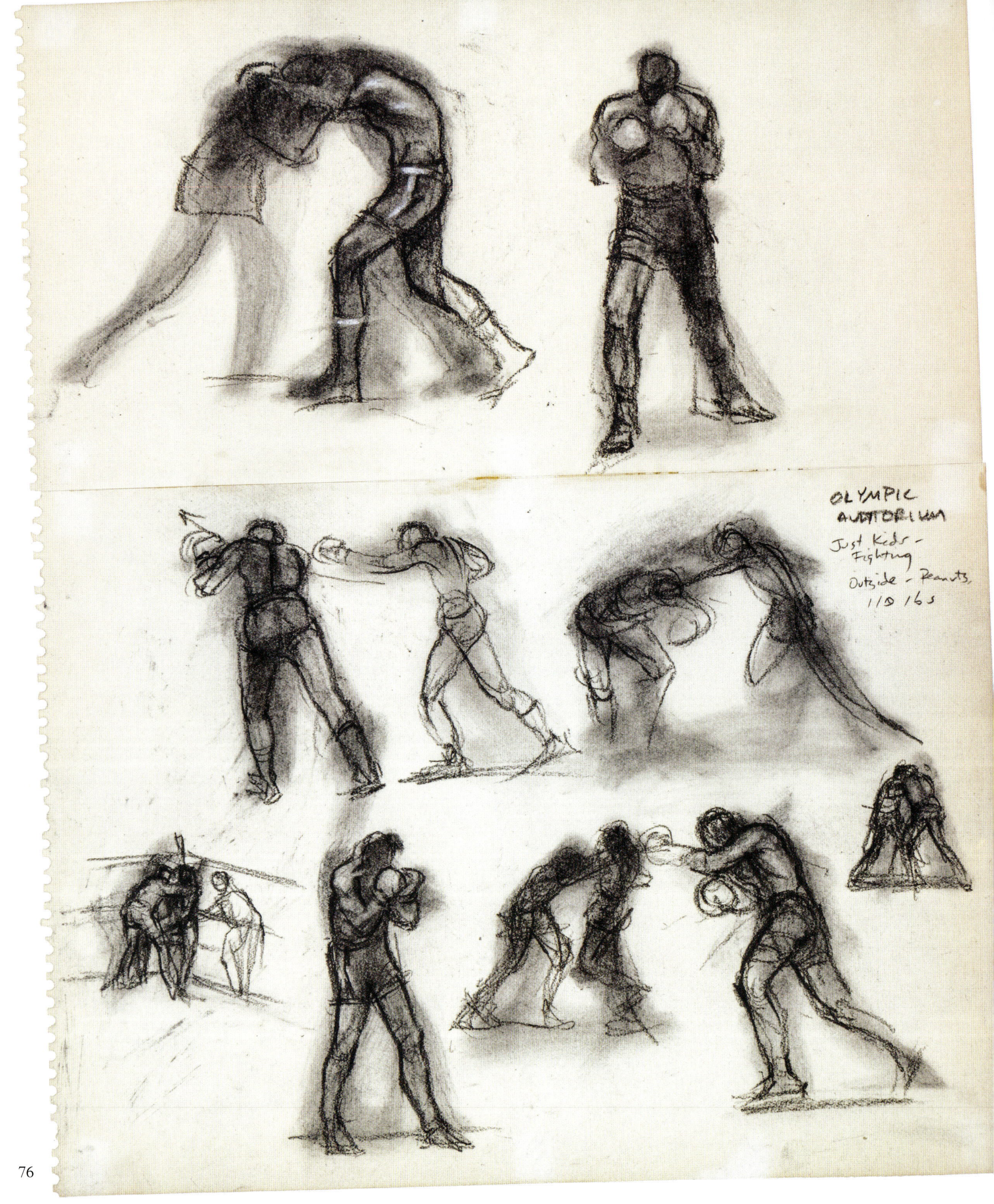
OLYMPIC
AUDITORIUM
Just Kids -
Fighting
Outside - Peanuts,

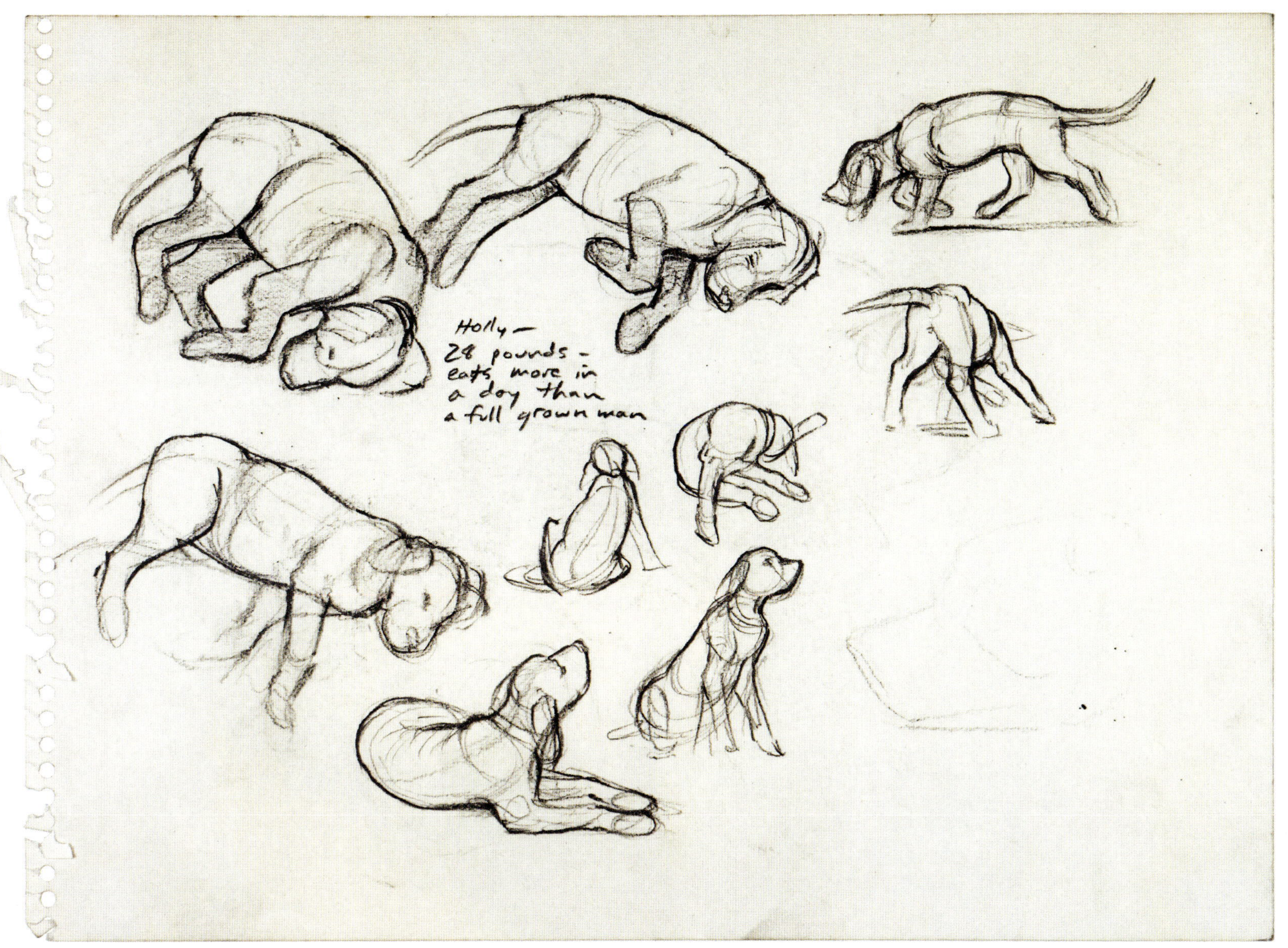

◀ **BOXERS,** *charcoal on drawing paper, 14" x 17". The tonal mass technique for motion sketching makes possible a very loose foundation in tone upon which to develop specific details in line. Because of the softness of the tones, the result has a moody feeling. The approach I used was to load a 6-inch square of cotton rag with charcoal dust, which I had ground up on sandpaper at home and had carried on location in a plastic film can. With the charcoal-impregnated rag held over the tip of my index finger, I watched the action closely, and when I saw an interesting pose, I quickly scrubbed the overall gesture on the absorbent paper. The next step was to reinforce the pose with a sharpened 6B charcoal pencil. Only the important lines were defined; I didn't describe the head or the gloves as anything more than simple, rounded shapes. Finally, on some of the sketches, I used a kneaded eraser to pull out key forms inside the silhouette that help to explain the action. The two interlocked figures at the upper left show how this process looks at every stage of development, from the scrubbed tones indicating the legs of the left figure to the more finished rendering along the torso of the right figure. —JG*

▲ **SLEEPING PUPPY,** *pencil on drawing paper, 9" x 12". No matter how relaxed and quiet a sleeping animal appears, you can bet it will move out of position as soon as you begin to sketch it. You never can know in advance how long to expect the pose to last. To make this situation work to my advantage rather than letting it frustrate me, I kept each of the sketches on the page small and simply started a new sketch whenever the puppy changed position. —JG*

the subject moves, make the situation work to your advantage. You have at least four options:

1. If the pose is only slightly different from the last, superimpose it directly over the original drawing. For instance, if you are sketching a person sitting at a pew in church, and all of a sudden, he stands up to sing, you can go ahead and draw the standing posture using the same pair of feet that you used for the sitting posture. The feet won't have moved significantly. What you will feel when you look at that sketch is the impression, as your eye shifts back and forth from one position to another, that the subject is moving. This is a powerful way to get a sense of motion into your sketches.
2. Leave the half-finished sketch, and start a new one on the same page. Start yet another one if the subject moves again. Before you know it, the subject will return to that original pose again, and you can then refine that first sketch from observation. This method works well with such things as caged animals, which amble from one pose to another in a very predictable fashion. At one moment you see a side view, and at another you watch as the animal turns around. In this way you can develop five or six different sketches simultaneously.
3. Make a composite figure from a collection of fragmentary poses of separate people or animals around you. Let's say you are in a waiting room and you have begun a sketch of a woman on the far bench, slouching half-asleep, a prime candidate. By the time you have laid-in the main shapes with your pen or pencil, and then have begun to describe the details of her purse and heavy overcoat, you hear a voice from inside the office: "Next!" She leaves. Here's what you do. Look around and see if there is someone with a head that you can graft onto the original torso, or a foot that you can graft onto the original leg. Even if you end up with a curious looking sketch, you'll feel the satisfaction of having completed something.
4. Leave the fragmentary sketch alone until you get home, and then try to reconstruct the missing details from memory. You'll be surprised how much you can remember, especially of the significant details, such as the tilt of the head and the position of the arm. Whether or not the coat was buttoned doesn't really matter. If you can't really remember, go ahead and make it up. You'll find that sketches finished in this way from memory will have a consistency that purely observational treatments often lack.

PLACES TO GO FOR MOTION SKETCHING

Wherever you see people and animals, you will find people and animals on the move. But some places are better than others. At first you will want to find a place where actions are repeated enough times that you will have a chance to really observe them. Certain sports like bowling and tennis are ideal for repeating motions. Football, by comparison, tends to have motions that don't repeat and are difficult to see. Other team sports like hockey, basketball, and soccer offer a constant supply of varied action.

Every form of dance will provide you with a motion-sketching paradise. Ballet, in particular, features a highly stylized kind of human motion with a graceful line of action. Folk and popular forms each have a finite number of distinct motions which are repeated in different combinations.

Have you ever tried sketching from the television? Most programs have plenty of interesting movements to keep your sketchbook filled. And like real life, the motions are absolutely unpredictable.

If you want to try sketching animals in motion, go to the zoo, and look for the ones with the restless cage habits—the monkeys, the big cats, and the elephants are especially rewarding. If you live near a horse ranch, you'll find horses walking, trotting, galloping, and jumping. But even if you have nothing more than a pet dog or cat, you have a wonderful opportunity for sketching.

Everyday life is full of many interesting motions that are easily overlooked. Can you picture in your mind right now exactly how you put on a coat? When one arm is passing through the sleeve, what is the other arm doing? Try it. If you are standing up, you will most likely shift your weight from one leg to another halfway through the motion. You can make similar observations of such things as combing your hair, getting into a car, stretching, reaching for a can from a high shelf. To sketch these, act them out yourself, or have a friend do so, and try to capture in your sketchbook two or three phases from the entire motion.

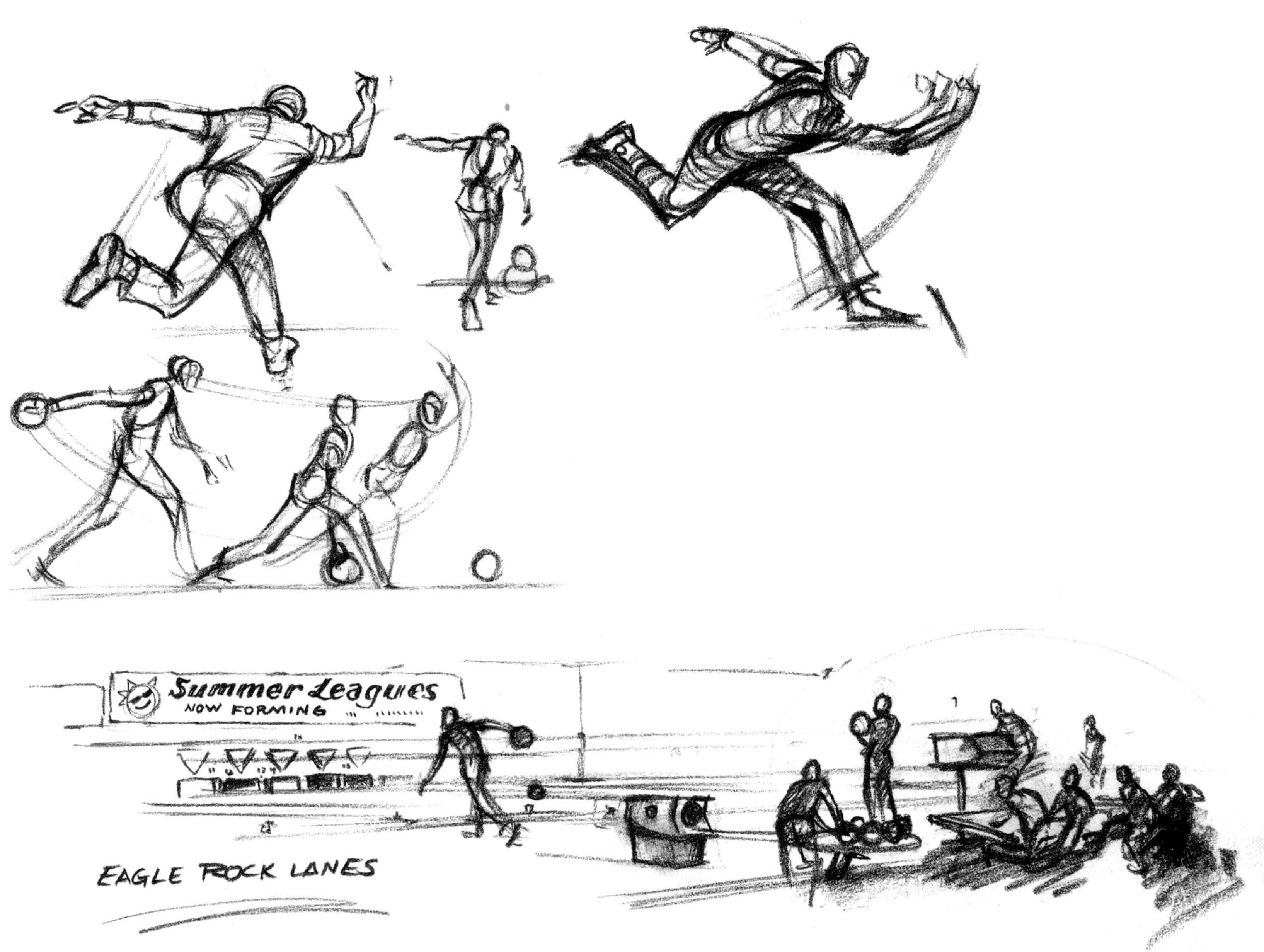

FIGURES IN BOWLING ALLEY, *charcoal on bond paper, 8½" x 11". You don't have to travel far to find moving subjects for sketching. On any busy downtown streetcorner, you are likely to find people walking, gesturing, and reaching to open doors. But to find motions that are more dynamic, it's worthwhile to visit places where people dance or play sports. Not only are the actions more extreme than in everyday life, but they also tend to be repeated again and again so that you can really study the motion. This repeated action makes bowling alleys some of my favorite motion-sketching spots. Over an extended period of time, I can study the approach and delivery of each individual bowler from a variety of angles. —JG*

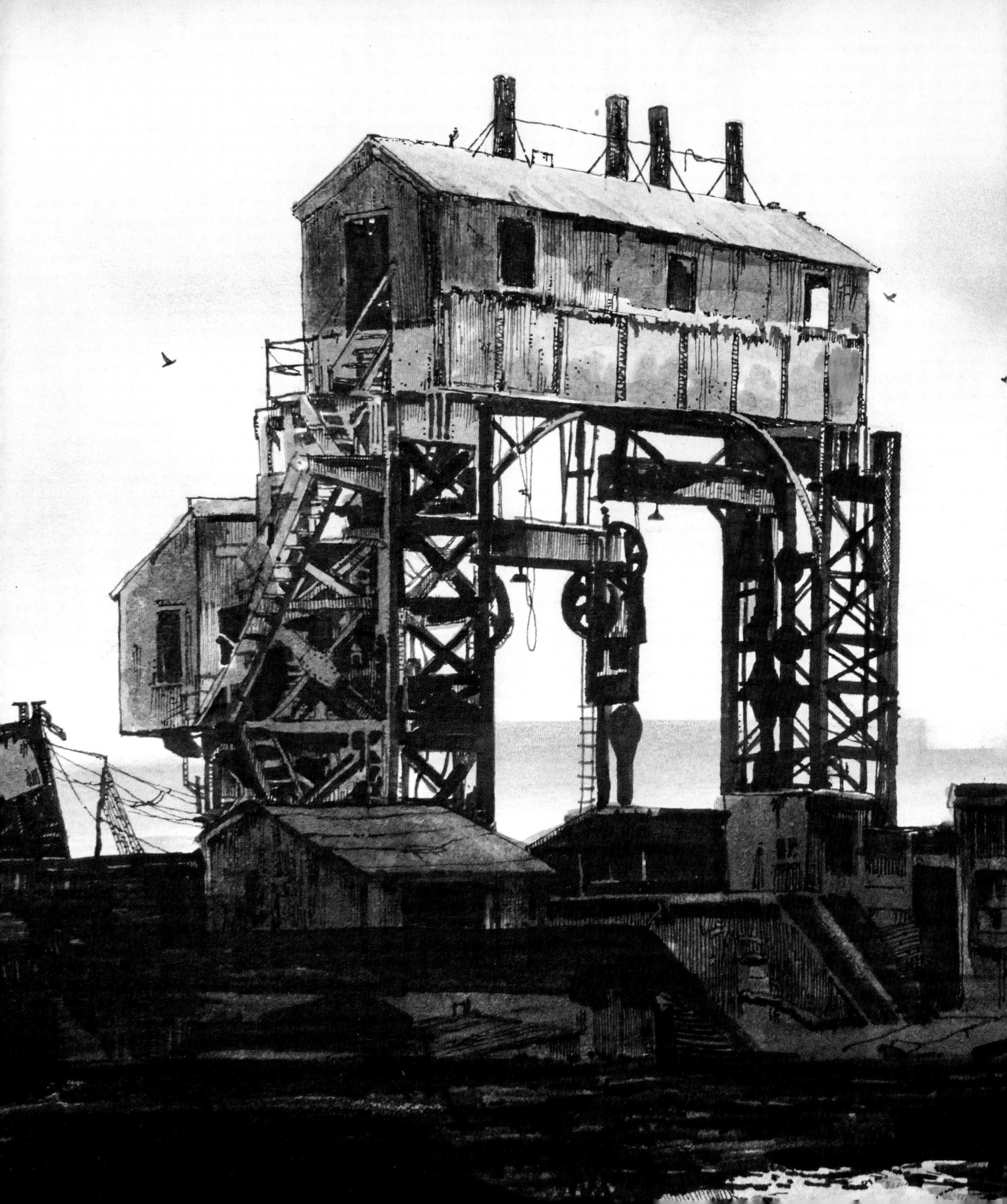

Creating Mood

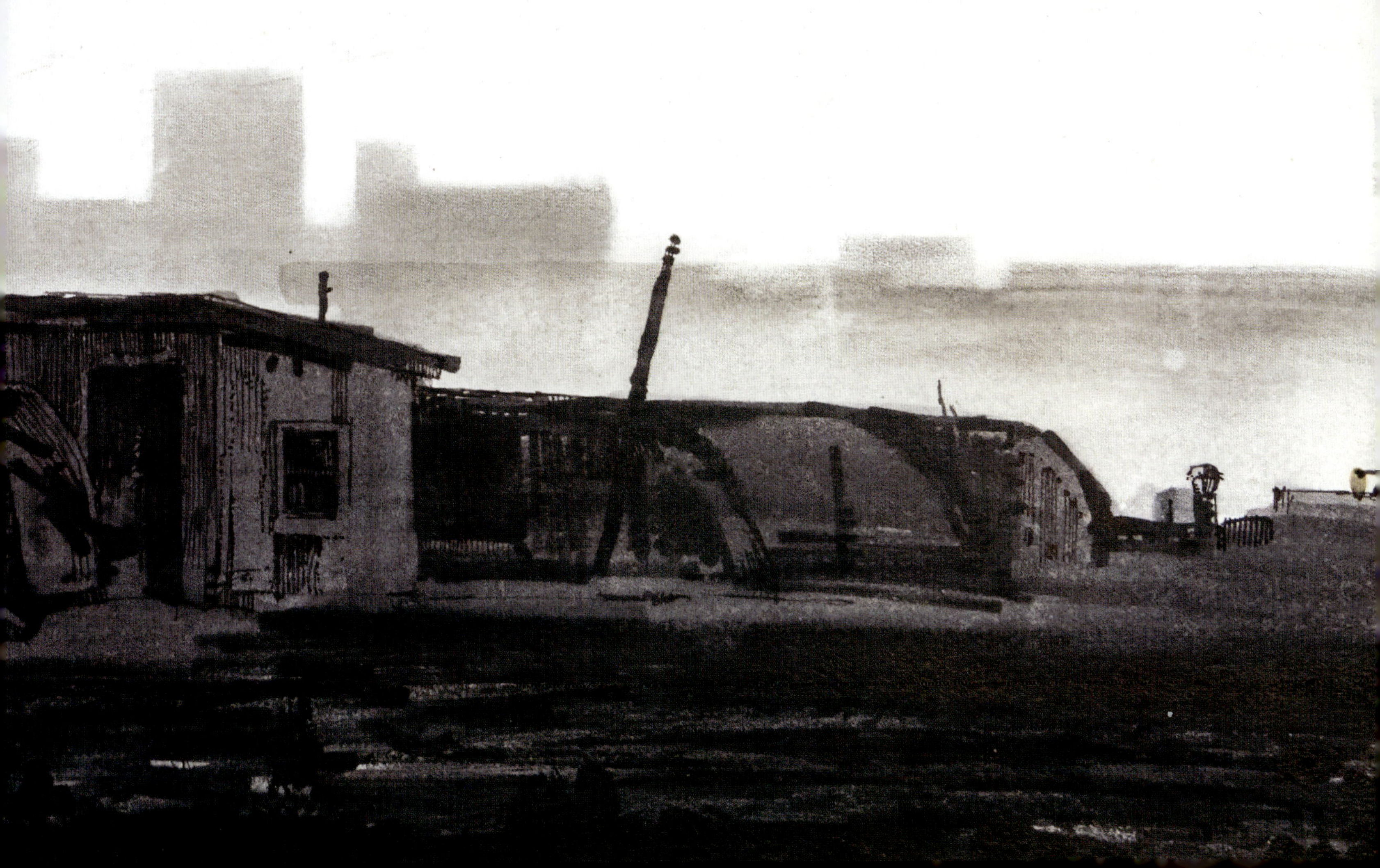

◀◀ **DOCK MACHINERY,** *markers and charcoal on cold-press illustration board, 11" x 17". This sketch was begun in the early afternoon and finished around dusk. At first I intended using a strong midday light source, but as the afternoon progressed I became intrigued by the deep shadows of the foreground areas and decided to use that effect instead. In so doing I was able to group the sketch into two value areas—the dark foreground structures and the light sky. This kind of simple tonal arrangement is the best way to add drama to your sketch. To achieve accuracy in the complex forms of the standing structure, I used a thirty-minute underdrawing involving a complete perspective grid (see Chapter 3, "Achieving Accuracy"). —TK*

HAVE YOU EVER seen the fading glow of sunset behind the darkened scaffolding of a half-constructed building? Or sat on a rocky perch overlooking the ocean and sensed the power of the thundering waves or the delicacy of the distant fog? Life offers a constant flux between moods of tranquility and moods of exuberance, moods of drama and moods of restfulness. Learning to capture these moods in sketches is a valuable ability that enables you to document the special moments you encounter daily or to add potent emotion to sketches of even the most ordinary subject. In this chapter we are going to take a hard-edged look at the rather nebulous subject of mood. We will offer you some of the methods we use to define our feelings about a subject and transfer those feelings to paper. These methods are simple ways to harness mood and use it as a tool to add interest to your sketches. But keep in mind one simple underlying idea. You will need to change the actual appearance of your subject in order to create the mood you want. Every sketch in this chapter has involved changing the subject for the sake of creating mood. This is your prerogative as a sketch artist.

CHOOSING A SUBJECT

Mood can be used to improve sketches of any subject. For example, think of something not usually considered good subject matter, such as a corner phone booth. By using the principles of mood, you could create a sketch that entices the viewer's eye to the area of the phone booth that interests you, and also expresses any feeling you might have about the phone booth. A simple, everyday phone booth could be dramatic, delicate, or mysterious depending on how it is treated. Similarly, the principles of mood can help you devise fresh, exciting ways to interpret even the most overused subjects.

With a little ingenuity, mood can make any subject into an interesting sketch. For this reason, you never should feel you have nothing worthwhile to draw. Think over the types of things you see each day—the mailbox, the supermarket on the corner, the old warehouse on the way downtown, the trees in your backyard. Everywhere you go you accumulate impressions of the world around you. Have the attitude that anything is potentially good subject matter for a sketch. Follow your vague inclinations and far-off hunches. Don't feel you have to be absolutely clear about your feelings and how to express them at first. That clarity will come once you have taken the time to sit before your subject and observe it carefully.

NOTING IMPRESSIONS

You have found an interesting subject and have sat down to draw it. Now, how do you go about using mood to make an exciting sketch out of what you see? We've found that before beginning with the underdrawing, it is helpful to clarify your impressions of the subject so that your artistic decisions can have direction and unity. The best way to do this is to make quick written notes that summarize in a few words your emotional reaction to what's before you.

Spend a few moments contemplating your subject. Look carefully around you and notice the overall atmosphere surrounding the subject. Is the area agitated or calm? Is there much noise? Do the weather and light suggest any particular feelings or warm memories? Absorb these features consciously. They may seem obvious, but they will have a profound effect on the way you depict the subject.

Try to isolate two or three words or a phrase that describe your impression of your subject and note the words down on a scrap of paper or directly on your sketch. If a brook strikes you as "a quiet place—a place to feel peaceful" or if a vacant lot makes you feel "claustrophobic" and "lonely," note these

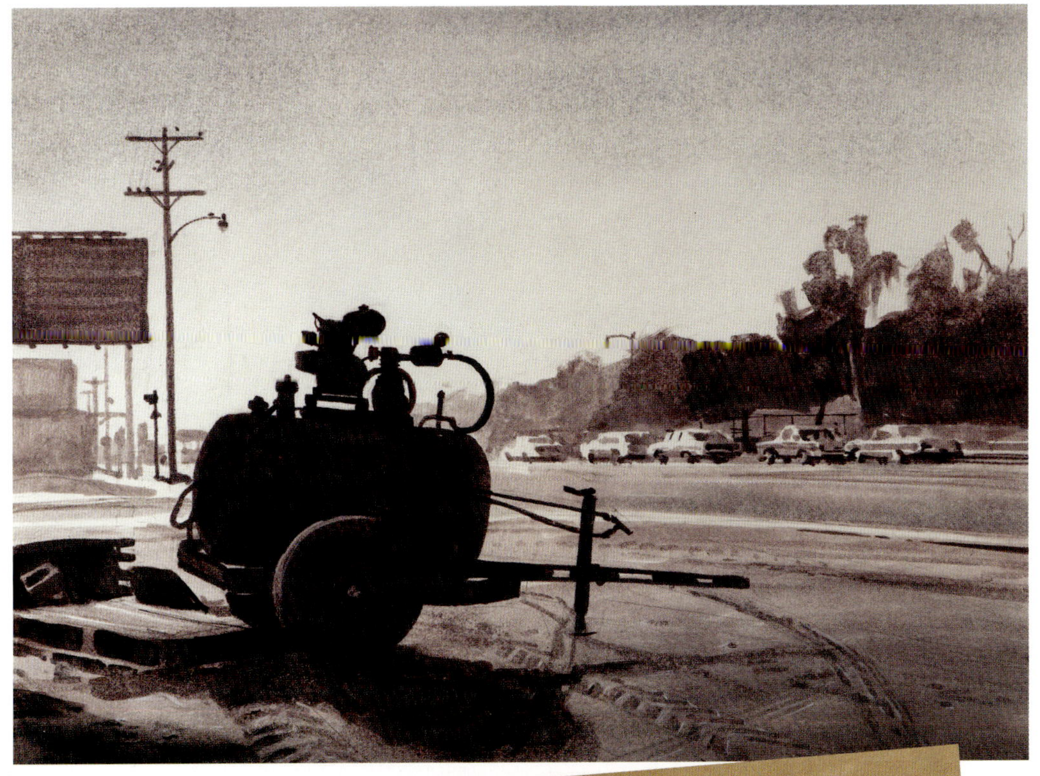

◀ **ASPHALT MACHINE,** *gray markers on bristol board, 11" x 15". An exciting aspect of mood sketching is that even the lowly, humdrum objects of the everyday world can be interpreted in very dramatic terms. This oily, steaming contraption caught my eye one morning as I walked past a construction area. The men on the road crew told me that it was nicknamed the "soup machine" and was used to spray a layer of gluelike tar for joining sections of a road surface. Too busy to stop and sketch at the time, I returned with my sketching materials on the following Sunday, when the place was deserted. As I began the process of making thumbnails, I realized right away that a low vantage point would bring the machine into dramatic compositional focus by silhouetting it against the sky. The tire tracks, road, cars, trees, and poles all lead to the center of interest—the blackened engine mounted on the tank. To convey the feeling of the smoggy day, I lightened the values of the more distant areas. Notice how the trees and cars on the right become progressively lighter as they move back in space. To gradate the sky, I used a cotton rag that had been charged with black marker dye and then gently rubbed across the surface. —JG*

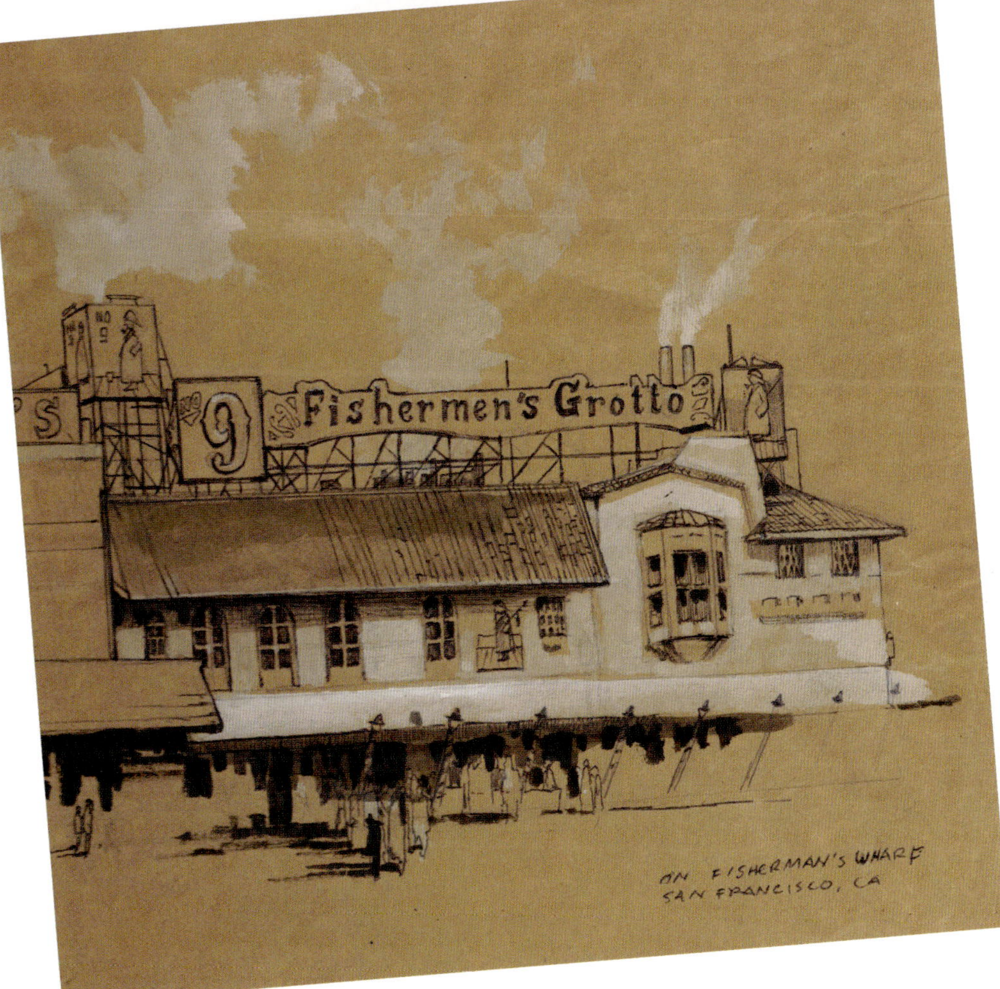

◀ **FISHERMAN'S WHARF, SAN FRANCISCO,** *ballpoint pen, gray markers, and white gouache on brown paper, 11" x 14". Before beginning this sketch I sat back on my stool for a moment and absorbed the scents and sounds of the area. The pungent aroma of fresh-baked French bread was in the air and all around were the sounds of the wharf: seagulls, shouting fishermen, street musicians, and an occasional foghorn. In addition, bright sunlight and a crisp breeze provided the perfect weather for enjoying the scene. I found myself entranced by the nostalgic ambience of the wharf, and I decided to try to capture my impressions by using brown paper and a combined linear and tonal technique that would allow for both specific detail and overall mood. I used pen lines to capture the detail, while the tone markers and white gouache suggest the sunlight on the building and the wispy clouds that were present that morning. To this day, this sketch serves as a vivid reminder of a very pleasant experience. —TK*

impressions down. Keep the notes handy and refer to them often as you work.

Isolating your impressions of the subject in words first gives you a foundation on which to build your visual interpretation of the subject. In other words, after you have narrowed down how you feel about your subject, it becomes much easier to decide how to draw it.

COMPOSING WITH THUMBNAILS

After isolating your impressions in words, you may want to make a few small preliminary sketches to find the most effective way to translate your feelings into visual terms. These sketches, called thumbnails, should be kept small—no more than 2" x 3".

They can be drawn in another notebook or directly on the page you intend for the finished sketch. Medium-width black felt pens are perfect for making thumbnails because they allow for an immediate two-value (white and black) notation of the subject. Fairly soft pencils (HB or softer) are also suitable.

To execute thumbnails, begin by sketching out three or more small rectangles of the approximate proportions of your sketchbook page. Then simply begin scribbling! Fill each rectangle with a different idea about the way to arrange the subject on your page. The thumbnail on these pages demonstrate the variety of options you have even with a simple subject. Experiment with different ways to crop your subject, whether to draw it in a horizontal or vertical format, which areas to make dark and which to make light, etc. You can quickly generate dozen of unexpected compositions and usually hit upon something much more effective than your first idea.

For achieving mood, thumbnails are a way of warming up to what you see and becoming familiar with the subject's visual potential before beginning the underdrawing of your actual sketch. Making thumbnails, like noting impressions, takes a moment or two to do. But it's time well spent. There' no comparison to the confidence that spending a moment planning your sketc can give you. You will undoubtedly be much more satisfied with the results you get if you take the time to decide your direction.

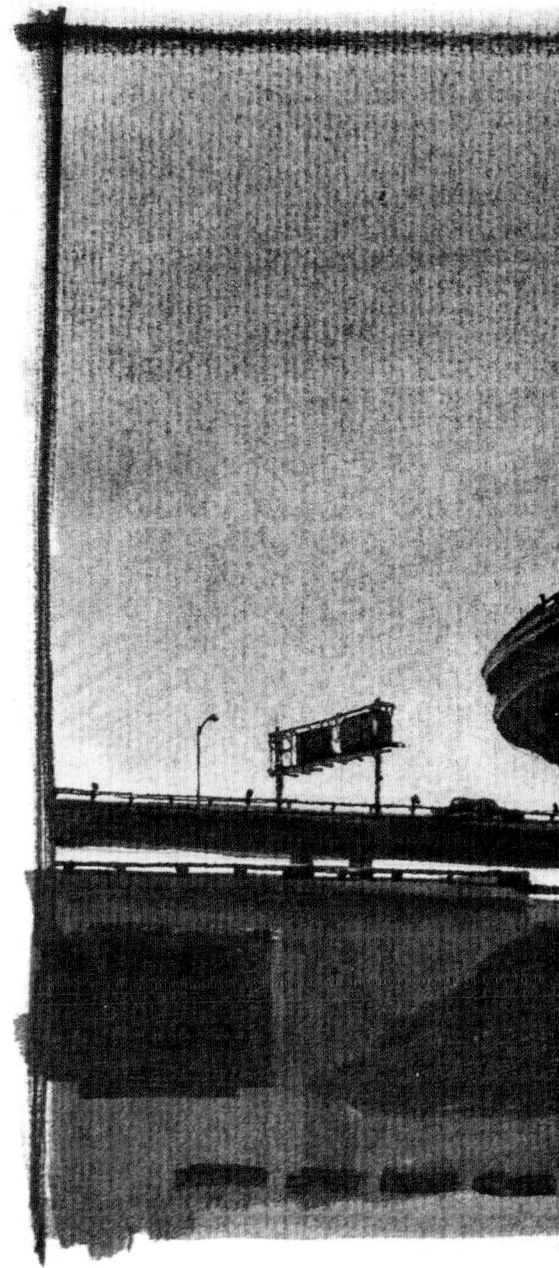

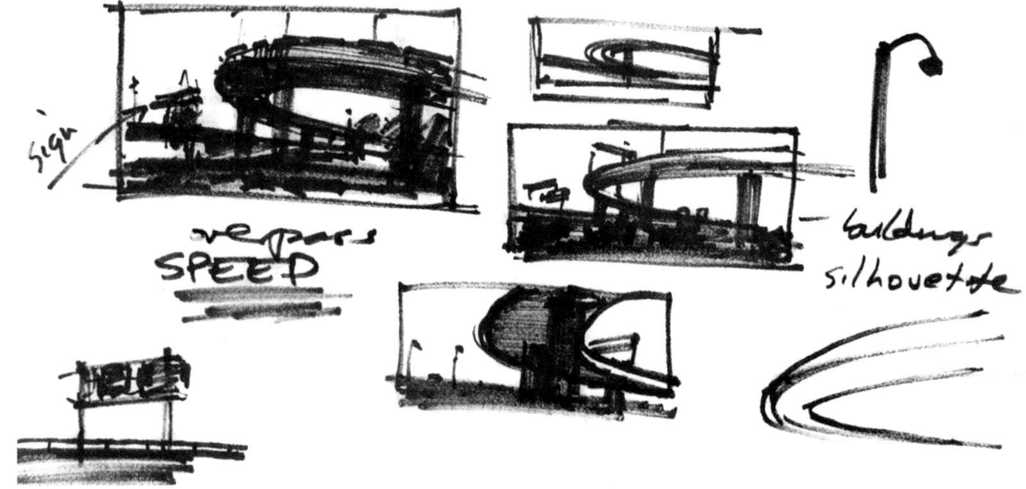

▲ **FREEWAY OVERPASS,** *markers and charcoal, 11" x 17". It often takes a little experimentation at the thumbnail stage to arrive at a design that really conveys the original impression. My interest in sketching these freeway forms was to capture the feeling of speed and expansiveness, the headlong race of man-made forms across the landscape. I tried several compositions, but they seemed to lack the drive and the simple movement through space that the final result has. The first thumbnail on the left, which is very similar to the actual scene, is too cluttered with trees and poles, and the overpass lamely dips out of the picture, rather than surging out. In the final sketch, I allowed the eye to follow the movement of the overpass into the middle ground space and accented this area with strong value contrast, hard edges, and very small shapes. —JG*

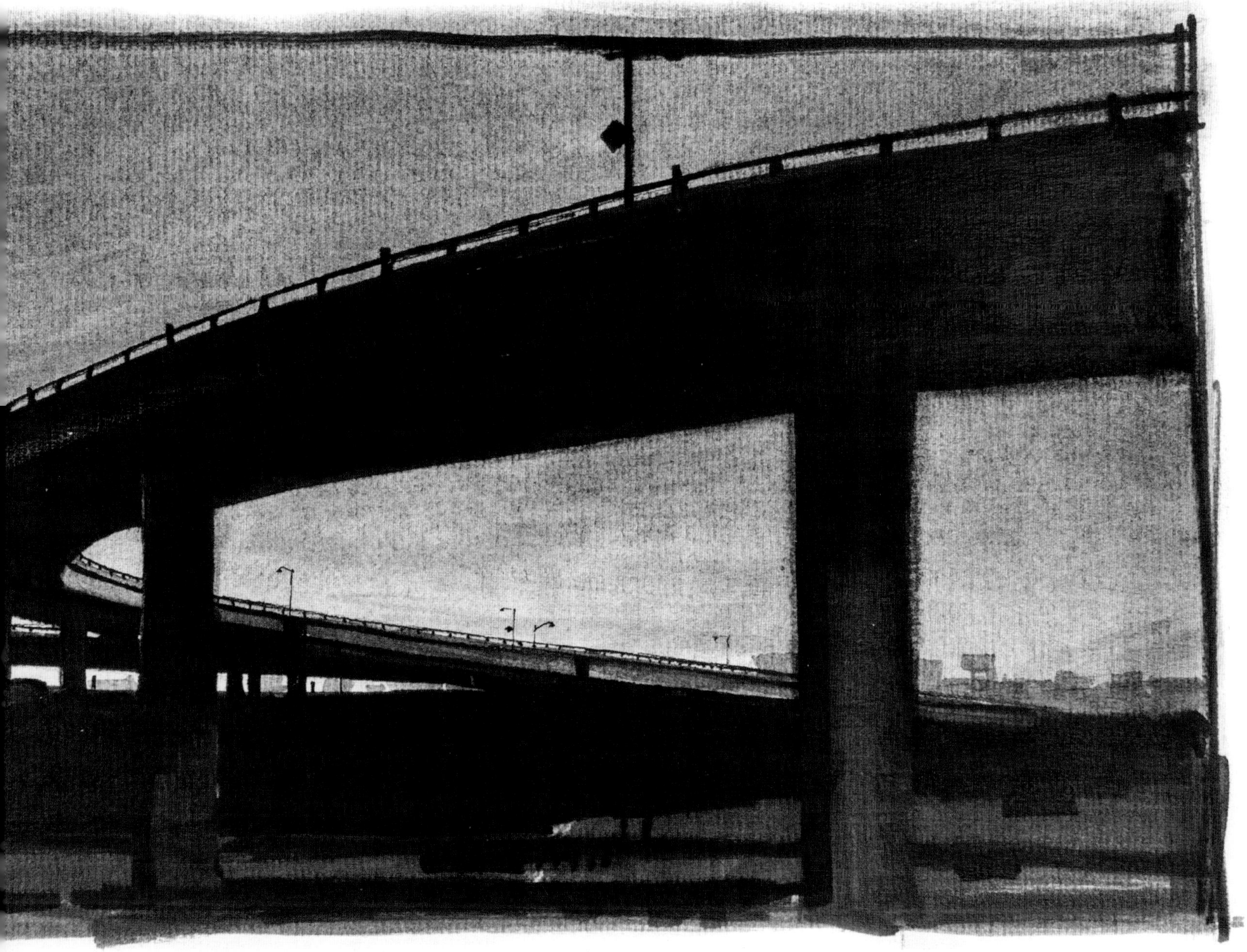

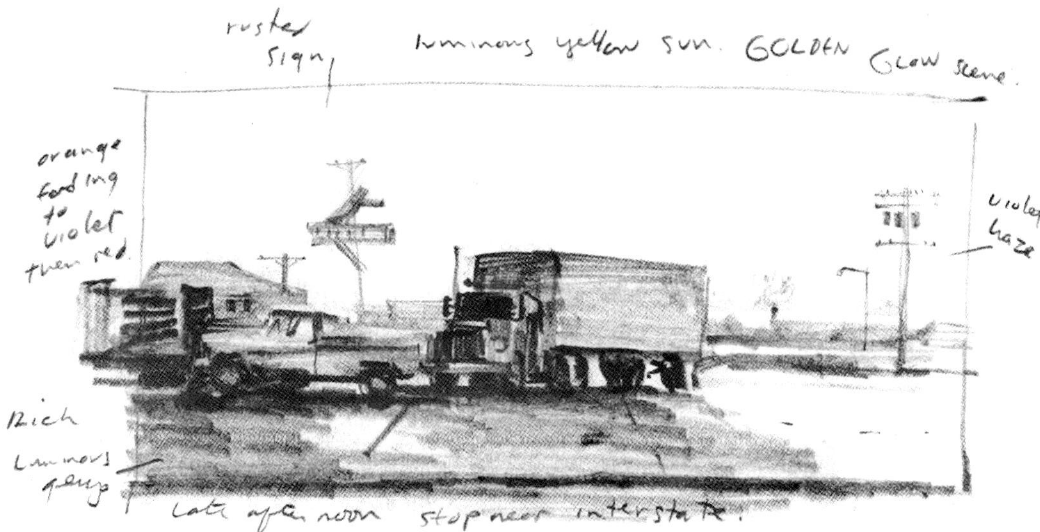

◀ **TRUCK IN PARKING LOT,** *pencil on bond paper, 2" x 5". Whenever I pull off the highway for a rest from driving, I enjoy the opportunity to absorb the unique beauty of roadside scenes. This brief notation is little more than a thumbnail, yet even the quickest sketch can capture mood. I made this sketch while staring beyond my greasy chili dog at a small diner in the Southwest. The sun had begun to set and the entire scene radiated a warm yellow glow. I included many color notes to remind me of the visual impression, in the event I decide to do a painting from my sketch sometime in the future. —JG*

SELECTIVITY

Selectivity is the process of deleting the unimportant. What you leave out of a picture is a more important factor in achieving mood than what you put in. As you begin your actual sketch, you have to decide which elements of your subject contribute to your impression and which do not. Don't just draw something "because it is there." Feel free to remove whatever detracts from the effect you want to achieve.

For example, let's imagine you were sketching a little motel on the outskirts of town and wished to get across a feeling of quaintness and tidiness. You might want to ignore the pickup truck full of old tires and the crisscross of telephone lines, and instead focus your attention on the hand-lettered sign and the carefully pruned bushes. Be selective in accordance with ideas you wish to express, not by random choice. When you make purposeful decisions, your sketches will be simple and consistent with your original impression.

In addition to deleting those elements you don't want, you also rearrange the aspects of your subject so that all the elements that interest you appear within the sketch. If a car down the street would look good in front of the building you are sketching, by all means borrow it! If something that you wish was there isn't—make it up. Your goal is to make an interesting sketch, not to be absolutely faithful to your subject. Like a good novelist, the sketch artist bends the reality of his subject to make it more powerful.

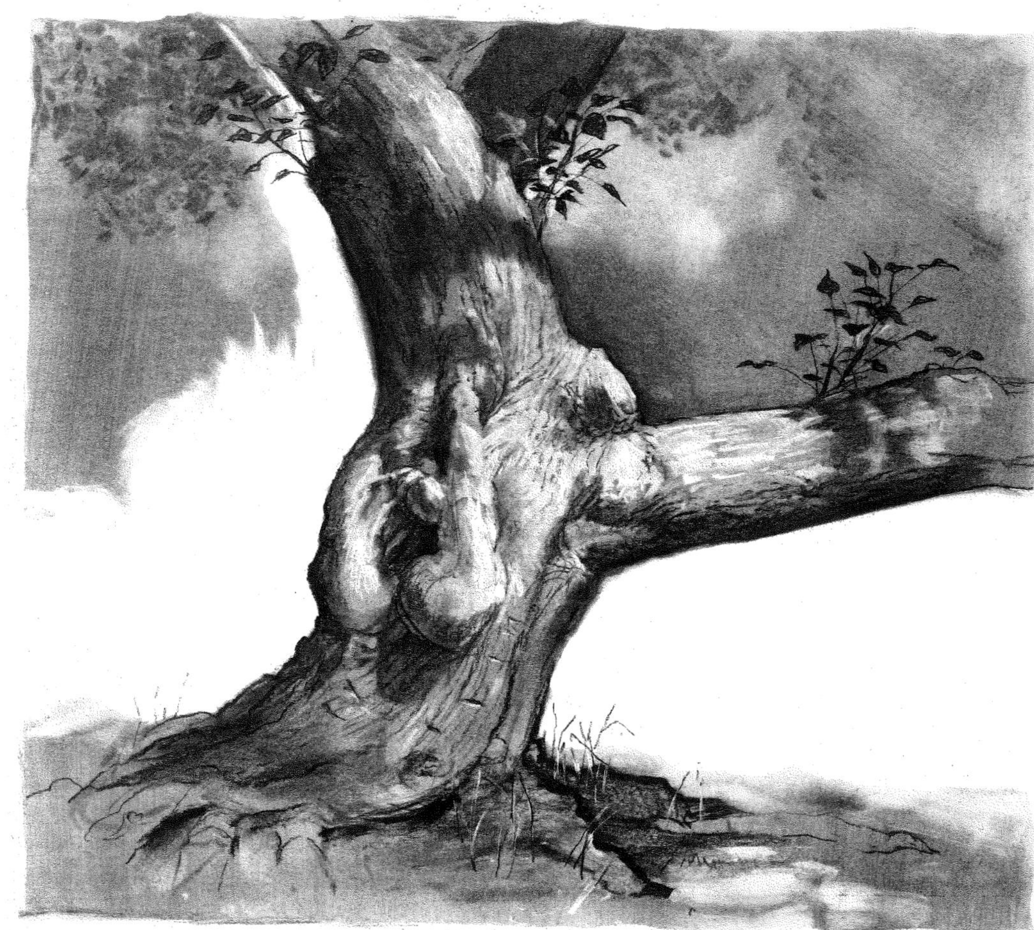

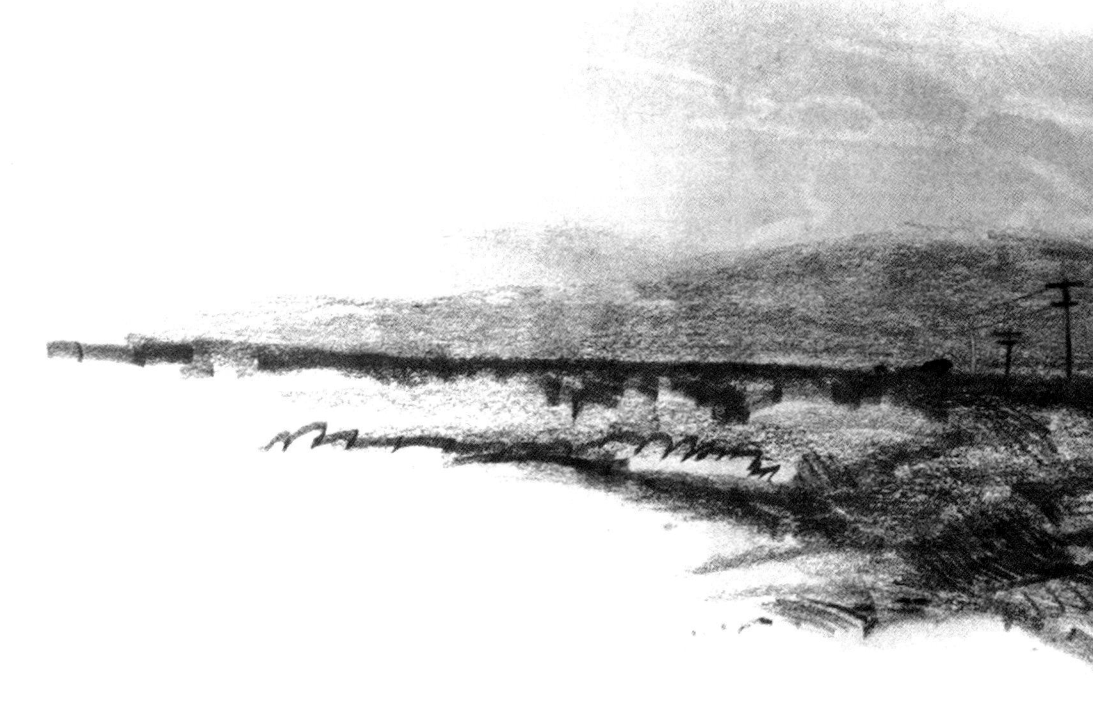

◀ **GROTESQUE TREE FORM,** *charcoal on tracing paper, 8½" x 9". This sketch is primarily a study in selectivity. I rendered only the areas that interested me and summarized or eliminated the rest. The background was really a maze of distracting details of bushes and parked cars, while the entire upper area was cluttered by intricate patterns of foliage. Even the ground detail has been greatly simplified. The focus of the sketch becomes the strange lifelike forms and textures of the tree trunk. —JG*

▼ **NUCLEAR REACTOR,** *charcoal on smooth drawing paper, 8" x 16". In this sketch I was primarily interested in the huge spherical forms that seemed so out of place in the rolling coastal hills where the reactor is located. To emphasize the obtrusiveness of the spherical forms, I softened the background areas and eliminated the parking lot and various buildings from the foreground. As final touches, I included a few telephone poles to suggest the scale of the spheres. —TK*

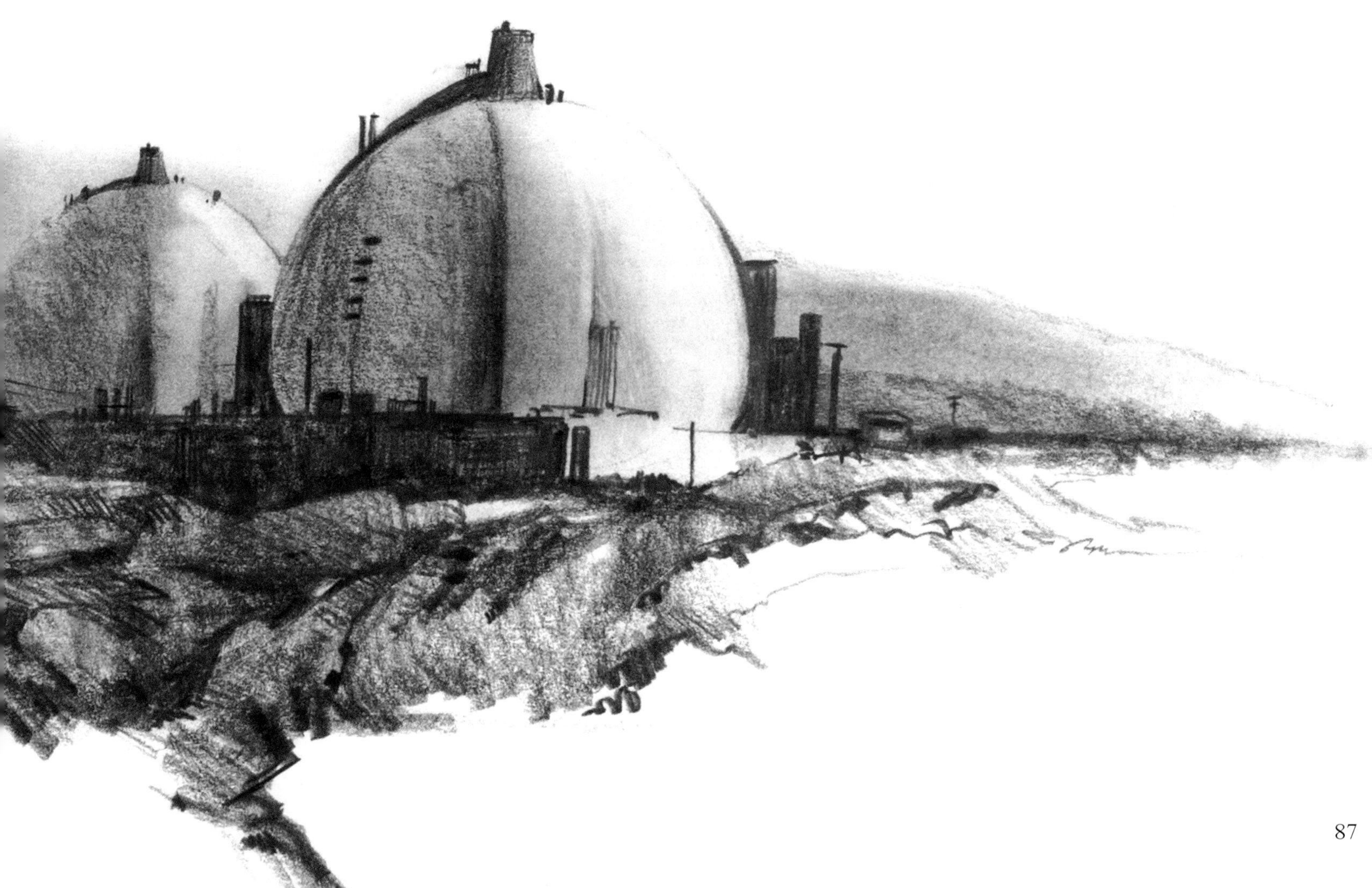

CENTER OF INTEREST

In addition to selectivity, another useful device for organizing your sketch and increasing mood is to establish the center of interest. Where do you find yourself looking most often as you view the subject? Why do you keep returning to it? You can create a similar focus in your sketch so that the viewer can have a home base from which to explore the less important elements. This focus allows you to emphasize the old, red soda pop machine that is catching the light of the afternoon sun. The soda pop machine, with its associations of nostalgia and refreshment, echoes the feeling of quaintness. The soda pop machine is your center of interest.

How do you make something the center of interest? Accent it with the darkest dark, the lightest light, or the most detail. Aim toward it with the key lines of your composition. Invent a figure to lean against it. Put an area of black behind it. Meanwhile, restrain yourself in the supporting areas of the picture: hold back on darks and highlights and crisp details. Allow your center of interest to be the star of the show. The subordinate areas of your subject may attract your eye and you may want to include them; however, it is usually a good idea to make it clear which area is dominant. Creating an order to the areas of interest gives structure to your sketch and makes it easily accessible to the viewer.

Even in delicate pen-and-ink sketches in which the viewer's eye is allowed to wander over a web of complex outlined details, it is still useful to create some sort of focus. Sketches with no emphasis tend to be somewhat decorative and flat. The viewer has no resting spot and, as often as not, doesn't bother to untangle the maze of pen lines to fully explore the detail.

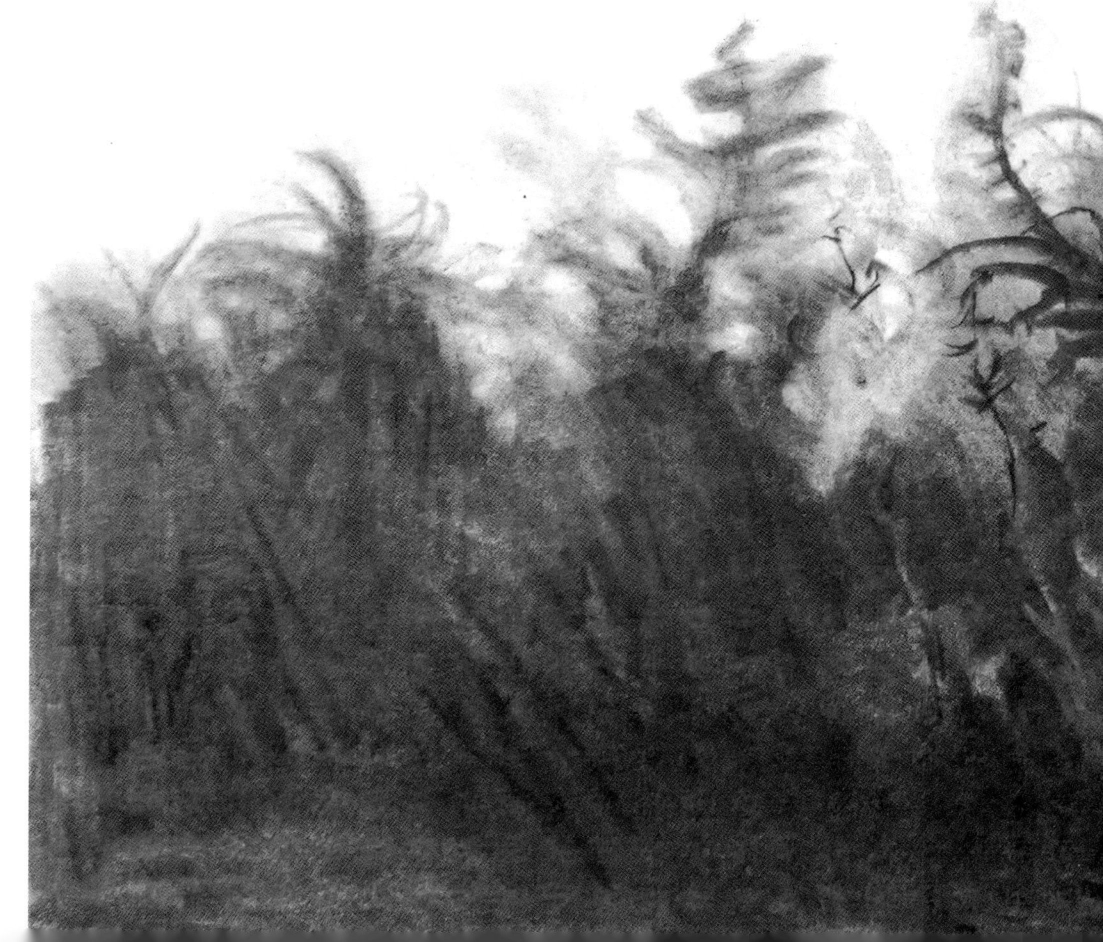

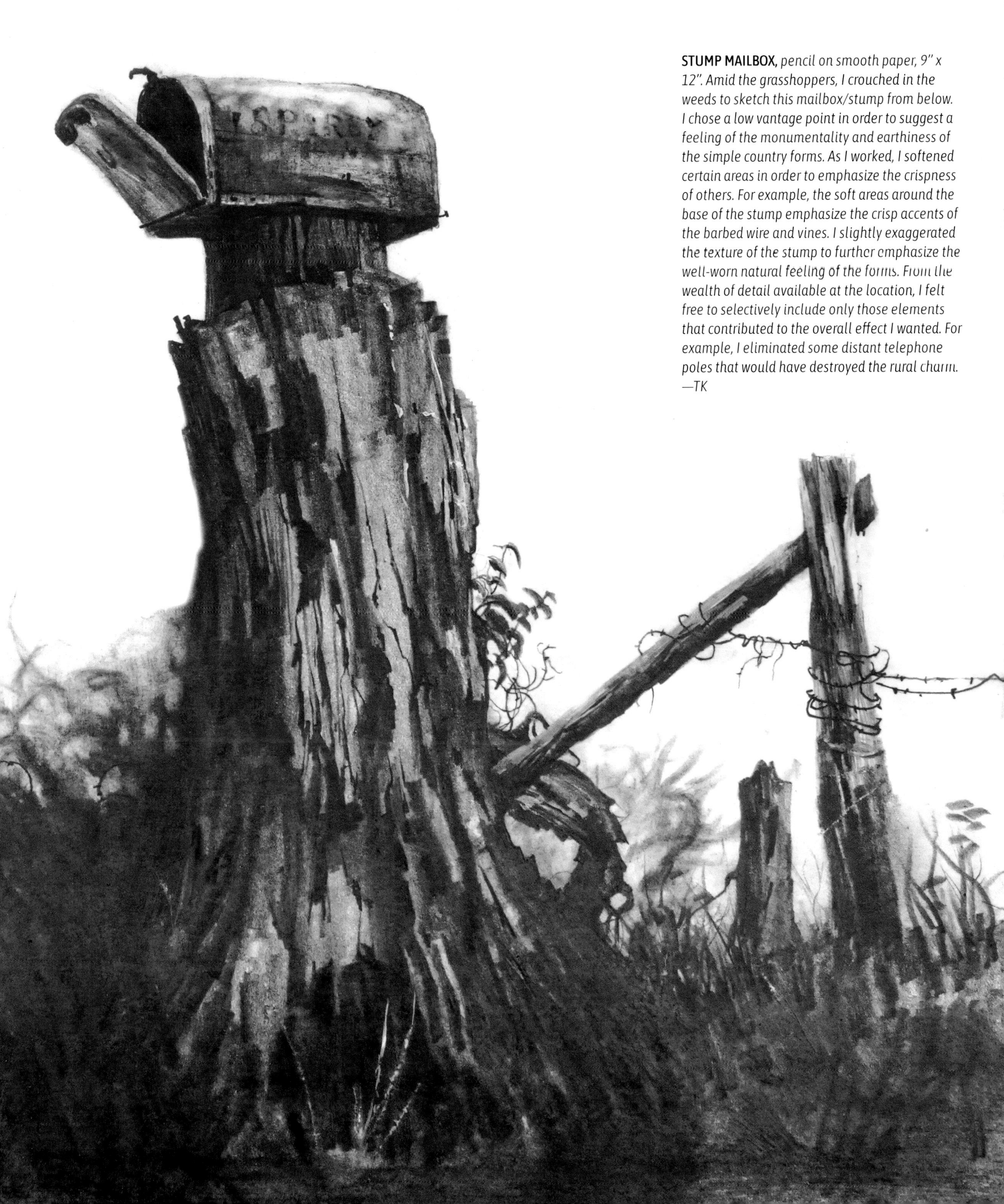

STUMP MAILBOX, *pencil on smooth paper, 9" x 12". Amid the grasshoppers, I crouched in the weeds to sketch this mailbox/stump from below. I chose a low vantage point in order to suggest a feeling of the monumentality and earthiness of the simple country forms. As I worked, I softened certain areas in order to emphasize the crispness of others. For example, the soft areas around the base of the stump emphasize the crisp accents of the barbed wire and vines. I slightly exaggerated the texture of the stump to further emphasize the well-worn natural feeling of the forms. From the wealth of detail available at the location, I felt free to selectively include only those elements that contributed to the overall effect I wanted. For example, I eliminated some distant telephone poles that would have destroyed the rural charm. —TK*

NASHVILLE FREIGHT YARD, *fine-line and gray markers on smooth paper, 9" x 11". In this sketch I increased the drama by opposing the dark, detailed areas in the lower sections with the lighter, less cluttered areas above. I use contrasts such as these—thick versus thin, cluttered versus sparse—to organize my sketch and create impact. If I had treated this subject by using only fine pen lines, it may have retained most of its interest, but it certainly would have lost most of its power. —TK*

DRAMATIC OPPOSITION

The principle of dramatic opposition is simple: create impact by simplifying the contrast between pictorial opposites such as light and dark, dense detail and openness. The word *simplifying* is crucial to the concept of dramatic opposition because, although all sketches contain oppositions, dramatic opposition involves consciously organizing these contrasts into a *single* visual effect.

The way this is done depends on whether the sketch is linear or tonal. Let's consider our imaginary example again. Suppose you were sketching the quaint roadside motel using pen and ink. In purely linear techniques, dramatic opposition is achieved by making one area densely detailed and leaving the rest of the sketch fairly open. In the sketch of the motel this might mean that the old, red soda pop machine is drawn with every button and lever in place and perhaps a stack of weathered bottle crates behind it. Then, if you contrast the intricacy of these areas by treating the porch below the soda pop machine with only minimal outline, you have created visual drama.

If you were making a tonal sketch of the quaint model, you have more options for creating drama. In general, it is most effective to organize your sketch into two or three major value groupings. For example, since the soda pop machine is the center of interest, perhaps you will render it in medium grays and allow the rest of the sketch to remain basically white. Or you could render the soda pop machine in light grays and make the supporting areas dark gray or black. Here's where your thumbnails really come in handy. If done properly, the thumbnails can help you determine how you want to organize your sketch tonally. With a bit of forethought, tonal organization can be a powerful way to create dramatic opposition.

DELICACY

Some subjects lend themselves to a more restrained handling. You may, for instance, want to convey a feeling of tranquility, softness, fragility, grace, or reverie. These moods depend not on dramatic opposition but on subtlety. Contrasts do exist, but they are understated.

Surprisingly, almost any subject can be handled delicately—even such typically dramatic subjects as fire trucks and fallen trees. How do you create a feeling of delicacy? Technique is one way. Ultra fine-line markers and technical pens produce very delicate results. When using these, strive for a slow, patient, linear style. Use outline only—avoid heavy cross-hatching and brushed-in black areas. A well-sharpened hard lead pencil also works well. We usually use a 2H pencil on smooth paper for delicate pencil work. Shading is a nice addition to a delicate pencil sketch if done with reserve.

With all linear techniques, strive for a feeling of overall subtlety in the forms themselves. If you are drawing a plant, exaggerate the family of curving lines: S-curves, C-curves, ellipses, and spirals. All of these convey a feeling of grace and serenity since they carry the eye in a flowing pathway throughout the composition. Clouds, drapery, and antique automobiles also lend themselves well to curvilinear exaggeration.

To achieve delicacy in tonal techniques with wash, charcoal pencil, or gray markers, use effects that give a feeling of a soft, luminous atmosphere. For example, if you keep the tonal range high—that is, generally *light*—with just a few accents of darker tone, you can give the illusion that a gentle light source is suffusing all the forms. To accentuate the effect, soften all but a few of the edges. Allow each form to subtly bleed into the surrounding areas. This effect is especially easy to achieve with smudgeable media such as charcoal and pencil. A few quick smudges with the end of your thumb and you have an instant effect of delicacy.

JEWELRY STORE, MANHATTAN, *technical pen on drawing paper, 9" x 12". I chose a delicate pen treatment of this subject as a means of suggesting the overall clutter and density of detail. Using a fine-point technical pen forces you to increase your sensitivity to subtle nuances of line in shape. When I use technical pens I put myself in a slow, meditative frame of mind and carefully explore every inch of my subject with the pen point as my guide. Nevertheless, I do find it helpful to use a brief pencil underdrawing in these treatments rather than to begin directly in pen. By using an underdrawing you can inject a touch of accuracy into your sketch, which helps prevent your careful observation from being hindered by overall inaccuracy of form. —TK*

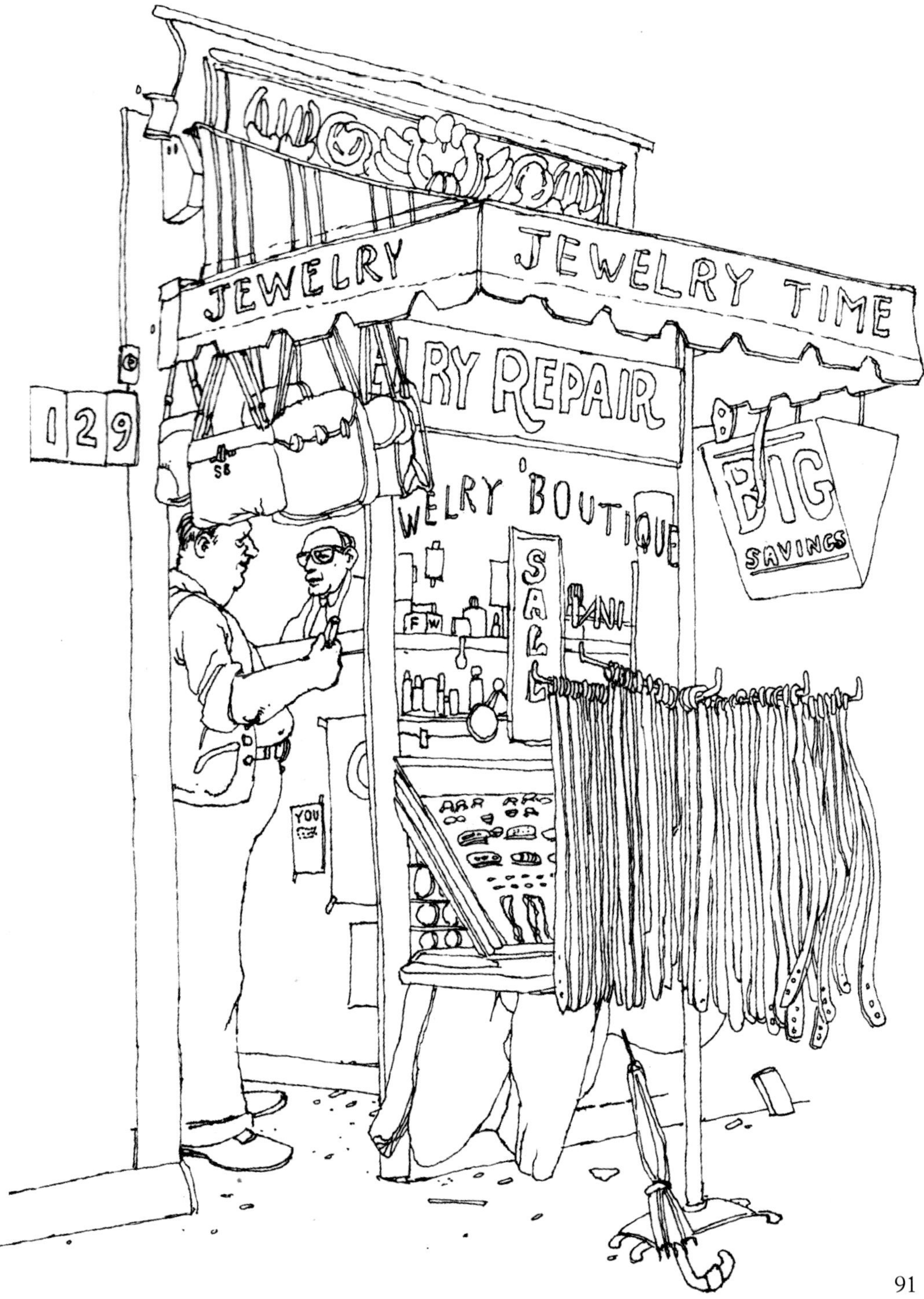

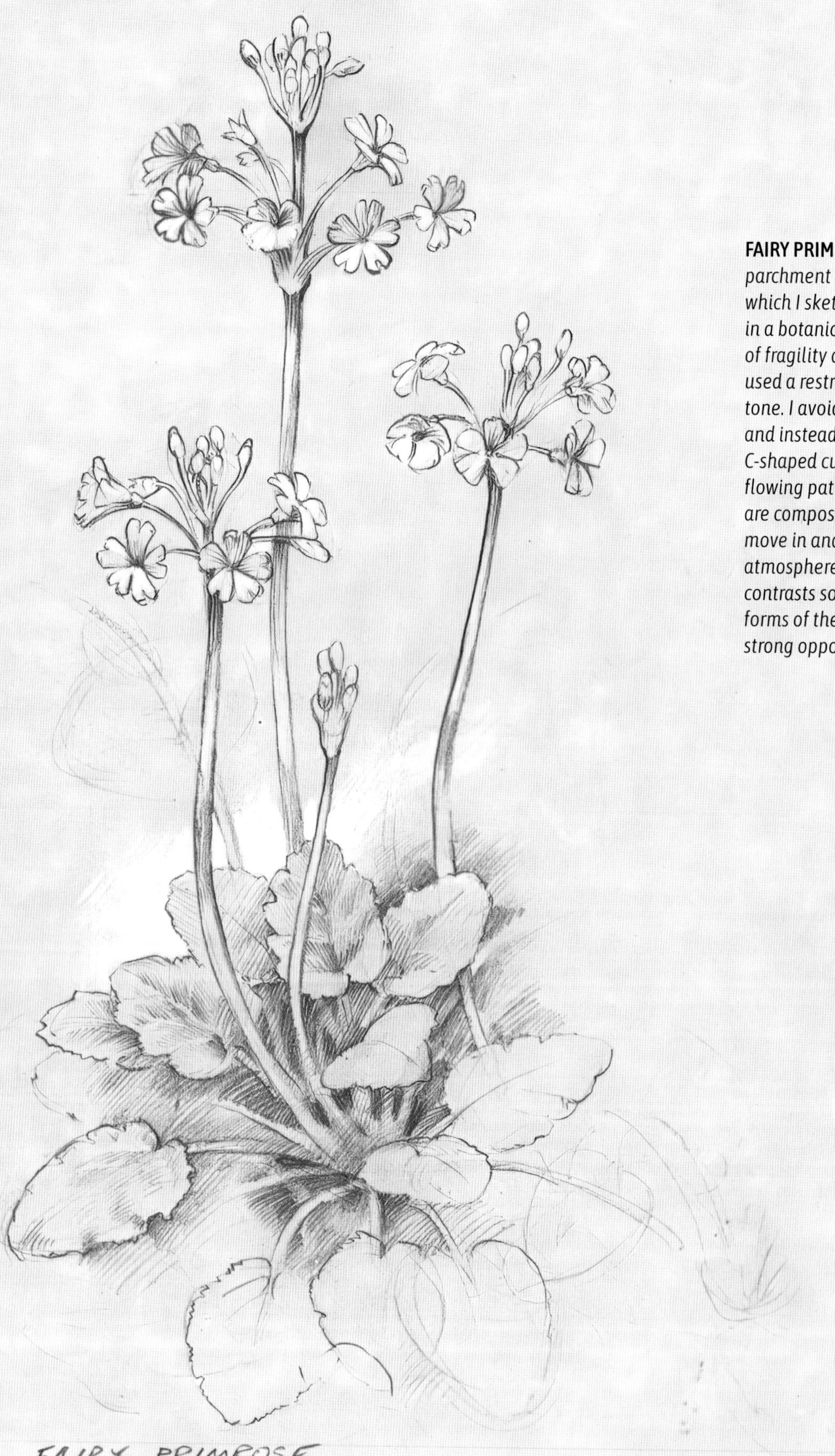

FAIRY PRIMROSE, *pencil and white gouache on parchment paper, 8½" x 11". These tiny flowers, which I sketched right after a gentle rain shower in a botanical garden, gave me an impression of fragility and grace. To convey this mood, I used a restrained handling of both line and tone. I avoided harsh, straight lines in the stems, and instead gave each of them an S-shaped or C-shaped curve; these lines carry the eye in a flowing pathway throughout the picture. The tones are composed of closely spaced parallel lines that move in and out of the forms like a soft, luminous atmosphere. I avoided using pure blacks or strong contrasts so that the eye could move around the forms of the plant, without feeling the tension of strong opposing forces. —JG*

MYSTERY

A fundamental principle of creating mood is mystery, the suggestion of the unseen. Too much clarity can be emotionally unexciting. But if you can make your viewer feel that there is something barely visible, just out of view, you will involve their imagination and hold their interest.

Using mystery is important because it is at the heart of some of the most compelling moods: grandeur, awe, sublimity, ominousness, gloominess, and expectation. Ironically, there's nothing mysterious about creating mystery. The methods we've found most successful are rather straightforward and can be used for just about any kind of sketch, from a ten-minute plant study to a three-hour rendering of a parked airplane.

The most basic method to achieve a sense of mystery is to suggest elements beyond the boundary of your sketch. You can suggest that the world extends beyond your sketch by showing only a selected part of the subject within the picture's borders. For instance, in the sketch of the base of the clown sign you will notice that by including only a small portion of the sign the viewer is allowed to speculate as to the full size of the sign. The net effect is that a sense of monumentality is achieved in a much better way than if the sign had been fully depicted.

Another way to achieve a sense of mystery is to block off part of the subject with a foreground element. A row of trees, for instance, might permit only a glimpse of a farmhouse behind them. Or a doorway might show just a pair of feet belonging to an unseen figure. You may have to recompose the elements of the scene a bit, but if you can achieve an interesting juxtaposition in your sketch, the overall interest is generally increased.

BASE OF CLOWN SIGN, *gouache on illustration board, 8" x 13". I get a special satisfaction from composing mood sketches inside a standard rectangle, rather than always using informal ragged-edge vignettes. To establish the borders for this sketch, I taped off the outer margin of the illustration board with 1-inch drafting tape, and then removed the tape after the painting was finished. I took advantage of the rectangular borders in the way I chose to compose the sketch. Instead of rendering the entire clown sign, I cropped the image down to a mysterious fragment that leads the viewer's imagination to speculate about what lies outside the border. To emphasize the immense scale of the sign, I invented a figure to sit beneath it. —JG*

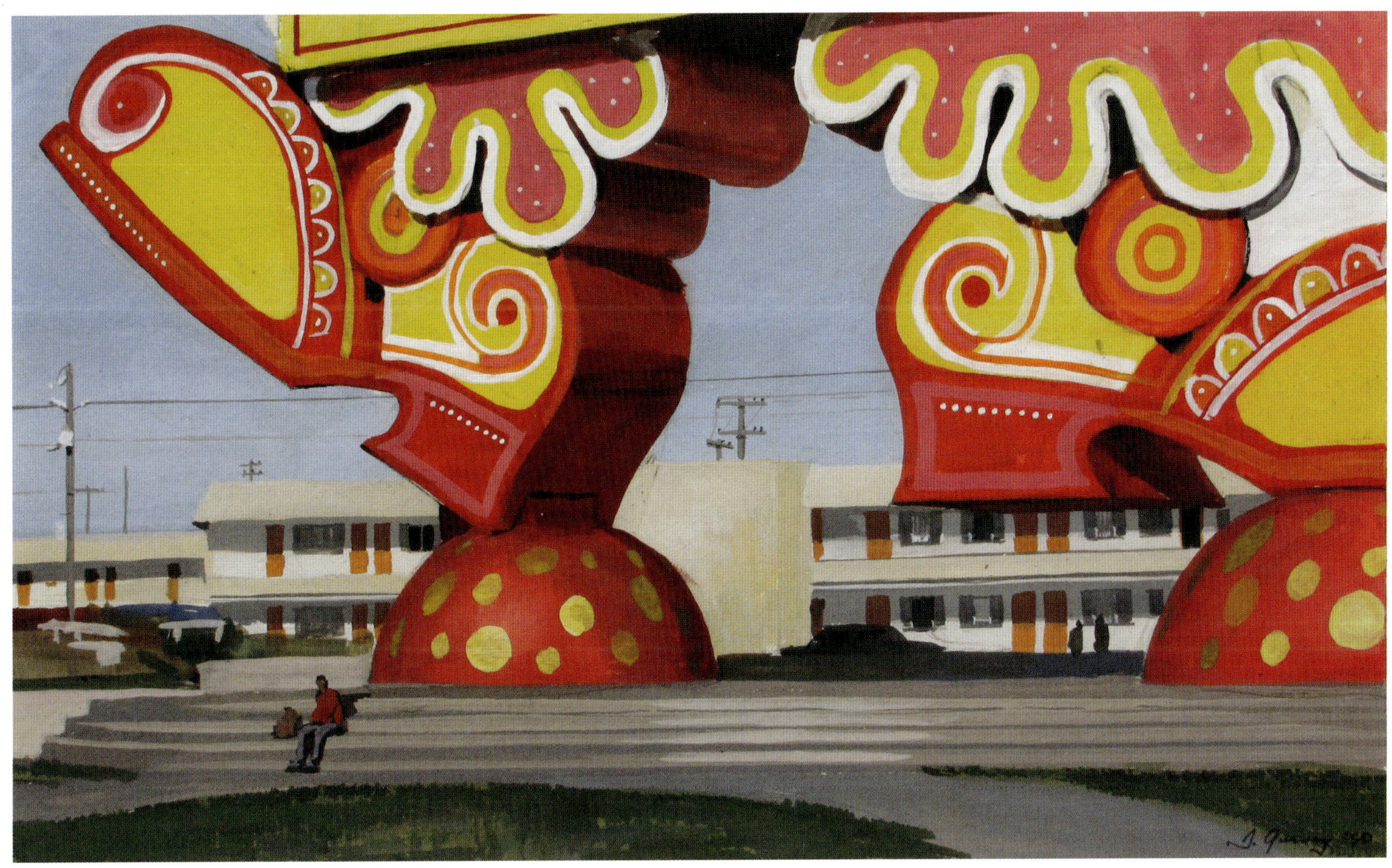

Fog and mist shrouding distant objects also creates mystery. A harbor becomes magical when ships suddenly disappear into a veil of fog. Mountain ranges seem infinite when their peaks are lost in clouds. Fog and mist, like all water vapor, will lighten the value and soften the edges of anything that recedes into it. Once you have actually observed and sketched these atmospheric conditions from life, you will understand these principles well enough to be able to improvise them in your sketch.

Many mysterious effects depend upon lighting conditions. As you can imagine, it would be difficult to create mystery if you were to copy a scene that was illuminated by a bright sun directly overhead. But let there be shadows and darkness, and the same scene will leave much to the imagination. In an afternoon landscape, for example, shadows will often be cast into the scene by buildings, trees, or clouds. When a foreground is darkened by a cast shadow, the viewer becomes aware, consciously or unconsciously, that something large enough to block a great deal of sunlight is situated beyond the frame of the picture. Cast shadows can also benefit a sketch by simplifying the values of the composition and eliminating a great deal of unnecessary detail. Feel free to invent cast shadows even if they don't exist in what you see.

The lighting effects of sunset and twilight are among the most intriguing. As the sun sets, the earth darkens relative to the sky. Everything that intercepts the sky becomes a silhouette. Some objects may be defined only by a sharp edge of light surrounding it, while the rest of the form is lost in shadow. These effects can convey not only mystery, but also, through association, calmness, peacefulness, restfulness (the end of the day); or dread, expectation, apprehension (the beginning of night).

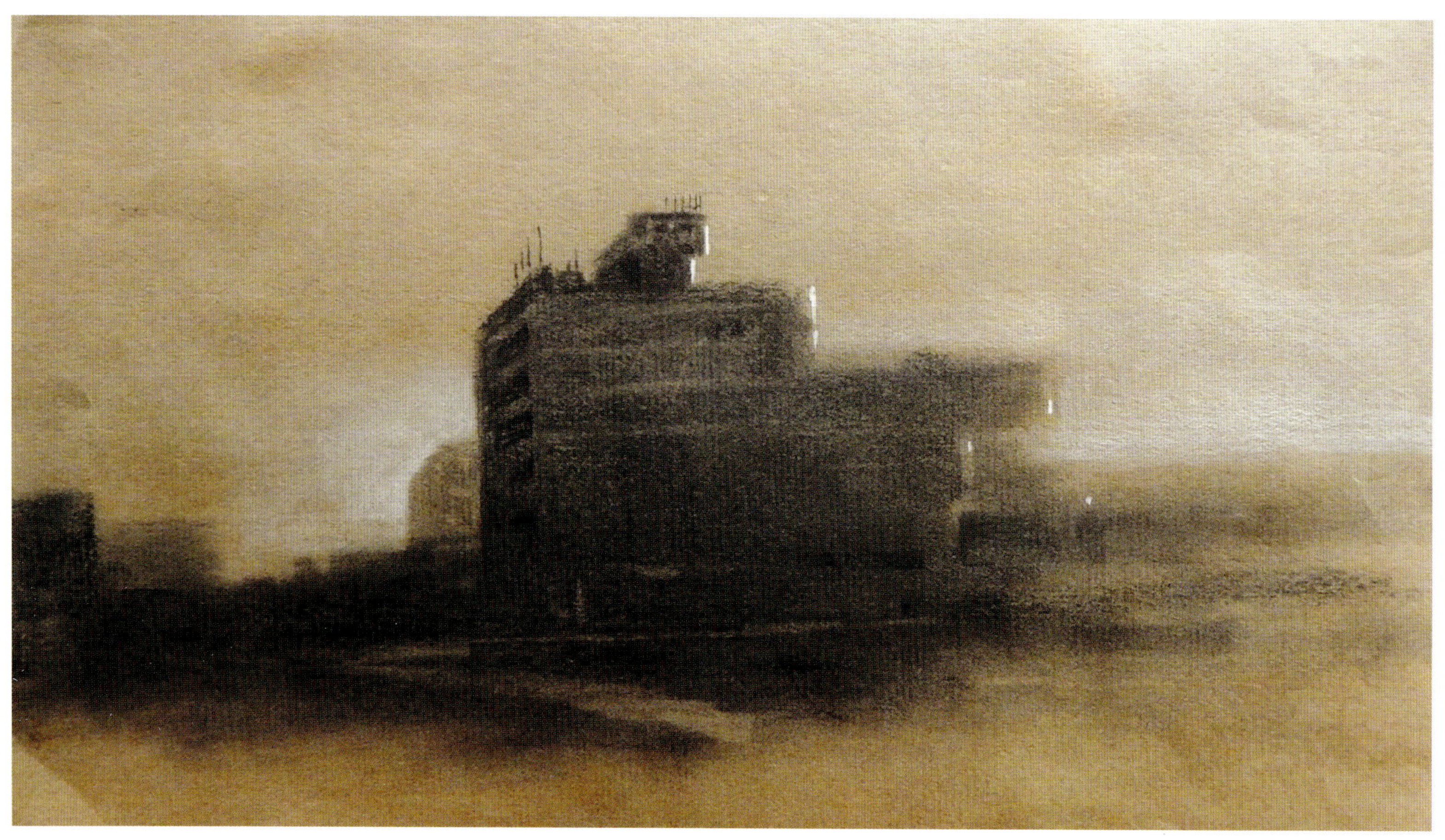

PARKING STRUCTURE, HAZY AFTERNOON, *charcoal and white CarbOthello pastel pencils with touches of white gouache on brown paper, 7" x 11". I find that softness as a pictorial effect works best when it is offset by a few crisp touches. In this sketch I used a simple pencil underdrawing to establish the eye level and basic shape of the building, and then I gradually applied charcoal, using a charcoal pencil and a paper stump. I then used a kneaded eraser to pick out a few of the details of the subject, such as the sidewalk area and the lines on the side of the main building. At this point the sketch was ready for some added crisp touches. I added the small vertical pole-like details first, and then began to add the white highlights and the subtle white tone in the sky. I avoided adding details to the building forms as a means of increasing the mystery of an otherwise ordinary subject. —TK*

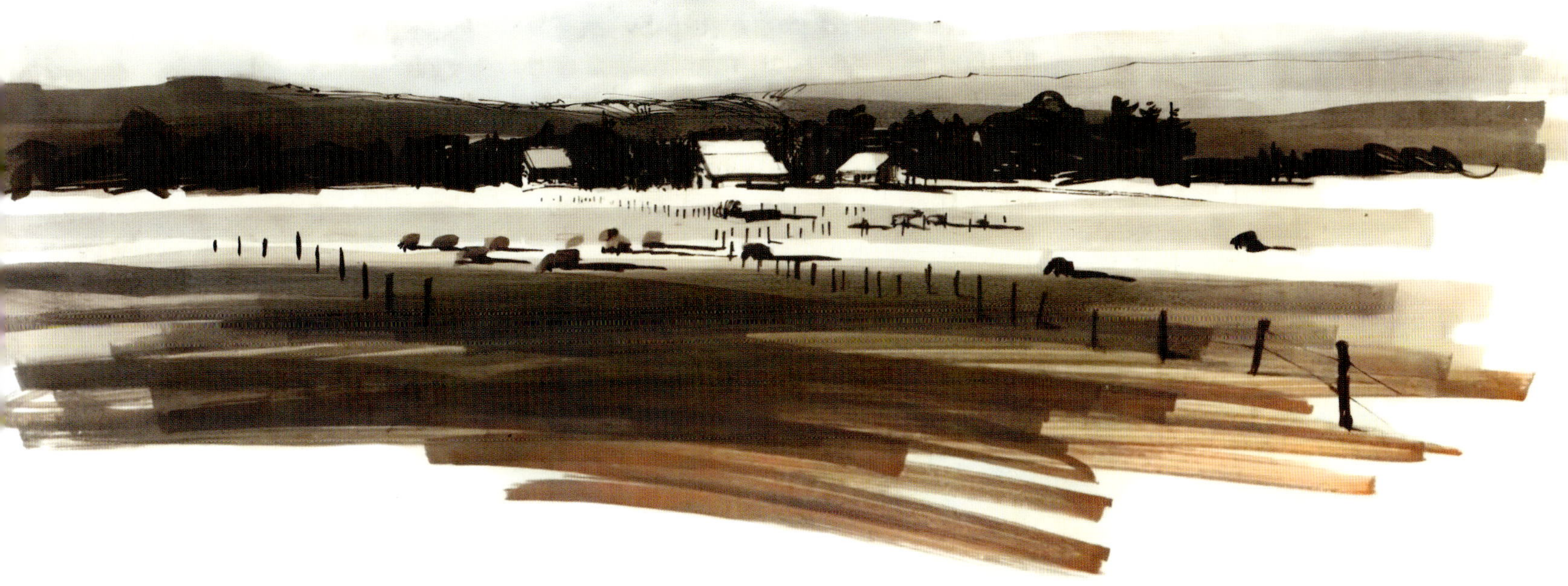

▲ **SMALL FARM, NORTHERN CALIFORNIA,** *gray markers on smooth paper, 9" x 14". This kind of rolling hill and flat meadow scenery is typical of the foothills of the Sierra Nevada in northern California. Tranquil, spacious subjects such as this call for broad areas of tone with only a few sharp accents added for contrast. I used a #1 cool gray marker to indicate the distant mountains, and a #2 and #4 for the sweeping foreground areas. Final touches, such as the shadows from the grazing cows and the distant trees, were added with a black calligraphy marker. The fence posts relieve the overall horizontal feel of the sketch by providing staccato vertical accents. —TK*

▼ **CALIFORNIA FOOTHILLS,** *watercolor and touches of pastel, 7½" x 14". The silent approach of a storm inspired the treatment for the sketch. I often use skies as a device to suggest emotions in landscapes. In this case I had originally intended to do a detailed nature study of the forms of the rocky foothill. As I worked, the sky began to deepen with the rich, transparent darkness of storm clouds. It was as though an ominous presence had apprehended the landscape. I immediately set to work to capture the effect. I was no longer as interested in the specific forms of the foothill as I was in the emotional power of the whole landscape. I softened the left-hand edge of the foothill to add mystery and to also bring the pictorial focus to the crisp right-hand edge. To balance the crisp edge of the foothill to the right, the tiny farm laborers were added. They also serve as a human touch to suggest man's efforts in contrast to the monumental power of natural forces. —TK*

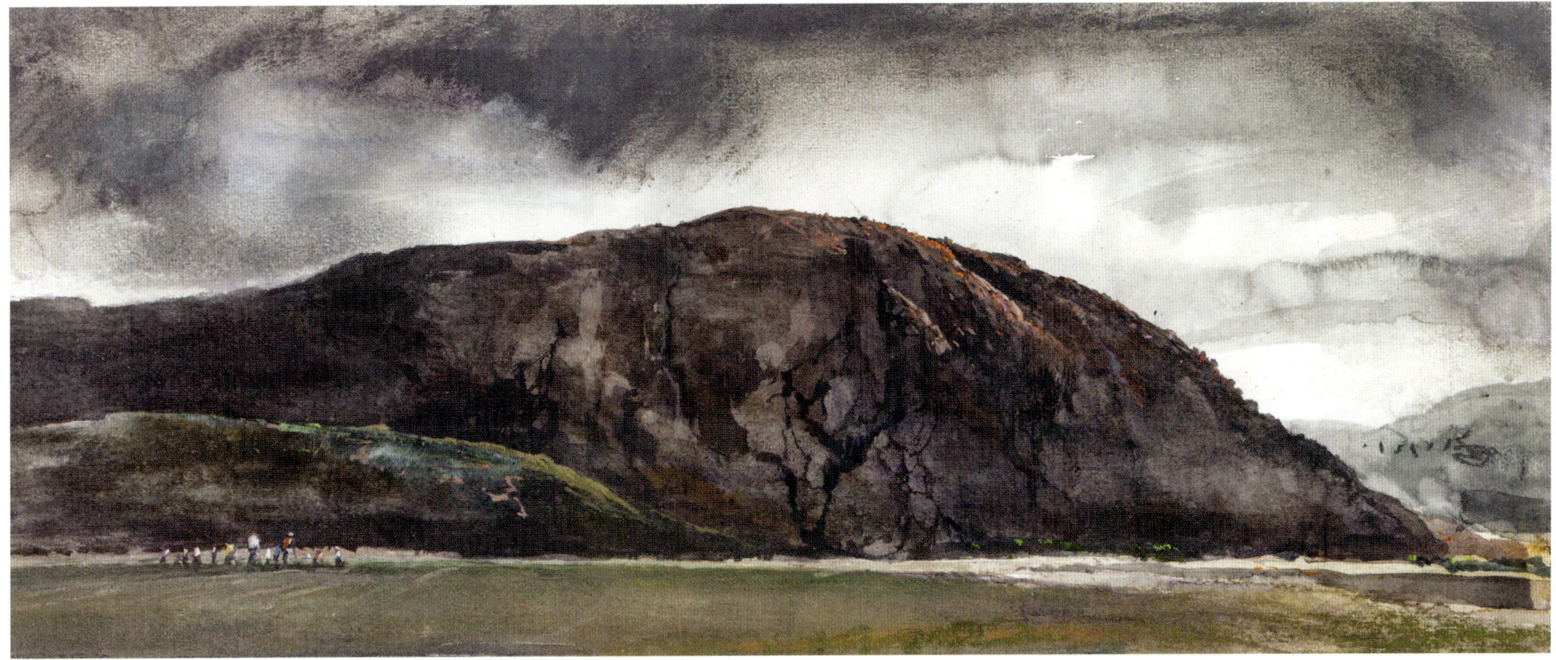

STRUCTURE AND EXPRESSION

Someone might ask why it is necessary to be consciously aware of specific methods for communicating feelings. Isn't it better to regard mood as something beyond our conscious control—something we achieve only through intuition and impulse?

In our experience, freedom of expression is not hampered by specific methods; in fact, it thrives within them. For example, in this chapter we have offered you a step-by-step method to note your impressions and develop them into thumbnails. Using these methods will not hinder your freedom to express yourself; in fact, like a traveler with a good map, you will be free to consider a variety of destinations before embarking, and

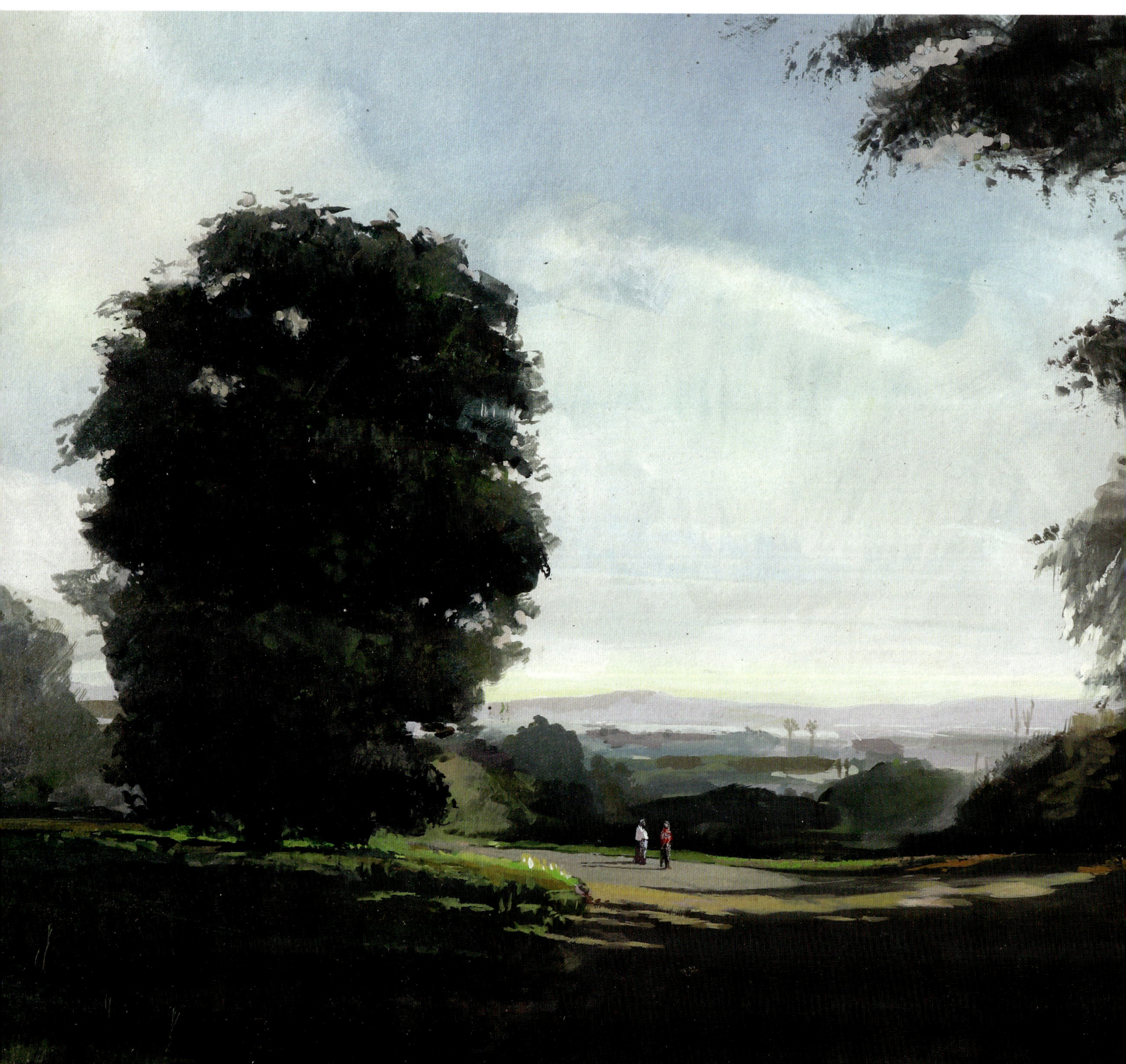

then travel confidently in the direction you want to go. This is certainly better than feeling a vague apprehension at not knowing where you are. We've looked at some principles of pictorial organization: selectivity, center of interest, dramatic opposition, delicacy, and mystery. These are tools that you can use to add excitement to a sketch in progress or else to organize your thinking before you begin a sketch.

We do not intend this chapter to be a rigid formula for creating mood. We are simply offering you the methods that we use to add mood to our sketches. You will undoubtedly pick and choose from these methods in accordance with the needs of each sketch. However, by applying yourself to consciously think in the ways we suggest, you will soon find yourself able to organize your sketch and create mood with little or no conscious effort. When you reach that point, you will have expanded your ability to be truly expressive beyond the point of intuition or impulse.

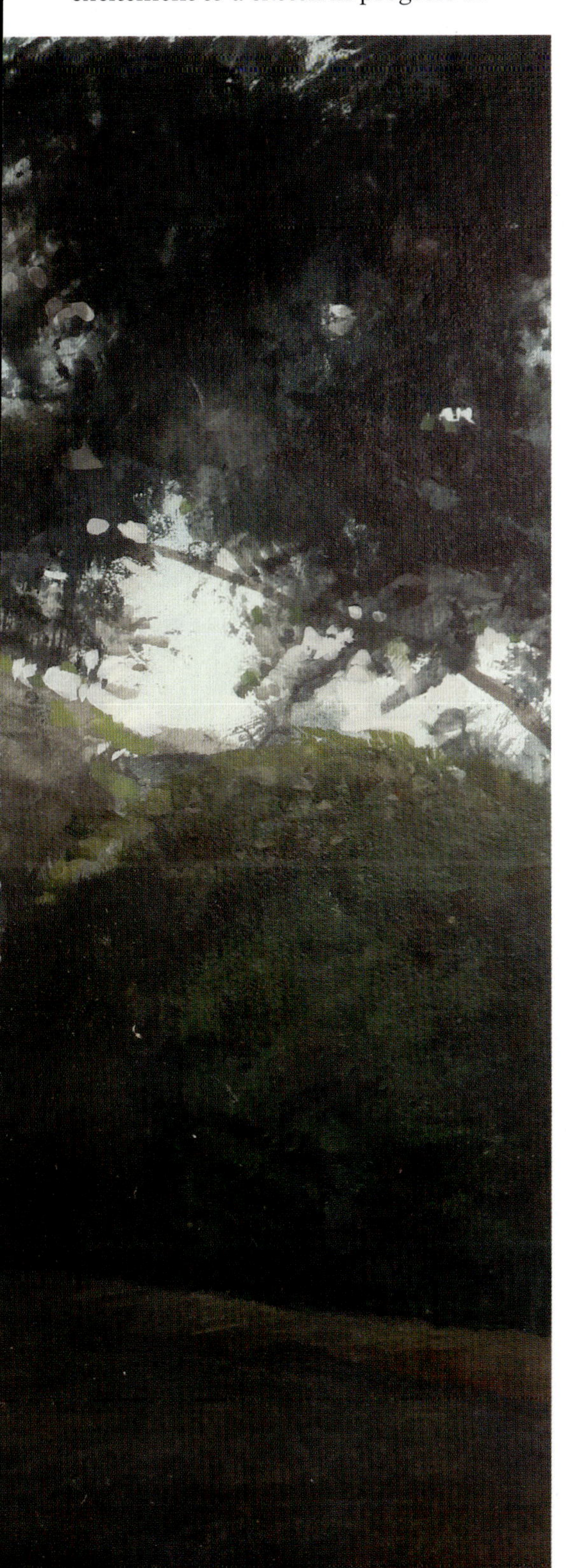

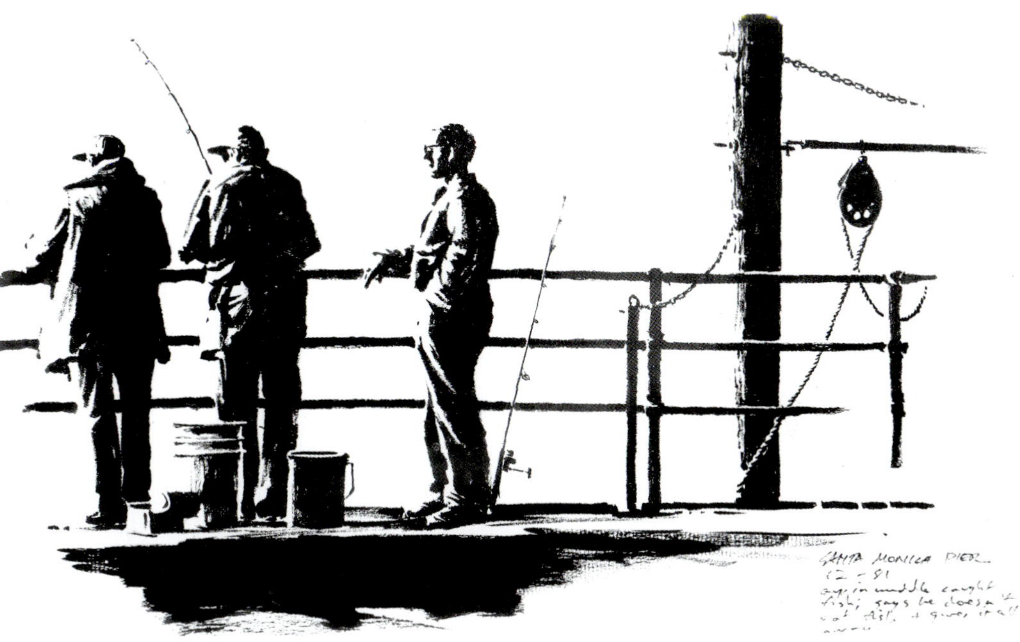

▲ **FISHERMEN ON A PIER,** *brushpen on charcoal paper, 11" x 17". In this sketch I used a technique that has an effect similar to a high-contrast photograph. Everything in shadow is grouped into a pure black, and everything in light becomes white. A line along the light side of forms is not necessary because the viewer's eye can easily supply the missing information. Just make sure that the sun is bright enough to create a clear separation between light and shade. Do your pencil underdrawing as you normally would to get the gesture, proportion, and perspective accurately. Then begin with the brush, drawing along the shaded edge of the form, and also along the dividing line between light and shade. This technique is effective for creating mood because it automatically suggests the low light of late afternoon. —JG*

◀ **TREE-LINED ROAD,** *gouache on cold-press illustration board, 15" x 18". In this sketch I took great liberties with the scene before me in order to enhance the mood of peacefulness. The biggest change is the arrangement of the trees and the addition of the foreground shadow, all of which are used to frame the central deep-space area and stabilize the composition. The tones were organized by grouping them into either the light area or the dark area. The sky is all light, and the ground and trees are all dark—except for the one area where the sun shines through to illuminate the road. I broke up the edge where light meets shadow to give a feeling of the dappled light that always occurs where trees cast shadows on a road. —JG*

Using Imagination

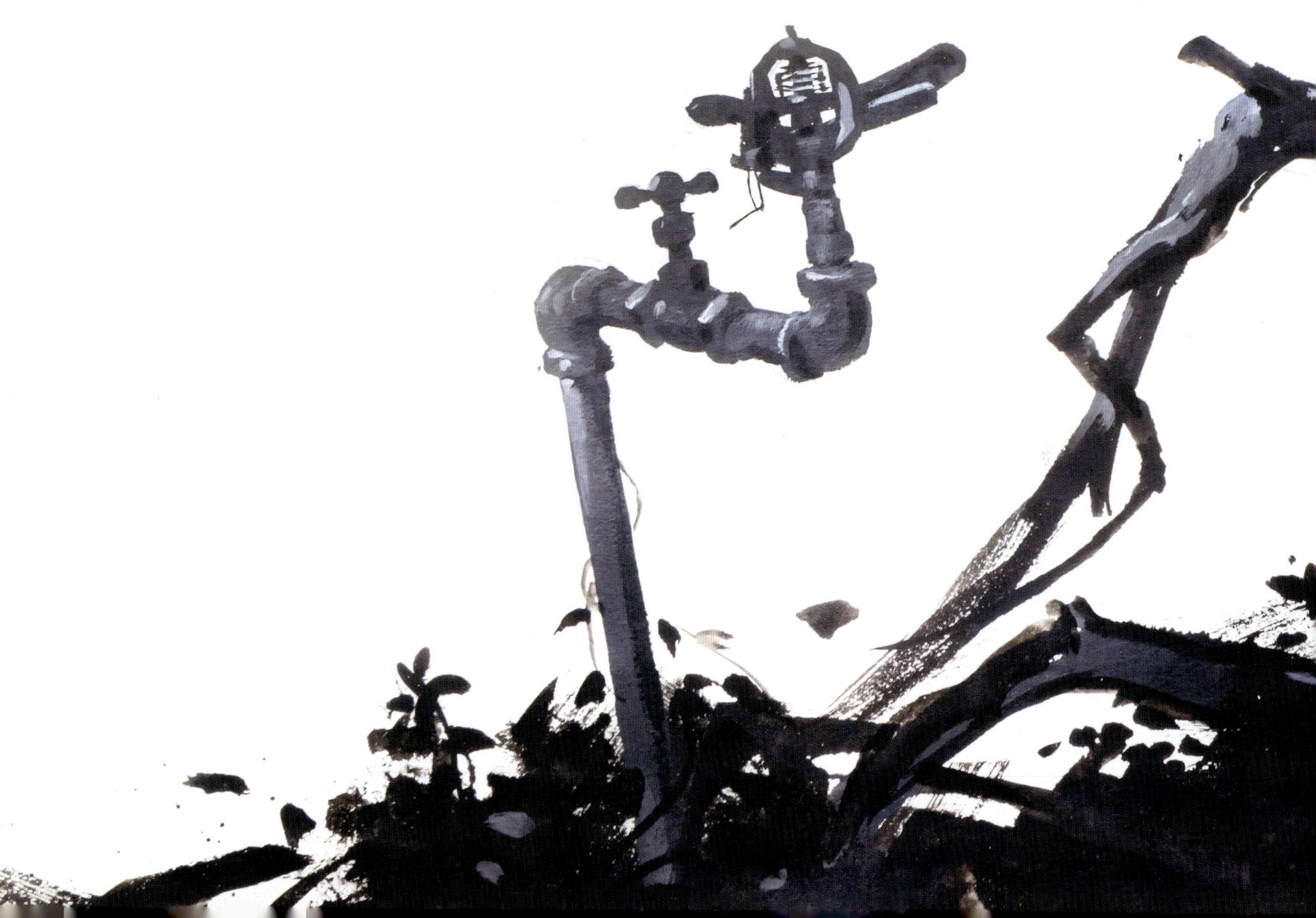

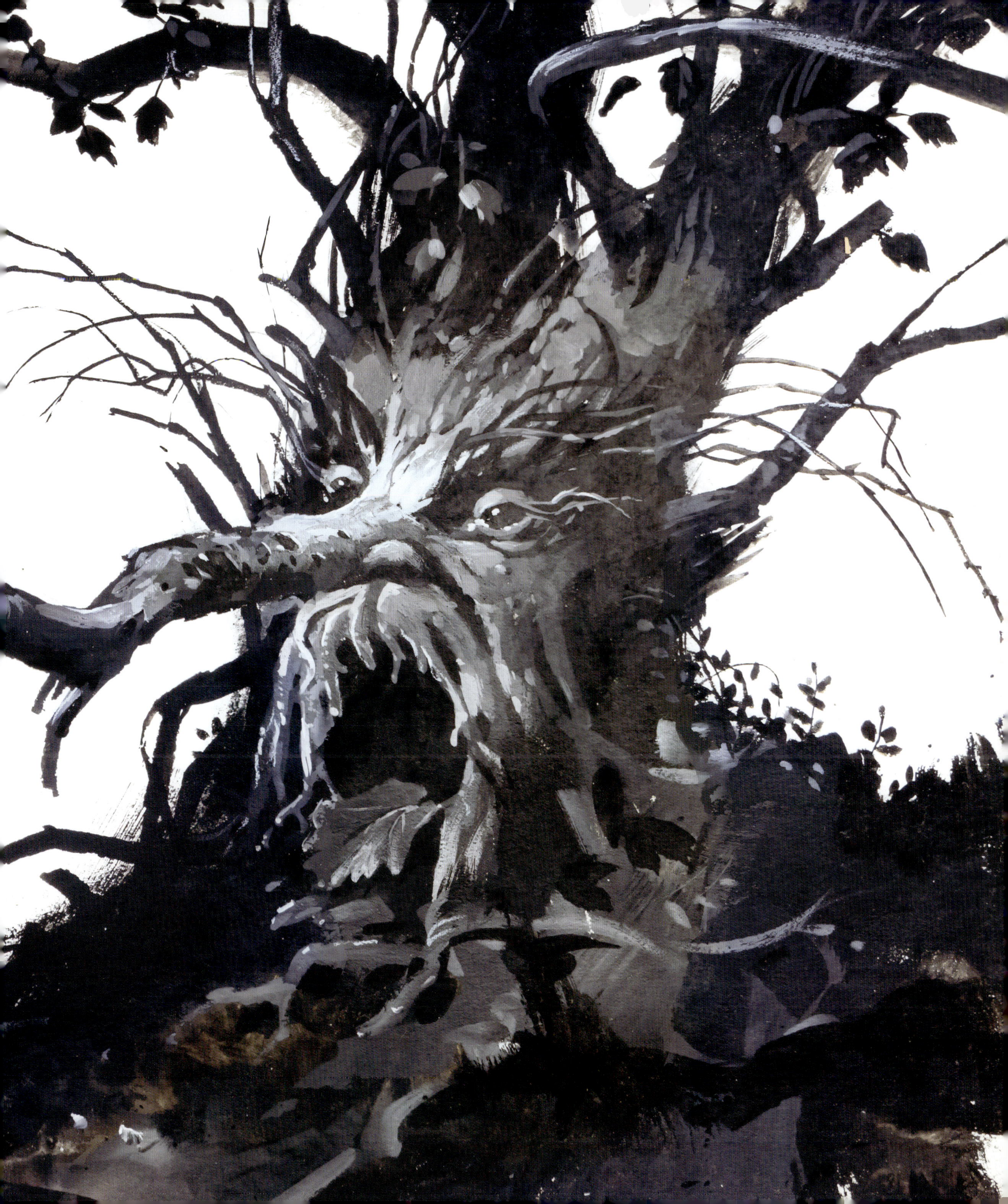

◄◄ **TREE STUMP CREATURE,** *gouache on illustration board, 14" x 20". When I left home to go sketching one morning, I expected to return with a serious nature study. But the place I chose to go was a weed-infested lot, humming with mosquitoes. When I got there, I came across a stunted tree whose branches suggested a fanciful face. Instead of recording exactly what I saw, I decided to coax the face out of hiding. Most of the ideas took place in the underdrawing stage—the long eyebrow-branches, for instance, and the wide-open mouth. In the painting I eliminated all the details of the background so that I could play up the silhouette. The sprinkler was an afterthought; I just happened to see it in another part of the vacant lot and decided to put it in as a contrast to the stump creature. A sketch like this, which looks like a finished illustration, is actually much more fun to do on the spot, amongst the weeds and mosquitoes, than it would have been in the barren walls of the studio. I like to think of the real world as a three-dimensional reference library for the imagination. —JG*

WHILE WE WERE SKETCHING at the zoo a few years ago, a small boy stopped in front of us and began diligently drawing the animals. As we watched him proceed, we noticed that he was launching into his own private world of fantasy. The buffalo, which we had painstakingly sought to render accurately, was being transformed into a magnificent alien monster, fending off flying saucers and meteors with no less than five horns. While we were trying to copy every detail before us, the boy was playfully exercising the magic of his unhampered imagination.

Comparing his sketch to our own, we realized how much we had limited ourselves. We had automatically decided that we were going to sketch the buffalo in a straightforward manner. Any humorous or fanciful idea that might have entered our minds had been squelched by our adult sensibility. We had stifled any potential to be creative, forcing ourselves instead to depict only what was there. That small boy with his buffalo monster made us realize that nothing prevents us from fully exercising our imagination while sketching on-the-spot. The approach described in this chapter involves using your own imagination in much the same way the child at the zoo did.

DARE TO BE CREATIVE

One of the biggest steps you are taking as you develop your ability in sketching is the realization that *you* are in control of your subject—not vice versa. This means you have the power to do anything you want to transform what you see as you sketch. When you use your imagination, you free yourself from any restrictions that you may have felt before.

As an artist you can take initiative and *dare* to be creative. Many artists seem to feel that it is somehow wrong to change what they see. It often boils down to a fear that the sketch will be ruined, but such fears are damaging to artistic growth. It's important to reach beyond old habits and take chances. Experimenting is the key to growth!

The goal in this kind of sketching is to look at your subject with the eyes of a child, allowing yourself to formulate associations and act upon whims. If an oak tree reminds you of a menacing bear, exaggerate it in that direction. Perhaps two prominent upper limbs can be transformed into extended forelegs complete with claws. Or perhaps you have always wanted to sketch an old abandoned rowboat. As you begin sketching, you imagine a group of tiny gnomes who have made this boat their home. Include them! Your sketch will not be ruined by this fanciful addition. If anything, it will be improved. You will have documented more than the abandoned rowboat—you will also have documented the wonderful idea that came while you were sketching.

The message is simple. Dare to be creative. You have a rich imagination that is waiting to be unlocked. Sketching can be your means to do that. Awaken yourself to the inner voice that constantly nudges your more serious mind with fanciful ideas. Follow a few of your whims. You'll be surprised at how imaginative you are.

BEING IMAGINATIVE ON THE SPOT

A friend of ours who specializes in surreal paintings once mentioned: "It's hard to use my imagination with all this reality around!" This statement indicates a misconception that we commonly find. The misconception is this: the only way to be creative is to be removed from any external input. When an art class is given an imaginative illustration assignment, many students lock themselves in a room for a weekend, frantically searching for ideas, only to emerge frustrated and discouraged on Monday with no solution to the assignment. They are convinced that they have absolutely no imagination and that they would be better off in another career. Yet what we discovered

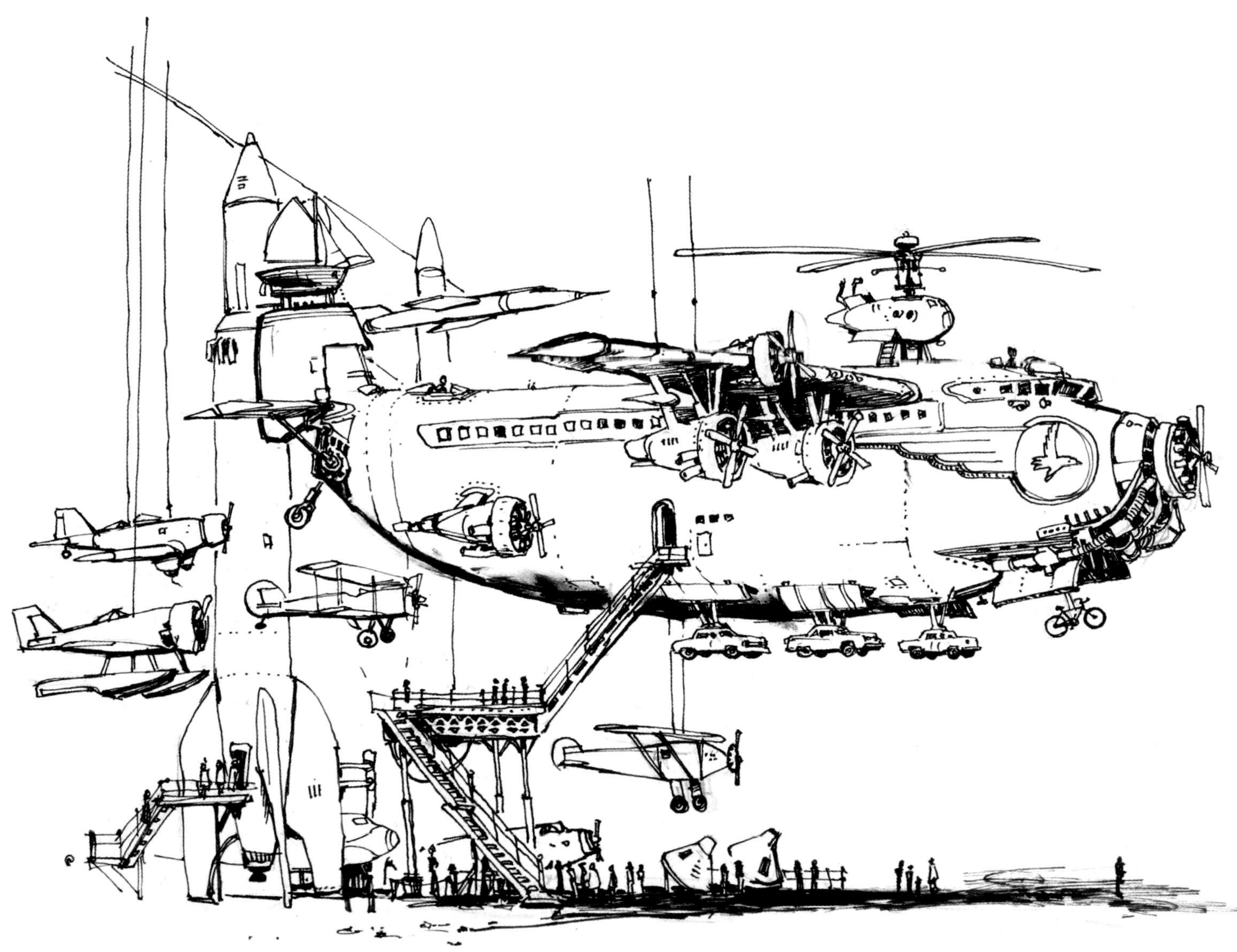

is that their imagination is not what is lacking. What is lacking is input.

The imagination is like an idea-producing machine that each of us is blessed with at birth. Like any machine, the imagination requires fuel for its operation. The more fuel you feed into your imagination, the more ideas it can generate. And that is precisely why imaginative sketching is so often the key to unlocking the imaginative potential that often lies dormant inside each of us.

Why was the surrealist artist frustrated with working on the spot? It was not only the fact that he had a misconception about the value of working on the spot. The problem for him was also that his imagination was overwhelmed by the sheer volume of visual input that he had to choose from. What he needed—and what we offer in this chapter—were specific techniques for getting beyond preconceptions, for seeing things in new ways, and most of all for taking the attitude that the details of reality are nothing more than raw material to be transformed by means of the imagination into something altogether new.

When is it appropriate to do an imaginative sketch? We find that in our experience, imaginative sketches are born of the most unlikely moments, when we're bored or tired or daydreaming. The creative mind is most active at these times. Also, an imaginative approach can be used to "save" a more serious sketch whose original inspiration has evaporated—especially with very ordinary

ANTIQUE AIRPLANE, AIR AND SPACE MUSEUM, *fountain pen on smooth paper, 8" x 10". This sketch is a team effort. The minute I got out my sketchbook on the upper balcony of the National Air and Space Museum in Washington, D.C., a group of about ten curious kids leaned over my shoulder and asked me what I was going to draw. "The Ultimate Airplane," I told them. Together we all thought of ideas for ways of combining different airplanes and helicopters together, and inventing ways to steer, propel, and land the monster flying machine. The sketch developed without a plan as we sat there, with detail piled upon detail. I was reminded of the fun that I had as a child when I allowed my imagination to take complete control of the picture. I find this kind of sketching to be a refreshing balance to the more careful and serious approaches that I spend most of my time doing. —JG*

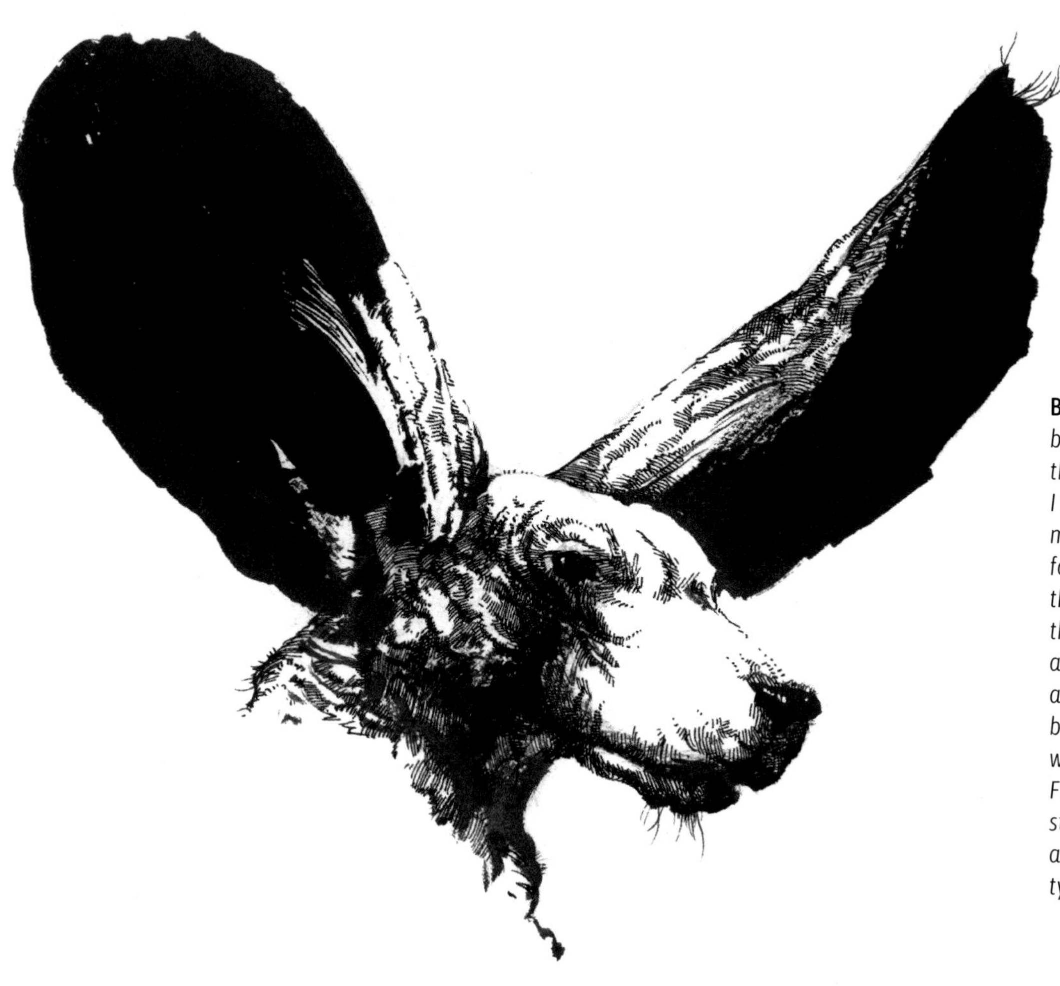

BIG-EARED CANINE, *technical pen on illustration board, 7½" x 10". With a good enough breeze, this creature could probably fly. At least the way I drew him he could. The actual animal had only moderately large ears, but anything is possible for the imaginative sketcher. I enjoy exaggerating the characteristics of animals, but I find that the best subjects for these sketches are stuffed animals rather than live ones. The motion of live animals somehow makes me feel obligated to be as accurate as possible in my sketch. This one was drawn at the natural history museum in San Francisco after a few hours of drawing more serious studies of the animals. Imaginative sketches such as this are a welcome diversion from the serious type of sketch I usually do. —TK*

subject matter. Don't schedule your imaginative sketches; let them grow spontaneously.

EXAGGERATION

When you made your first crayon drawings as a toddler, you were using a basic tool of imagination called exaggeration. A house was somehow *more* of a house when you drew it with curling smoke from the chimney and a bright green lawn in front. A wolf was somehow *more* of a wolf once you added those long fangs and red eyes. Even though the drawings may look crude to your eye now, they have a creative energy which is lacking in so many "realistic" drawings. This spark is exaggeration.

Exaggeration is the process of enhancing the essential characteristics of your subject. It can be used in any style of drawing, from the simplest childlike scribble to a very carefully rendered realistic drawing or painting. The first step you take to exaggerate something in a sketch is to look *away* from the subject and search your reserve of memories and associations for those characteristics that define the subject you are drawing.

If you are stuck trying to think of the essential characteristics, do this: look at the subject from many different angles (if possible). This will help to break you away from that fixed, inflexible image. As you walk around, consider what makes your subject *different* from other related objects. For example, a rowboat is not like a sailboat—it lacks a mast and a rudder and pulleys—instead it has oars and oarlocks and a seat in the middle. An oak tree is not like a pine tree—it lacks a straight trunk and sharp needles—instead it has heavy, twisted branches and small leaves. Obvious? Of course. But also very important, because if you can emphasize these things in your sketches, your viewer will have the delightful feeling that his own visual memory of rowboats and oak trees has been reaffirmed. Your sketch will seem more "right" than if you had been absolutely accurate.

Now the drawing part is easy, because you know what to emphasize. As you draw, eliminate or subdue those features that are not essential. Don't worry if the sketch looks childlike. See how far you can exaggerate any given characteristic. If a jet strikes you as sleek and powerful, add extra sweepback to the wings and make the nose more pointed. Another artist might see the jet as clumsy and ungainly; a drawing exaggerating those characteristics would show a stubby, sausage-shaped body with tiny wings and awkward-looking landing gear. In either case, the finished picture will look nothing like what you actually see. In fact, it may show the subject from a wholly different viewpoint.

Now you are exaggerating what you see, and, more likely than not, you are rediscovering the joy you had when you sketched as a child.

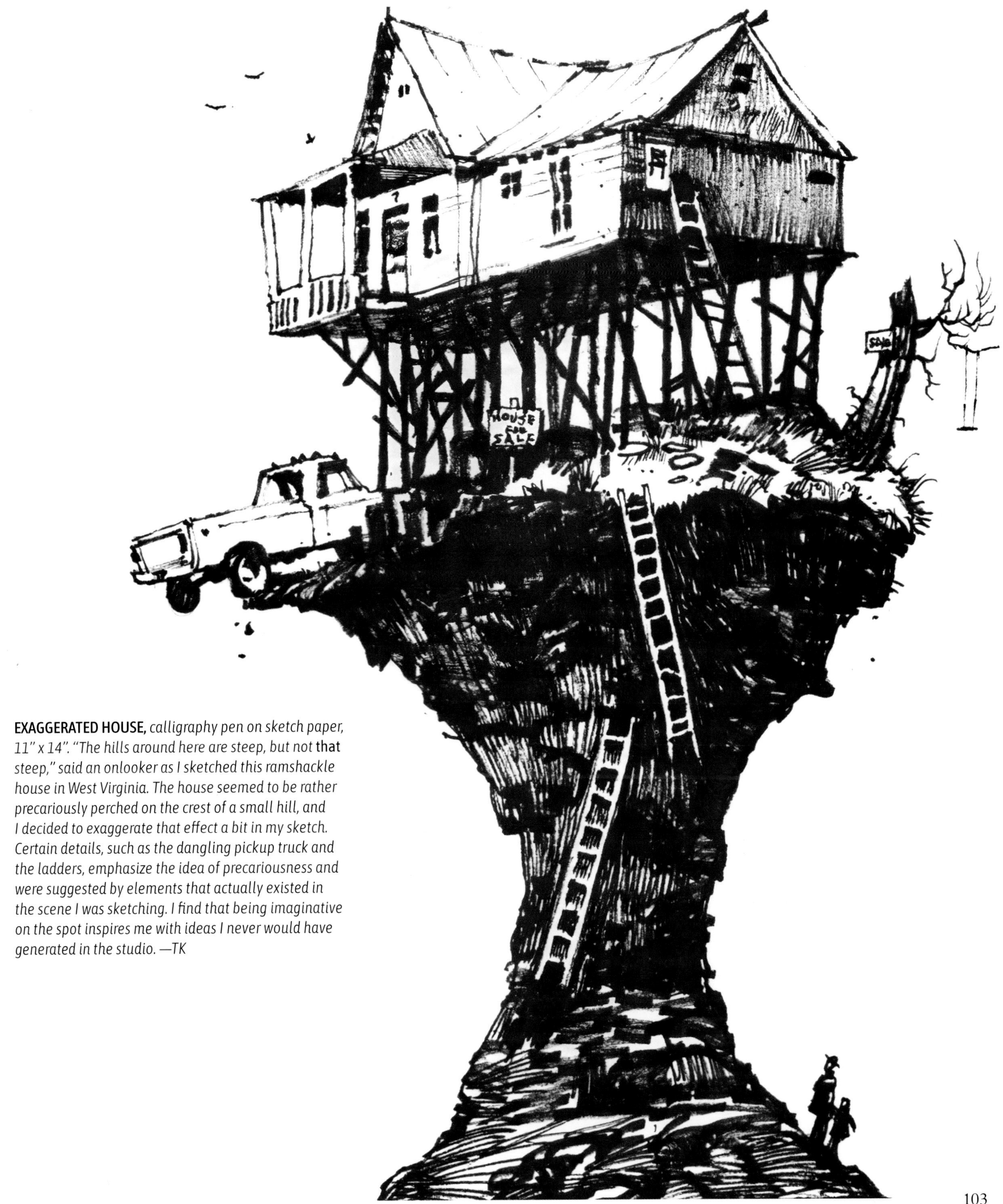

EXAGGERATED HOUSE, *calligraphy pen on sketch paper, 11" x 14". "The hills around here are steep, but not* that *steep," said an onlooker as I sketched this ramshackle house in West Virginia. The house seemed to be rather precariously perched on the crest of a small hill, and I decided to exaggerate that effect a bit in my sketch. Certain details, such as the dangling pickup truck and the ladders, emphasize the idea of precariousness and were suggested by elements that actually existed in the scene I was sketching. I find that being imaginative on the spot inspires me with ideas I never would have generated in the studio. —TK*

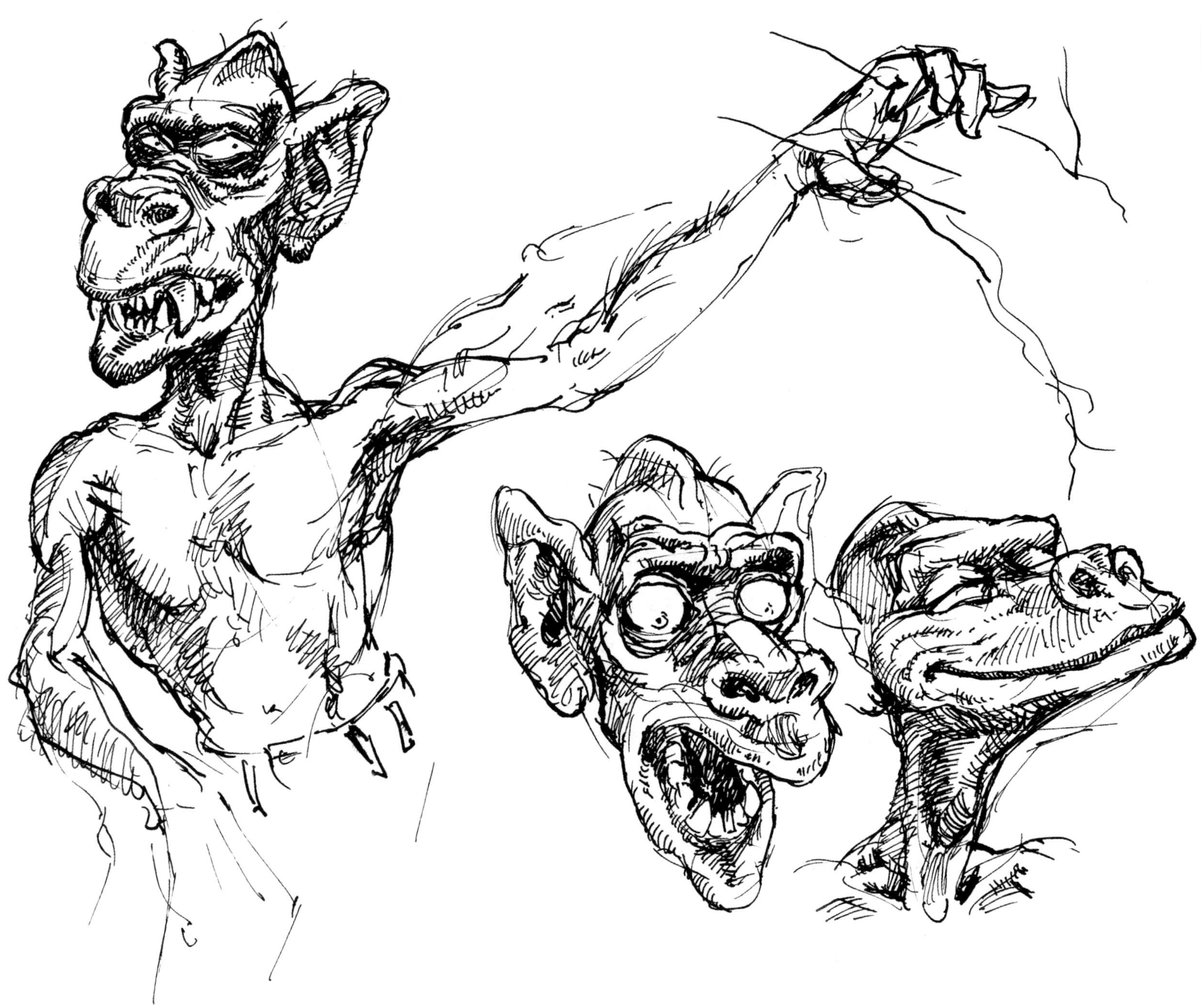

▲ **STRANGE CREATURES,** *fountain pen on sketch paper, 9" x 12". Sketching was my primary means of escape from dull lectures in college. These little studies, done without a pencil underdrawing, began as a very exaggerated portrait of a psychology professor, who was at that moment discussing the brain mechanisms of aggressive behavior. Although I couldn't see him very well from where I was sitting in the back of the class, I noticed that he would contort his face into all kinds of odd expressions to illustrate his points. I accentuated this in my creature. Also, in the back of my mind were some studies of a gorilla skull that I had sketched earlier in the week at the anthropology museum on campus. —JG*

▶ **FLOATING MERRY-GO-ROUND,** *fountain pen and gray markers on smooth paper, 11" x 14". I began this sketch one July afternoon, leaning against a wooden rail of the boardwalk in Coney Island, New York. I finished it three months later atop a stack of fish crates in Morro Bay, California. When I sketched the merry-go-round, I had no idea where or how I would eventually use it. I just had a feeling that if I left enough blank space around it on the page, I might later find some strange setting to put it into. I ran across the merry-go-round sketch as I was preparing to do what probably would have been a fairly conventional watercolor sketch of fishing boats. From this experience I have learned to take along several half-finished sketches whenever I go to a new location, in case I get an idea to add an unusual context. —JG*

CHANGING CONTEXT

Changing context involves taking any object you are sketching and drawing it in a setting where you would least expect to find it. An otherwise boring sketch can become interesting if you do this. Suppose, for example, you have spent hours meticulously rendering a statue in a town square. When you finish, there it is: a rather ordinary drawing of a rather ordinary statue. You needn't despair, for you have the raw material for a wonderful imaginative treatment. Ask yourself what would be the most unexpected place to find a statue. A supermarket aisle? Floating at sea? In either case, a minimal suggestion of background will suddenly transform the sketch into a startlingly improbable scene. A friend casually flipping through your sketchbook will stop on that page and ask you a flurry of questions.

We've found that when you remove an object from its context, it's best to go way beyond the bounds of plausibility for the sketch to be effective. A fire hydrant in the middle of the desert might be unusual—but a fire hydrant in the middle of a kitchen is absurd. Don't be afraid to push it to the limit.

There are many ways to approach a sketch involving a change in context. The first way is simply to do a careful drawing of an object in the middle of your sketchbook page, eliminating all of the surrounding environment. You may have no idea at the time how you will eventually use it. A day will come later when you are sketching in an entirely different location, and you discover that half-finished sketch of an object without a context. You might then get the idea of combining the prior sketch with the present location. This kind of accidental discovery seems to work best.

Another approach is exactly the reverse; you sketch a setting, such as the inside of an insurance office or the edge of a meadow, knowing that later you will insert some unusual object, like a newspaper rack or a gum machine or a helicopter. Of course, with this procedure, you will need to work in pencil so that you can erase the areas that will be overlapped by the object. Later, in the studio, you can refine the sketch more, if necessary, redrawing it in pen and ink on the original or on a separate piece of paper.

Another approach is to do the whole picture at one sitting. You may be sketching a dilapidated barn and notice a powerboat parked in someone's driveway down the road. Put the two elements together and something interesting can

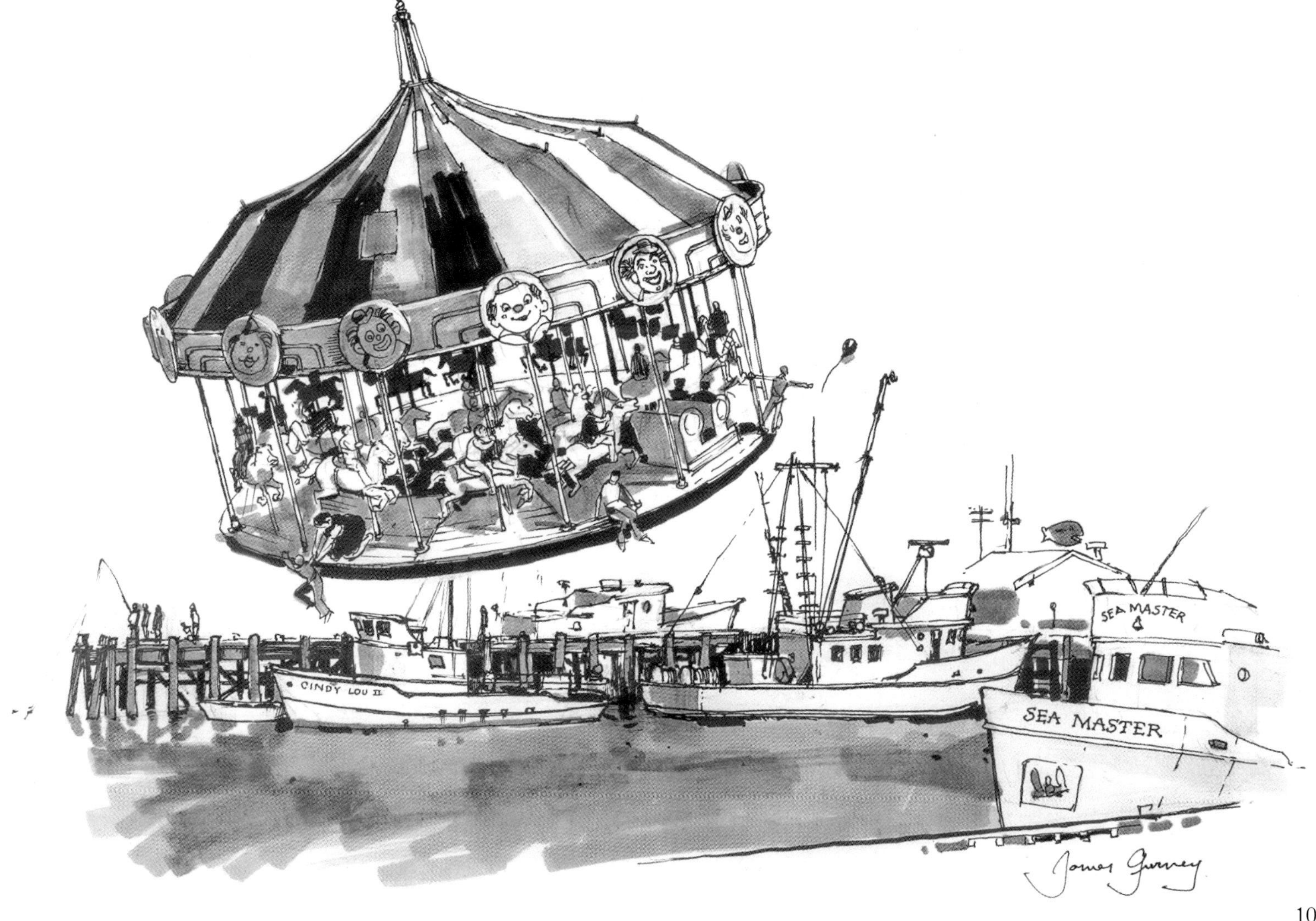

result. After all, when was the last time you saw a speedboat in a hayloft? You also have the possibility of *inventing* either the object or the setting as you sketch its counterpart from life. Most of us could make up a field of high grass. If that would make an interesting setting for your sketch of a staircase, then go ahead and add it. Similarly, your sketch of a basketball court may inspire you to make up a weeping willow to set right in the middle. Regardless of what method you use to change the context, keep this in mind: the more unlikely the combination, the more effective the result.

CHANGING SCALE

Changing scale involves altering the *relative* size of the objects you are drawing. The word *relative* is important here, because objects in your sketch will only appear larger or smaller than life relative to the things that are around them. It works best when you really exaggerate the variation in scale. For example, you may want to do an imaginative sketch in which you make a car look larger than life. Drawing the car to appear the same size as a house will probably look like nothing more than an error in perspective. But if you draw an entire city below its wheels, you will get a startling effect.

Include enough elements in your picture so that it is obvious which is the exaggerated element. For example, a tiny building next to a huge apple will not tell the viewer whether the apple is huge and the building is normal-sized or whether the apple is normal-sized and the building is tiny. Solve the problem by including other items that are in keeping with the scale of one or the other of your objects. If you put in more apples and leaves in scale with the first apple, you would suggest that we are seeing a miniature building in an apple orchard. On the other hand, if you stayed with a single apple, and surrounded the building with appropriately scaled telephone poles, driveways, and trees, we would understand that the apple is colossal in size.

The simplest and surest way to establish an unusual scale situation is to include figures. Viewers of a picture automatically put themselves in the place of the figures you have included. Viewers join in with the others to marvel at the magnificent ink bottle that has just appeared on the city skyline.

Remember, too, that the viewpoint from which you present objects will give a great deal of information about scale. We are all accustomed to seeing the world from a height about five or six feet above the ground. Generally, we look down at small things and up at large things. If you want to make a small object look large, hold it above your eye and actually look up at it, as if you were only a fraction of an inch tall. This alone, even without other scale references, will give the object a feeling of hugeness. Similarly, always take advantage of any situation where you happen to be sketching from a high viewpoint, such as from an upper-floor balcony or atop a mountain. The houses and streets and trees will already look tiny and can easily be drawn to appear as a miniature world inhabiting the palm of your hand or surface of a baseball.

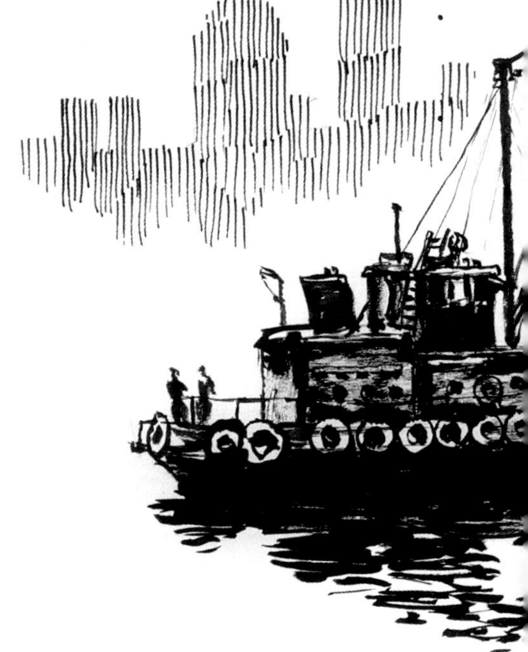

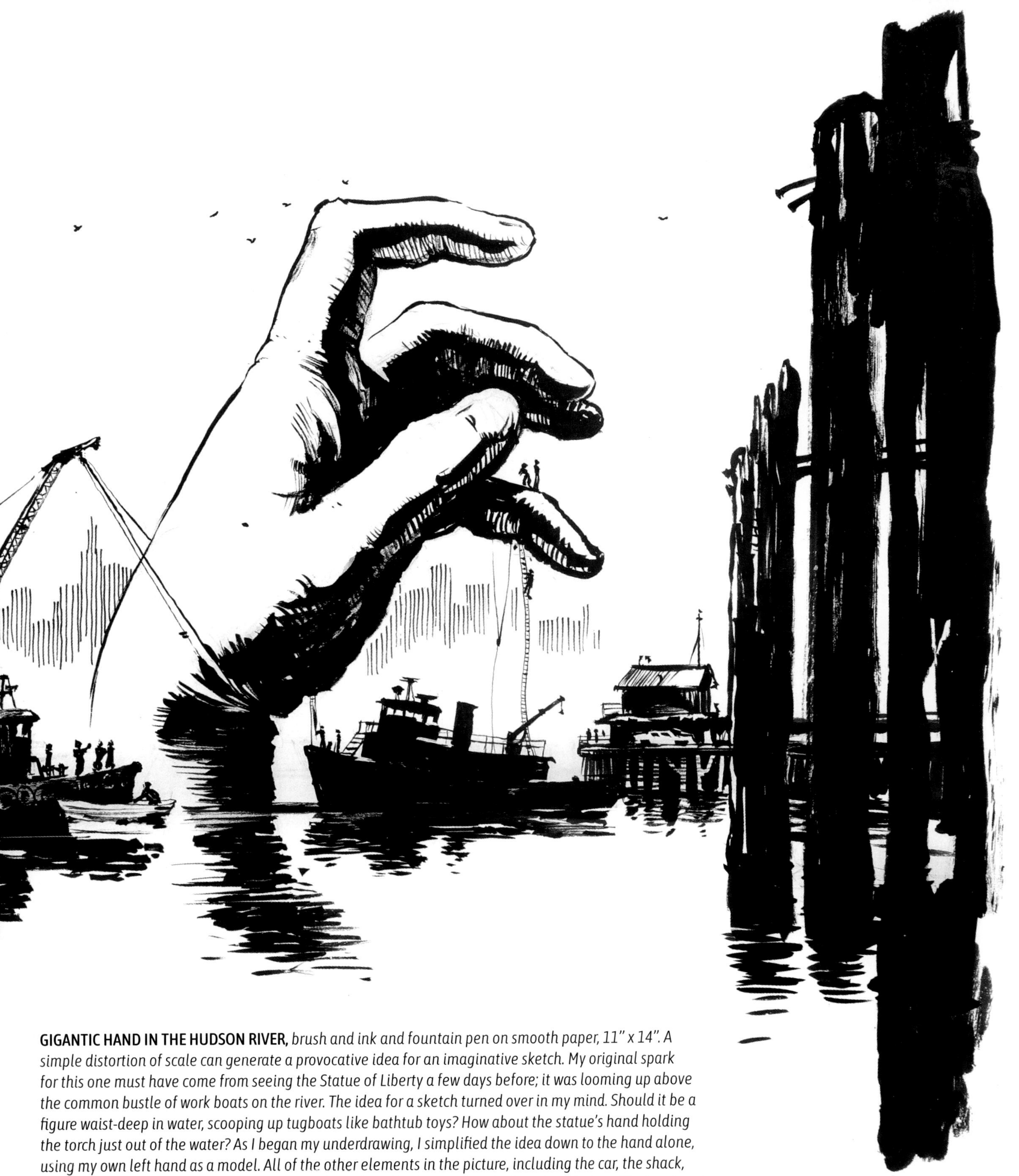

GIGANTIC HAND IN THE HUDSON RIVER, *brush and ink and fountain pen on smooth paper, 11" x 14". A simple distortion of scale can generate a provocative idea for an imaginative sketch. My original spark for this one must have come from seeing the Statue of Liberty a few days before; it was looming up above the common bustle of work boats on the river. The idea for a sketch turned over in my mind. Should it be a figure waist-deep in water, scooping up tugboats like bathtub toys? How about the statue's hand holding the torch just out of the water? As I began my underdrawing, I simplified the idea down to the hand alone, using my own left hand as a model. All of the other elements in the picture, including the car, the shack, the birds, the figures, and the boats, are in scale with each other, making it clear that the hand is the absurd element. Had I designed a composition of only two large hands and a boat, it might have appeared to be the hands of a normal person playing with a model. —JG*

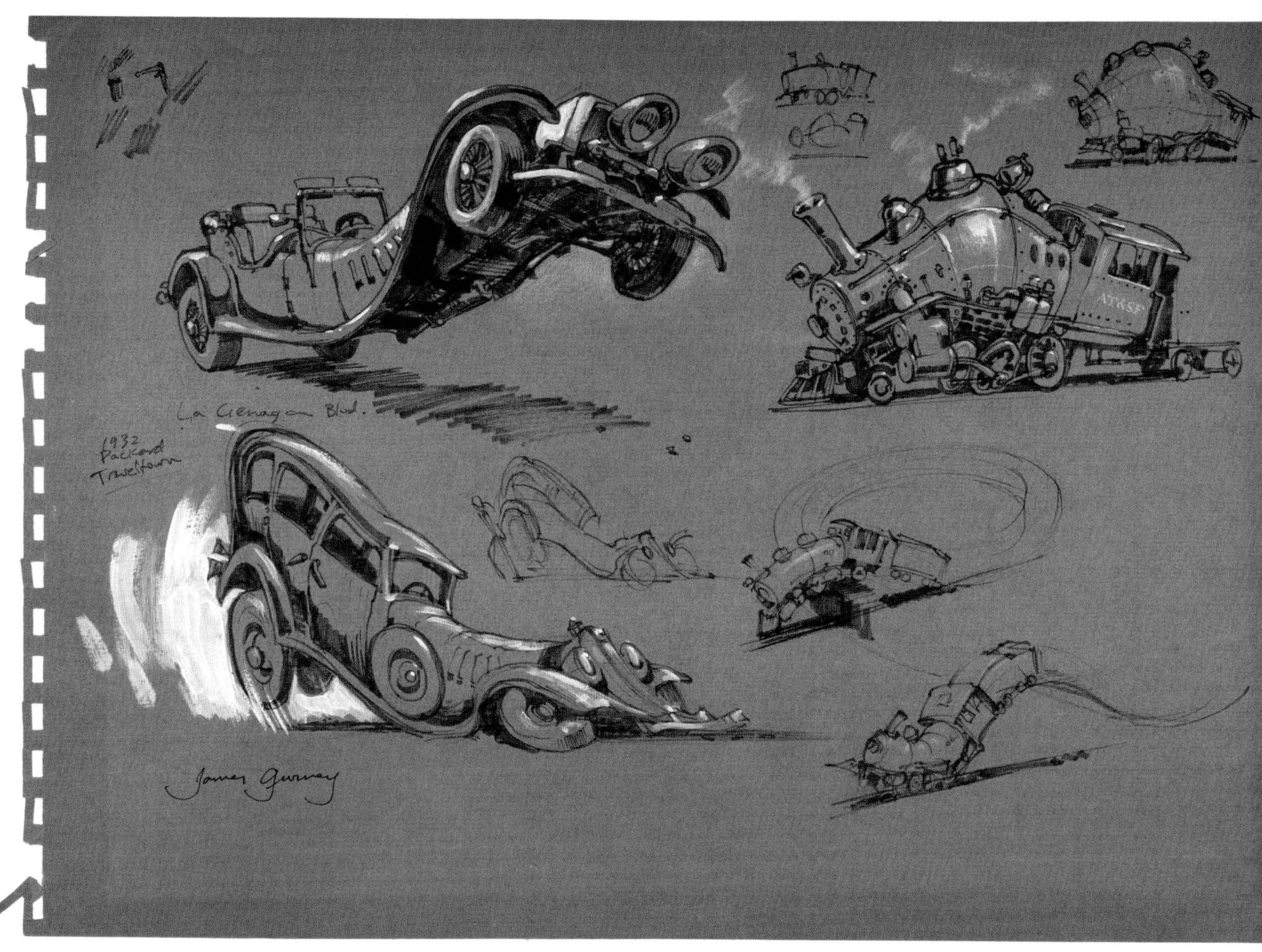

LIFELIKE CARS AND TRAINS, *calligraphy marker and white gouache on brown paper, 11" x 14". One reason I love imaginative sketching is that it allows me to defy the laws of nature. Within the special realm of the sketchbook page, solid steel can be twisted, stretched, and raised up off the ground. Inanimate objects can be made to live and breathe. When I sat down to sketch each of these cars and trains at a historical museum, I posed in my mind "what if?" questions: What if a car reared up on its wheels or flopped down on the ground like a dog? What if a steam locomotive inhaled a deep breath of air into its boiler? These questions helped me to focus on the single point I wanted to make with each sketch, rather than making arbitrary changes in the forms. I found that it helped to walk around each of the objects several times, looking at them from all angles. Interacting so closely with the things I was drawing excited my imagination because it made me feel actively creative rather than being just a passive observer. —JG*

USING ANTHROPOMORPHISM

Anthropomorphism is the attribution of human characteristics to nonhuman things. As a sketcher, you can use anthropomorphism to create humorous twists on reality. Look closely at what you are drawing. Do the limbs of that tree suggest human arms? Does the front of that truck look like an absurd caricature of a face? Let the associations flow. You will discover that almost anything can appear vaguely human in one way or another.

Animals are particularly good subjects for anthropomorphic sketches. Artists all through the ages have developed ingenious ways to make animals reflect human traits. Today, the tradition of humanized animals is carried on by children's book illustrators and film cartoonists. You can look to these sources for ideas about how to make the forelegs look like arms, how to use clothing, and how to make animals look natural on two legs. Then, when you are at the zoo, look for the individual characteristics of each animal you sketch. Exaggerate these characteristics by putting them in human terms. If a polar bear seems lazy, you might try clothing him in a bathrobe and slippers, and giving him a recliner to sit in. A giraffe might appear to you as an aloof intellectual. A pair of glasses and a book under his foreleg will convey the idea. Have fun with this the next time you are at the zoo. For many of our sketch club members this is the most enjoyable form of animal sketching they have tried.

Manmade objects such as vehicles and buildings make especially good subjects for anthropomorphism. Look for arrangements of shapes that suggest faces. Just about any pair of headlights or windows can be stretched by the imagination to look like eyes. Any opening could form a mouth. When you recognize a face hidden in your subject, try to coax it out just a little more in your drawing—enough so that it is evident to the viewer, but not so much that you lose touch with the original forms that first sparked your imagination.

Whether or not you want to add a face or a pair of arms to an inanimate object, you can suggest a very convincing sense of life by twisting and stretching the form. Imagine that the form you are drawing is completely pliable, as if it were made out of a kneaded eraser. You can bend it, twist it, compress it against the ground, stretch it into filaments, and even inflate it like a balloon. Whether you are sketching a refrigerator, a patio chair, or a delivery van, these changes in the physical properties of the material will suggest that the form is responding to strong, lifelike internal forces just like a living thing.

ADDITIONS AND COMBINATIONS

Additions and combinations are two imaginative methods that can be used in almost any circumstance and are among the simplest to do. Additions are simply any invented element included in your sketch. In an earlier section we mentioned adding elements out of context. This is certainly a type of addition. More commonly, we prefer to use strange fantasy additions such as elves and dragons, especially when we are drawing natural subjects with a fairytale feel. There need not be any logical or narrative connection between the thing you have sketched and the thing you add. Any juxtaposition is acceptable and, indeed, the more bizarre the better.

You can make additions after the sketch is finished. We often stop by coffee shops after a day's sketching to browse over the day's work. At that time, we sometimes get inspired to make additions. Don't be afraid to make additions to old sketches. A little imaginative reworking can greatly improve an otherwise bland sketch.

In a combination sketch you join two or more objects seen on location to form a strange new object. The results are surreal: a policeman with a parking-meter face or a jukebox on wheels. Try to avoid *seeking* subjects to combine—in other words deciding beforehand that you want to draw a tree/automobile combination and then running out to find each subject. Part of the joy of combinations is the unpredictability of what you will end up uniting.

FEEDING THE IMAGINATION

To enrich your imaginative sketching, expose yourself constantly to the imagination of others. Your local library is a rich storehouse of creative imagery. Children's books are full of fine examples of everything we have mentioned in this chapter. Borrow a few children's books from your library and browse through them, paying special attention to the way the illustrator has used anthropomorphism, exaggeration, and changes in scale.

Fantasy and science fiction novels offer another source of inspiration. Many great imaginative artists have been avid readers of fantasy and science fiction. The reason is simple—such novels force you to conjure images that are beyond your day-to-day reality. Your imagination is inevitably developed through such exercise.

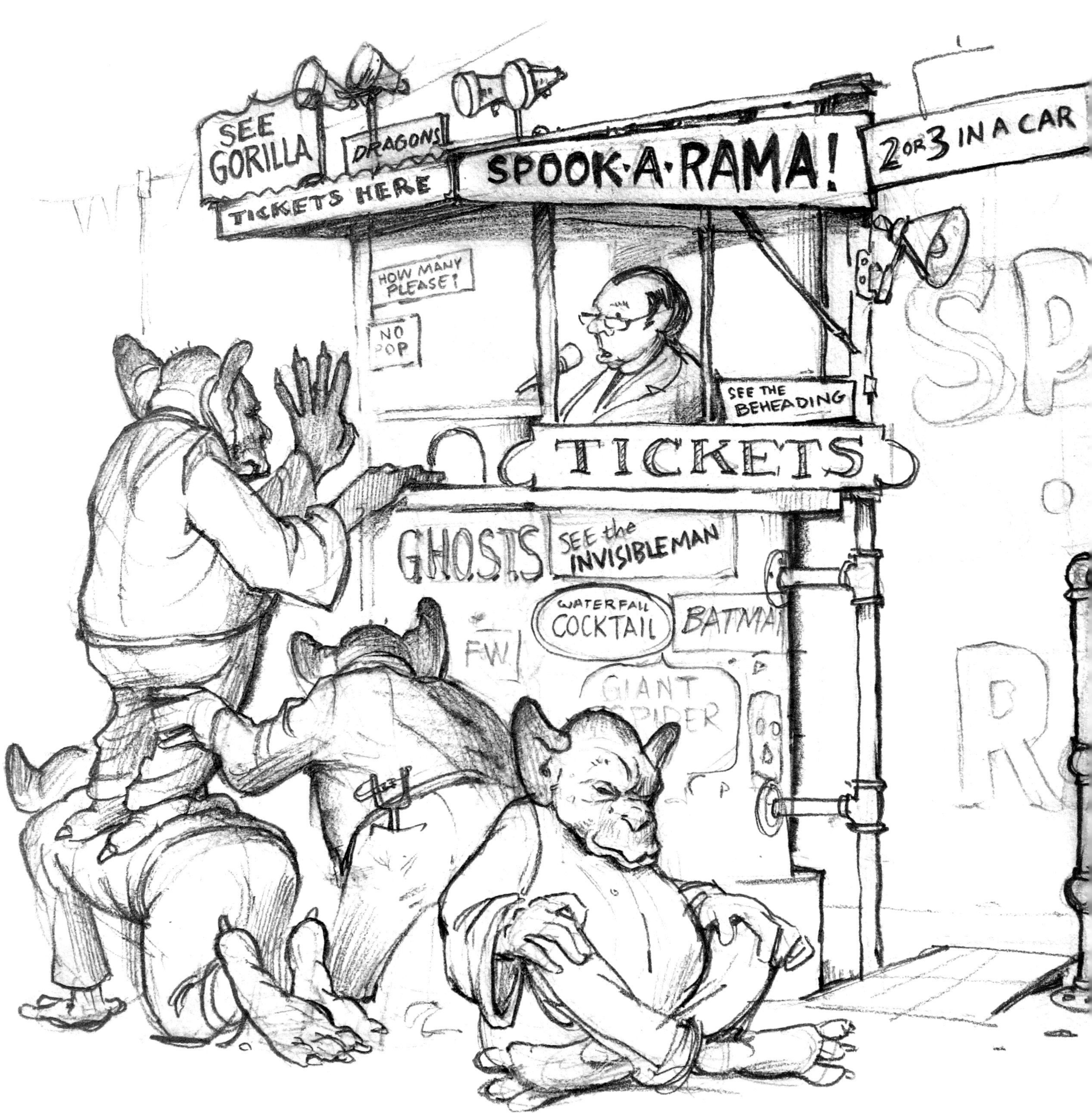
SEE GORILLA
DRAGONS
TICKETS HERE
SPOOK·A·RAMA!
2 OR 3 IN A CAR
HOW MANY PLEASE?
NO POP
SEE THE BEHEADING
TICKETS
GHOSTS
SEE the INVISIBLEMAN
WATERFALL COCKTAIL
BATMA
GIANT SPIDER

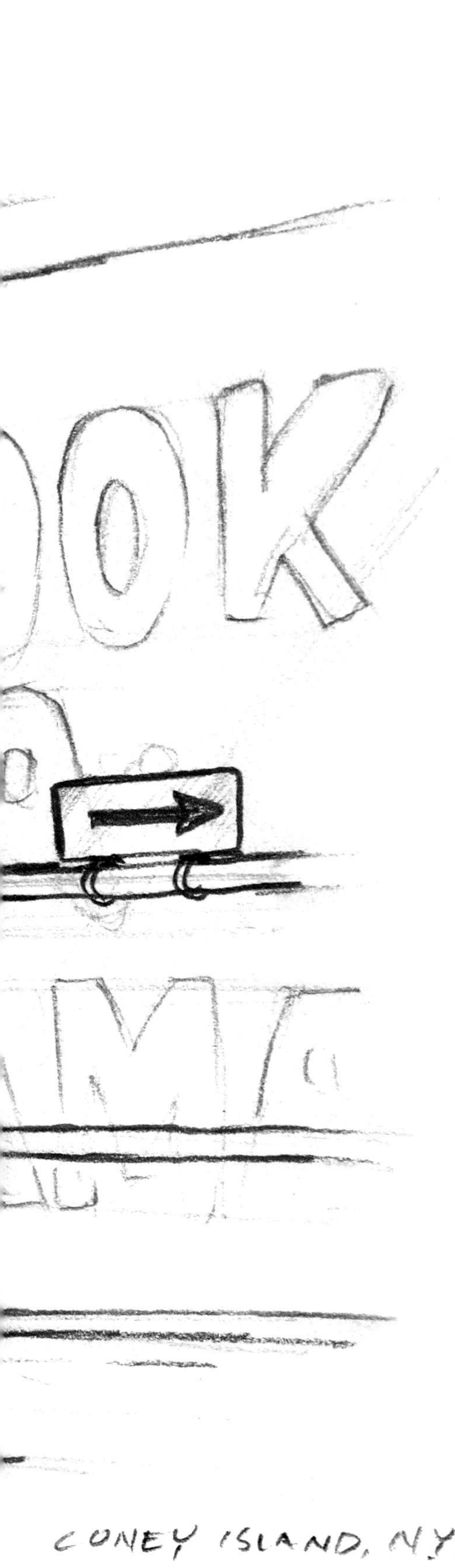

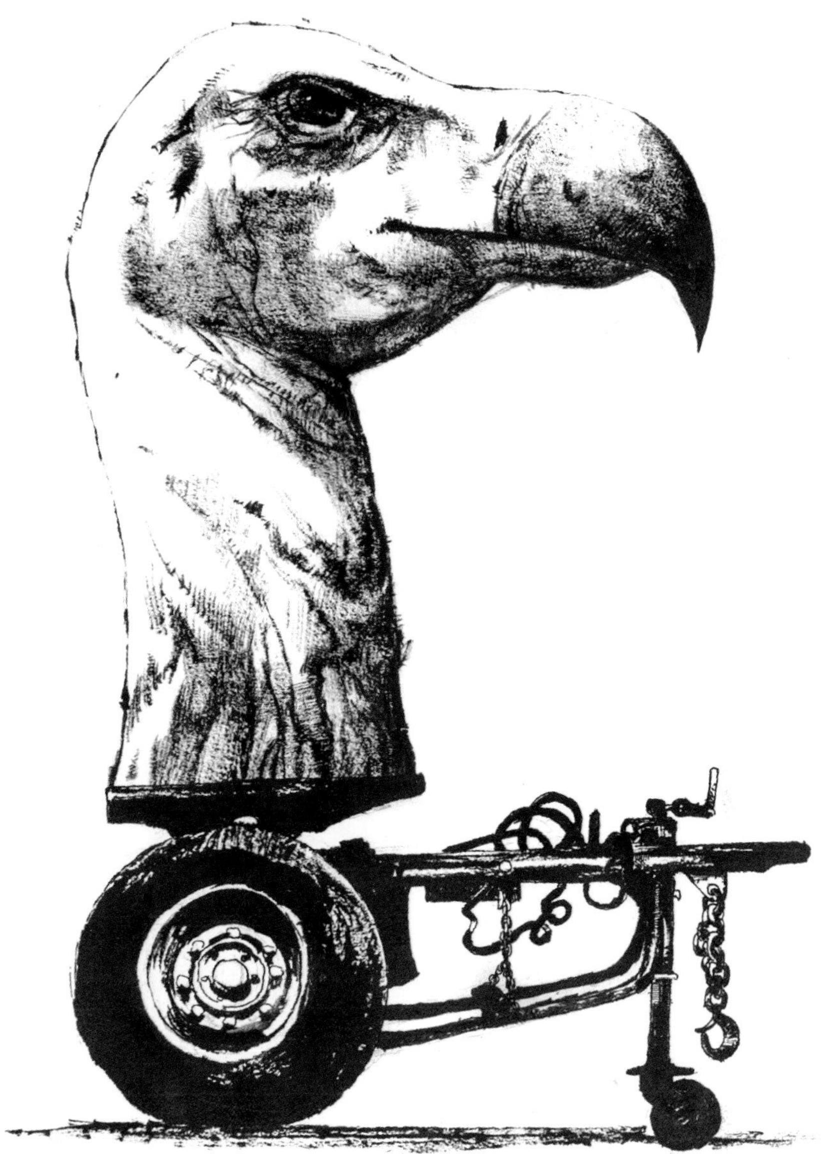

▲ **VULTURE/TRAILER-HITCH COMBINATION,** *dry brush on illustration board, 6¾" x 10". When I sketched the trailer hitch I had no idea that it would eventually be used as a transport for a giant vulture head. But this kind of odd combination is what happens when you allow your imagination to do the decision-making. After drawing the trailer hitch, I found the sketch rather boring, yet because I had no immediate ideas on how to improve it, I stuffed the sketch in between the pages of another sketchbook. Later that day at the natural history museum, I stumbled upon my earlier sketch and was inspired to find something appropriate to mount on the hitch. The stuffed vulture virtually cried out to me as I passed by. How could I resist? The worn, leathery texture of the vulture made a perfect contrast to the rather crisp forms of the trailer hitch. —TK*

◀ **CONEY ISLAND SCENE,** *pencil on drawing paper, 9" x 12". All by itself, the ticket booth for Coney Island's dilapidated horror show would have been made a plenty interesting subject for sketching, with all of its odd signs and spotlights. But something in me reacted to the absurdity of the entire setting—where I had set up to sketch. Giant green plaster spiders and leering one-eyed statues watched over me as I worked. It seemed only natural to include a few spooks out of my own head to add a little twist to the scene. I sketched them in lightly with the #2 office pencil before reinforcing some of the lines with a softer graphite pencil. To keep the area around the seated creature's head from becoming too cluttered, I lightened up on the pencil lines describing the signs and strengthened the lines bordering his head and ears. The same trick was used around the four-fingered hand of the standing creature. —JG*

BECOMING MORE IMAGINATIVE

Once you become sensitive to the dormant imaginative potential of ordinary objects and places, your mind will be constantly active, transforming what you see into future imaginative sketches. You may find yourself speculating about the world around you in ways you never have before. "What if bedspreads were made of ivy leaves?" "What if radios grew on trees?" "What would a pineapple the size of a delivery truck look like?" And the most enjoyable aspect to these speculations is that they provide you with an ever-increasing reserve of ideas for sketches. It becomes a self-sustaining cycle. The more you sketch imaginatively, the more you will notice interesting twists on the things you see. And the more interesting twists you notice, the more you will want to sketch imaginatively.

If you lack confidence about your ability to be imaginative, don't feel alone—many others have felt the same thing at first. Yet the fact is that most of the artists who initially felt hesitant later discovered that being imaginative on-the-spot renewed their excitement about sketching in a way nothing else could. Give yourself the opportunity to become excited about imaginative sketching.

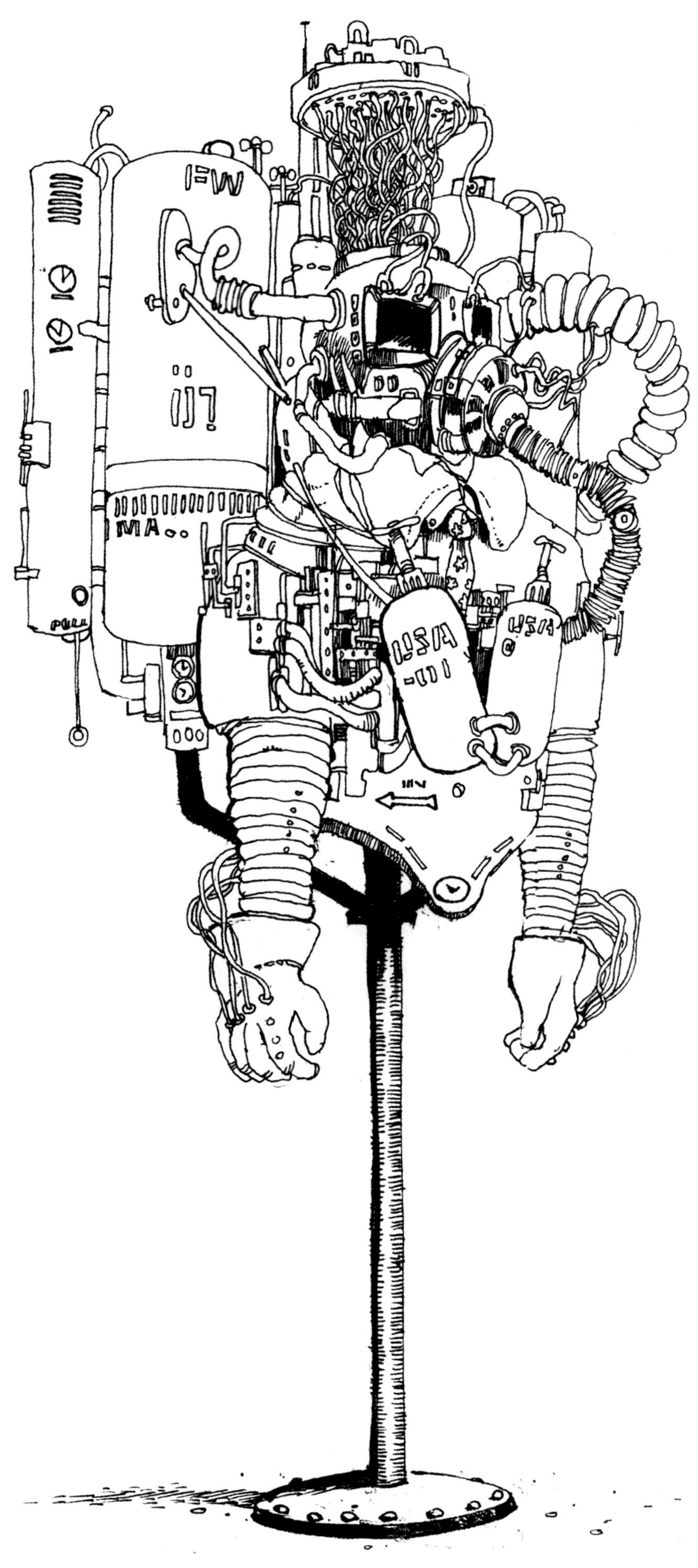

◀ **ABSURD FLIGHT SUIT,** *technical pen on smooth paper, 7½" x 11". The complexity of an old-fashioned flight suit on display at the Smithsonian Museum in Washington, D.C., fascinated me, but as I sketched it, I found it tedious to record factually detail for detail. So, on top of a rather complete underdrawing of the actual suit, I began improvising details that the original designers of the suit had never dreamed of. More than one casual browser of my sketchbook has been stopped cold by the oddness of the forms. In detailed sketches like this, I enjoy picking a theme and repeating it as a means of unifying the elements of the subject. In this sketch I repeated the theme of the spaghetti-like wires both above the head and near the hands. The segmented tube form also appears in numerous places throughout the sketch. —TK*

▼ **STUMP WITH AXES,** *technical pen on smooth paper, 7" x 9". I left my studio one afternoon with the intention of sketching tree-bark texture for use in a painting I was working on. What I ended up with was altogether different. The tree I had chosen to sketch looked so weathered that I imagined it as a stump. So I drew it as one. I began texturing the bark and I got the idea to add a woodsman's axe stuck in the top of the trunk. I penciled it in lightly, but as I did I got the idea for a smaller axe beside it. For balance I penciled in another axe on the left-hand side, and then another one in the middle, and so on until I ended up with the drawing you see here. I was dissatisfied with my sketch in pencil, so I decided to use pen and ink as a means of accentuating texture. By this time the sun was setting and I returned home, where within two hours I had completed the stump sketch. —TK*

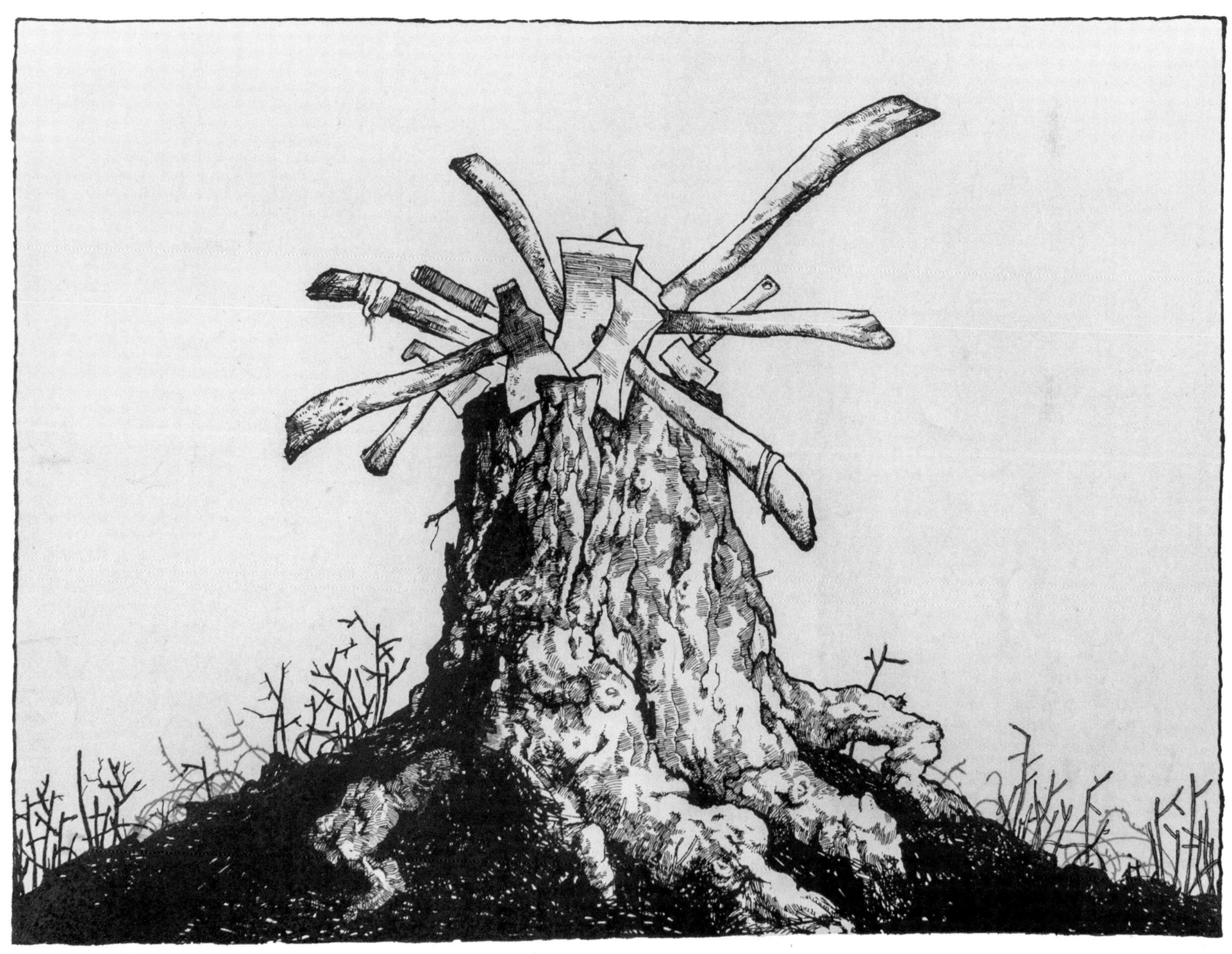

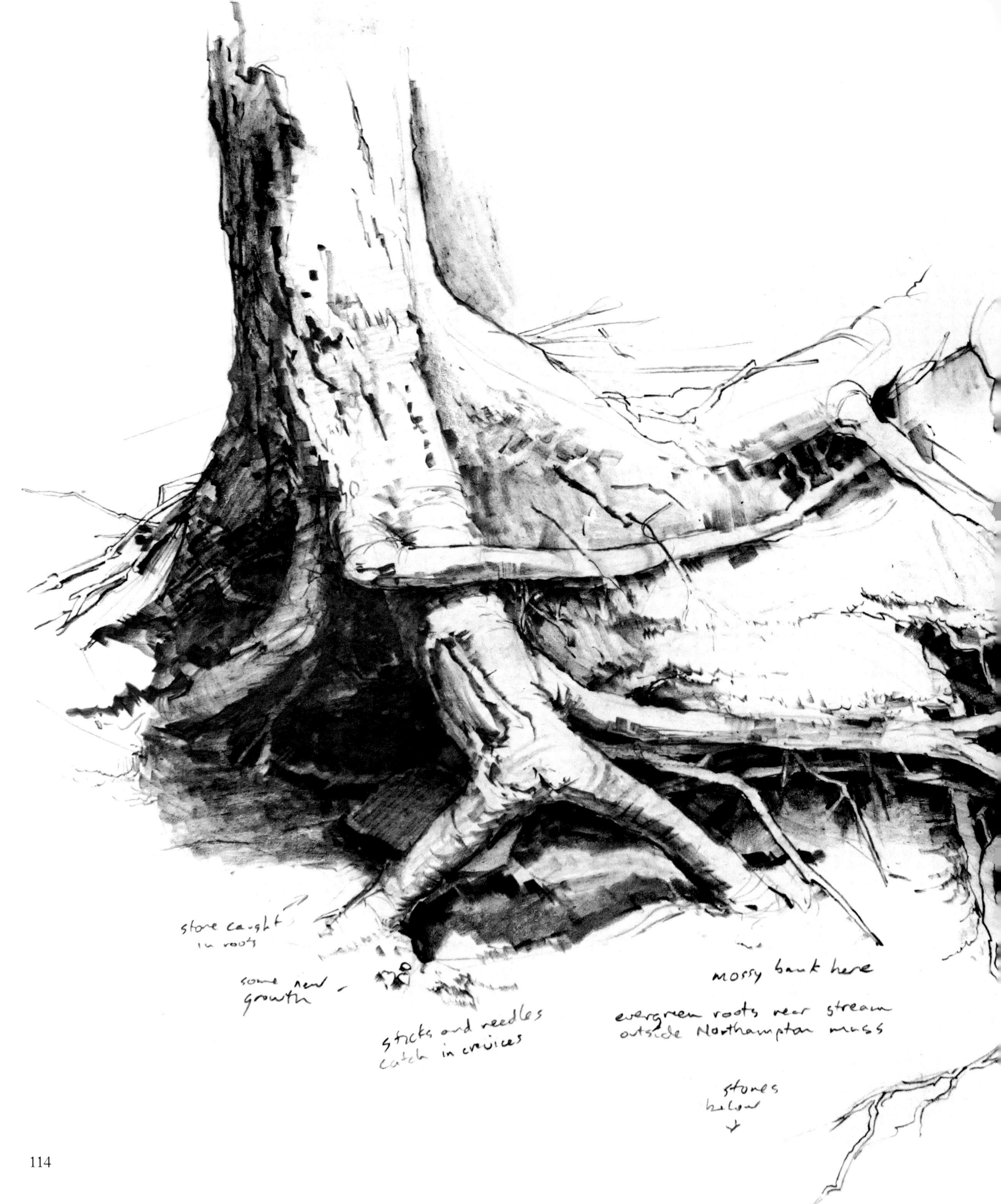
stone caught
in roots
some new
growth
mossy bank here
sticks and needles
catch in crevices
evergreen roots near stream
outside Northampton mass
stones
below

Studying Nature

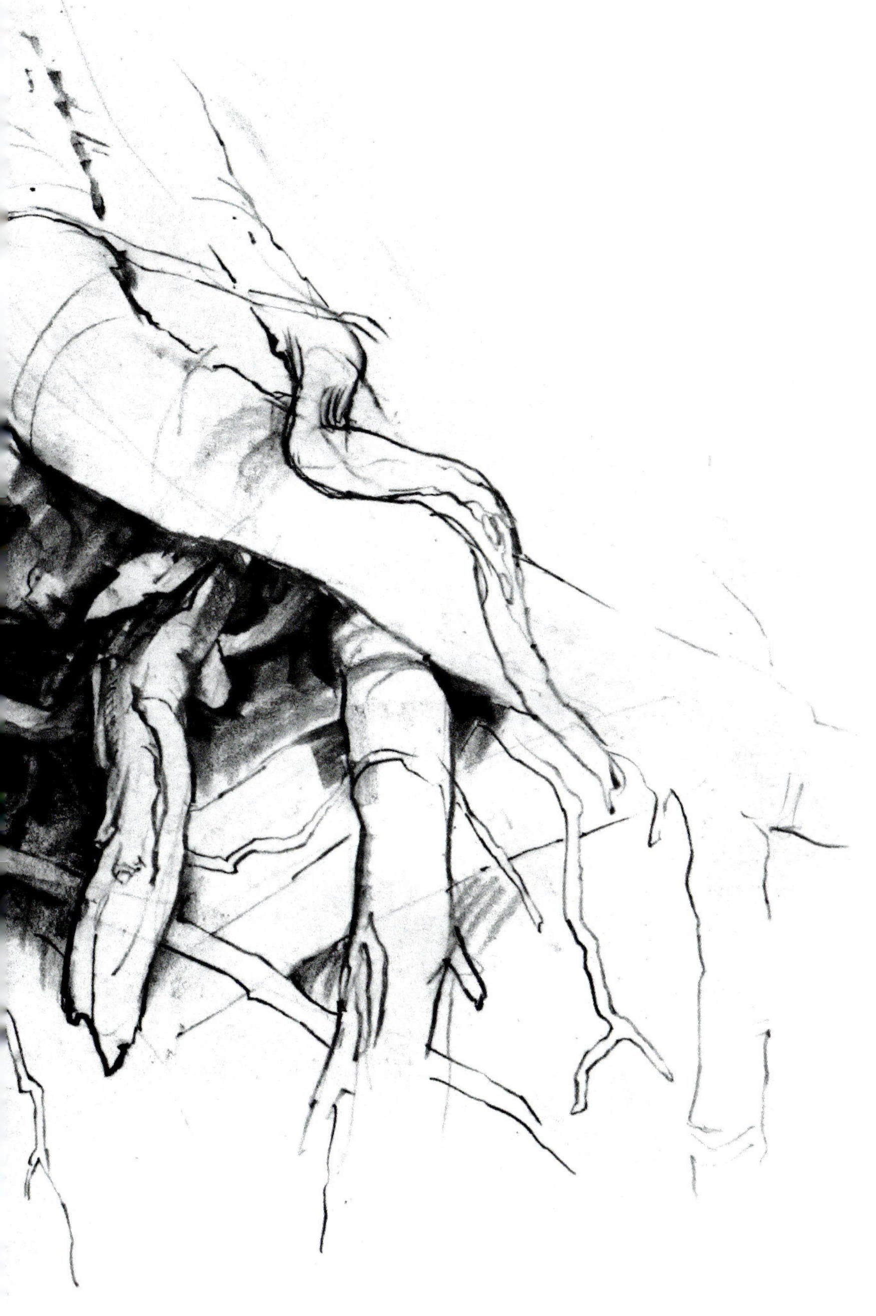

ROOT FORMATION, *hard and soft pencils on smooth paper, 11" x 14". Far from the noise and hurry of the city, I wandered down a dry stream bed in eastern Massachusetts. I discovered this arrangement of tree roots, which had been undercut by the current. For the next two or three hours, I explored the miniature landscape before me, with the overlapping tendrils reaching into the soft shadows under the bank. I was seeing with the eye of the naturalist and the artist simultaneously. My goal was to draw what I saw objectively, but at the same time I was appreciating the beauty of its structure. —JG*

SWERVE NOT FROM NATURE, for Art stands firmly in nature," advised the great master of the northern Renaissance, Albrecht Dürer. For Dürer, studying nature was fundamental to the creation of art. Are things any different for us today? Although our world has changed greatly, no one can deny that something special still happens when you stand before nature with nothing but a fountain pen and a sketchbook. Your senses sharpen as a brisk breeze sweeps over your face. Your breathing relaxes; your mind clears. You realize that with little more than a few brief motions of your wrist you will record forever the beauty that you see before you. Yet you will have done more than document what you see. You will have learned something about the way the natural world is constructed. You will have paused, perhaps for the first time, to really *observe* the twisting of a tree trunk or the growth patterns of a rosebush.

In this chapter we will discuss some of the insights we have gathered from doing on-the-spot nature sketching. The information deals with mental attitudes as well as practical techniques. Both of these will help you get the full benefits of nature sketching.

NATURE: YOUR PERSONAL DRAWING WORKSHOP

Most people respond very well to on-the-spot sketching from nature. Some say they have made more progress in one afternoon sketching a tree root or a cluster of rocks than they had in months of traditional figure and still-life lessons in the studio. Why? Perhaps in the face of nature we are less self-conscious, less subject to conventional thinking, less apt to rely on formulas. Nature demands a patient, selfless approach that allows us to break away from the mannerisms that can keep us from growing. Also, the forms of nature are quite forgiving. There is more allowance for error when you draw a gnarled tree than when you draw a building or a person. When you sketch a bush, for example, you have none of the worries about "getting a likeness" that can impede your progress as when you make a portrait of a friend. And nature meets you at your level. If you are drawing for the first time, you will discover a great deal about basic shapes, light and shade, and proportion. If you are a more advanced artist, you will find in nature a wealth of knowledge about such things as edges, reflected light, and value control. Further, if you have a scientific turn of mind, and a knack for drawing, you will observe and record the processes and forms that until now you have studied only in books. Nature will fulfill you no matter what you bring to it.

THE EXPERIENCE OF NATURE SKETCHING

Friends have told us that they look forward all week to the chance on Sunday to sketch another grove of trees in the park. It's easy to see why. When you are in nature, you feel tranquil, peaceful, contented. The worries of the routine life seem to slip away. Time stands still. Hours pass like minutes. Perhaps you've heard people say the same thing about fishing. The real joy for both fishermen and nature sketchers alike is the chance to be outdoors with no schedule. The experience is an end in itself. You may come home with a good catch or two, but even if you return empty-handed, your time is well spent.

The special state of mind of nature sketching is important not just because it is enjoyable, but also because it helps to create good sketches. Nature seems to require a certain attitude from you when you sketch. Patience is the cornerstone. You can't hurry a study from nature, because you will overlook too much. If your time is limited, you can patiently observe one small detail. For example, suppose you have a few minutes to spend waiting in a friend's living room. You notice a fishtank across the room. Do

▶ **STUDY OF A TREE AND BUSH,** *watercolor and wash on illustration board, 15" x 20". This sketch is a view of a hillside done in preparation for an oil painting. My interest was in the bush and tree, so to focus on these, I deleted a whole forest that extended behind both of them. After a minimal pencil underdrawing to establish general forms, I began by briskly brushing in a suggestion of the foliage, using a large brush and a medium-value wash. Strands of grass were scratched into the wet wash with the end of my brush. When everything was dry, I used a small brush to begin adding details. The tranquility of the environment inspired me to occasionally set aside my sketch and simply lie flat on the meadow, absorbing the warm sunshine and hushed sounds of the nearby forest. —TK*

you have your sketchbook? If so, you can do a quick nature study. Concentrate on drawing a single fish. Observe its motion and form. Even a couple of minutes is enough to learn something new. Imagine what you could do with two hours at the aquarium next Saturday.

So, the first requirement is patience. You are thinking "study," not "sketch"; "observing," not "looking." The second requirement is that you set aside the desire to make a "pretty picture." Your goal should be understanding, not self-expression. All the rules of composition and the methods for creating mood are important in their own right, but they can interfere with a fresh way of seeing that is needed to get deeply involved with what you see. If you are doing a study of a rose, for instance, it's best to avoid the temptation to add a graceful curve to the stem or to eliminate the withered petals. Although other chapters in this book describe methods to change what you see for certain purposes, what's important here is that you closely observe what is actually there.

John Constable, the great nineteenth-century landscape painter, called this objective state of mind the "pure and unaffected manner." Paul Cézanne put it this way: "Whatever may be our temperament or our power in the presence of nature, we have to render what we actually see." When you approach nature, keep these things in mind, and you will experience the same joy in being in nature that has delighted many artists from earliest times till the present.

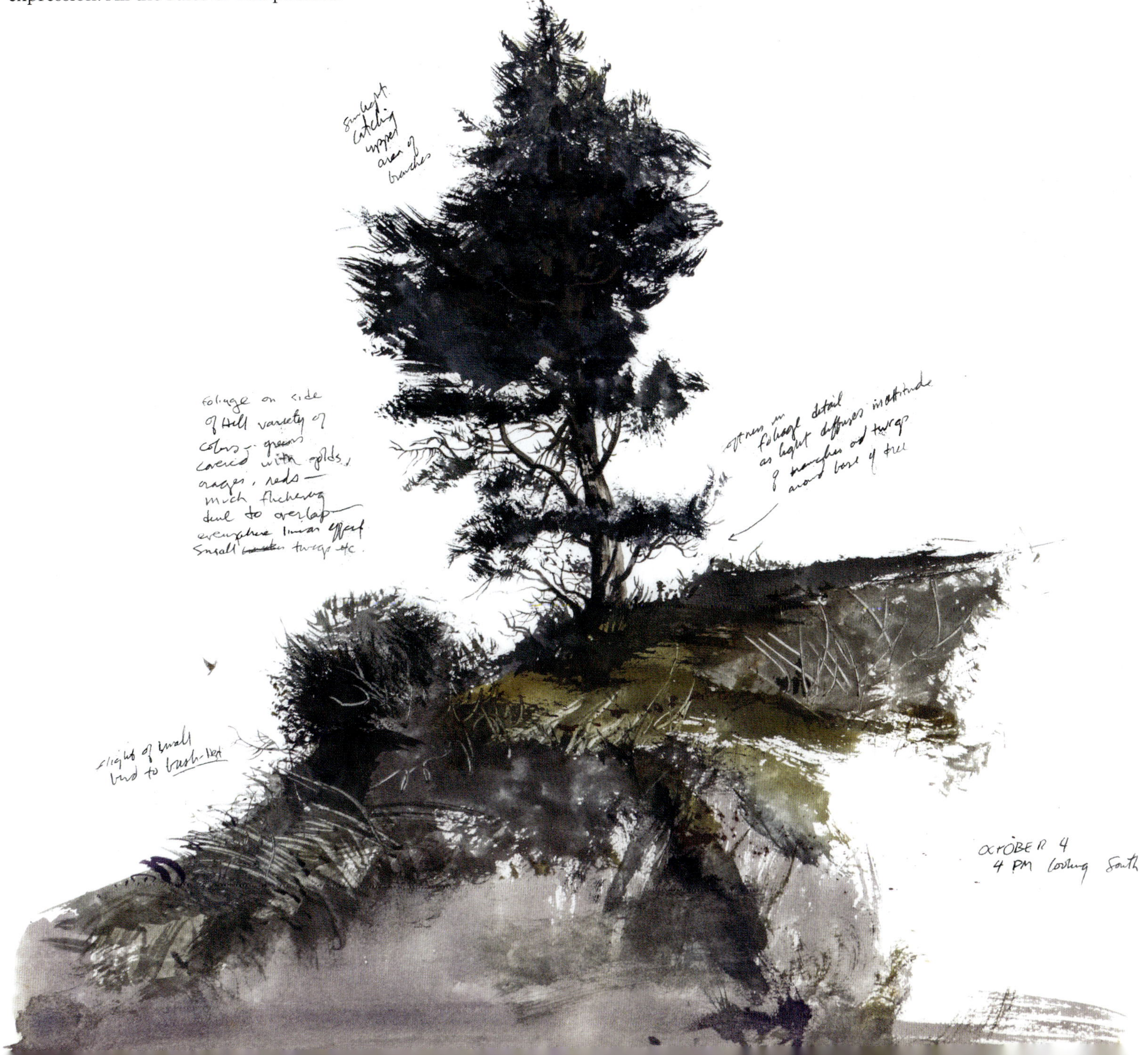

PLANTS

Plants probably attracted you early in your development as an artist. Can you remember your first careful drawing of a flower or a tree branch? Plants are a good place for the nature sketcher to begin. Of all the forms in nature, plants are the most forgiving to inaccuracy. Also, plants are static, allowing you to concentrate on form without being distracted by motion. Most of all, plants are accessible no matter where you live.

Choosing your subject matter is an important factor in sketching plants. Most students try to tackle something large and complex like a tree, and then proceed to begin detailing leaf by leaf. Before long, the sketcher feels frustrated in the confusion of detail, and often resorts to technical gimmickry to finish the sketch.

The way to avoid this problem is to begin with simple subjects. An acorn, a leaf, a branch with a few leaves on it, even a carrot from the supermarket are all ideal. We recommend you begin with a pencil on smooth paper. Use the pencil directly on your paper, following the contours of your subject as carefully and patiently as possible. When you drop branching or leafy forms, it helps to think in terms of construction. Draw the central stem first, and then add the adjoining twigs and leaves. If you do this, you will be sensitive to the way the plant actually grew and developed. A sensitivity to structure gives you confidence as you draw by helping you understand what you are drawing. It seems obvious, but you would be surprised at how few remember to do it.

An excellent approach for sketching a tree is to render it in silhouette only. This means that all the forms are drawn in black, as if they were cut out of paper. This is one of the easiest ways to sketch a tree, because you don't have to worry

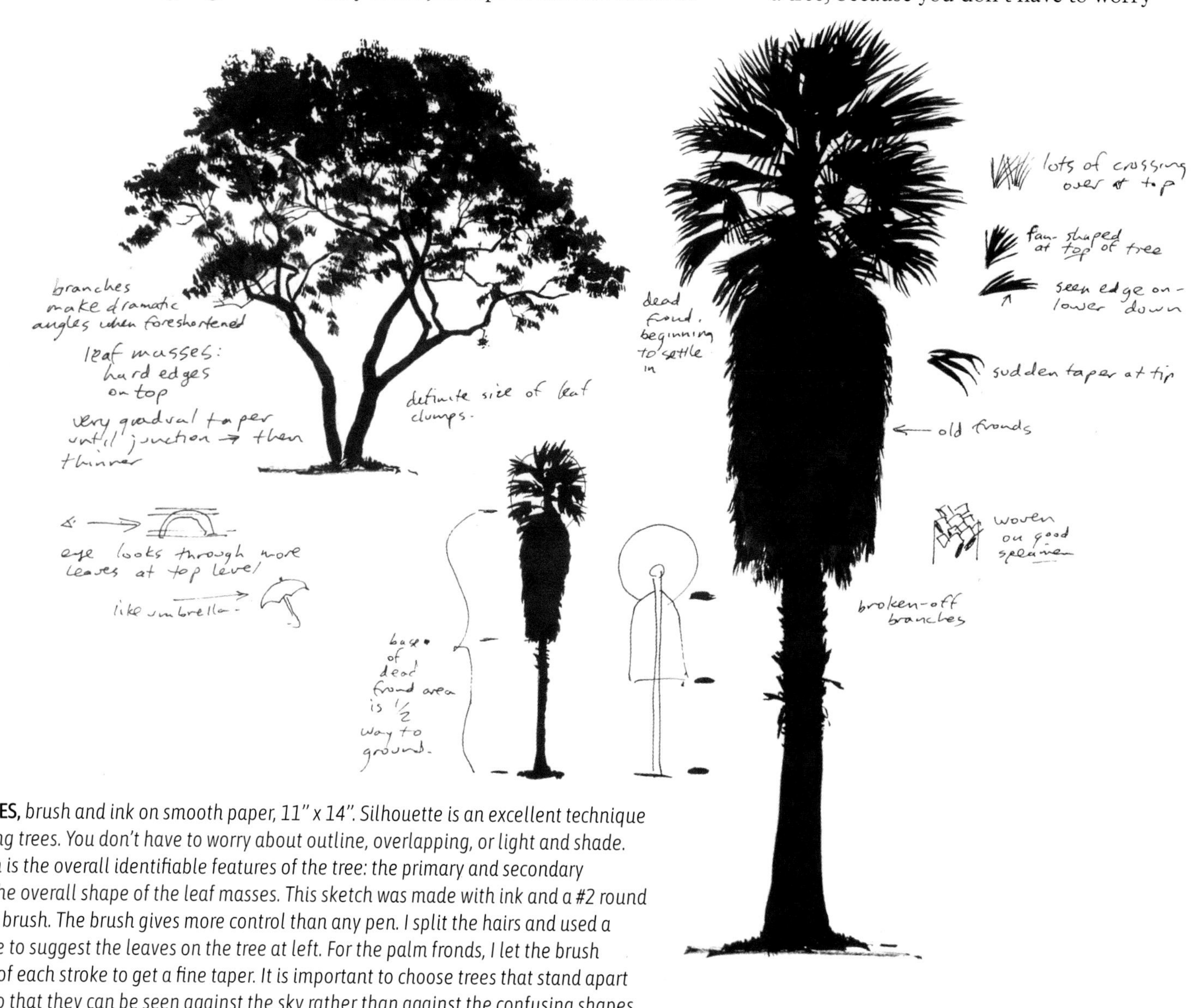

TREE SILHOUETTES, *brush and ink on smooth paper, 11" x 14". Silhouette is an excellent technique to use for studying trees. You don't have to worry about outline, overlapping, or light and shade. The only concern is the overall identifiable features of the tree: the primary and secondary branching, and the overall shape of the leaf masses. This sketch was made with ink and a #2 round sable watercolor brush. The brush gives more control than any pen. I split the hairs and used a stipple technique to suggest the leaves on the tree at left. For the palm fronds, I let the brush gently glide out of each stroke to get a fine taper. It is important to choose trees that stand apart from all others so that they can be seen against the sky rather than against the confusing shapes of other trees. It also helps to work during the hours of twilight, when everything falls naturally into silhouette. —JG*

about overlapping or outline. All the large masses of leaves fall right into place, and the overall shape of the tree comes across very clearly in the drawing.

Here's how you go about it. You can select any tree, as long as it stands clearly against the light of the sky. In a grove or a forest, you may have a difficult time seeing where one tree ends and another begins. But at dusk or early morning, in a park or a field, the conditions will be ideal for seeing the silhouette. Be sure to sit far enough back from the tree so that you can comfortably see the entire form without turning your head. We find the best medium to use is brush and ink, because it allows you to vary the thickness of line quite easily, an advantage when you are drawing tapering branches. The brush can also be used as a stippling tool to suggest the masses of leaves. Be aware of not only leaf masses, but also "sky-holes," the areas in which you can see the sky behind the tree. In nature there is a judicious balance between the sparse skeleton and the opaque lollipop. Pay attention to balancing these two tendencies and your trees will look convincing.

Keep these silhouette studies of trees. They will be valuable to you when you do landscape paintings in the studio. As a result of your tree studies, you will have engraved in your mind some of the basic rules that nature has established. For example, you'll intuitively remember next time you draw or paint a tree that a branch tapers gradually along its course, thinning at each point where another branch splits off from it. At the same time, you will be acquiring a sense of the enormous variety of tree shapes. You don't have to know the Latin names of the trees or get involved in any extensive botanical theory for this study to be meaningful to you. In practice, this new knowledge will help you evaluate your own work and enable you to see what "looks right" or "looks wrong." If your interest carries beyond that into the area of research, by all means pursue it.

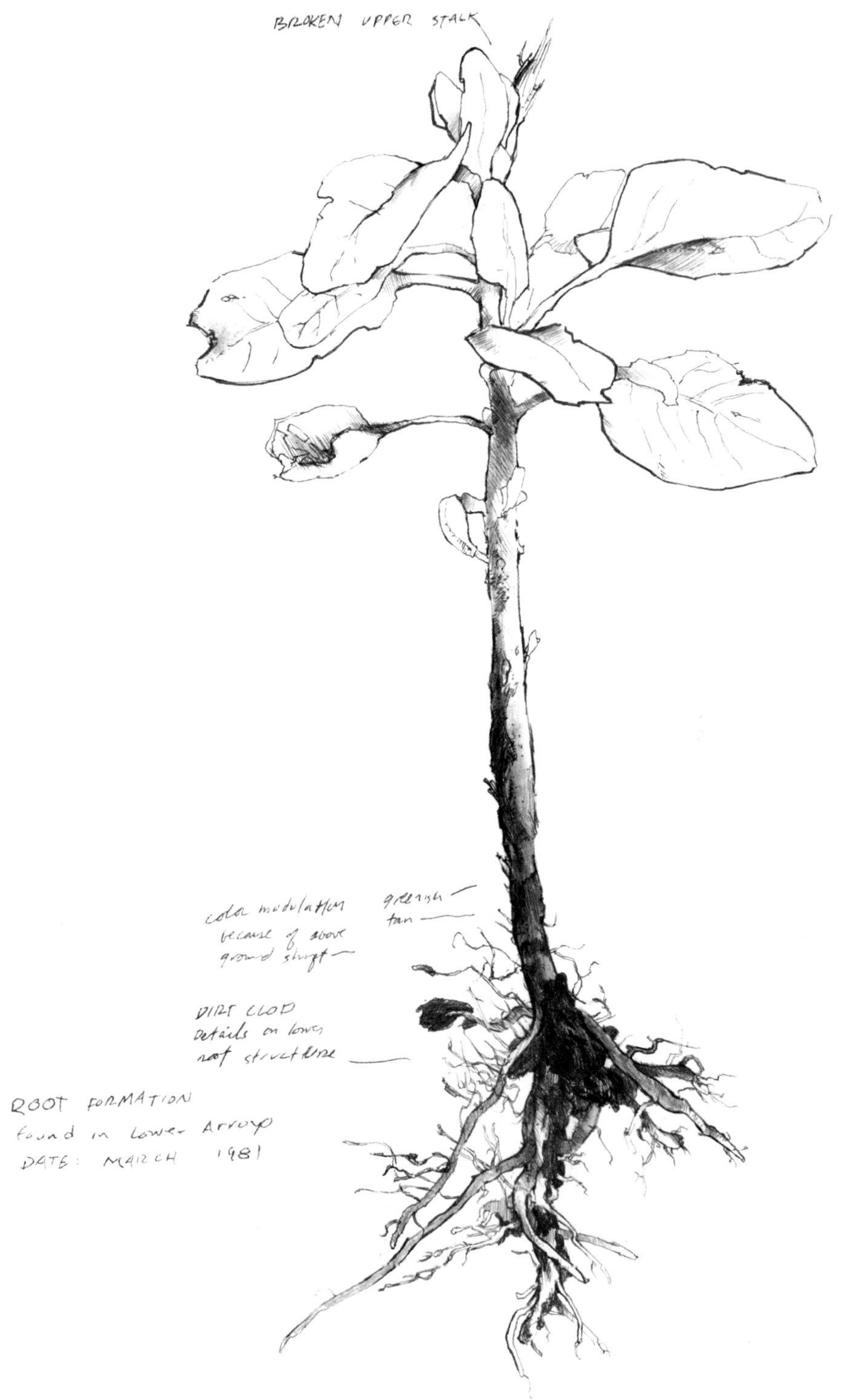

PLANT STUDY, *pencil and ballpoint pen on smooth paper, 11" x 14½". Even a vacant lot can yield a wealth of subject matter for studying nature. This plant was found in a lot located in a suburban area. The locals would have probably referred to it as a weed, but to me the plant was a fascinating example of the structure of roots and the arrangement of leaves on a stalk. To make this sketch, I began with a simple pencil underdrawing to indicate the size that I wanted the plant to be on my page. I enjoy drawing large enough so that I can capture details, but not so large that I lose a sense of intimacy with the sketch. After establishing size, I drew a few of the key details lightly in pencil and then went directly into ballpoint pen, working slowly so as not to lose accuracy. After a linear drawing was complete, delicate tones were added with a 2H pencil. —TK*

▶ **PLANT STUDIES,** *gouache on illustration board, 11" x 14". My most rewarding studies of plants are often made from those simple, easily overlooked subjects, rather than the exotic specimens at botanical gardens. All the plants on this page were found in a friend's yard. I made a special trip out to the yard for three consecutive Saturdays, allowing myself about an hour for each study. The section of geraniums on the right was embedded in a larger bush, and would have been impossible to distinguish if I had not placed a piece of white cardboard behind it. Even though I have looked at geraniums all my life, I only really observed them for the first time when I sketched them, understanding how the new leaflets grow up from clusters, and then as they mature, hang down below the main stalk. —JG*

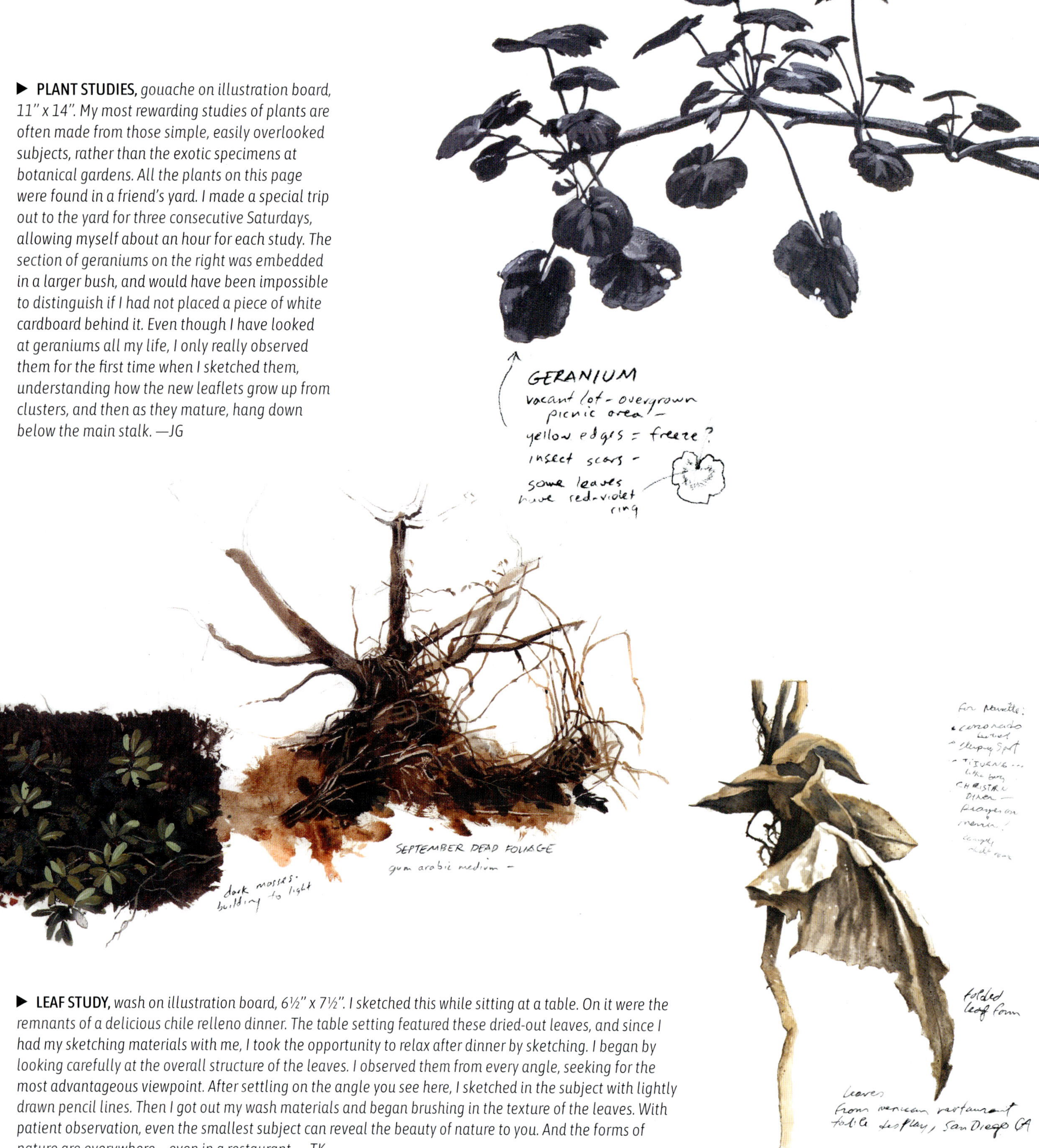

▶ **LEAF STUDY,** *wash on illustration board, 6½" x 7½". I sketched this while sitting at a table. On it were the remnants of a delicious chile relleno dinner. The table setting featured these dried-out leaves, and since I had my sketching materials with me, I took the opportunity to relax after dinner by sketching. I began by looking carefully at the overall structure of the leaves. I observed them from every angle, seeking for the most advantageous viewpoint. After settling on the angle you see here, I sketched in the subject with lightly drawn pencil lines. Then I got out my wash materials and began brushing in the texture of the leaves. With patient observation, even the smallest subject can reveal the beauty of nature to you. And the forms of nature are everywhere—even in a restaurant. —TK*

ANIMALS

We said earlier in the chapter that sketching from nature is like fishing. In nothing is this more true than in animal sketching. You never know what you are going to catch. You learn to be a sly, alert, resourceful observer. You will very quickly acquire a kind of confidence that will keep you undaunted by any failure that you might experience. Every bad sketch buys a dozen good ones with the lesson that it gives. So if you are like most people, you like animals but have never really had the chance to draw them from life. Take that chance now. In very short order, your drawing ability will surpass that of those who resort to the snapshot or who resign themselves to drawing only those subjects that never move.

Since this chapter is called "Studying Nature," you might think we mean you have to draw only animals found in the wild setting. In actuality, your pet dog or cat has as much to teach you about the animal kingdom as does anything else. In overall structure, all mammals share the same basic structural plan, which assumes a variety of manifestations from one family to another. For a fully detailed examination of animal anatomy, you can turn to any of the several excellent books currently available—but for now at least be aware that the experience you gain sketching a dog or cat is transferable to other animals.

Keep a small sketchbook on the coffee table at home in order to record any of your pet's poses that strike you as interesting. Whenever they bite a flea, or curl up by someone's feet, or stand with their nose in the dinner bowl, be ready. In any case, if you own any pet, be it a bird or a lizard or a fish, you've got a handy model for animal sketching.

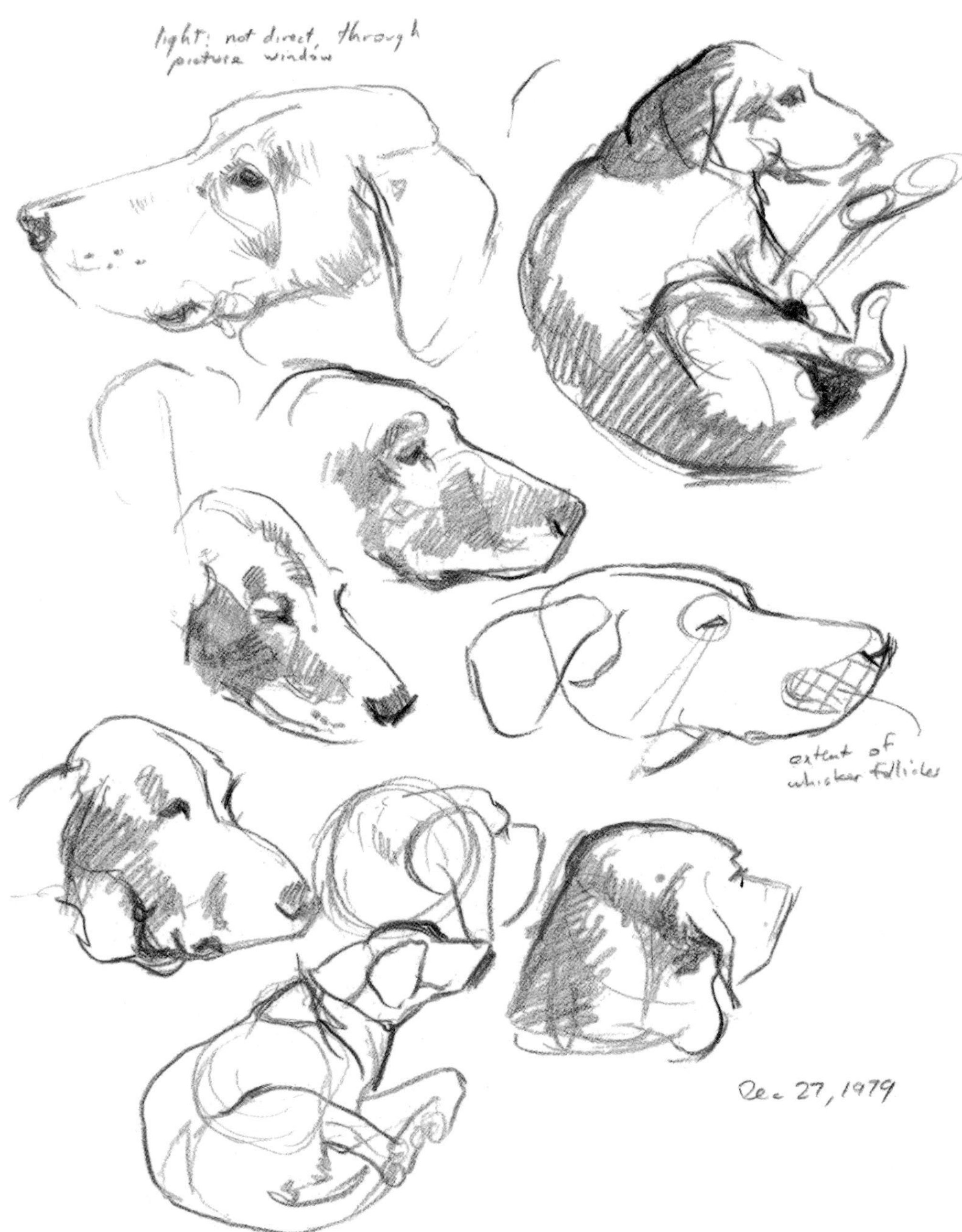

STUDIES OF A DOG'S HEAD, *pencil on drawing paper, 9" x 12". If you own a dog or cat, you have the best opportunity for animal drawing you could possibly ask for. I made dozens of pages of studies of this dog, who seemed to enjoy posing for me. On this page I was interested in the overall structure of the head from a variety of angles. A lot of quick two-minute impressions such as these can be as valuable as a single long, involved study, because they solidify your understanding of the simple shapes. —JG*

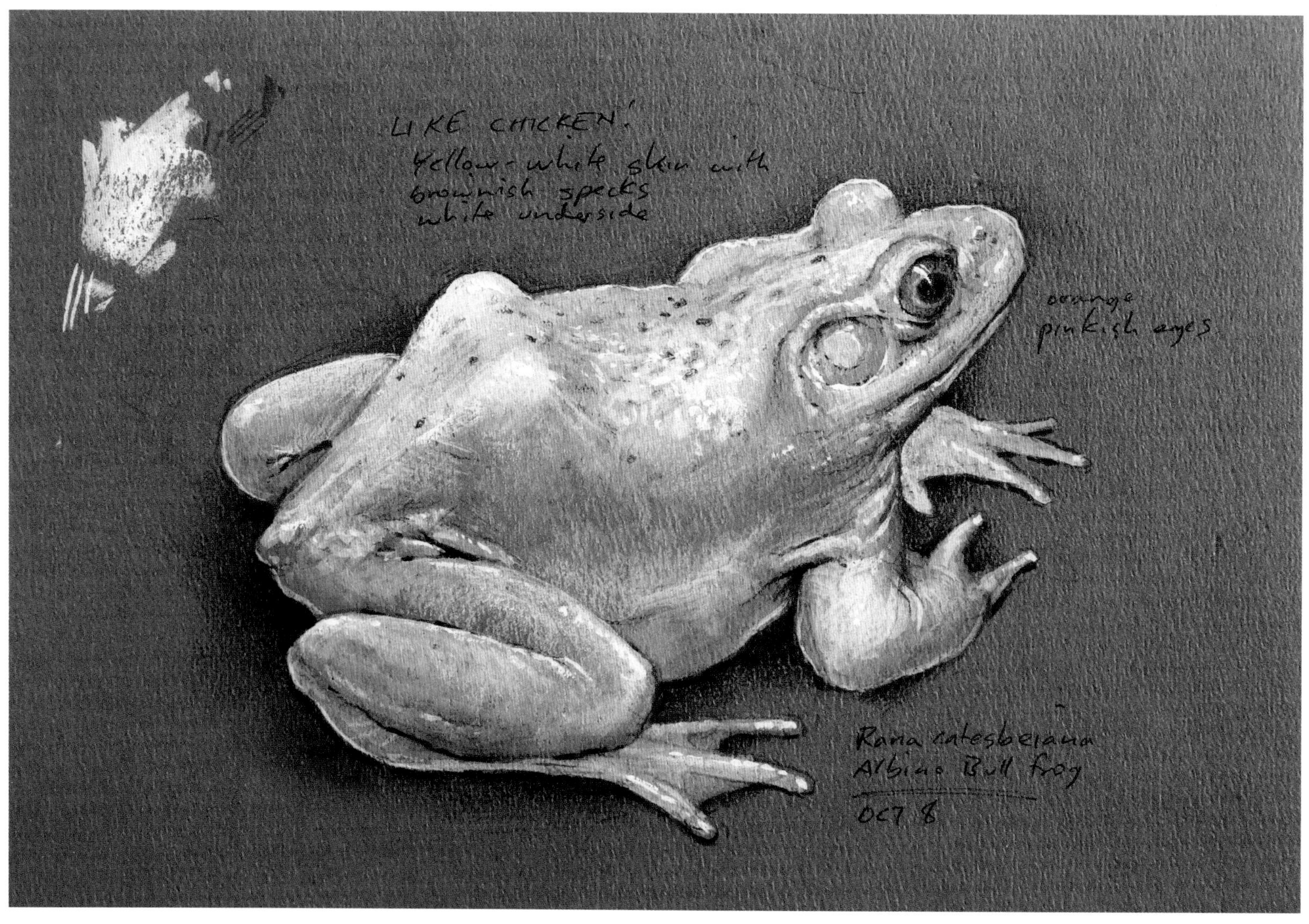

▲ **ALBINO BULLFROG,** *pencil and white gouache on gray mat board, 8" x 9½". This sketch made use of a spare piece of mat board that I happened to throw in with my sketching kit before visiting the aquarium one Saturday. When I found this pale, yellowish specimen of a bullfrog, I knew that I had not only the perfect subject, but also the perfect materials. Using the white gouache very thinly at first, I built up the planes that faced toward the light so that they were lighter than those facing downward. Pure white was saved for the highlights on the pelvis and the eye. After modeling the whites, I used a soft graphite pencil very sparingly to add darks inside the eye and underneath the belly, as well as occasional accents throughout the form to suggest creases and spots. —JG*

▶ **CROCODILE,** *ballpoint pen on drawing paper, 11" x 14". One of my favorite tools for careful studies of line and texture is the ordinary ballpoint pen. In this sketch, it was just as useful for the quick sweeping lines on the crocodile's tail as it was for the scaly skin texture on the close-up studies. In addition, the ballpoint pen is perfect for adding the written notes that always seem to accompany my nature studies. The closest equivalent to the ballpoint pen would have been a #2 office pencil, but unlike the pencil, ballpoint pens never need sharpening. —JG*

SKETCHING AT THE ZOO

The zoo is a paradise for animal sketching because it offers a chance to see, close up, a variety of animals not usually seen elsewhere. You can observe not just the *forms* of the animals, but also their behaviors. During a good day at the zoo you can expect to bring home about eight or nine pages of sketches of varying quality. Students frequently report that they have had a breakthrough with regard to something that had been frustrating them before, and in exchange have been intrigued by a new challenge that had not interested them prior to that.

Most people make the best early progress with elephants, camels, and rhinoceroses. There is no question that these are among the most fun to draw, perhaps because of their clearly defined forms or their rather comical appearance. These animals are also rather slow moving and seem to have a kind of patient understanding of the sketcher, obligingly holding very awkward poses, and eyeing you curiously as you draw.

If you want to try some of the methods that we talked about in Chapter 4, "Capturing Motion," the zoo is a perfect place to go. You can help yourself enormously if you take a few minutes to watch a moving animal before you begin drawing. Here's the reason. Zoo animals have cage habits, which are repeated behaviors that they have learned in captivity. The big cats, for example, with roaming instincts from the wild, tend to pace back and forth in a figure-eight pattern inside their cage. Bears often sit on their haunches to beg for food. Gibbons swing by their arms along the top of the cage. Since these motions are repeated consistently, you can be sure that you will have a chance to observe a given pose a number of times. If you start six or seven sketches on the same page, each of a different pose, you will never have to wait for your model to get back into position.

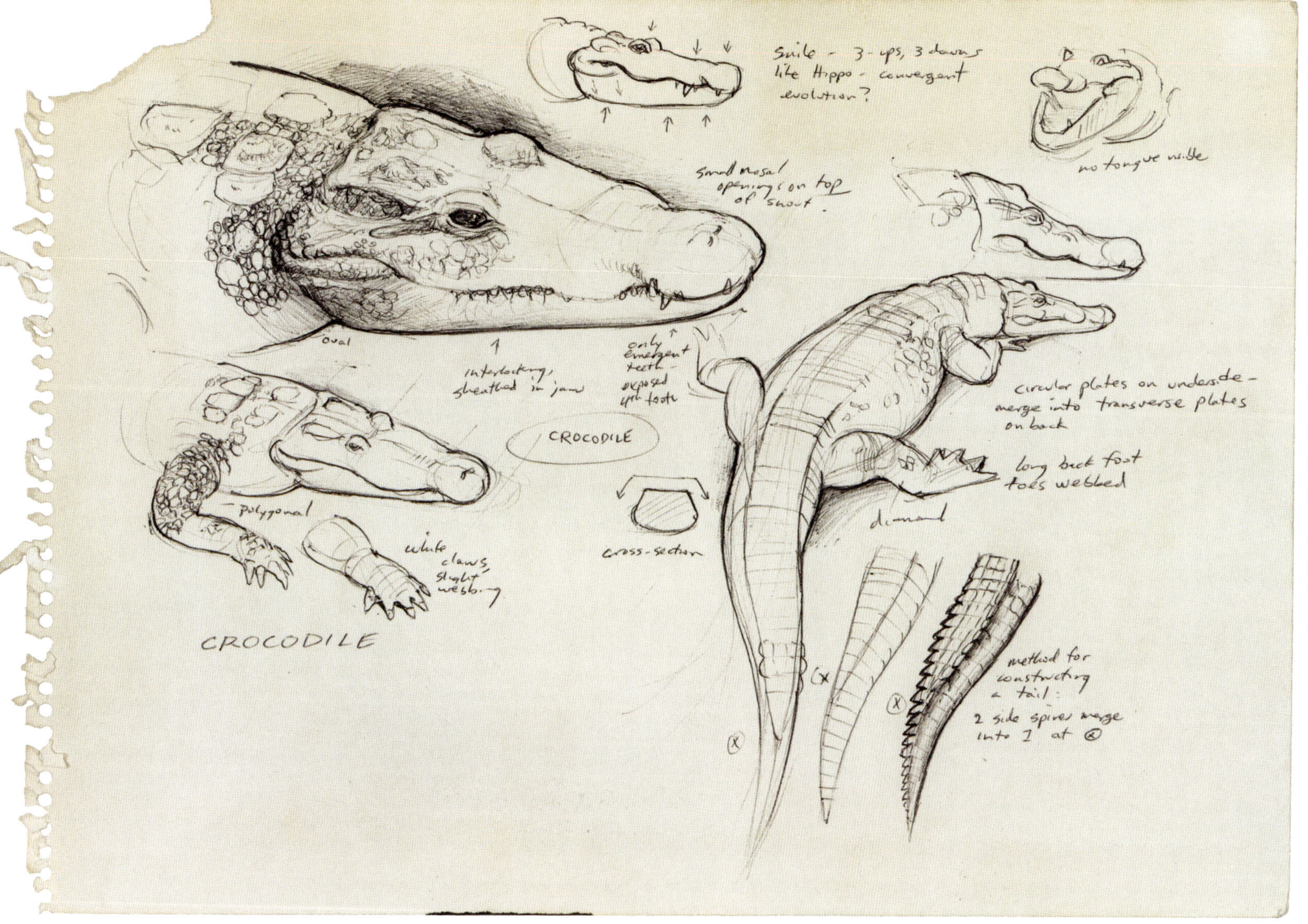

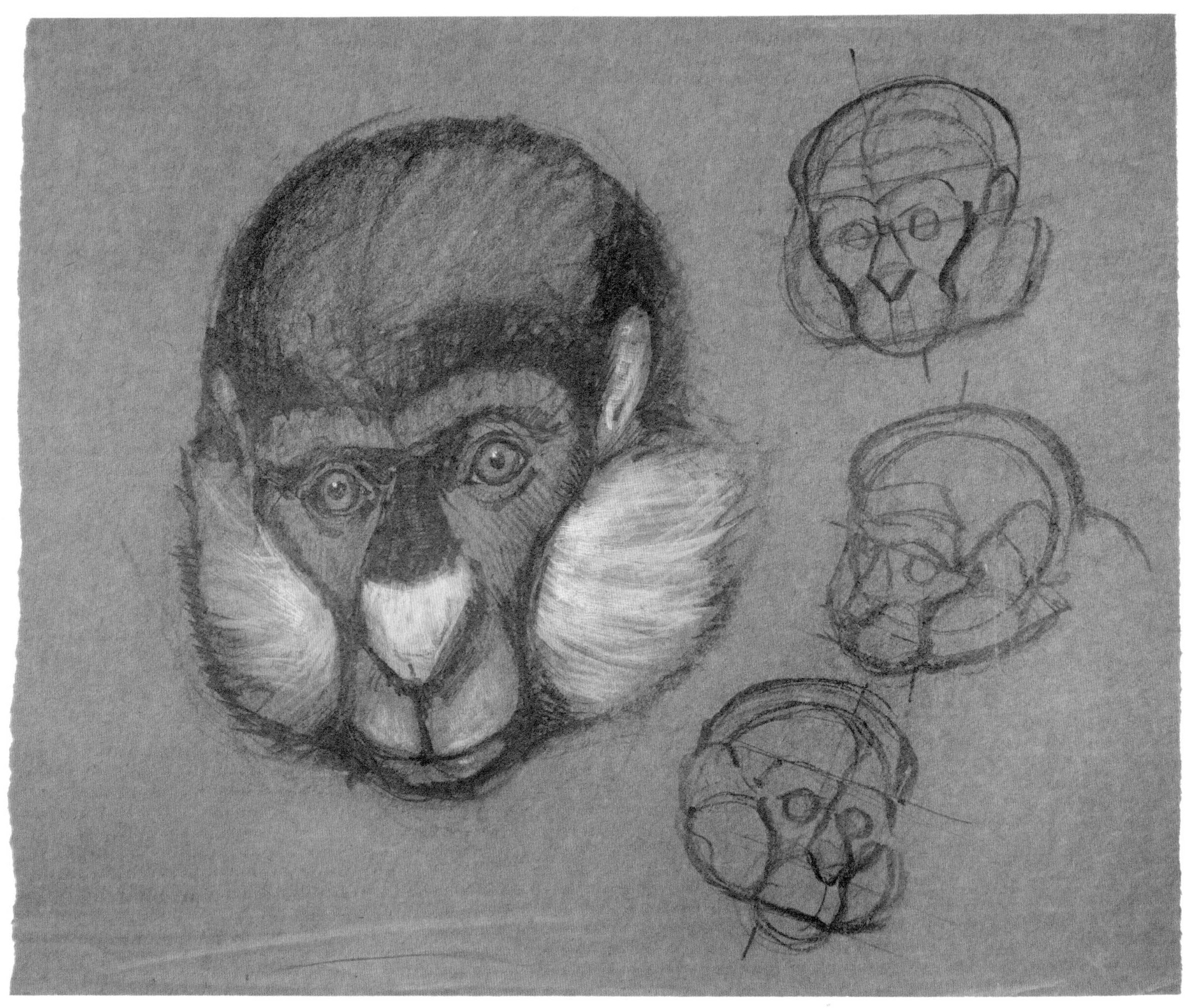

▲ **WHITE-NOSED GUENON,** *pencil and white gouache on brown paper, 12" x 14". How do you get a restless monkey to sit for a portrait? I must have made every kind of strange noise to keep this one against the chain-link fence watching me intently as I drew him. Having him before me, always changing position, was actually an advantage, because I was able to see the shape of his head from every angle, and this gave me a full understanding of its structure. —JG*

▶ **COMPARATIVE STUDY OF HORNS,** *soft pencil on drawing paper, 12" x 18". Wherever an assortment of related species of animals are gathered in one place, I enjoy making a comparative study in which I draw a full page of variations on a theme. This approach could be used to study any feature—hooves, tails, markings, etc. Here I was interested in the three-dimensional spiraling of the horns of African big-game species. Each little drawing is made with an absolute minimum of line and tone. I held the pencil in my fingertips with the palm facing down, in much the same way you would hold a screwdriver. I find that this position gives the hand enough freedom to shift quickly from the point to the side of the lead for making both lines and broad tones. —JG*

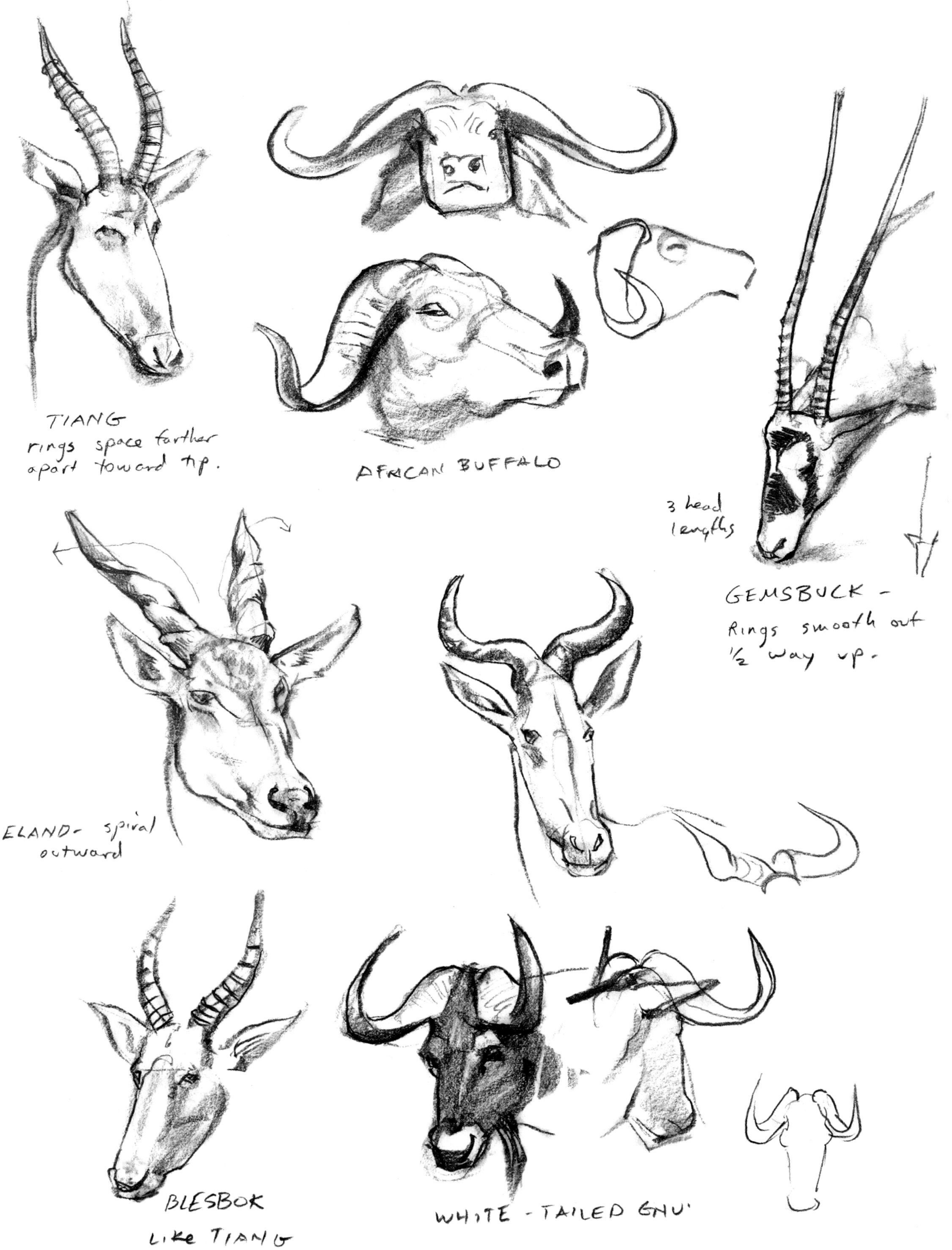
TIANG
rings space farther apart toward tip.
AFRICAN BUFFALO
3 head lengths
GEMSBUCK - Rings smooth out ½ way up.
ELAND- spiral outward
BLESBOK
Like TIANG
WHITE-TAILED GNU

NATURAL HISTORY MUSEUM

As an alternative to drawing the moving animals at the zoo, the mounted animals at the natural history museum offer you a chance to do more in-depth work with your sketchbook. In addition, you have an opportunity to get a close look at insects, reptiles, amphibians, birds, and fish. The only handicap is the lighting in most natural history museums. It's usually quite dark in the exhibit halls, but if you tilt your sketchbook a little bit forward, you can get enough light to sketch by.

This is the place to draw the animal that frustrated you at the zoo, or to study your favorite animal in detail. Look closely at its markings and the direction of its fur. Try drawing the same pose from two different angles. In your mind you will be making constant comparisons between what you are drawing and what you just drew. Somehow this process paints in your visual memory a firm understanding of the animal's form.

Most natural history museums also feature mounted skeletons, which can be very rewarding to sketch. To get the most out of it, we recommend you avoid copying the complex pattern of light and shade on the bones, and instead try to capture the overall gesture and proportion. Try to develop your own simplified mannequin, which can then be used the next time you sketch at the zoo.

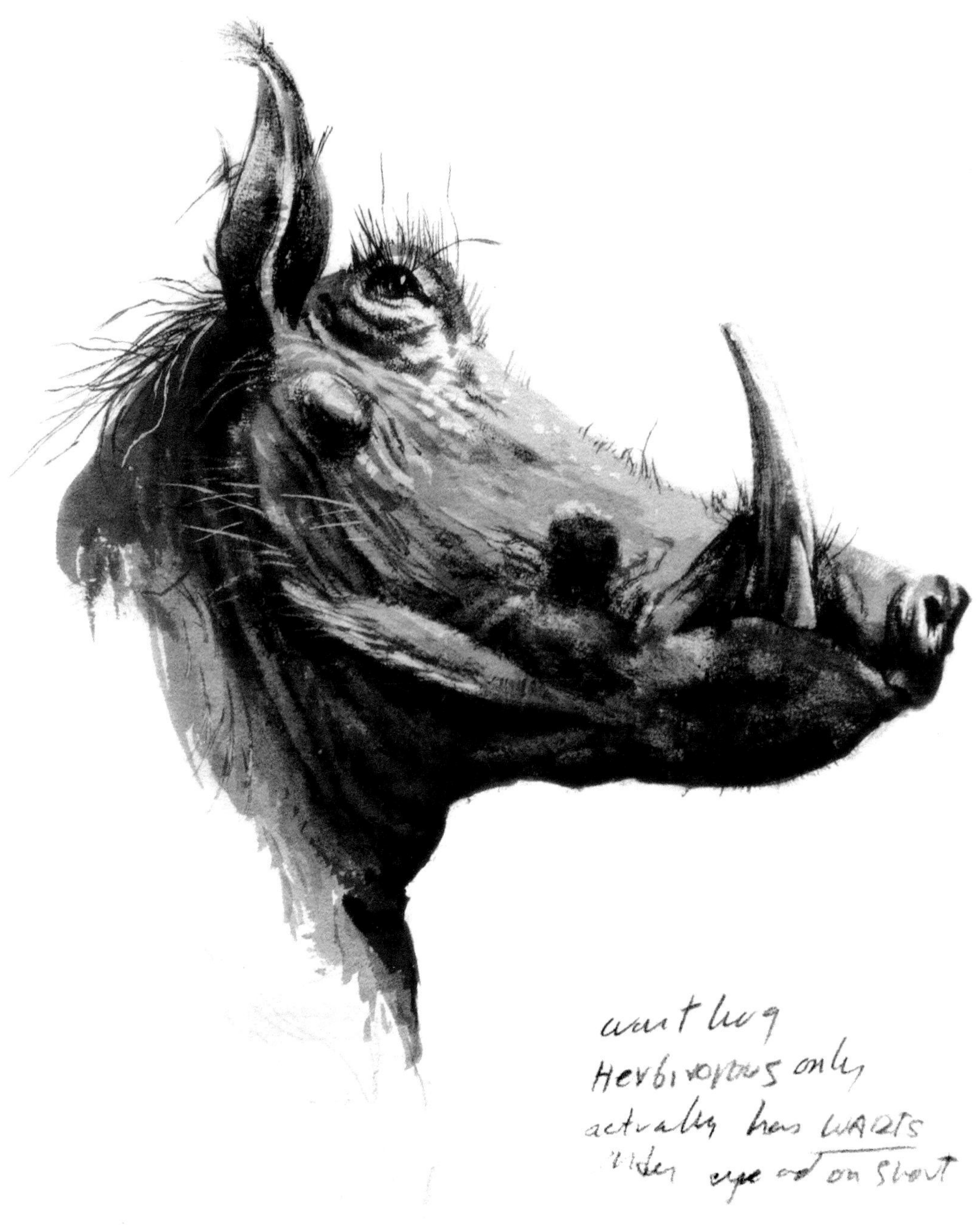

WARTHOG, *wash on illustration board, 6½" x 10". Warthogs are known to be vicious, and luckily for me I didn't have to coax this one into holding still—someone had already done that by mounting him on display in the natural history museum. My chore was simple by comparison: sketch him. To do that I set up my stool as close to the glass display as I possibly could. I picked an angle that minimized the reflection from the glass. Since the form is basically conical, the underdrawing was simply a geometric shape for the head and a few brief indications of such details as the eye, ear, and horn. The texture of this creature was what fascinated me most, and I focused on the wrinkled, leathery skin and the spiny hairs as I applied the delicate gray washes. —TK*

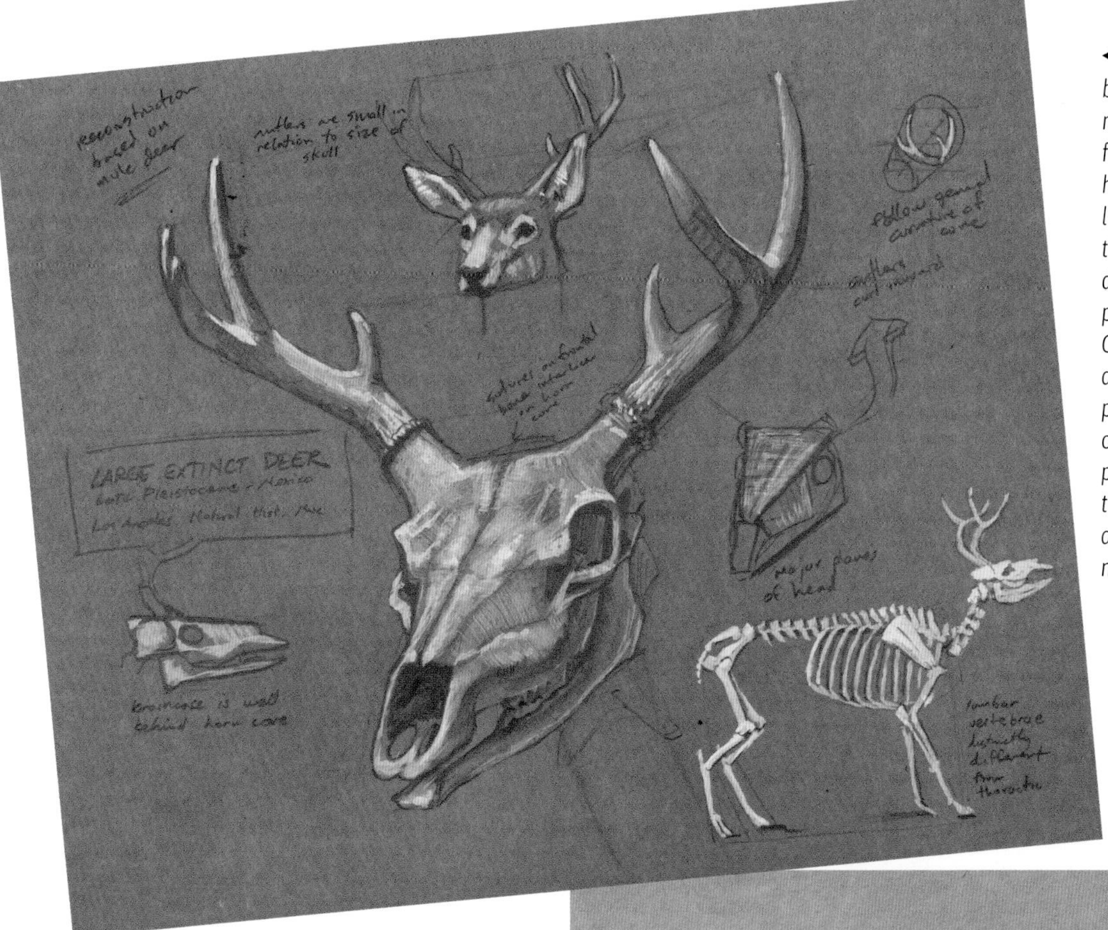

◀ **SKELETAL STUDY,** *pencil and white gouache on brown paper, 11" x 14". In the hallways of most natural history museums, you can usually find a few good mounted skeletons. This deer skeleton happened to be positioned under a single strong light source, so I couldn't resist making a study of the skull in light and shade. Here's a seemingly difficult form that can be mastered in the early pencil stages using the methods we describe in Chapter 3, "Achieving Accuracy." I made sure the antlers cross-checked from tip to tip in the same perspective as the rest of the skull. The sketch of the complete skeleton at right captures the proportions of the whole animal. After observing the bone structure from a skeleton, I have been able to sketch the same animals at the zoo with much more authority. —JG*

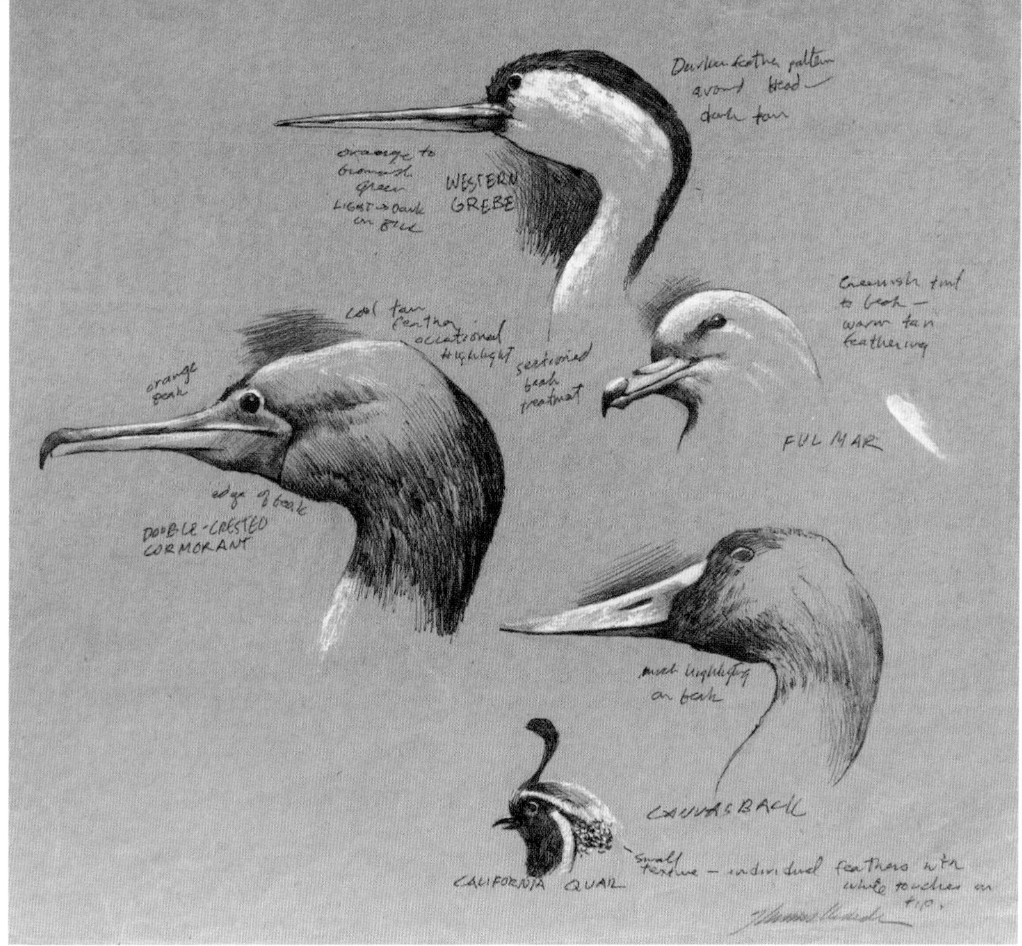

▶ **HEADS OF BIRDS,** *ballpoint pen and white gouache on brown paper, 12" x 15", Bird beaks have never been an overwhelming interest of mine, but through the eye of a sketcher, all nature is fascinating. These comparative studies began as a single study of the cormorant, but as I looked around at the other birds on display at the natural history museum, I became amazed at the variety. If more time was available, I could have done ten times this number and still not have exhausted the supply. To make the comparison as effective as possible, I used the ballpoint pen and white gouache to suggest the texture and coloring of the birds. The written notes serve to remind me of significant features of the birds in the event that I ever need to research any of these for a personal painting or illustration assignment. —TK*

CLOUDS

On those beautiful days when the sky is inhabited by large billowy clouds, we often drop whatever project we happen to be working on and rush to the top of any nearby hill and begin sketching. If the hills are far from where you live, find the highest point in the nearby landscape or the top of a building to perch yourself on. Of all the subjects available for nature studies, clouds are perhaps the most personally inspiring. John Constable referred to clouds as "the chief organ of sentiment" in his landscape paintings, and referred to his constant habit of sketching skies and clouds as "skying." The benefit that Constable received from sketching clouds is still available to us today.

A good technique for cloud sketching is pencil and white gouache on gray or brown paper. The middle tone of the paper corresponds to the value of the blue sky, allowing you to develop the lighter tones of the clouds with the white gouache. Otherwise, using white paper, you would have to draw around all of the light values and laboriously establish the middle tone of the sky with your pencil or marker. The middle-tone paper technique also lends itself to very fast rendering procedures, an advantage when working from observation since most clouds will change drastically in as little as ten or fifteen minutes.

Once you have chosen a given configuration of clouds that interests you to sketch, study it for a moment. What direction is the light coming from? Where is the separation between the light side and the shadow side of the clouds? How close is the value of the shadow side of the cloud to the middle value of the sky? How are the major masses of cloud forms arranged? Now you can begin by lightly indicating these cloud forms with your pencil. This is done only to give you a reference point for applying your paint. We usually use a fairly hard (2H or 3H) pencil to avoid making dark lines on the paper.

Following your pencil underdrawing, begin applying gouache with a #4 red-sable or sabeline watercolor brush. Experiment with different ways of applying the paint. It helps to use a fairly dry paint application to avoid going too opaque too quickly. You want to save your pure whites for the brightest accents of sunlight on the clouds. If you have difficulty achieving enough softness with the gouaches alone, use a white pencil like a CarbOthello or Conté white.

Be aware of unusual cloud sketching opportunities. If you have a window seat on a daytime airline flight, you have a grand view of the clouds that would have overawed the nineteenth-century landscape painters. From this vantage point, you can easily observe the variations in altitude of different cloud types, the boiling masses of a thunderstorm, and the rippled texture of an ordinary overcast cloud layer seen from above. In this situation, it would probably not be wise to risk spilling any white paint inside the airplane, so you may want to rely instead on white chalk or Conté on middle-tone paper, or else simply use a ballpoint pen

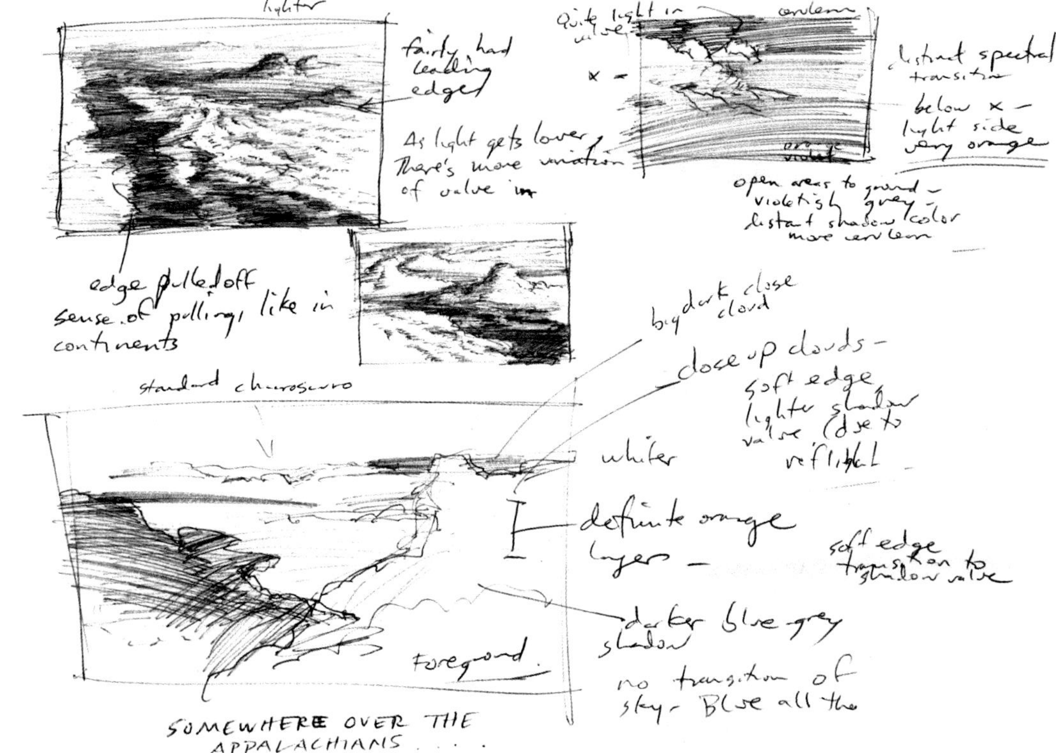

◀ **CLOUD STUDIES,** *ballpoint pen on drawing paper, 9" x 12". By contrast to the previous cloud study, this page of sketches represents a very analytical approach—the why rather than the what. I made the observations while looking out the window of a jet airliner. Over a period of about two hours, I made about six pages of studies like this one, sketching and writing as fast as I could to capture the fleeting effects. The written notes are at least as important as the drawings in helping to refresh my memory of what I observed. —JG*

▶ **TWILIGHT IN GOLDEN CANYON,** *pencil and white gouache on brown paper, 8½" x 11". This craggy silhouette caught my attention during an evening hike in Death Valley. Like many parts of the Southwest, this region contains dramatic rock forms free from the blanket of vegetation. —JG*

or pencil on white drawing paper. Since you are moving so fast, you will have to limit your observations to very quick two- or three-minute mini-studies, but certainly your time spent observing firsthand will make you more sensitive to the subtlety of shape and color of the clouds than the person who carried only a camera onboard the flight.

ROCKS AND LANDFORMS

Although rocks and landforms are an important part of nature, many sketchers overlook them as subjects for sketching. The majority of people who go nature sketching find themselves attracted to plants. But once you begin to sketch geological forms, you become sensitive to the variety of cracking and weathering and the contrast between the jutting angular forms of rocky outcroppings and the rounded shapes of stream boulders. The kind of knowledge that you will gain about rocks through sketching is not the same as that of a geologist—you won't be as concerned with technical scientific terms like sedimentary, igneous, and metamorphic as you will with descriptive characteristics of rock types. Sketching actual rock forms gives you an intuitive visual sense of what looks right and wrong, which will guide you in any landscape work that you do in your studio and allow you to rearrange and compose the rock forms and still keep them looking convincing.

The technique you decide to use depends on what aspect of the rocks you want to concentrate on. A patient line drawing will reveal the cracks and contours of your subject. If there is a clear source of sunlight, you might want to concentrate more on form and texture. With larger rock formations, like the face of a cliff or a pile of broken rubble, it helps to conceive of your subject in terms of simple geometric planes. This will lend an overall solidity and authority to your sketch. To do this, simply look for the simple blocklike forms in your subject and sketch it in these simplified terms. Cubes and pyramids are the forms most frequently found in all kinds of geological structures. After establishing this basis, you can concentrate on the textures and subforms.

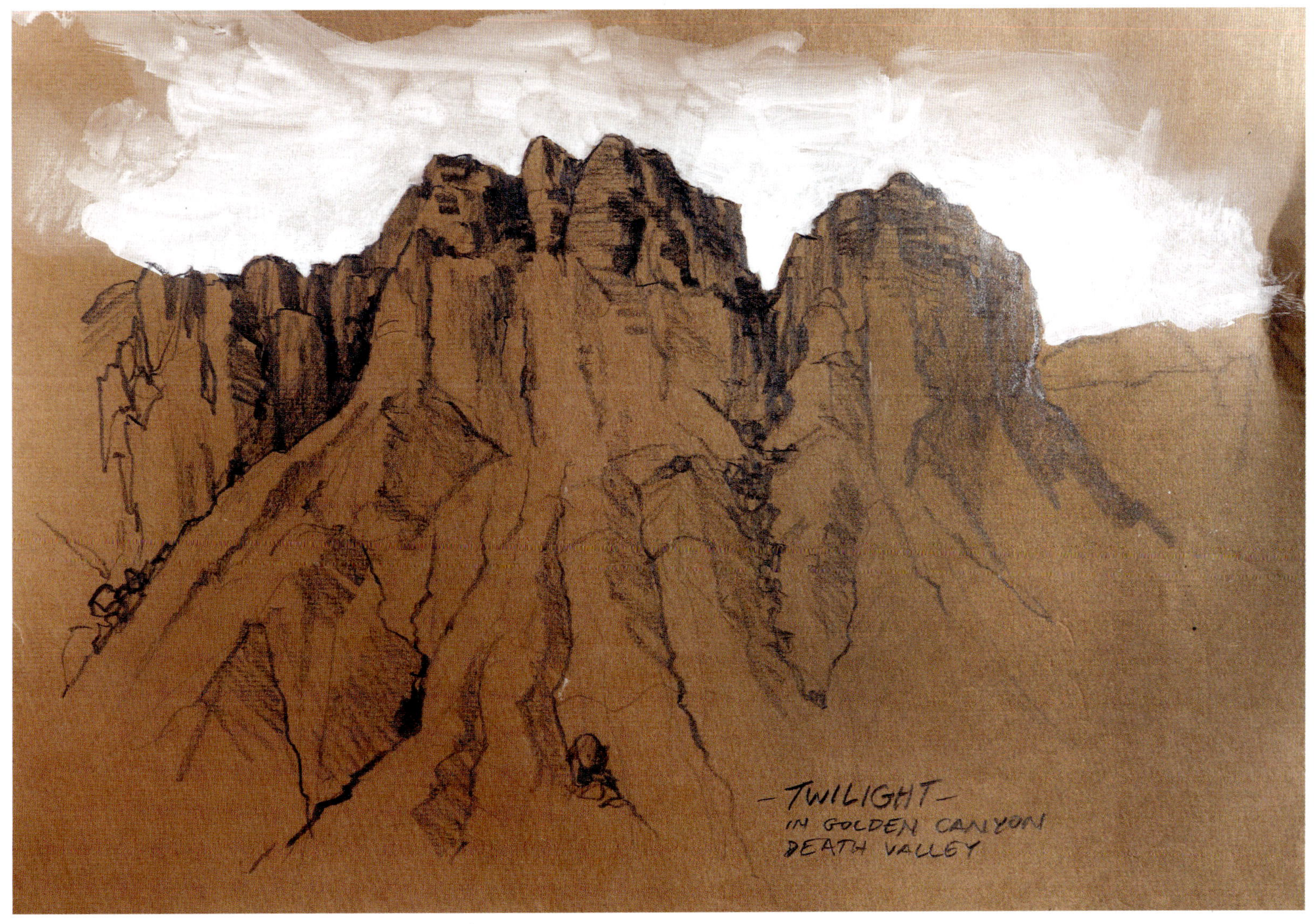

THE BENEFITS OF STUDYING NATURE

Sir Joshua Reynolds, leader of England's Royal Academy and great art theoretician of the eighteenth century, declared that "the study of nature is the beginning and the end of theory." This statement has as much relevance to us now as it did in his day. Whether you have had training in academic art theory—composition, color, rendering, light and shade, etc.—or in the theories of natural science—anatomy, botany, geology, etc.—you will find that nature puts everything you have learned to the test. And nature will reveal to you subtleties that no textbook could ever begin to suggest. If you are an artist wanting to learn more about natural science, or a scientist wanting to learn more about drawing and painting, you can make your study of nature into an exciting opportunity for broadening your interests.

It's a good idea to keep a special sketchbook that's reserved for nature sketching alone. Use a small one—8" x 10" or smaller—and carry it with you whenever you go hiking or camping, or even when you go downtown to the park or the natural history museum. Unlike the quick fleeting impressions that you may do in other approaches to sketching, save this book for the close-up scrutiny of the intricate patterns and forms of the natural world. Make every drawing as careful and precise as you can. In this way, you will advance your ability as an artist very rapidly and see your progress demonstrated in each page of your sketchbook.

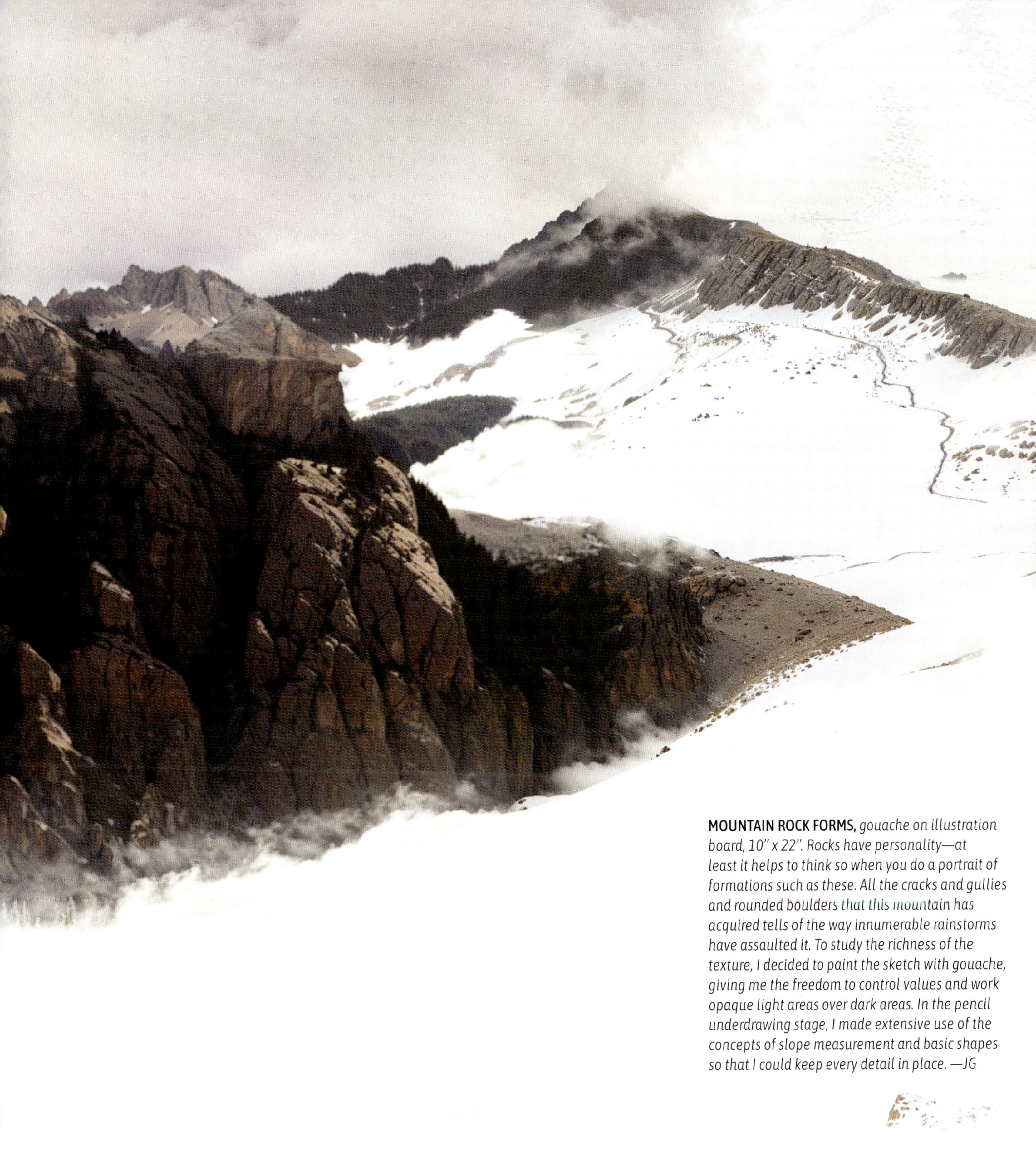

MOUNTAIN ROCK FORMS, *gouache on illustration board, 10" x 22". Rocks have personality—at least it helps to think so when you do a portrait of formations such as these. All the cracks and gullies and rounded boulders that this mountain has acquired tells of the way innumerable rainstorms have assaulted it. To study the richness of the texture, I decided to paint the sketch with gouache, giving me the freedom to control values and work opaque light areas over dark areas. In the pencil underdrawing stage, I made extensive use of the concepts of slope measurement and basic shapes so that I could keep every detail in place. —JG*

Sketching People

COUNTRY PREACHER, *pencil on smooth paper, 11" x 14". A man of patience, this country preacher held perfectly still for me as I sketched his portrait in his living room. To aid in my concentration, he even volunteered the vocal talent of his three redheaded daughters, who sang old-style gospel tunes as background music. The light source was the reading light beside him. Unfortunately, the lighting on my sketchbook wasn't very good, and so I leaned forward to catch the light coming from the same lamp he was reading by. I used a single #2 office pencil for the entire drawing, from underdrawing to final sketch. —TK*

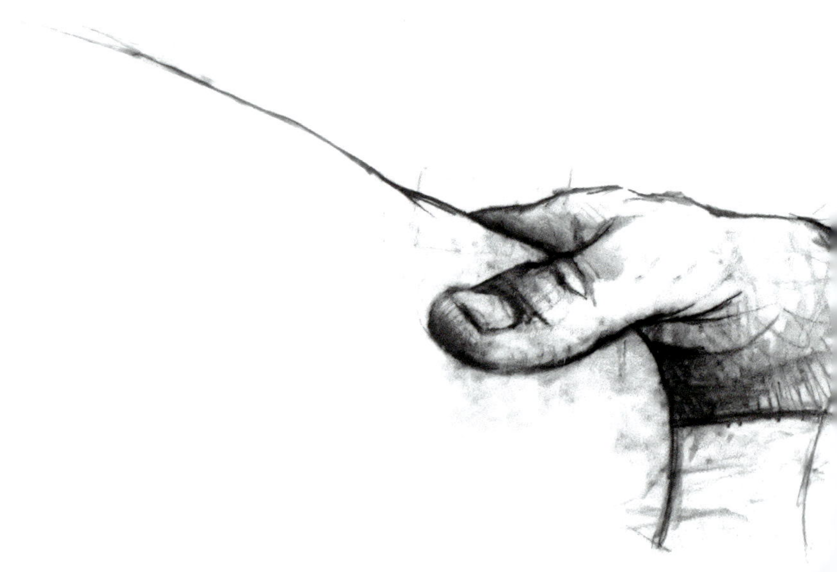

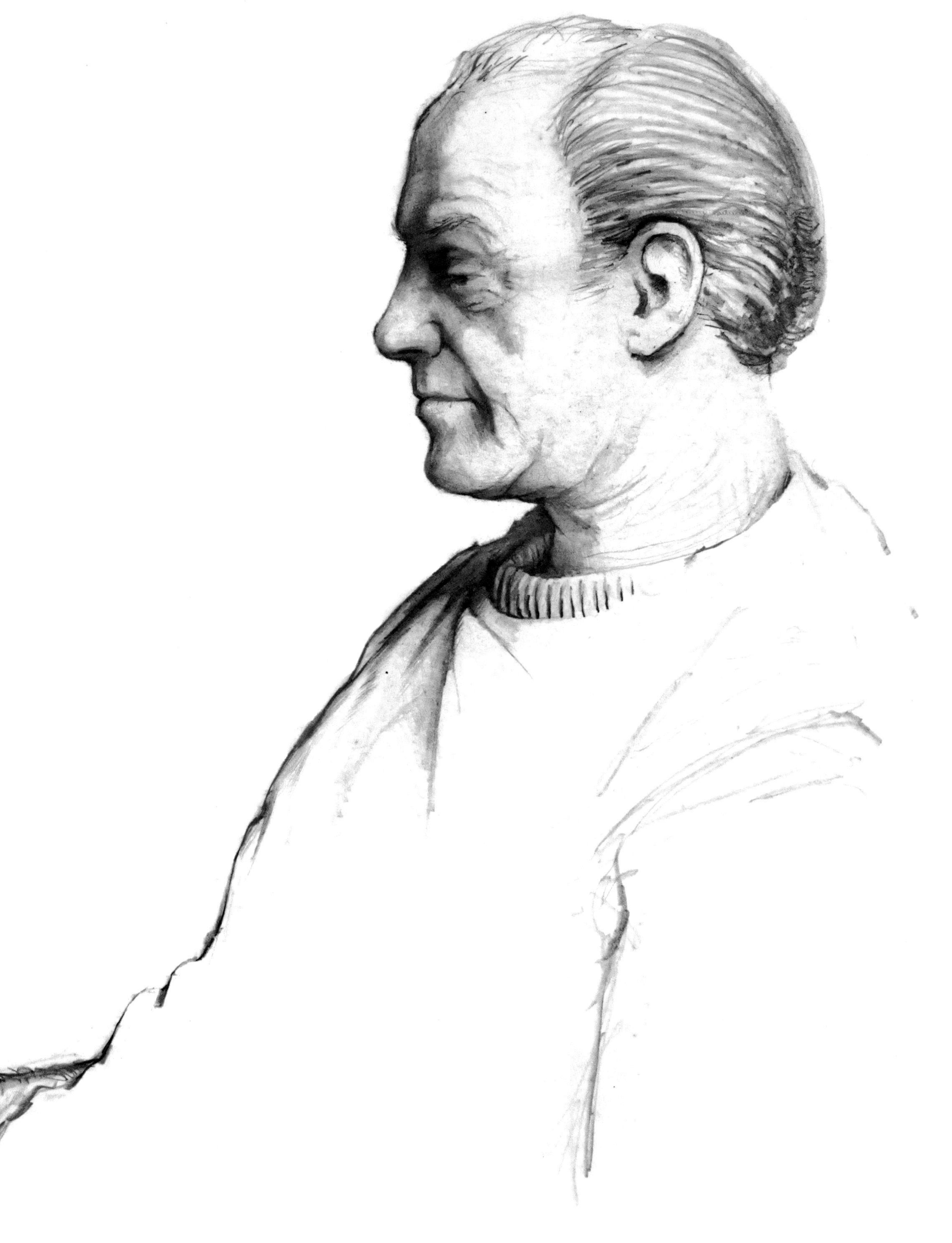

SUPPOSE YOU were searching through an art school catalog for the ideal class in portrait and figure drawing. What would you look for? Certainly you would want a good variety of models, people of all ages and types. You'd want them to be expert at posing in a relaxed, natural way. It would be nice if they wore authentic costumes and if they used realistic props. You'd also want the models to be lit with different types of lighting rather than just the usual overhead spotlight. And ideally you would prefer to have no other students to crowd your view, no rigid limitations on what you'd like to study, and of course no tuition fee.

Where can you find a class like this? It's all around you each time you sketch people on the spot. Regardless of whether you are beginning or advanced, you are guaranteed to progress rapidly. If you consider yourself the shy type, you can sketch people without being noticed. If you are gregarious, you can take advantage of the willingness of the average person, given the right encouragement, to pose absolutely still for you. Even without leaving the comfort of home you can find models among your family and friends.

This chapter is a guide for those of you who want to sketch people on the spot. Unlike many instructional books, which discuss drawing people from a standpoint of anatomy and proportion, our emphasis is on character—how to give your on-the-spot model a distinct personality. Whether you are doing a casual figure notation or a serious portrait, a concern for character will keep you from getting overwhelmed by the confusion of lines and tones that you find in most human subjects.

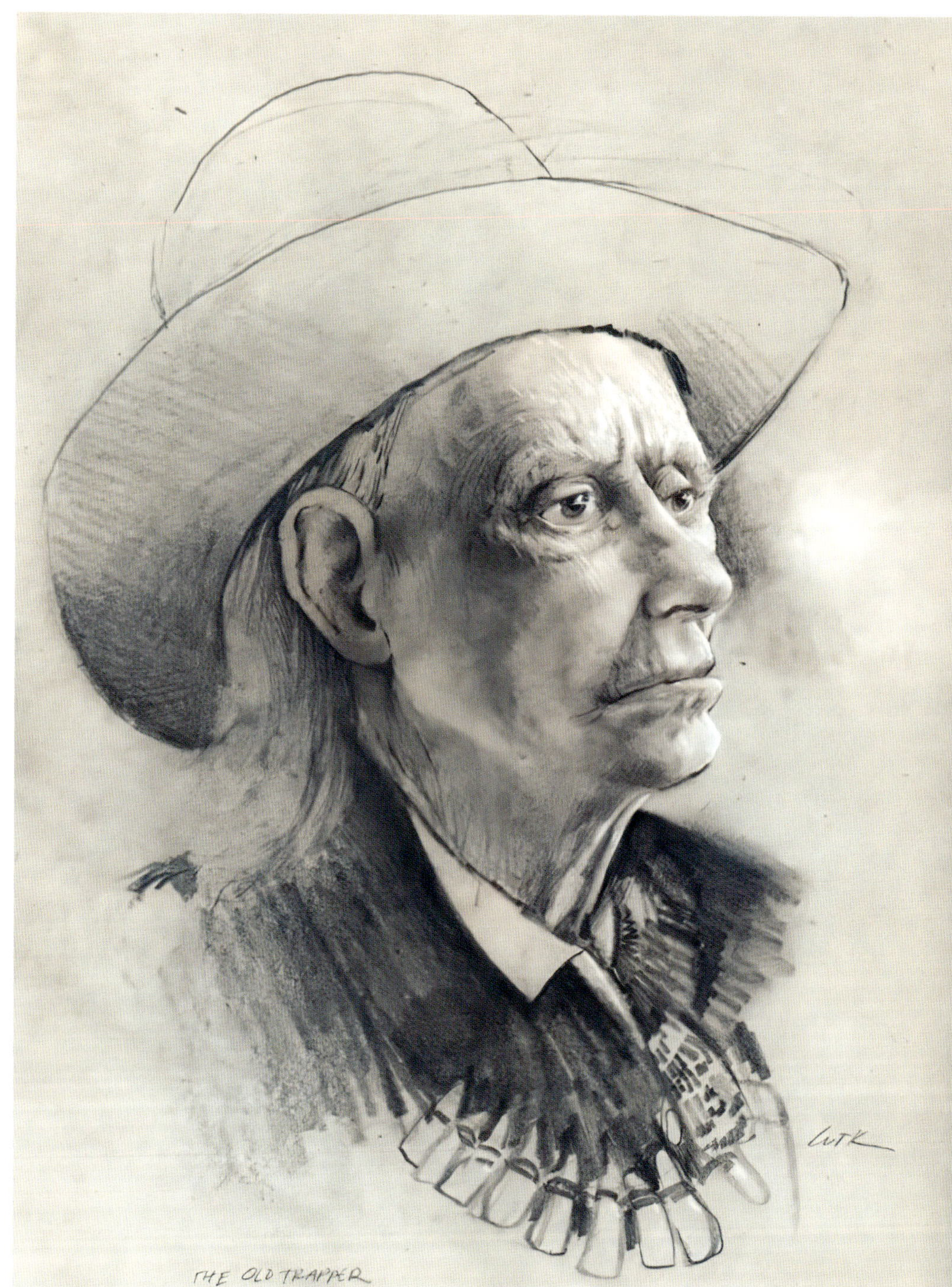

THE OLD TRAPPER, *gouache and pencil on gray paper, 9" x 11". Descended from the earliest trappers of the Rocky Mountains, this elderly gentleman ran a unique hotel featuring bearskin rugs and deer trophies. To his family and friends he was known as "the old trapper." Though his words were sparse, he revealed his inner strength in the pose he took for the hour or so that he sat for this on-the-spot portrait. I have found that most people feel honored at the chance to sit for a portrait. I usually keep the materials as simple as possible when drawing people, because too many materials intimidates the subject. Working on gray-toned paper, I began this sketch with a #2 office pencil and then added white Prismacolor touches to suggest the areas that were in direct light. —TK*

FINDING RAW MATERIAL

You don't have to travel far to find people to sketch, especially if you live in the city. At first you'll want to try places where people are sitting fairly still and where you can remain inconspicuous as you sketch. For this, the best hunting grounds are

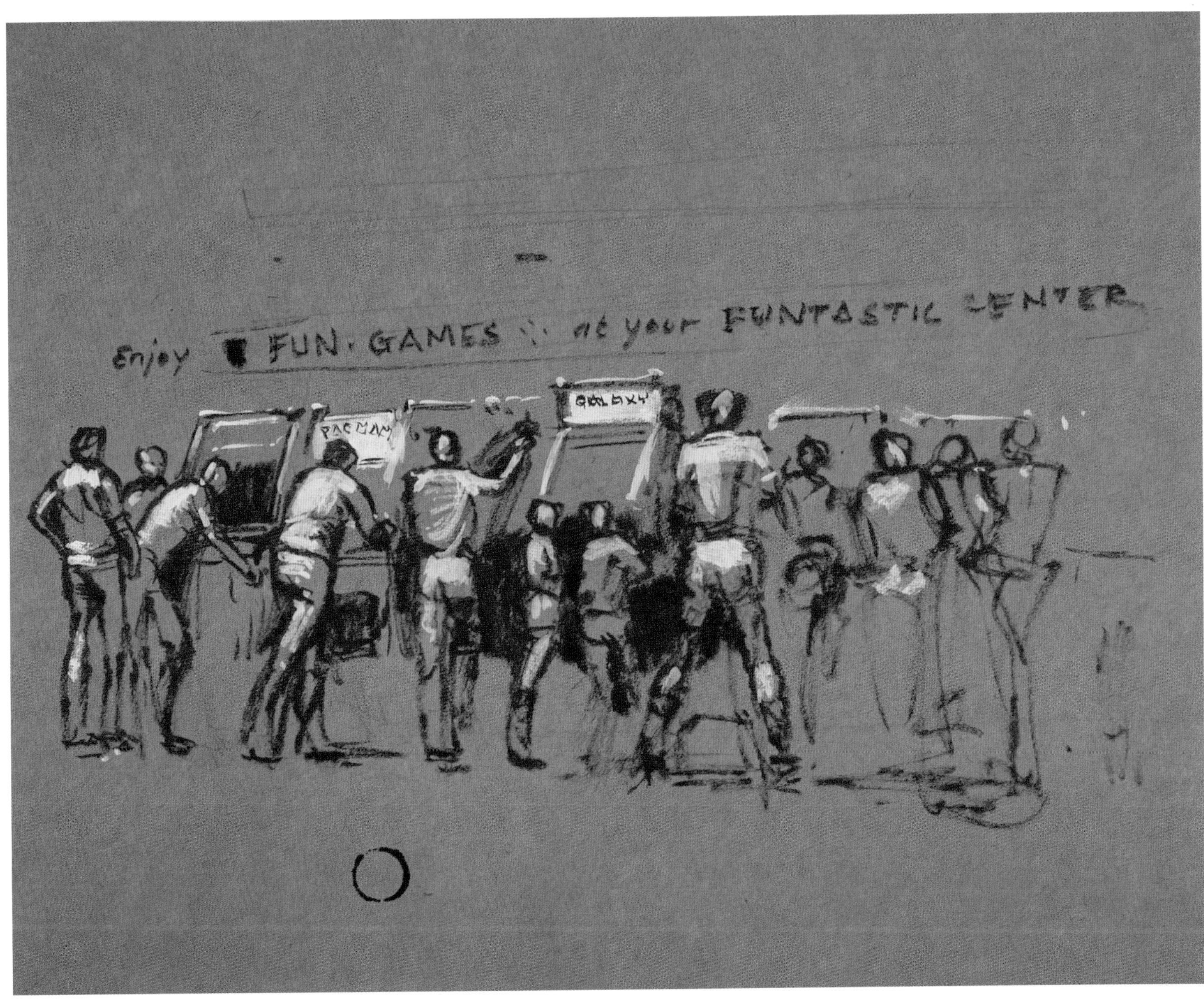

places where other people are seated and relaxed, such as bus stations, laundromats, and courtrooms. Subways, buses, and trains allow you to sit near enough to your subjects so that you can see them clearly.

Some of the best people-sketching opportunities are in more public situations. It takes some time to develop confidence sketching in a place where people may flock around you asking questions. (Chapter 1, "The Experience of Sketching," contains a discussion on how to deal with curious spectators.) It's really just a matter of developing a positive attitude and becoming familiar with the experience of being watched. With this new confidence, you can try out some of the gold mines of people-sketching. Weekends bring people outdoors to parks, playgrounds, beaches, and zoos, or indoors to bars, nightclubs, and theaters. At a ball game you can sketch hot dog sellers, athletes, and fans. Be open to any opportunity to sketch people by keeping a small sketchbook with you always, especially during lunch hour and on weekends.

FIGURES AT AN ARCADE, *brush pen and white gouache on brown paper, 11" x 14". Raw material for people-sketching is everywhere. Public places where people are preoccupied with something allow you to sketch without anyone noticing. I made this sketch from a booth in a bowling alley. The sketch was developed from left to right, using poses as I saw them. Instead of defining individual characters, I used a fairly standard figure-construction formula with an egg shape for the head and a blocklike torso. The white tones help to bring the forms forward. —JG*

EXAGGERATING CHARACTER TRAITS

You are sitting at a diner looking across your table at an elderly gentleman on the other side of the room. You have decided to sketch him and have discreetly gotten out your pad and pencil. How can you make this sketch go beyond an ordinary head drawing and capture something of his personality? We find that it helps to think along the same lines that a novelist would if he were developing a character for a story. By combining observation with imagination, a semi-fictional interpretation can emerge on the sketchbook page. Your concern in this kind of approach is to identify and exaggerate those qualities that set your subject apart from all others, that make him or her an individual.

To do this, identify a single dominant trait that can then translate into your drawing. If you are verbally minded, it helps to express this trait in one or two words. It might be an emotion (proud, disgusted, contented) or an action (slouching, strutting, tottering). It might be something that you associate with particular mannerisms, conversation, or dress—for example, most people have a particular character trait in mind when they think of businessmen or mechanics. Write down a few words relating to the character directly on your sketchbook page. If the elderly gentleman in the diner looks like a very proper Englishman, you might write: stiff, sober, hands folded, leans forward to eat.

If you are more of a nonverbal person, identify the abstract visual qualities of the character. One person might strike you with a hard, angular feeling, another might seem rounded and soft, and another sparkling and radiant.

When you begin the sketch, use these impressions of character to guide you as you subtly exaggerate the facts of what you observe. As soon as you begin to lay in the basic shapes for the head and the body, think of how the verbal or abstract visual traits would translate into the specific forms of the head and figure. For the Englishman, you might want to emphasize straight lines, especially verticals, wherever you could. The nose could be made straight and pointed, the lips thin and pursed. Try to reflect the dominant trait in all of the incidental details besides the face. If your character is sleepy-looking, exaggerate the droopiness of everything about him—from his eyebrows to his socks. Make the hair say sleepiness by having it limply sag down over the forehead. Make the clothes a little baggier, and use lines that have a lazy character of their own.

CHAMBER MUSICIANS, *soft pencil on drawing paper, 9" x 12". I've always noticed that musicians take on the characteristics of the instruments they play. At a chamber recital I attended, the person behind the graceful, sinuous sound of the viola was herself graceful and sinuous. To suggest this, I emphasized the S-shaped folds in her satin dress, and softened the tones around her hair and legs. The values were kept very light, except for a few black accents made with the side of the pencil: at her feet, under her sleeve, and on the viola itself. On the other hand, the clarinet has always struck me as an absurd, ducklike instrument. Sure enough, the clarinetist was a funny, balding fellow with a mismatched suit of clothes, featuring a tuxedo coat and old plaid pants. In my sketch, I exaggerated very slightly the forward slouch, the long sideburns, and the rounded nose. To make him look pale, I avoided darks in the face and hair, instead placing them in the bow tie, clarinet, and jacket. —JG*

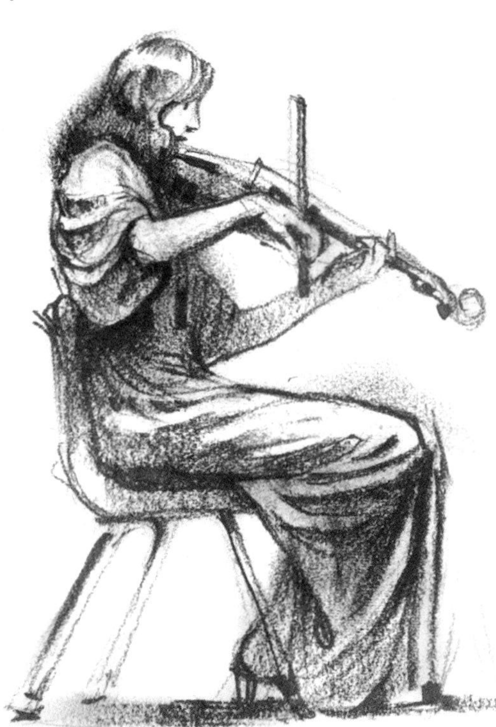

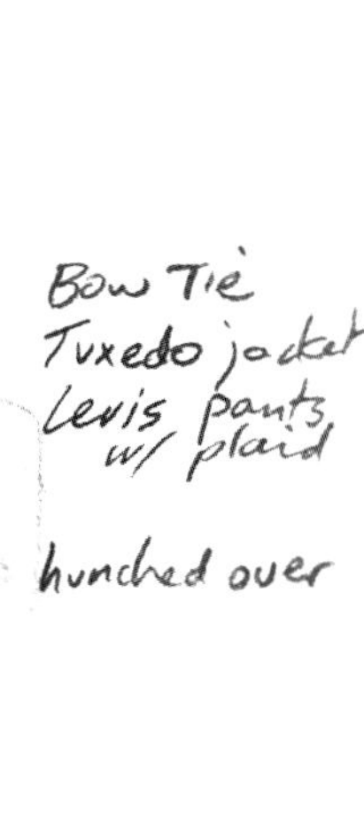

THE CARTOON APPROACH

When a person strikes you in a distinctly comical way, you might want to try a more cartoonlike approach. The difference between a cartoon and an observational drawing is that the cartoon is based on a stylized vocabulary of features—a particular way to draw eyes and noses, for example. You probably know some cartoon systems already; if not, the best way to learn is to copy the single-panel cartoons found in many major magazines. You really have to keep the cartoon formulas memorized, so that you can draw figures and faces from your imagination.

When you work on the spot, you still are working from memory for the most part. The character that you see only serves as a springboard for your imagination. For example, let's say your formula uses large balloon-shaped bodies and small pointed feet. Everyone—businessmen, old ladies, and truck drivers—would have to be adapted to that formula, and yet within that formula, you could go wild with exaggerated traits, even to the point of making up props to help suggest the character. A holster and a cowboy hat, for example, would turn someone into a cowboy character. As you sketch in this way, you will spend most of your time looking at the page, and only occasionally look up at your model.

A cartoon approach to characters should exaggerate the dominant trait to the point of absurdity. If you were on a college campus sketching a brainy, bookish physics student, you'd want to make the glasses as thick as beer mugs, and the neck as thin as a broomstick. Someone looking at the sketch should be able to tell immediately what you are trying to get across.

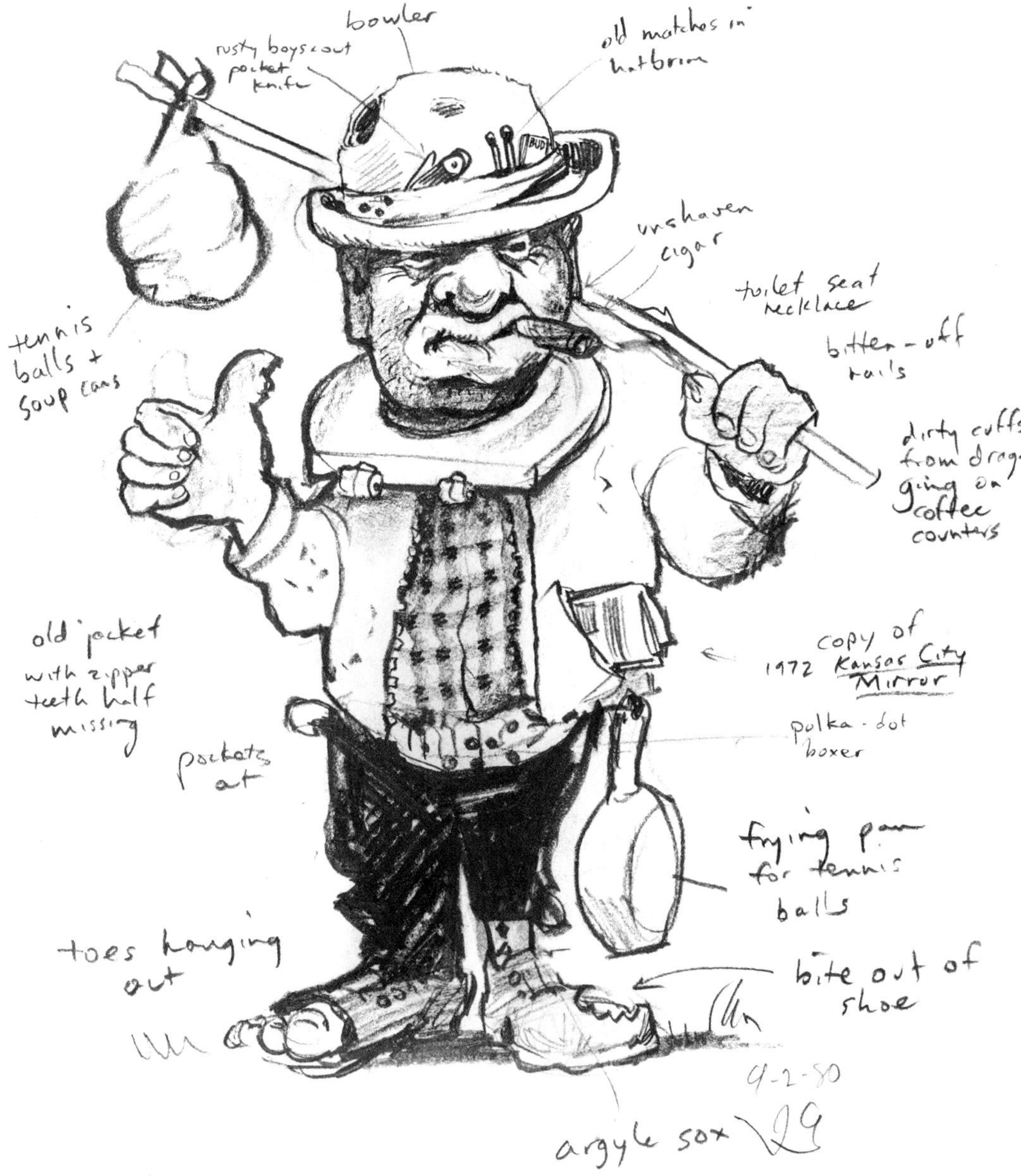

THE TRAMP, *soft pencil on drawing paper, 11" x 14". People sketches don't have to be realistic, nor do they have to be done completely from observations. In this case, a person walking by as I was sketching suggested a particular character type: the tramp. Based on the movies and cartoons I have seen, I have a definite stereotype of the tramp, including all the old clichés—the cigar, the matches in the hat brim, the old frying pan used for tennis ball soup. While I sat there sketching, I had fun adding my own variations on the theme. A cartoonlike approach such as this uses a set of stylized drawing rules, such as the oversized head and the short legs. I enjoy using these rules for any occasion when I'm sketching people in a humorous way. —JG*

PORTRAYING PEOPLE IN THEIR ENVIRONMENT

Whether you use a realistic or cartoon approach to drawing people, you can enhance your picture by adding suggestions of a surrounding environment. The conceptual approach is exactly the same as it was for the figure. Your goal is to reinforce and clarify the dominant trait of the character. Every line, tone, and detail should echo that trait.

For example, suppose you are at a shopping mall, discreetly sketching a woman loaded with packages who has sat down a moment to rest. The dominant trait that you have chosen is "weary." To suggest this, you may emphasize the forward-leaning posture and the droopiness of the head. Make her eyes halfway shut and perhaps dangle her arm at her side. In the figure alone you can convey the dominant trait of your subject. Yet by including a few details of setting you can go beyond this and make your sketch tell a story. Those packages she was carrying—how about exaggerating them a bit? Try enlarging them and drawing in more of them than there really are. This will suggest the fact that she has been shopping and that she has been worn out by the weight of her burden.

Now let's carry it a bit further. Look around and isolate one or two features of the shopping mall that sum up its visual qualities. Perhaps a few of the hanging shop signs catch your eye. Or perhaps a particular trash can with a design on the side interests you. Include these things. A few key details really help to identify the location. Be selective and don't think you have to draw a blank wall behind your subject just because that is what happens to be there. Invent, arrange, pick and choose. You are creating a setting that will complement your sketch of a person. Don't feel bound by the appearance of reality. *Use* what is there to create an environment which suits your purpose.

The opportunities for setting to enhance character are richest when the person you are sketching is at home or at work. There they are most comfortable with their surroundings, and the objects around them are of their own choosing and arrangement. Imagine the possibilities of an old man in an antique store, a portly mother sitting beneath a clothesline, or a college student in her dormitory room with posters and stereo and hanging plants around her. These are settings that tell the story of the character all by themselves. Settings such as these can answer questions about character, telling you what he eats, how much he is concerned about his appearance, how his time is spent.

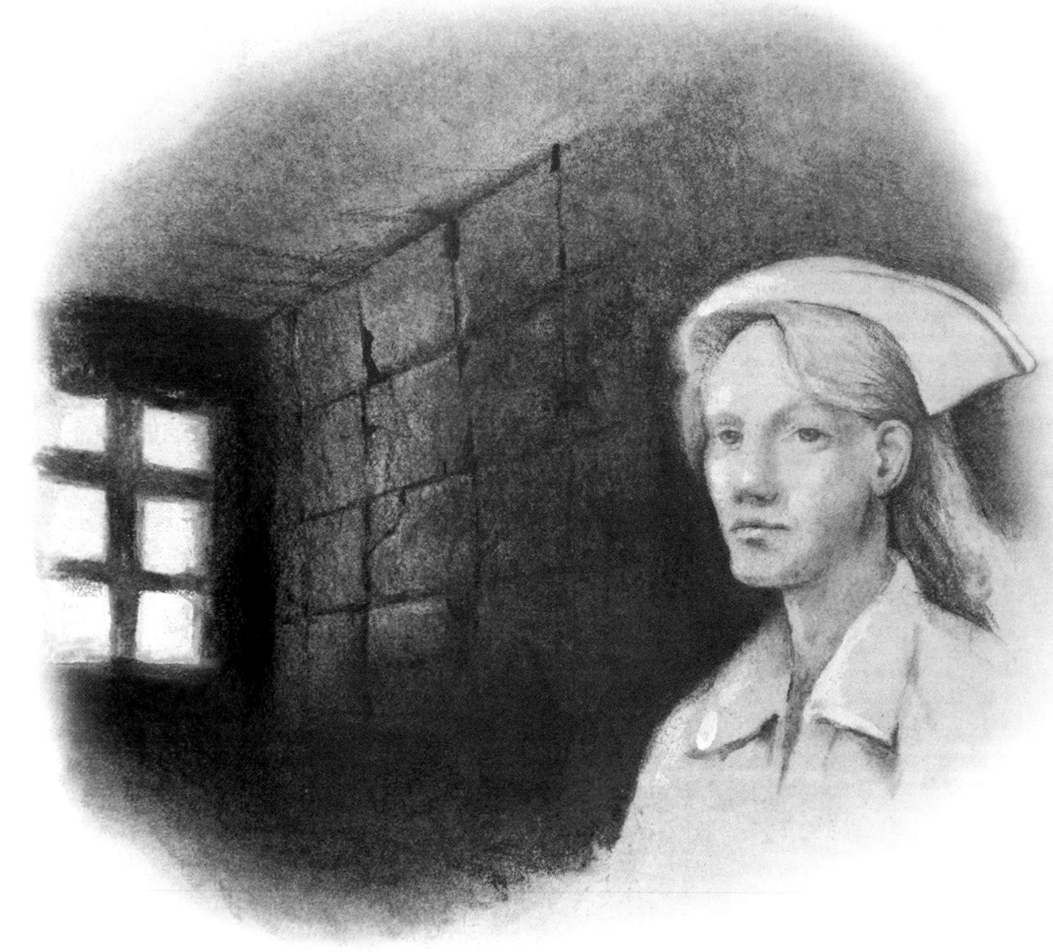

NURSE AND BARREN ROOM, *charcoal on smooth paper, 11" x 14". I was impressed by the softness and delicacy of this nurse's face. To accentuate these features, I decided to invent a harsh setting as a means of contrast. Placing your subject in a setting that contradicts his or her characteristics can add either poignancy or humor, depending on the degree of absurdity of the contrast. In this sketch I contrasted the whiteness and perfection of the nurse with the darkness and dilapidation of the setting to create a solemn, somewhat evocative mood. The technical procedure for the sketch involved extensive use of smudging and erasing to create the soft tones of the face and walls. —TK*

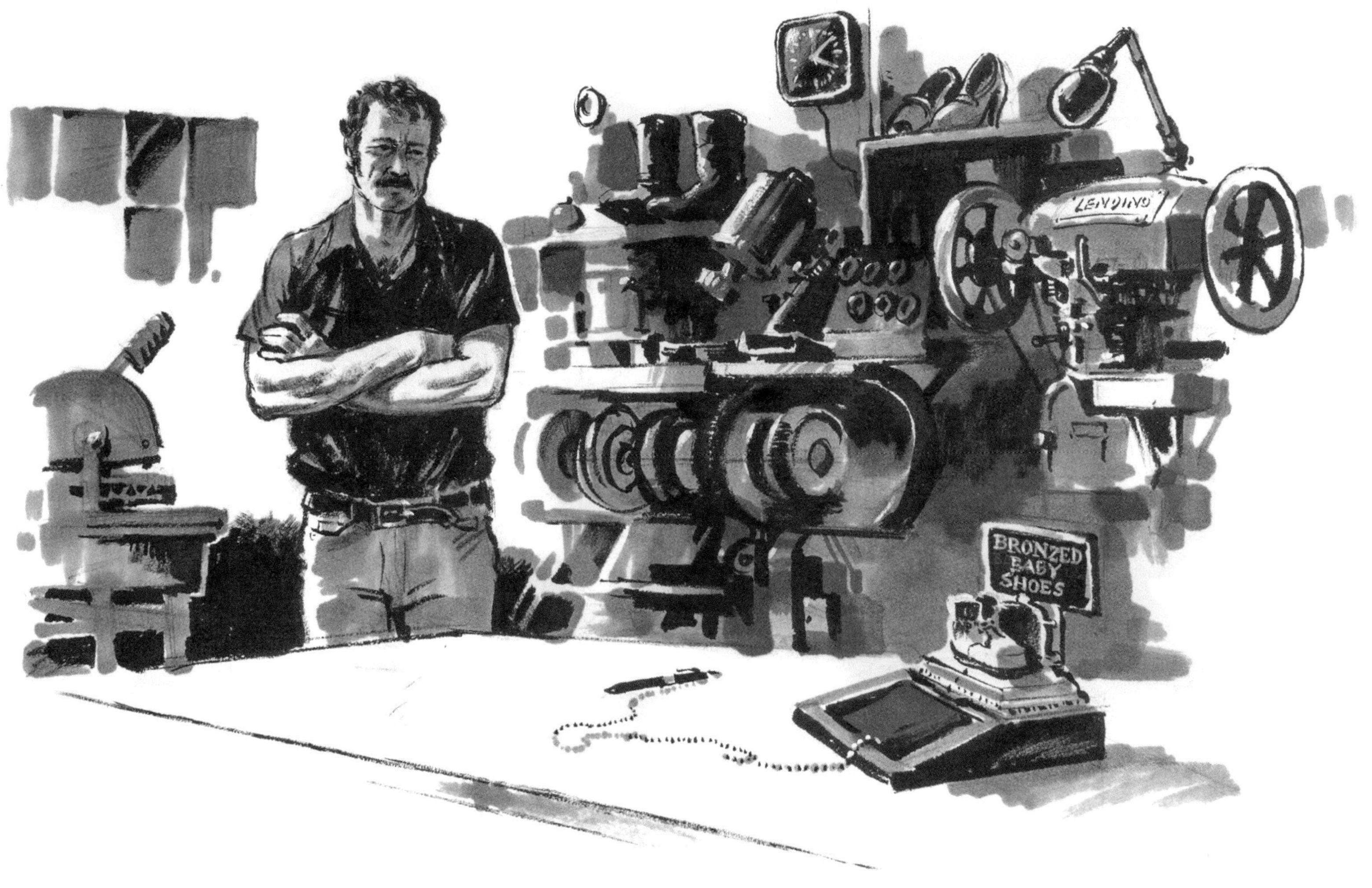

When you see a person you would like to sketch, always look for objects associated with him or her which in themselves have character. The packages mentioned earlier are a good example. The same is true of other things, such as a tuba, chihuahua, a lacy parasol, or an old trunk.

We have talked about how setting can *reinforce* character, but it is often humorous when a character is in a setting that *contradicts* their personality. Have you ever seen a wealthy, elderly lady in front of a pawn shop, for example, or a burly man waiting for his wife in the lingerie section of the department store? These juxtapositions happen so often in day-to-day life that we don't even notice them most of the time. Make a conscious effort to look for odd character/setting situations.

SHOE REPAIRMAN IN HIS SHOP, *brush pen and markers on drawing paper, 11" x 14". People at home or at work surround themselves with things that reveal aspects of their character. In this case, I chose to portray this Armenian shoe repairman amid the tools of his trade. He was proud to show me the powerful industrial sewing machine at right, given to him by his father, and the line of specialized buffing wheels behind him at waist level, which he used to polish different kinds of leather. These tools, which suggest long years of working with the hands, echo the steady, resolute pose of the worker. I chose to include the bronzed baby shoe display on the counter because it indicates by association perhaps a more gentle, paternal side to the repairman. I carefully designed the sketch so that the figure seems a part of the surrounding detail without being overwhelmed by it. The technique I used was gradation, the lightening of values as one area turns behind another. Notice how the blacks drop out of the background rendering, and the details soon translate to impressionistic abstract shapes before reaching the right-hand edge of the figure. A similar gradation occurs at the outer edges of the vignette all the way around. A simple black tone behind the repairman's legs connects him directly to the lower areas of the machines, and at the same time helps to define the upper edges of the counter. Finally, notice how the rendering behind the baby shoe display gradates to an even gray so that the strong blacks and whites of the sign can stand out with no confusion. —JG*

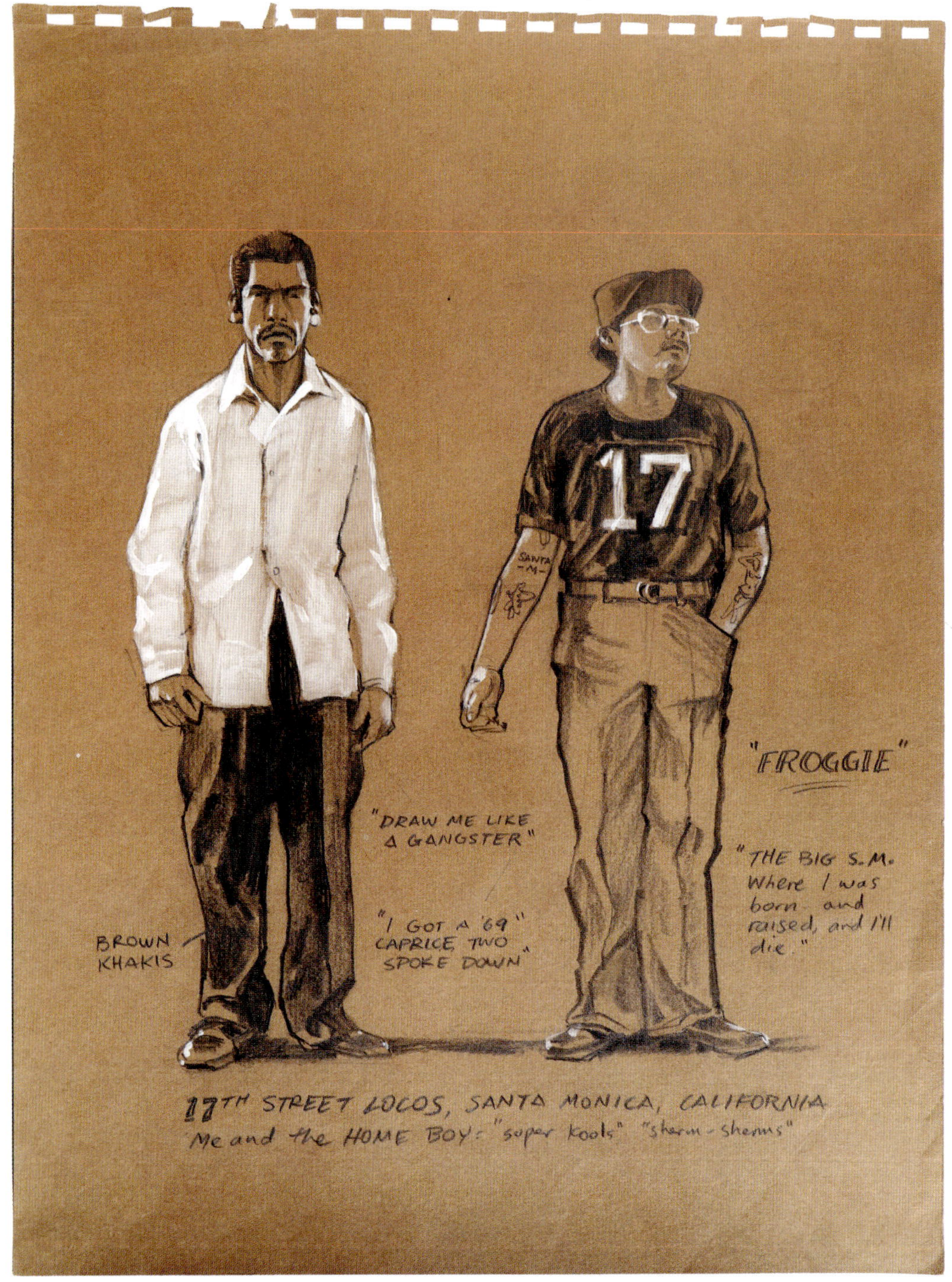

TWO YOUNG GANG MEMBERS, *pencil and white gouache on brown paper, 11" x 14". "Draw me like a gangster," said the fellow on the left, the leader of the Santa Monica Locos, a gang in California. He had been watching over my shoulder as I sketched the boardwalk. I let him strike a pose without any direction on my part to see how he would choose to reveal himself to me. His friend, nicknamed "Froggy," on the right, stood less defiantly, and was most concerned that I record all of the tattoos on his arms: "I got all kinda tattoos on me, all tacked down, you know." As dangerous as these characters look, they actually became friends of mine as I sketched them. They were as fascinated to hear me describe the way I draw as I was about the way they had fixed up their "lowrider" cars. Sketching opened the door into these people's lives in a way that nothing else could. —JG*

TWO CHARACTERS

Any character that you draw will become much more interesting if you juxtapose him or her with another character of an opposite dominant trait. A weakling looks weaker beside a ruffian. A rich man makes a beggar seem poorer. An introvert shrinks deeper into himself when he is seen sitting beside an extrovert.

Whenever you do a sketch that combines two people, keep in mind the concept of opposition. Of course what you draw will be based on observation, but your goal will be to consciously exaggerate each character in opposing directions. Little details have a big effect. If one person's shirt is untucked and the other's isn't, the viewer will notice it, because his eye will be shifting back and forth from one person to the other, comparing them.

You might also find it helpful to think in terms of roles and relationships when you are sketching two characters. Failing to do this often yields sketches of people in haphazard poses, looking off into meaningless areas of space. That can be just as boring to draw as it is to look at. But when the people in the picture are related in some way, hundreds of possibilities open up. Here are some examples of relationships, written in the form that we often jot down on the sketchbook page: clerk/customer, husband/wife, boss/employee, best friends, grandfather/granddaughter. Sometimes, in actual situations, this is a matter of speculation—you may not know whether a couple is married—but this kind of speculation is what feeds the imagination of the character sketcher.

Whenever the two characters you are sketching are conversing with each other, you have a special opportunity. In the empty space above or below the drawing, write a few lines of the actual dialogue that you overhear the people saying. Even if the lines sound banal at the time, they will take on a vividness later, recalling the character very strongly in your memory.

If you are too far away from your subjects to overhear any of their conversation, invent one. How can you reflect the dominant trait in words? Try it. And when you finish the sketch, take a look at it. Here are people interacting. We sense their actual presence.

GROUP COMPOSITION

When you sketch a group of people, it helps to think in terms of situation. Novelists use the word "situation" to refer to the predicament between characters that motivates the story. To you, the sketch hunter, a sensitivity to situation will give your multiple figure drawings a clear purpose. Here are some examples of situations: a child on a bus stop bench with a loud radio that is disturbing others, a collection of businessmen at a donut shop trying to make up their mind about what to order, a group of bird-watchers eyeing a fine specimen.

This kind of sketch is really an on-the-spot illustration or cartoon, and it requires a little planning. It helps to jot down a few thumbnail compositions before you start sketching. Also, a quick underdrawing with a pencil will help you to interrelate the figures in such a way that there is no confusion. But despite this planning, stay open to a spontaneous idea that you may get from seeing one of your subjects strike an unusual pose.

On-the-spot group compositions usually develop in a fairly haphazard, creative fashion. Once you have a basic idea in mind, you can improvise as you go, using whatever method works best for you to tell the story you had in mind. One method we use quite commonly is to redraw a single figure in several different positions, to create a group from one person. As your subject moves from time to time, all you do is quickly capture that pose in pencil, rendering as much as you can before he or she moves on to another pose. It helps you to place the figures if you make a brief indication of the setting or background before starting in with the figures. Here's an example: suppose you see a man across the street, waiting for the bus, shifting from one foot to another, leaning against the brick wall. You could very easily make a sketch of an entire group of bus riders using him alone. Just change his clothes each time, and try to get a different dominant trait with each figure.

Another approach that is fun to try involves expanding outward from a central focal point. You can do this with or without an underdrawing, depending on your preference. Find yourself a comfortable place to sketch near some object that attracts people for a short period of time, such as a cash register or a drinking fountain. These rallying points have a tendency to initiate situations. They make for good storytelling. Once you have drawn the central object, just build outward with the figures that will appear before you. When figures overlap in actuality, don't hesitate to draw one figure directly over another figure. You can get away with quite a lot of this without hurting a sketch; in fact, overdrawing often makes a sketch more interesting because it reveals the creative process to the viewer of the sketch.

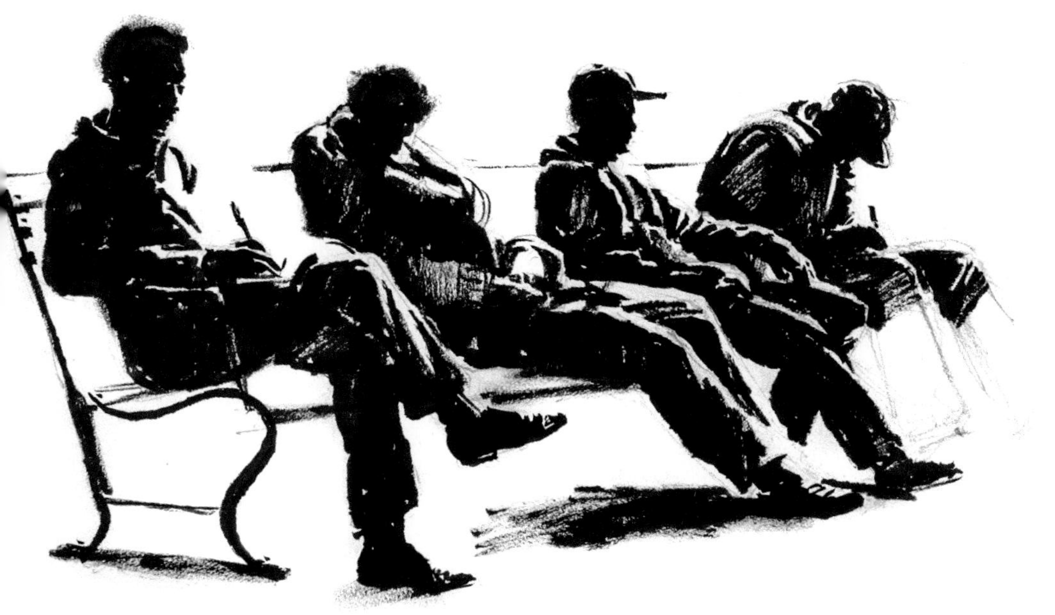

MULTIPLE CHARACTER STUDY, *brush pen on drawing paper, 9" x 12". A simple situation like people sitting on a park bench in the afternoon light can provide an exciting opportunity to do a comparative study of characters. I decided right away to use this dramatic light-and-shadow treatment because it forced me to express character in terms of posture alone, without depending at all on facial expression. For example, the man on the far left, with his legs crossed and pen and notebook in hand, is apparently a student, while the lanky man next to him might be one of the perennial inhabitants of the park, judging from the way he seems so at home on the bench. I developed the sketch from left to right, completing each figure before I moved on to the next. No matter how much you plan a multiple figure sketch, it has to be something of an improvisation, because any given figure may at any time change positions or leave altogether. —JG*

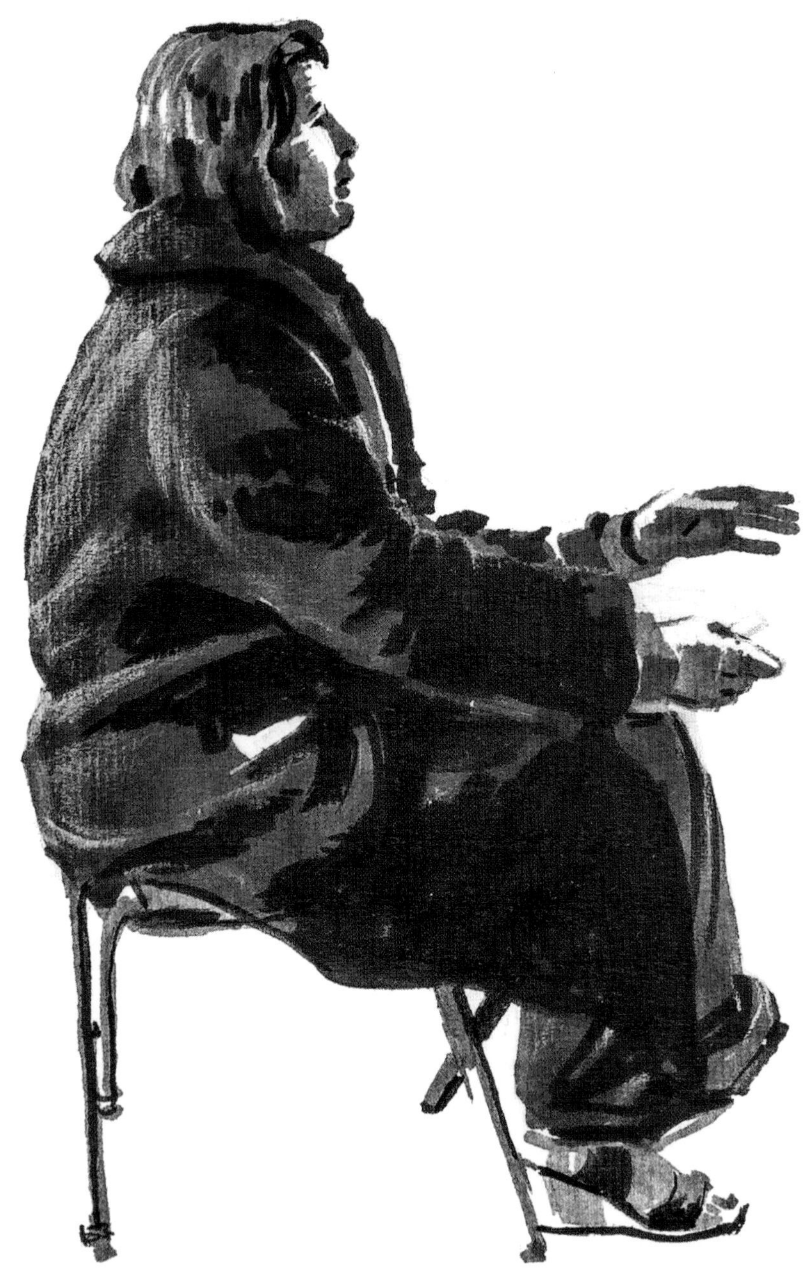

IMMIGRANT WOMAN, *markers and white chalk on charcoal paper, 6" x 8". This lady, who spoke broken English with a strong accent, was eager to pose for me, but I knew that she might move too much if I had her standing. So I let her take the folding chair that I usually use for sketching, and I sat on the ground next to a building. I initiated a conversation about her childhood memories, so that she could do most of the talking and allow me to mostly concentrate on drawing. I was attracted to the solidity of the dark overcoat mass, supported by the thin legs of the stool. The forms are lit from two sources: a low bright sun setting over to the right, and a soft cool light from behind, which fills out the form of her back. I purposely left out all details of the setting to give a feeling that she is detached from the world around her. —JG*

THE ON-THE-SPOT PORTRAIT

All of the people-sketching we have discussed so far has involved models who were never asked to pose. In fact, if you are like most sketchers, most of your subjects will be people you never even speak to, let alone ask to model for you. But if you want to make the most of the opportunities that people-sketching has to offer, it often takes some initiative on your part to establish rapport with a stranger. But here's the good news: people *love* to pose for a sketch. In fact, they usually feel honored. Many times we have had strangers actually line up for the chance to see their picture drawn.

Unlike conventional portraits, on-the-spot portraits are unique because they involve drawing a person you may never have seen before and probably won't see again. This very fact is what makes this type of portraiture so exciting. Here is your chance to become acquainted, if only briefly, with someone whose background is completely different from your own. A stranger, with fresh ideas, attitudes, and mannerisms awaits discovery by means of your sketch. We have talked fishing with fishermen, logging with loggers, and dress design with dress designers, all as a result of the interesting forum for interaction created by the portrait sketching process.

The key to getting someone to pose for a sketch is to develop rapport with them so that they feel comfortable holding still for you. This is true not only for strangers, but even for the closest family members, since most people are not used to being drawn.

Make friends with the person you'd like to draw before you ask him or her to pose. Show them any previous sketches that you might have with you; comment on the surrounding scene; talk about why you enjoy drawing people. In this way, you let them know what your intentions are as an artist, and they can feel that they know you a little already. Then let the conversation shift to their interests and spend some time getting to know them.

As you do this, you can begin considering how you want to approach the sketch. Do you want to use pencil, pen, or charcoal? Any of those would be fine, depending on what feels comfortable to you.

When you're ready to ask them to pose, do so casually, without making it sound like a big deal. It isn't. Say something like this: "Hey, are you any good at holding still? I'd love to sketch your picture." Make it clear that you're not trying to sell them a portrait, but just that you want to do it for your own sketchbook. If they say yes, get out your materials, which you have kept handy, and get ready to sketch.

Some people don't need any direction for posing. They'll automatically strike their own pose, sometimes defiant, sometimes introspective. If this happens, just tell them that they look perfect and ask them to hold still as best they can. These natural poses are priceless, because they reveal a person's self-image, how they want to be seen. Other people, however, need to be guided. The best way to pose someone is to tell them what to look at. If you want a frontal angle, tell them to look over your shoulder (not directly at you or you'll both feel self-conscious). For a profile pose, choose something in the scene for them to look at so that you can see them directly from the side.

Once the pose is established, immediately resume the conversation at the point you left off. Ask them about their hobbies, job, or favorite recreation. These subjects will involve more talking on their part than yours. You can then more easily concentrate on your drawing without having to do too much verbal thinking. However, listen closely to what your new friend is saying, and when you hear an interesting quote, write it down immediately. As you sketch, keep in mind the ideas of dominant trait and character that we discussed earlier. Allow yourself to form an impression of your model's character, and let that impression guide your hand as you draw. Your goal

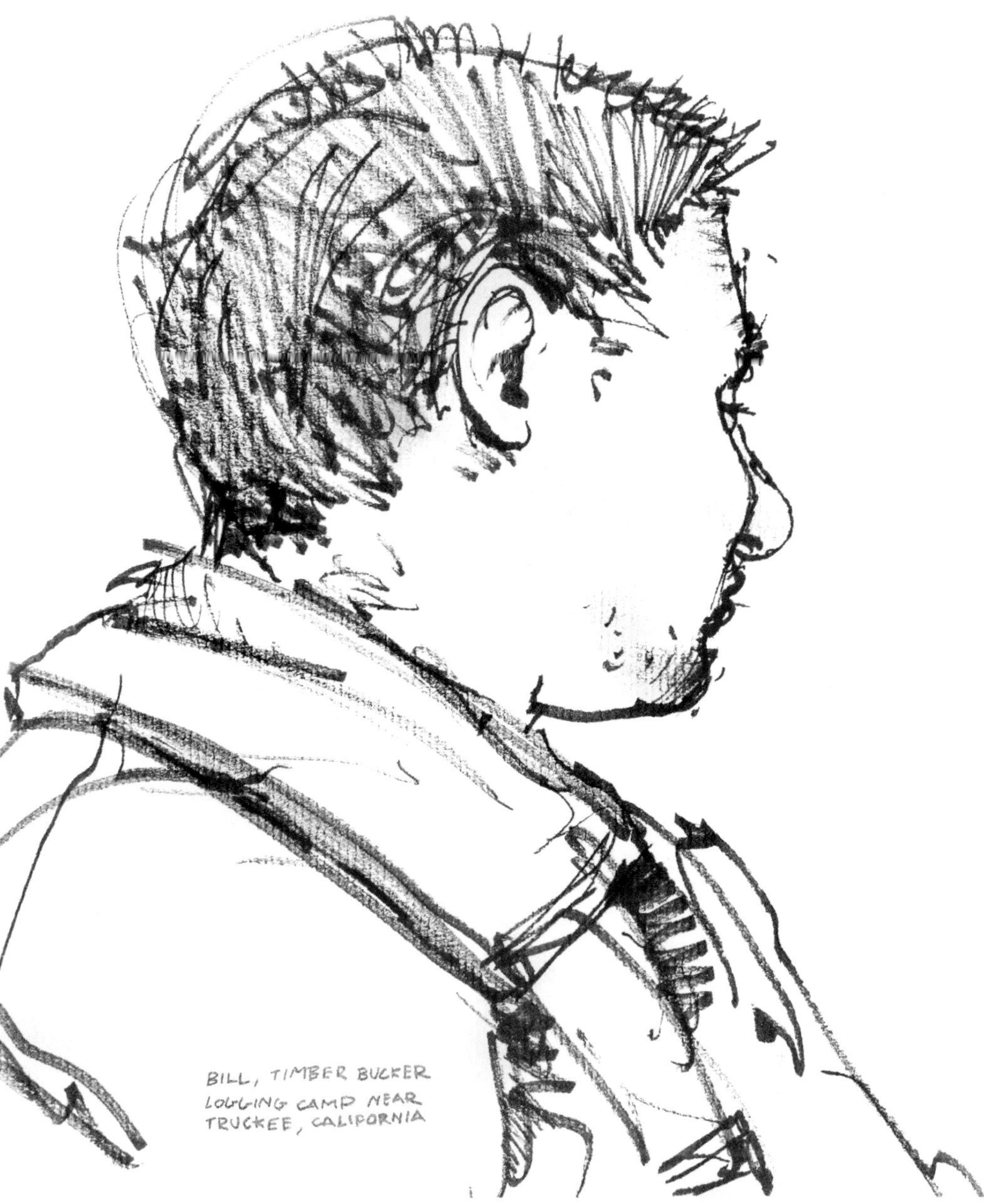

TIMBER BUCKER, *calligraphy pen on charcoal, 8" x 11". A hesitant model, this lumberman was reluctant to pose. I was having coffee with him after having sketched the logging camp where he worked. I brought out my sketchbook and began sketching while he looked the other way and talked about some of the dangerous aspects of his profession. I began the sketch directly in calligraphy pen to record an impression in the quickest possible way. To suggest his week-old stubble, I smudged the area of the chin, using a moistened finger rubbed over the calligraphy pen. —TK*

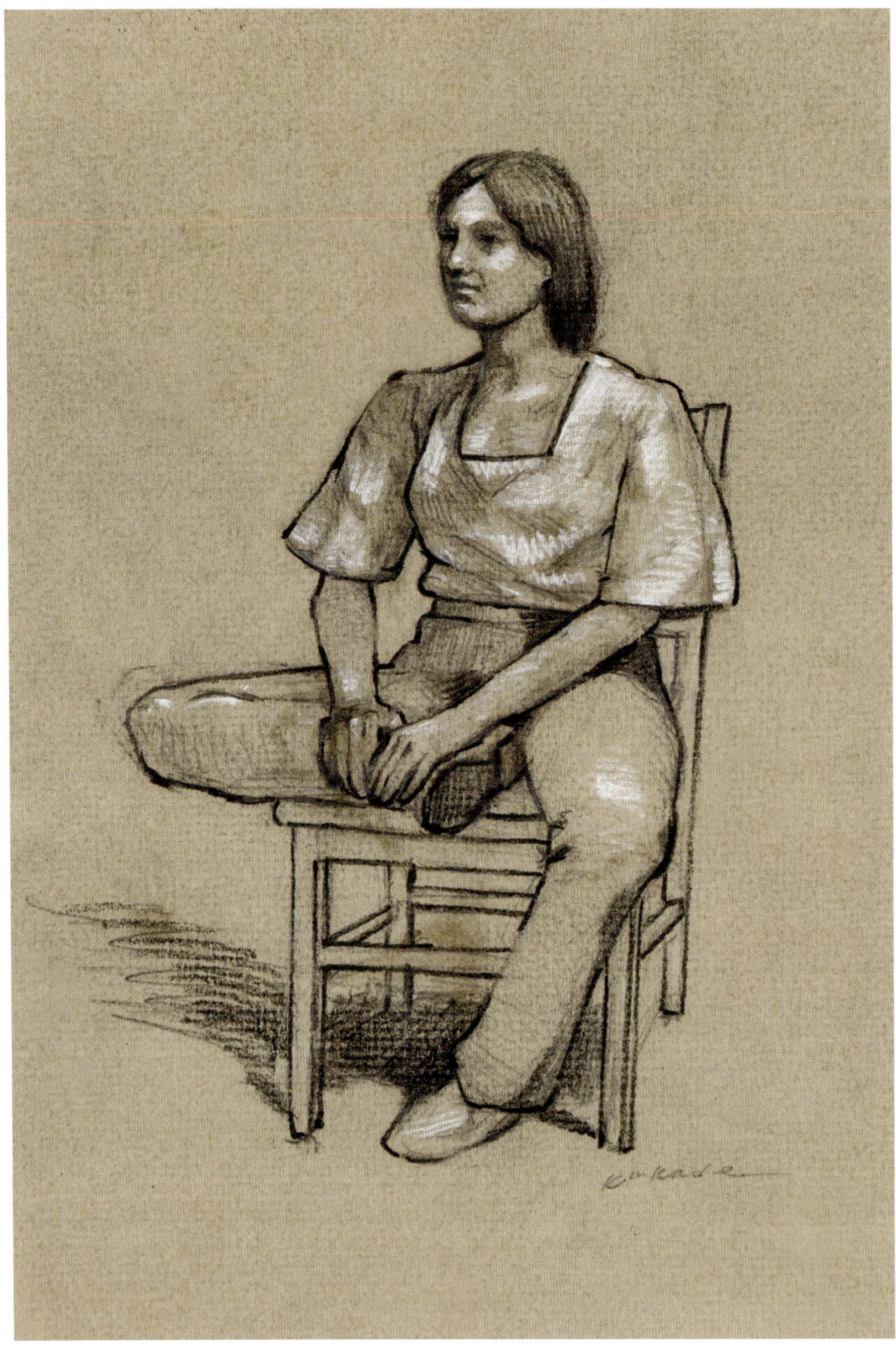

SEATED WOMAN, *black Prismacolor pencil, white CarbOthello, and white gouache on toned charcoal paper, 8" x 9¼". A good recruiting tactic for getting family and friends to model is to ask them if they would mind holding still during a half-hour television show. Most people have no problem holding a pose for that amount of time, especially when watching their favorite show. I prefer to be facing away from the TV—in other words, facing toward the model—so that my eye is not distracted by the insistent image of the video screen. To do this sketch I used a quick pencil underdrawing and then worked darker tones over that with softer pencils. White was added with Prismacolor pencil to further suggest form. —TK*

is neither to self-consciously flatter the person nor to try to photographically record them, but rather to sensitively interpret their personality by subtly exaggerating those characteristics that seem important to you. If you feel a woman has a graceful curve to her shoulder, make that line even smoother, and accent it so that the viewer of your sketch will notice it too.

After you finish, thank your model very graciously and show him or her the result, even if you yourself believe it to be unsuccessful. Chances are, your sitter will be impressed with your efforts and feel enriched by the experience of having been drawn.

MAKING PEOPLE SKETCHES COME ALIVE

To get the most out of people-sketching, be versatile and flexible. Try as many different kinds of approaches as you can. We all tend to get in ruts otherwise, repeating the same formula over and over just because we know that it works. Try a cartoon treatment if you haven't before. Or if you're used to doing only quick sketches of people in motion, take an opportunity to do a more careful portrait. If you have drawn one person's face many times from observation, try it again from memory and see how well you do. And by all means make a point of meeting someone new and sketching a quick portrait on the spot. You will generate some of your fondest memories that way.

When you don't have your sketchbook with you and you happen to be going about your daily affairs, standing in line at the bank or walking through the park on a weekend, be observant of character. You can think all you want about cylinders and planes and cast shadows, but don't forget that each person has a distinctive spirit reflected in everything he wears, says, and does.

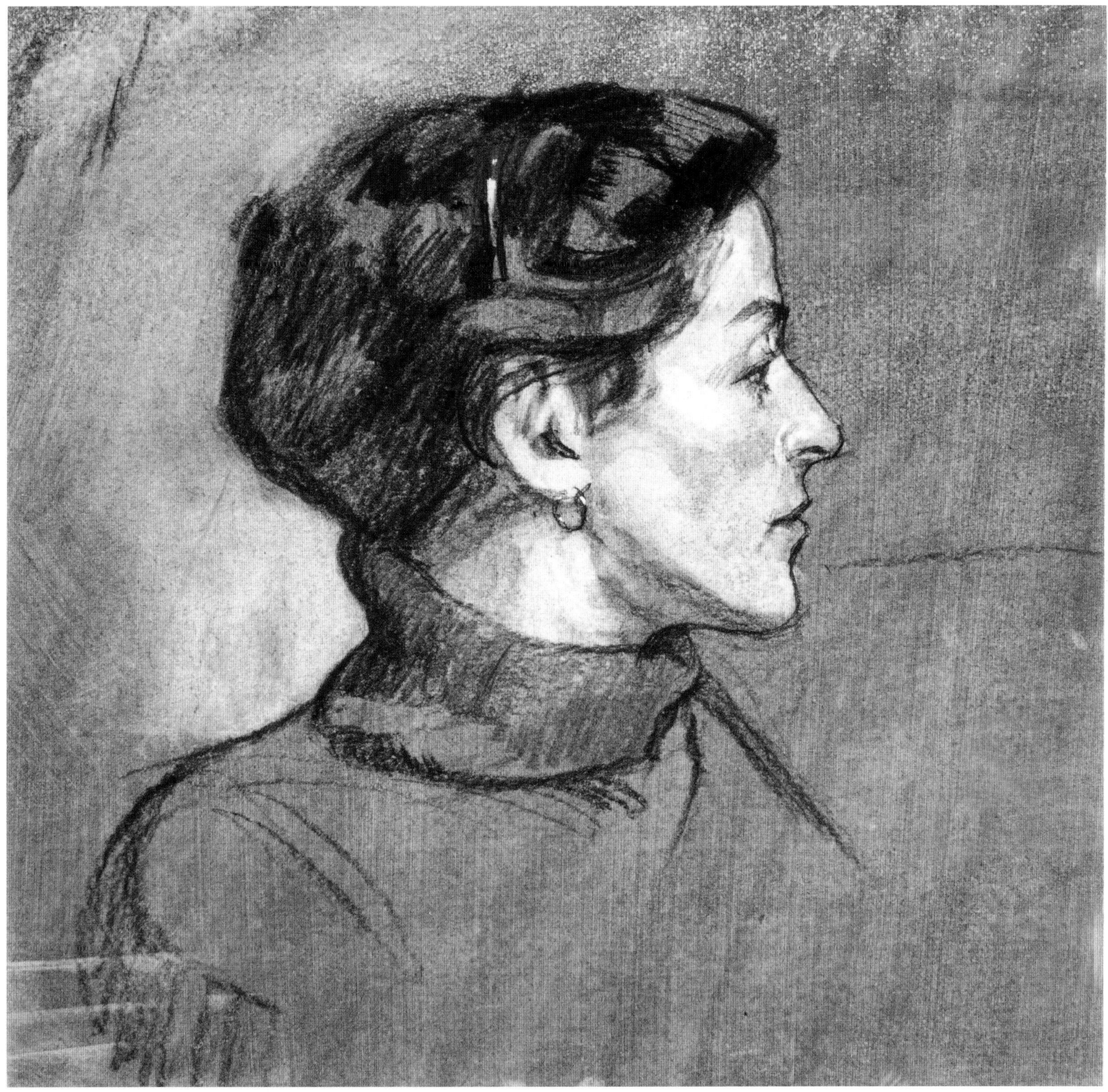

HEAD STUDY, *charcoal on tracing paper, 9" x 9". I enjoy sketching friends at home so that I can keep in practice. An art student friend of mine posed for twenty minutes while I made this profile study. The unconventional technique makes use of the nonporous coated surface of tracing paper. Any covering of charcoal settles only on the surface and can be erased back to pure white with just a touch of the eraser. Even the least touch of a finger will remove the dust, as you can see from the light streaks at lower left. The procedure begins with the application of ground-up charcoal dust with a housepainter's brush across the whole surface of the paper. Then, using a quick underdrawing with a 6B charcoal pencil, the light tones are modeled with a rag on the face and behind the neck. A kneaded eraser, brought to a sharp point, was used for the highlights around the eye and nose. Then, returning to the 6B pencil, with great care not to touch the delicate surface, I emphasized the dark lines in the hair, face, and sweater. —JG*

FAMILY AND FRIENDS: YOUR FREE MODELS

Between those times when you are sketching on the spot, you have some available, if not willing, models among you at home. Your family and friends are just as interesting to draw as anyone else. You don't even have to ask them to pose—just capture them at quiet moments, like when they are watching television or doing the dishes. After you have sketched them three or four times, they'll begin to tolerate you to the point that they hardly notice when they're being used as a model. You will rapidly acquire a collection of not only good figure-drawing practice, but also intimate memories of people that you love.

Occasionally, take an evening to do a more comprehensive portrait, where you ask a relative to pose for you under a good clear light. You may find that you have never really noticed the beauty of those close to you until you have actually drawn them. Each time you do a portrait, you discover new things not only about the forms of their face, but the secrets of their character that before had been hidden to you.

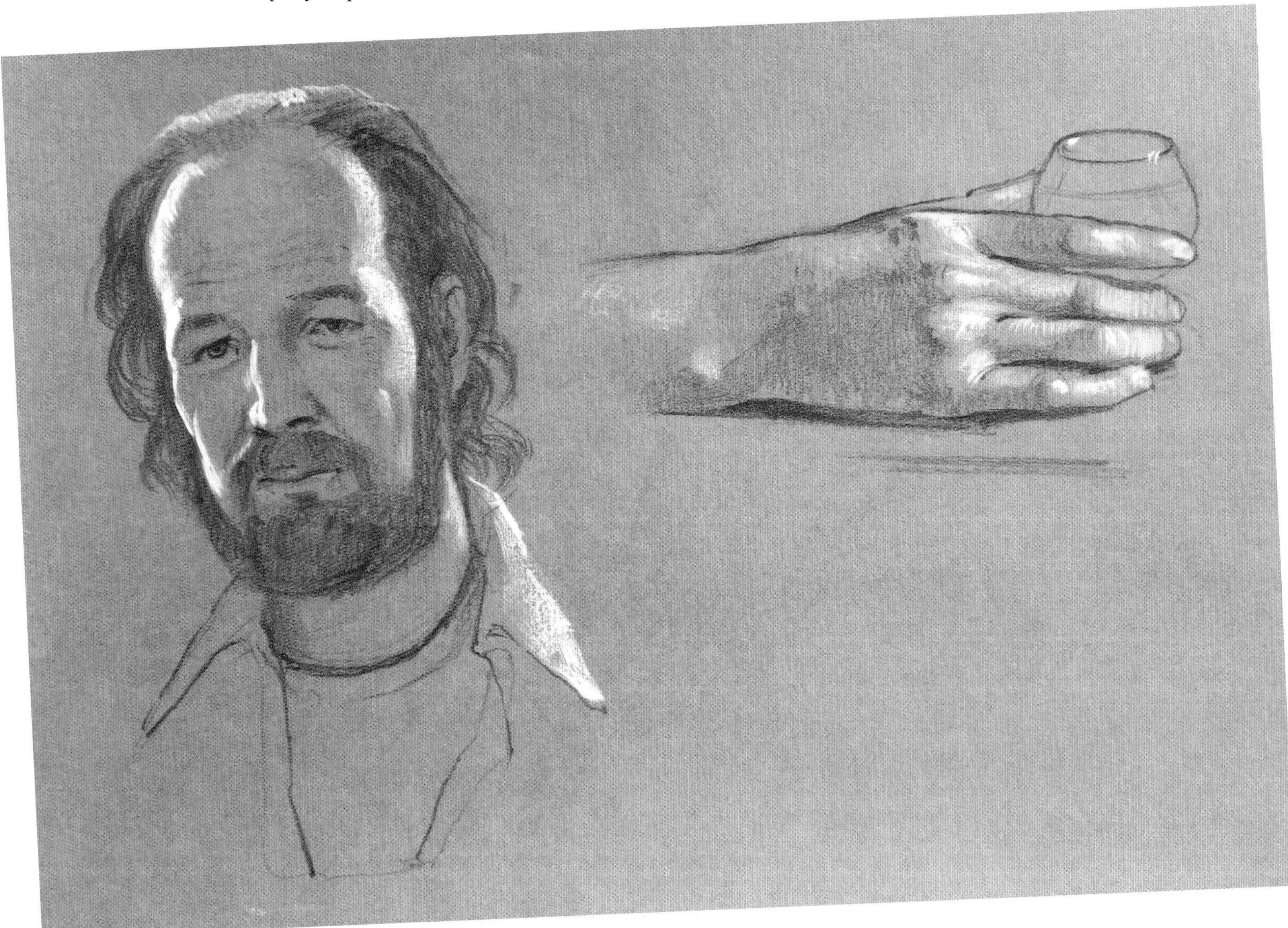

◀ **HEAD AND HAND STUDY,** *pencil and white gouache on brown paper, 8½" x 11". "I've been walkin' a tough road lately," this man told me as I sketched his portrait. He had been a friend of my family when he was in high school many years before, but had lost touch with all of us since then. When he appeared on our doorstep during a Thanksgiving reunion one year, he was offered a dinner and a chance to forget his cares. For me, sketching his portrait was a way to reopen my friendship with him. He posed at the dinner table with the light from a window behind illuminating the edges of his face. Never having been sketched before, he was a little nervous at first, but soon opened up, and after I showed him the finished picture, he seemed deeply touched. —JG*

▼ **SLEEPING WOMAN,** *watercolor on illustration board, 11½" x 16½". Some people make a better model asleep than awake. This sketch of a friend was done with drybrush watercolor in about an hour. In the middle of the sketch I was surprised to look up and see that she had changed positions in her sleep. It took all of my gentleness to coax her back into the original position without waking her. The drybrush watercolor technique I use is quite simple. After a detailed pencil underdrawing is sketched in, I use thin washes of color to establish the overall lighting. Then, with the brush tip dried on a paper towel, I scrub color onto the sketch in a delicate fashion, gradually bringing out the subtlety of form. I use a pencil eraser to lighten areas that need it and wet washes to darken areas that need it. —TK*

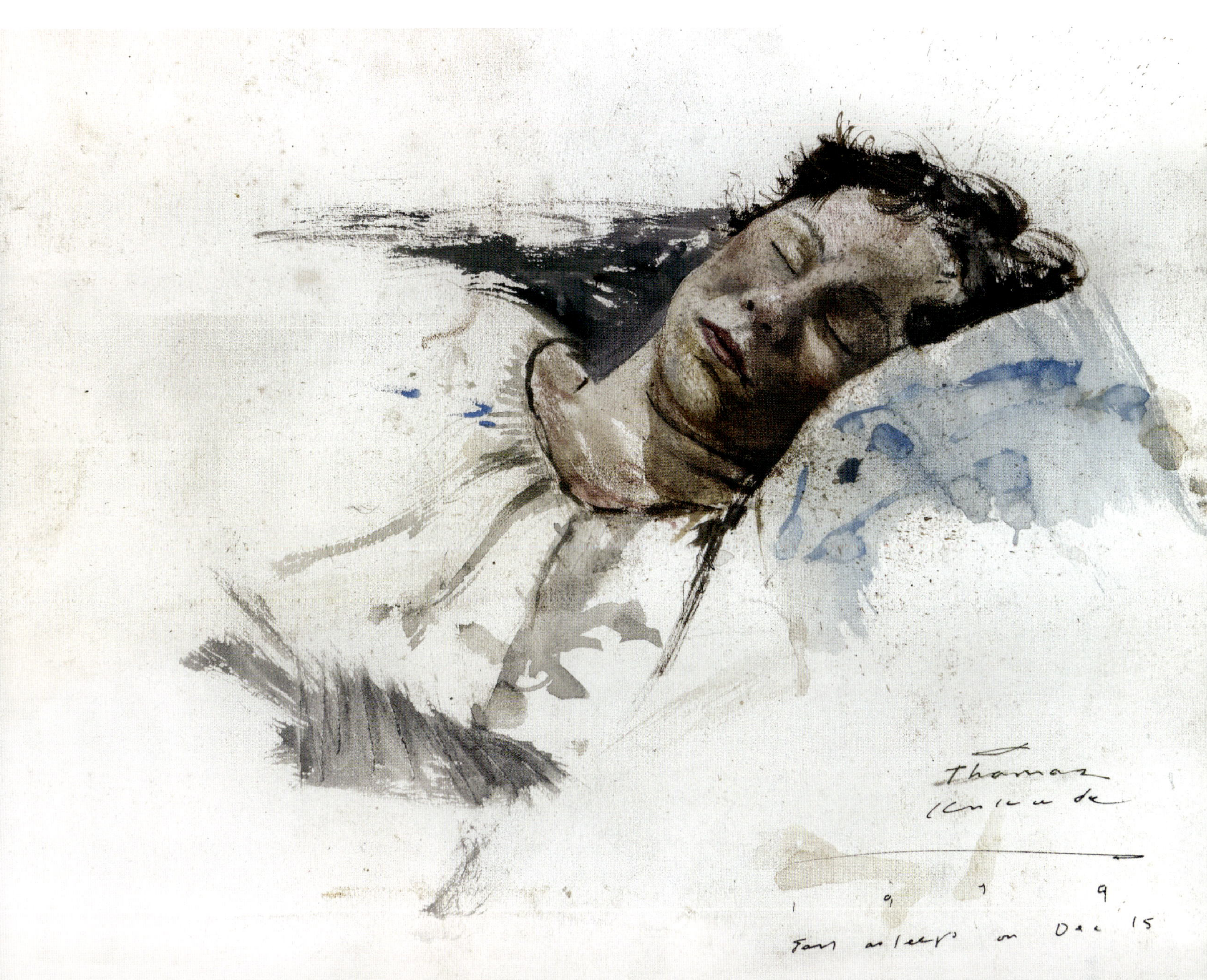

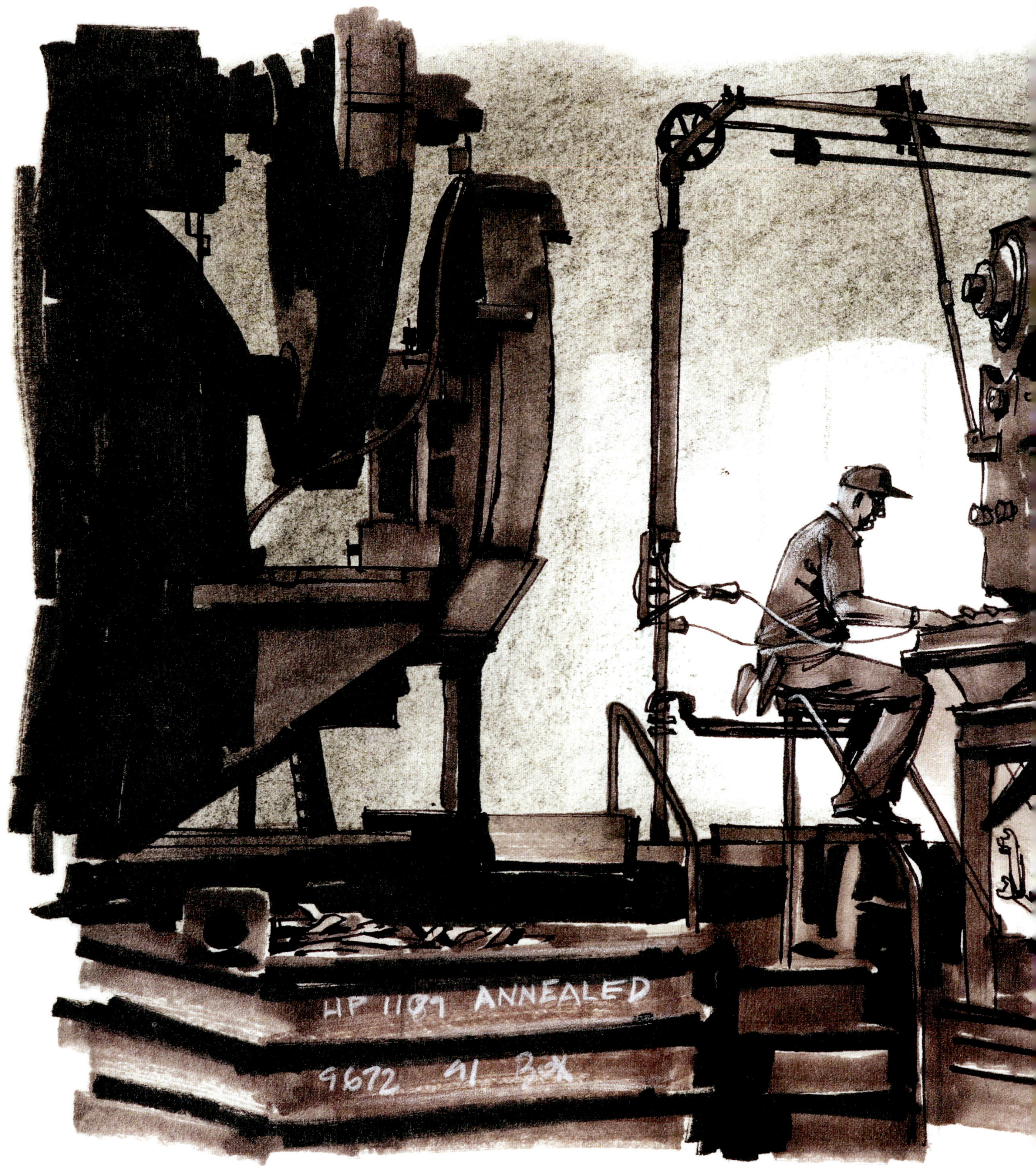
ANNEALED
9672 41

Exploring the Man-Made World

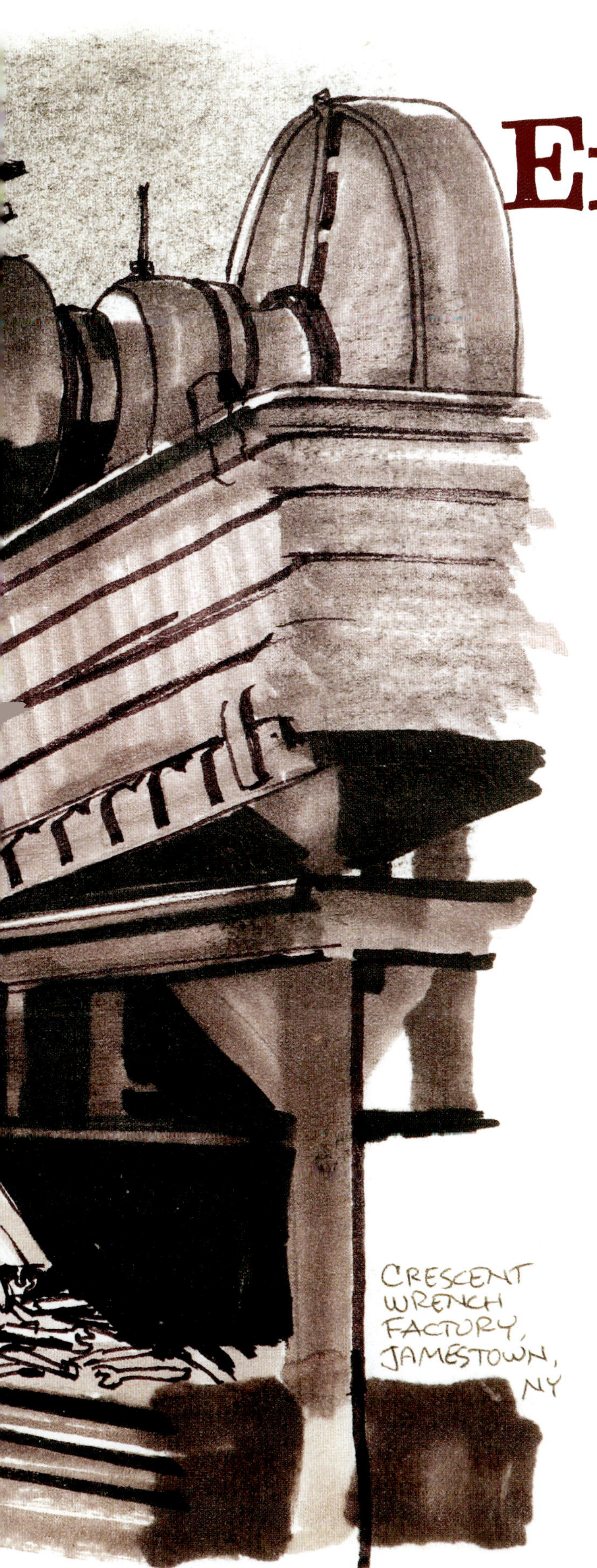

WORKER IN A STEEL FORGE, *calligraphy pen, gray markers, and charcoal on drawing paper, 11" x 14". Big tools make little tools in this drop-forge factory in western New York State. The big Czechoslovakian operator, with his hands held safe by restrainers, seemed as much a part of the machine as did the gears and hoses. I gained access to the factory by approaching the manager in the front office, who kindly gave me not only a visitor's pass, but also earplugs, goggles, and a hard hat to protect me from noise and danger. Fascinated by the looming black shapes of the machines, I chose a tonal technique that allowed me to sink arbitrary shapes into pure silhouette while rendering others more completely. When I worked on the areas on the left side of the composition, I paid special attention to alternating large against small shapes to give a sense of scale. I designed the silhouette so that the light gray negative shapes interlocked with the black positive shapes like pieces in a puzzle. The areas of the paper remaining white were carefully planned so that the viewer's eye would gravitate to the head of the worker, and then down the chute into the bin below. —JG*

THE STRUCTURES and objects that cover the landscape present you with a paradise of nonmoving subject matter for sketching. From the ancient to the modern, the pastoral to the industrial, the common to the exotic, you are bound to find something you would enjoy sketching within the realm of man-made objects. At first, you will probably be attracted to subjects for which you have warm associations—perhaps dilapidated barns or sailboats—but you'll soon discover that the range of subject matter that can interest you is unlimited. You may find yourself sketching city skylines, cement mixers, and drugstore facades with the same enthusiasm that you once only felt for more traditional subjects.

The key to enjoying sketching the varied subject matter of man-made objects is feeling confident about your ability to capture them on paper in an interesting way. In this chapter, we'll look at some of the methods we use to make any man-made form into a successful sketch.

BEGIN WITH THE COMMONPLACE

The best place to begin sketching man-made objects is with simple details of the everyday world, rather than big historic events or exotic places. For example, when you are downtown with your sketchbook, why not record something as ordinary as a gas station? You might be interested in the overall view, with the gas pumps and the garage, or just a small detail of it, such as a woman washing her windshield while waiting for her tank to fill. This is the kind of subject that most artists overlook as they trek off in search of the exotic. Yet the everyday things are what filled the sketchbooks of such great artists as Rembrandt and Toulouse-Lautrec. What they sketched is interesting to us because we are removed in time and space. But the things that we see daily are even more varied and interesting because the range of materials and technologies is far more elaborate than in any previous age.

The more you sketch, the more sensitive you will become to the commonplace. On the way to work or school or in the market, you will begin to take notice of all the little details that you may have overlooked before. By all means, follow your whims! Perhaps a rusted old neon sign that you had once considered an eyesore could end up being a prized addition to your sketchbook.

Keep track of the subjects that interest you by noting them regularly in a small notebook. Then when you have a free afternoon, a brief look through your notes will remind you of good locations for a sketching excursion.

SKETCHING IN THE HOME

Perhaps the most familiar subject matter can be found within the walls of your home. The kind of sketching we talk about in this book usually means going somewhere out-of-doors to draw, but with a bit of looking, you'll find plenty of fodder for your sketchbook right at home. Home is a good place to practice with furniture and small objects. When you draw them you can think about proportion or values or line—or you can think of nothing at all and just sketch absentmindedly while you are waiting for the laundry to finish drying. Drawing things at home is especially satisfying because it forces you to really look at those objects that you've casually used for years. Even a teapot or a lamp has nuances that you wouldn't be aware of unless you sketched them.

Home is the place for experimentation, because you have no spectators leaning over your shoulder, nor do you have to contend with the glaring sunshine. If you find a technique that intrigues you in any of the pictures in this book, you can try it first at home on a simple object. With the confidence that you have gained, you can then move on to more high-pressure situations, like on-the-spot portraits, and have a pretty good idea of what to expect.

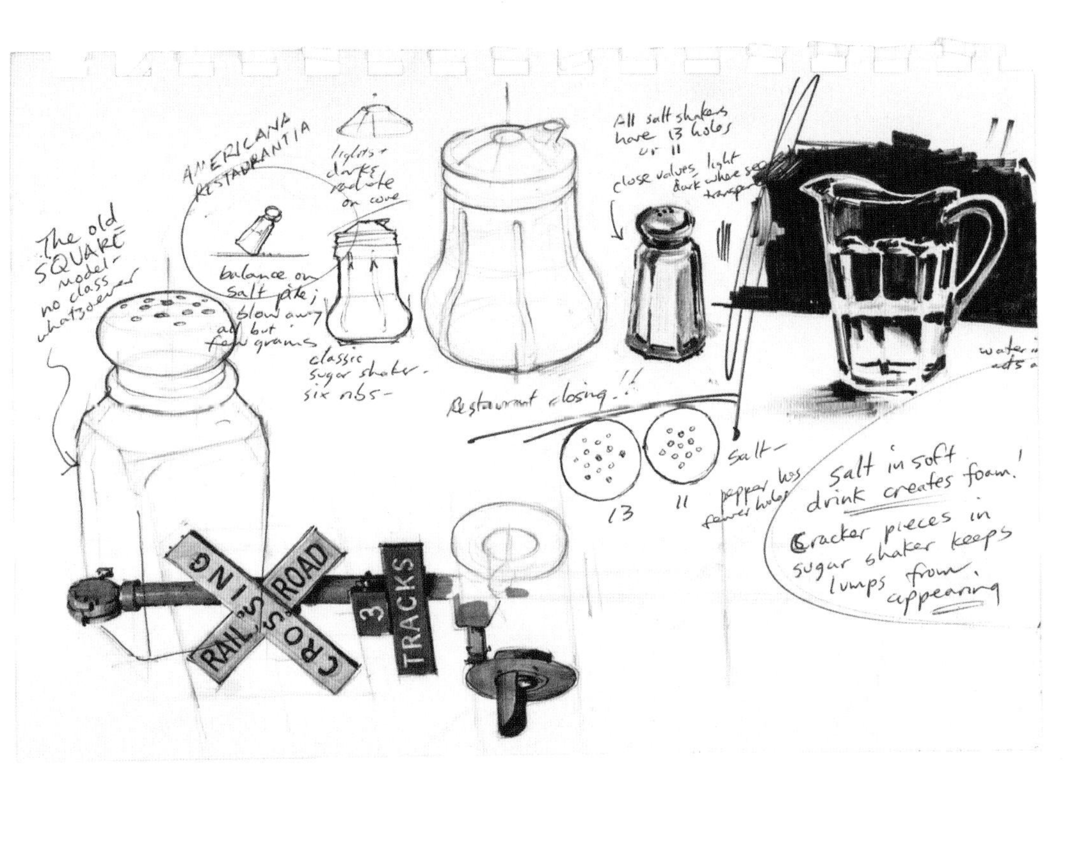

◀ **SALTSHAKERS AND CROSSING SIGN,** *pencil, calligraphy pen, and markers on smooth paper, 6" x 9". Did you know that most restaurant saltshakers have thirteen holes? Actually, that's if the holes are based on the hexagonal pattern—the star-shaped pattern has eleven holes. Not only that, there are at least two different designs for the body of the saltshaker. In some restaurants, they are six-sided, and in others they are four-sided. Before long I was learning about all sorts of everyday objects—sugar shakers, pitchers, and even railroad crossing signs, which I could see through the window of the restaurant. So it is when I see through the eyes of a sketchbook: the ordinary things I have looked at hundreds of times in the past reveal a wealth of fresh information. —JG*

▶ **ELECTRICAL TOWER,** *calligraphy pen on charcoal paper, 9" x 12". One person's eyesore is another person's delight. This electrical tower, for instance, was located behind some storefronts that were so elaborately decorated that I got the impression they were trying to disguise their backyard. I was unimpressed by the facade but found myself drawn instead to the electrical tower and the buildings surrounding it. The subject was simple enough that only a minimal underdrawing was needed. I only had a few minutes to sketch and I needed my time for the final sketch. Following the underdrawing, I completed the sketch with calligraphy pen, striving for a quick, indicative style that suggests details without actually delineating them. Electrical towers, telephone poles, and television antennas are overhead structures that few of us notice. However, they all make great subject matter because of the crispness of the struts and poles against the sky. —TK*

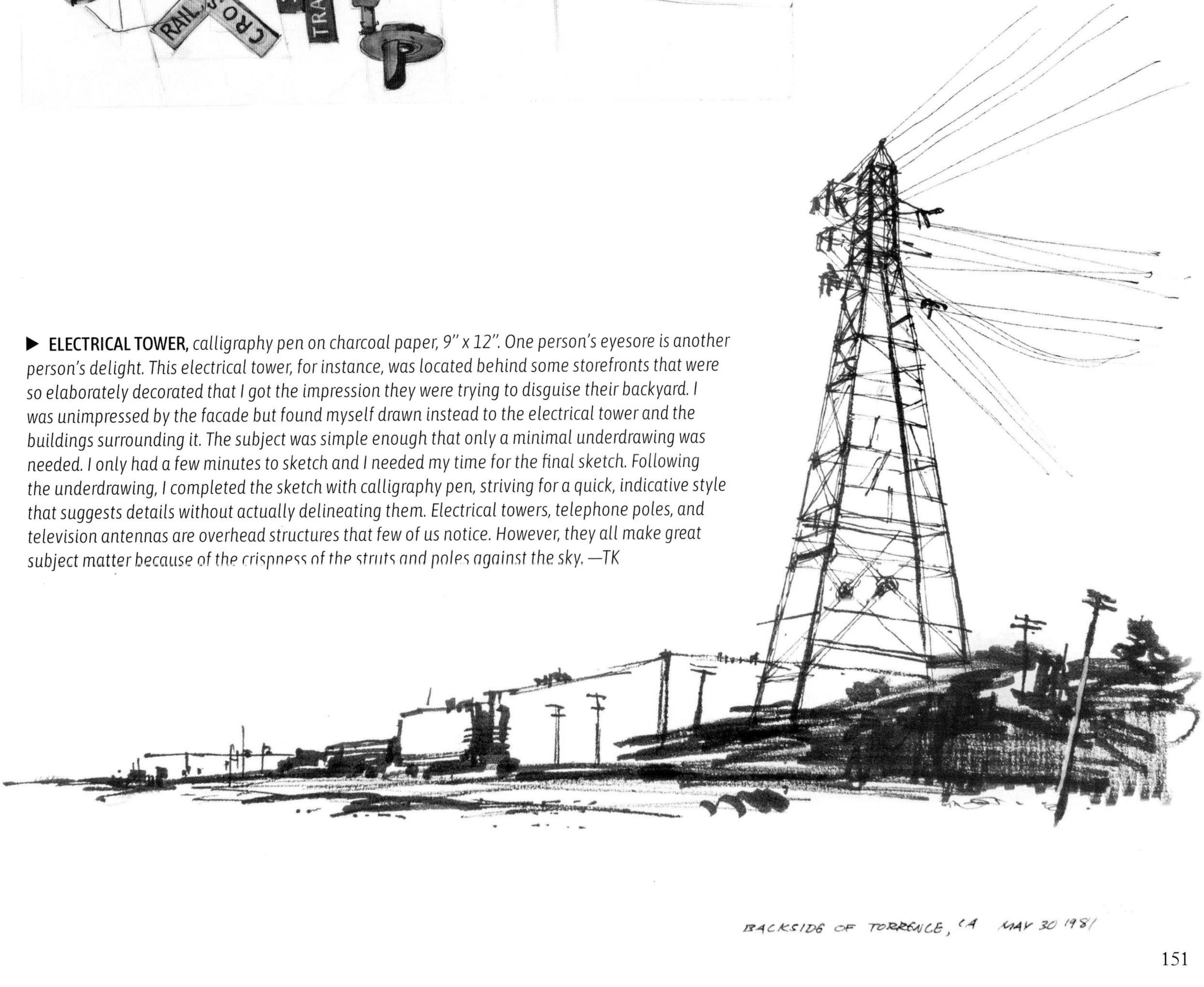

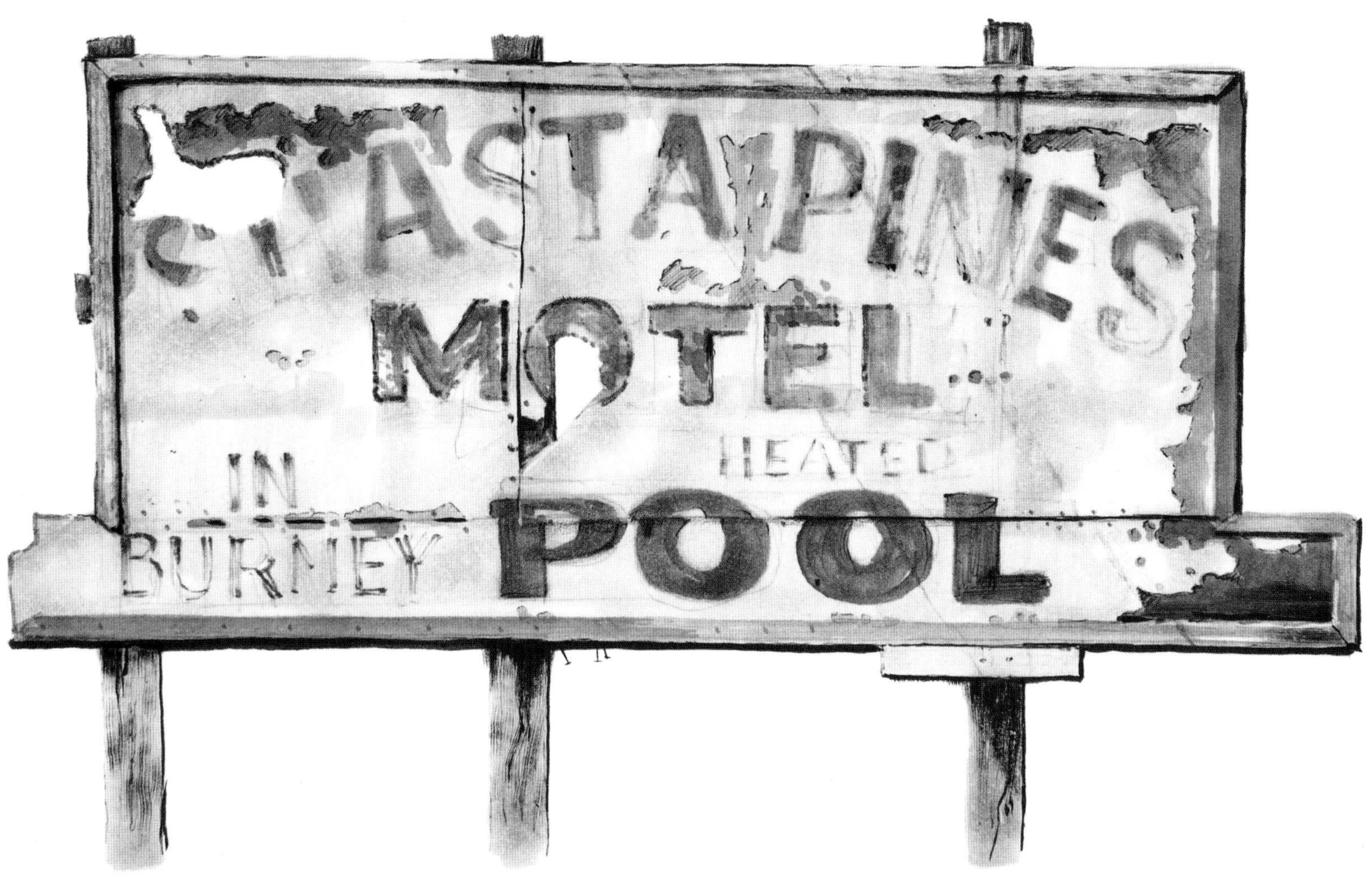

Sketching at home has a personal dimension as well, since any little vignette that you draw will be recorded forever. Later, when you rearrange the furniture or even move to a new home, your sketch will nostalgically call to mind the way it once looked.

INDICATING BUILDING EXTERIORS

Sketching building exteriors is no different from sketching any other man-made form if you see them in terms of pure line and tone and shape. The process for achieving accuracy, which we discuss in Chapter 3, can be used when you sketch anything from a chicken coop in the Ozark mountains to an ornate facade of a government building in Washington, D.C. But even though you will be working with a lot of straight lines, we recommend that you avoid using a ruler, to keep your sketches from looking harsh and cold.

You might be interested in a particular building for a number of reasons. Those of you studying architecture can find examples of cornices and friezes, as well as countless variations on window and rooftop details. For others, sketching buildings can be a way of documenting a particular region known for its distinctive building style, such as the brownstone buildings in New York City. The main reason we like to sketch buildings is simply for the joy in abstract shapes that every building is composed of. Just about any building, whether it's residential, commercial, or industrial, is visually made up of a variety of lines, short and long, of little details and large mass areas, and of textures ranging from rough stucco or brick to reflective glass or metal. Combined with figures for human scale and perhaps tree forms to contrast with all the straight lines, a building can be a visual feast.

The kind of sketching that we do where we convey this abstract variety in realistic terms is called indication. Unlike a rendering, an indication treatment suggests details without spelling them out. Bricks and windows can be hinted at with just a few strokes. Even a very complex form, like a Gothic church surrounded by scaffolding, could be handled easily with such a treatment.

Our favorite techniques for indication usually involve a drawing tool that can make either thin lines or broad strokes of black. For this we recommend using a soft pencil, like an Eagle Draughting pencil, which has been sharpened to a good point. The sharp point can be used

◀ **BILLBOARD,** *markers, ballpoint pen, and white chalk on smooth paper, 9" x 12". Copying signs is a good way to learn about letterforms. I'm always attracted to the old hand-painted roadside eyecatchers and to the neon extravaganzas fashioned decades ago by specialized craftsmen. Despite the fading and peeling paint on this billboard, I could still make out the shapes of the letters. Over a fifteen-minute underdrawing, I laid-in the marker tones, starting with the #2 and #4 in the light areas of the sign, and gradually working in the #6 in the darker areas. The black accents were added last with a ballpoint pen, which helps cure the fuzziness of a pure marker indication. I also added a few subtle touches of white chalk to further delineate texture. —JG*

▶ **GAS PUMP,** *gouache on illustration board, 8½" x 11". This gas pump seemed so animated and futuristic that no exaggeration was necessary to convey the robotlike appearance. I used black and white gouache as a technique in order to capture crisp details with a minimum of effort. I began the sketch with a half-hour underdrawing to clearly establish the subject in simple geometric forms. Following the underdrawing I used opaque gouache to render the pump area by area. After an hour the sketch was mostly painted but still somewhat crude in appearance. What was missing were the little touches of detail. I got out my #2 red-sable round brush and began to build up the detail, adding highlights on the hoses and pump handles, indicating the numbers and the display area, and adding sparkles wherever necessary. —TK*

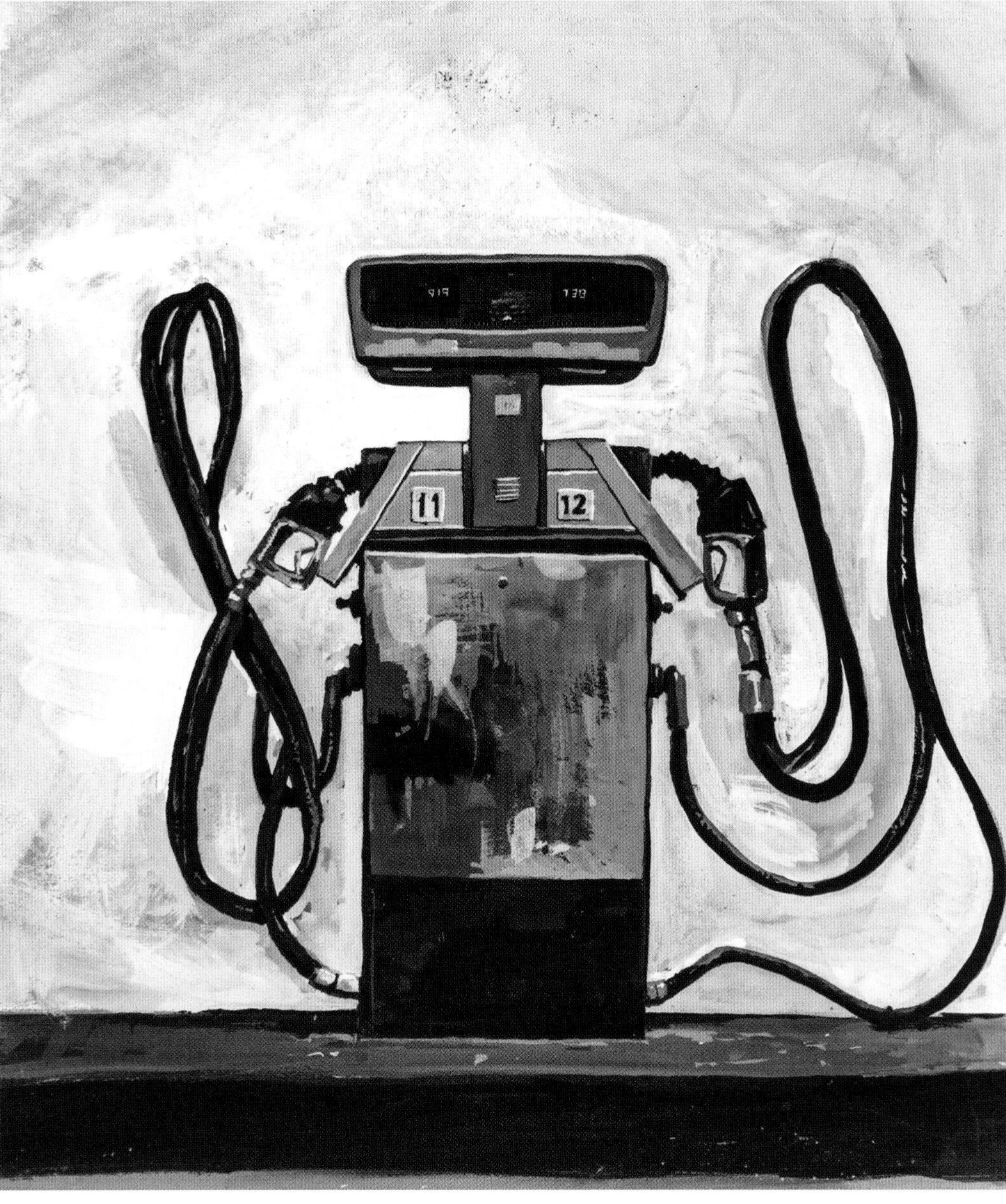

for lines; and the side of the lead, with the pencil held at a low angle to the page, can be used for wide strokes. Similarly, a calligraphy marker can make a variety of stroke widths, depending on whether you use the edge or the flat part of the chisel tip. Combined with a gray marker, or with charcoal, it can yield results that suggest the look of a painting in a minimum of time.

The main point to keep in mind when you are indicating is to avoid outlines, particularly around the side of the forms receiving the light. Also, alternate large shapes against small ones for the sake of variety. And use the biggest and the fewest strokes that you possibly can. If you sketch frequently with these ideas in mind, all your building pictures will breathe with a feeling of warmth and spontaneity.

SIGNS AND LETTERFORMS

Signs and letterforms are an effective device to add interest to a sketch, particularly to a larger street scene or interior. Even small signs in a sketch will grab the eye and help to tell a story. Taking the time to carefully render a sign may seem laborious, but the payoff is rich. A sketch of even an ordinary building takes on charm and interest through the use of signs. For example, imagine a sketch of a supermarket. If you chose to delete the various window signs and sale posters and simply drew the building alone, you would be left with a rather boring boxlike form with little character. Yet when the signs are added, and perhaps even exaggerated, your sketch will be more exciting.

If you have trouble making "lettered-looking" signs, then simply use your personal handwriting to indicate the signs you sketch. Even the crudest lettering can

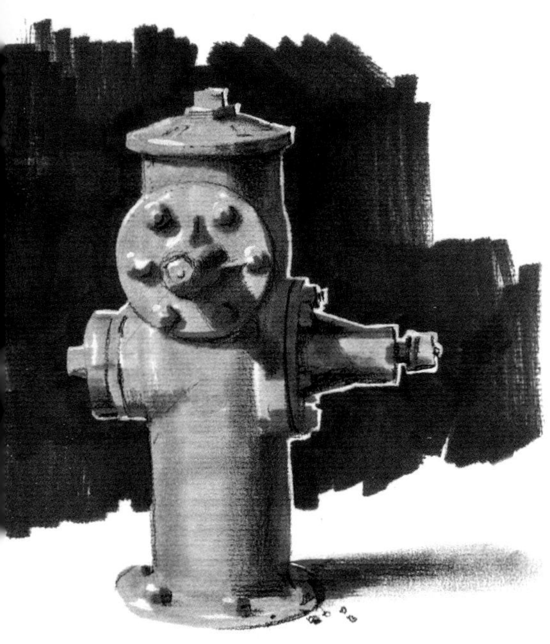

FIRE HYDRANT, *markers and charcoal on charcoal paper, 9" x 12". Nothing fancy or exotic, just a fire hydrant. But I was interested in it as a variation on the simple cylinder form in light and shade that I had practiced so many times in studio exercises. At the base of the hydrant, it's easy to see the light, the cast shadows, and the reflected light. The cast shadow from the frontal spout crosses over the protrusion on the right, suggesting that the angle of the sun is about forty-five degrees. I tackled the rendering with just two values of gray—#2 on the light side, and #6 on the dark side—with a black background to bring the whole shape forward. The white outline along the right-hand edge helps to separate the dark side from the background. Inside the form, a black charcoal pencil was used to accent the cracks and hollows. A few white highlights were added to the nuts to indicate their form without having to resort to using outline on the light side. —JG*

add great warmth to a sketch if it includes actual wording from the sign.

Furthermore, if you have an interest in calligraphy or typography, sketching signs is an excellent way to broaden your scope of letter styles. You'll run across letter styles on signs that never find their way to the printed page. Neon, for example, because of the requirement that the letterforms be continuous, has developed a graphic look all its own. The three-dimensional cutout letters that you find on old storefronts are also fascinating to draw because of the way the third dimension is used.

The layout of signs that you will find on the road is just as interesting from a graphic standpoint as are the letterforms themselves. There's a special beauty to the old diner signs, in the way that they stack the letters vertically and steer the eye with neon arrows. If you live near an old arcade or boardwalk, there are plenty of the densely packed circus posters and other cluttered layout forms that make great subjects.

Adapt whatever technique suits your temperament. We suggest you start with a fairly careful pencil underdrawing to establish horizontals for the upper and lower cases, as well as the slant of italics. Then go in with gray markers or calligraphy markers. Make written notations of colors to refresh your memory if you plan on making a painting later from your sketch. Lighted signs at nighttime can be easily sketched with the tone paper technique that we use throughout the book.

A NEW LOOK AT MACHINES

Wherever people work outdoors, there are usually opportunities for sketching machines. Road construction crews, for example, use a fascinating variety of heavy machines for leveling the surface and laying on gravel and tar. Building contractors have their own equipment, usually including an assortment of cranes and cement mixers. Neither of us knows much about construction, yet for some reason we have both always loved to sketch complex gadgetry. Perhaps the fact that we *aren't* experts about these machines and that we don't know what all the hoses and gears are for allows us to indulge in the pure joy of drawing form for the sake of form. What's more, the big machines that you find on the job are designed according to the law of pure function, not style, which makes them seem more earthy and honest.

Our machine-sketching obsession has even taken us into several factories, where we have set up our sketching stools amid the pungent wood pulp steam of a paper mill, or the thundering crash of a steel forge, or the silent concentration of a design shop for precision race cars. The process of how things are made would be fascinating in itself, even if we had no sketchbook, but to spend a moment to study the details of the factory makes the experience even more memorable.

Generally, the smaller factories are more willing to allow sketching than are the big corporate factories, which usually try to safeguard trade secrets. However, if you approach the front office, telling them that you are an artist with a desire to sketch machines, you'll usually get clearance to set up in an inconspicuous area where you won't disturb the workers. For this kind of sketching, take a very simple load—a folding stool, a 9" x 12" pad, a few pencils and markers.

RENDERING SMALL OBJECTS

One motivation for sketching man-made objects is simply to sharpen your technique. Rendering from still lifes in the studio or copying from photographs can never equal the satisfaction of working outdoors from real objects, because the natural sunlight illuminates form far more clearly than does artificial light, and the forms that you sketch can be touched, studied from all sides, and measured. You can use just about any of the tonal techniques that we referred to in Chapter

2, "Materials" markers, gouache, wash, pencil, or even ballpoint pen, depending on what feels most comfortable to you.

It is usually best to render on a sunny day because the clear light causes a definite pattern of light and shade. However, overcast days are also good if you are more attentive to subtlety of shading. Choose something small enough that you can walk around it and study it from different angles. Such things as fire hydrants, parking meters, rural mailboxes, and automobiles can be found anywhere, and make good subjects for careful rendering.

In renderings, a pencil underdrawing is particularly useful. Outline all the major shapes, and be sure your perspective and proportion is accurate. When you do begin laying-in the tonal media, do so gradually, and try to fix any mistakes as you go. Don't worry if the sketch starts looking overworked; your goal is to achieve a realistic likeness, complete with all the texture and shadows and small details. This disciplined practice will provide a good contrast to the kind of sketching you do when you want to capture motion or jot down a quick mood thumbnail.

USING CLUTTER

Certain subject matter seems to call for a semi-cartoon approach that emphasizes decorative detail and holds the interest of the viewer. It's the opposite of the stark minimalism of a simple monumentalized object lost in mystery. A Victorian house, or an antique shop, for instance, could be sketched in such a way. To some, this look in a sketch seems false and cluttered; to others it's an honest response to the subject matter. In any case here are some ideas about ways to achieve that look if you want to try them:

1. Try to keep your drawing linear, using either a technical pen or a fountain pen. The effect of clutter is related to delicacy more than to

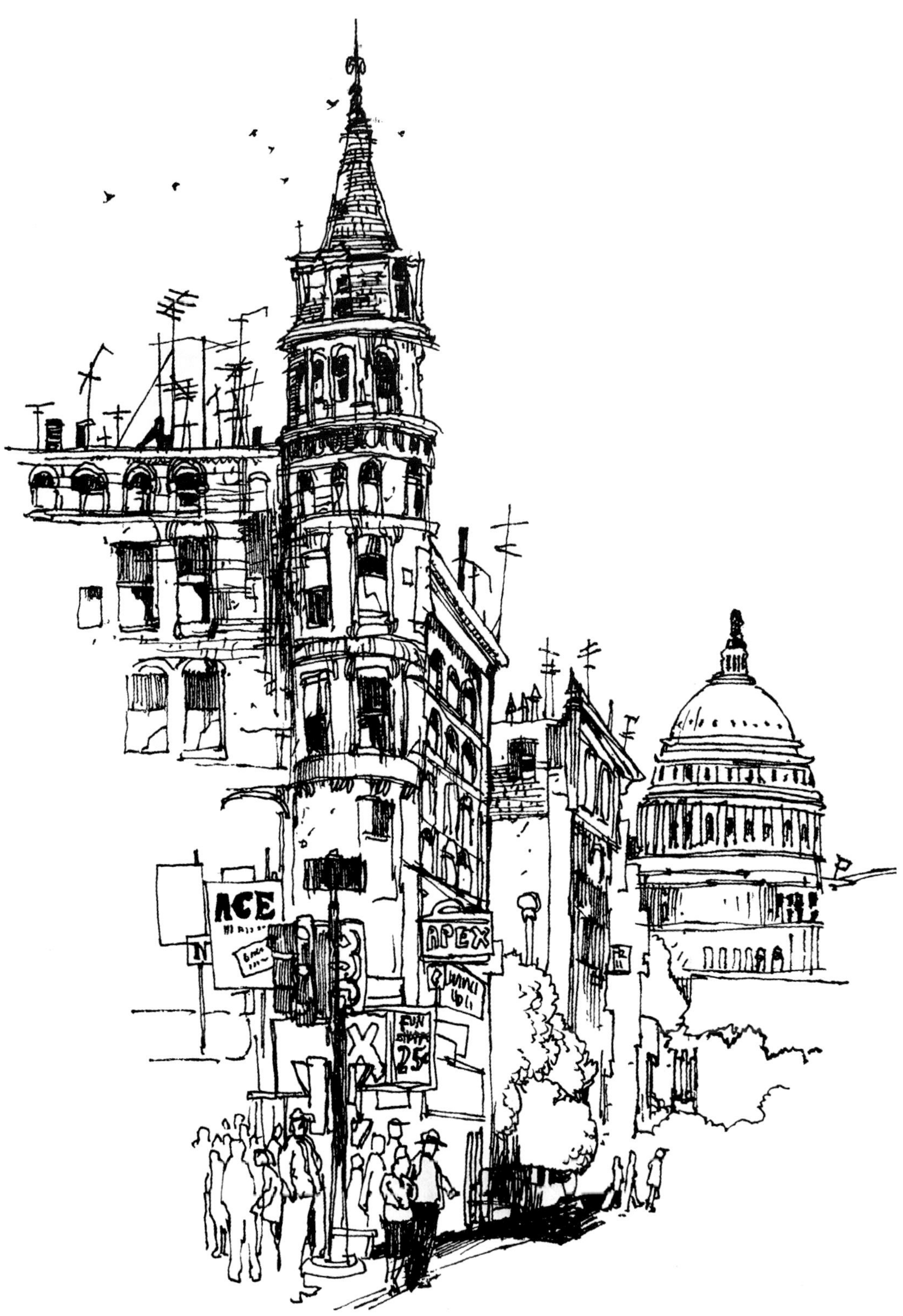

STREET SCENE, WASHINGTON, D.C., *technical pen on sketch paper, 9" x 12". To me, a cluttered sketch, like an overfilled bookcase, has a charm all its own. I've found that certain subjects lend themselves well to the cluttered look: broken-down buildings, coffee shop tables after a meal, parking lots; however, any subject can be given a feeling of clutter with the right approach. To achieve the effect, I allow myself to continue drawing details beyond the point of my artistic common sense. Also, as I work, I keep in mind a focal point where the detail is packed the tightest. In this sketch I chose to focus on the tower in the center of the sketch. The further an area is from the tower, the less detail I gave it. —TK*

drama or mystery. A lot of toning or use of heavy black seems to kill the effect.

2. Keep your pen to the paper as much as possible, without lifting between strokes. Like cursive writing, the lines will then take on a sense of verve.
3. Pack in the detail, even past the point of good taste. Try to keep a single focus, though, so it doesn't look scattered. If a certain area of the scene you are sketching seems dry, borrow forms from elsewhere in the scene.
4. Repeat elements in the scene, improvising variations as you go. On a fire truck, for example, you might make a hundred dials and levers rather than the ten or twenty that might actually be there. Don't worry about actuality—try to go beyond the fact, as you would in exaggeration (see Chapter 6, "Using Imagination").

ON-THE-SPOT RESEARCH

Do you know how many windows there are on the side of an average city bus? Or how the fruit and vegetable scales are hung in a supermarket? Or what a policeman wears on his belt? Some people have photographic memories, but we sure don't. The best way to find out is to observe firsthand and to record your observations with a sketchbook. If you are an illustrator or a cartoonist, you may not be able to find photographic reference for many everyday details, and often the deadlines are too tight to allow you to take your own photos. Many of the great illustrators in the past have been those who have compiled, over the years, thousands of sketches of ordinary things around them. Most of the sketches were made with no specific use in mind, yet one way or another, just about everything found its way into a finished illustration.

Take the extreme case of the newspaper sketch artists around the turn of the century before the invention of the halftone process for photographs. Artists like F. R. Gruger and George Luks and William Glackens would be required to report to the scene of some big news event, like a hotel fire, and record it in pen and ink in two or three hours for the next edition of the paper. Needless to say, they had no time to do a lot of observing for the first time. They had very well-trained visual memories, and more importantly they had sketchbook after sketchbook of little details like fireplaces and barber chairs that could be used to reconstruct a scene later. Because of their extensive sketching experience, it was no problem for someone like Gruger to do complex, detailed illustrations purely from his head.

We like to think of the idea that every artist has a "visual vocabulary," a mental stockpile of forms that he or she has become familiar with through sketching. With or without photographs, it is the artist with the larger visual vocabulary who will be able to construct the most believable scenes in his or her paintings and illustrations.

And on a more personal level, there's a joy that you feel in knowing about the rich texture of your world, at seeing things that everyone else overlooks in their haste to get from one place to another. Putting those sketches to use is almost beside the point; it's the doing of them that's so enjoyable.

One good way to approach this kind of form research is to compare and contrast subtle variations in a single type of object—a streetlight, for example, or a drinking fountain. If you are so inclined, start a page in your sketchbook especially devoted to "variations on storefront awnings," or whatever. Whenever you run across a new one, open up your book to that page and jot down the new style.

USING WRITTEN NOTES

As we've seen with other kinds of sketching, written notes can help you clarify your response to a man-made subject and carry it beyond the limitations

HAIR STYLING SALON, *calligraphy pen and white CarbOthello pencil on brown paper, 8¼" X 11". Surrounded by loud music and the whine of a hair drier, I sat in this futuristic barber shop and sketched the tools of the hair stylist's trade. For me, sketching blow dryers and sinks and futuristic barber chairs was a means of learning about their form and adding them to my mental catalog of shapes. I often sketch unusual objects just for the sake of understanding them. In this sketch, I used a brief underdrawing in pencil to establish the general shapes and then began detailing with a calligraphy pen. White was added with a CarbOthello pencil to further suggest the light on the edges of the form. Written notes helped to clarify the color and material of the subject. —TK*

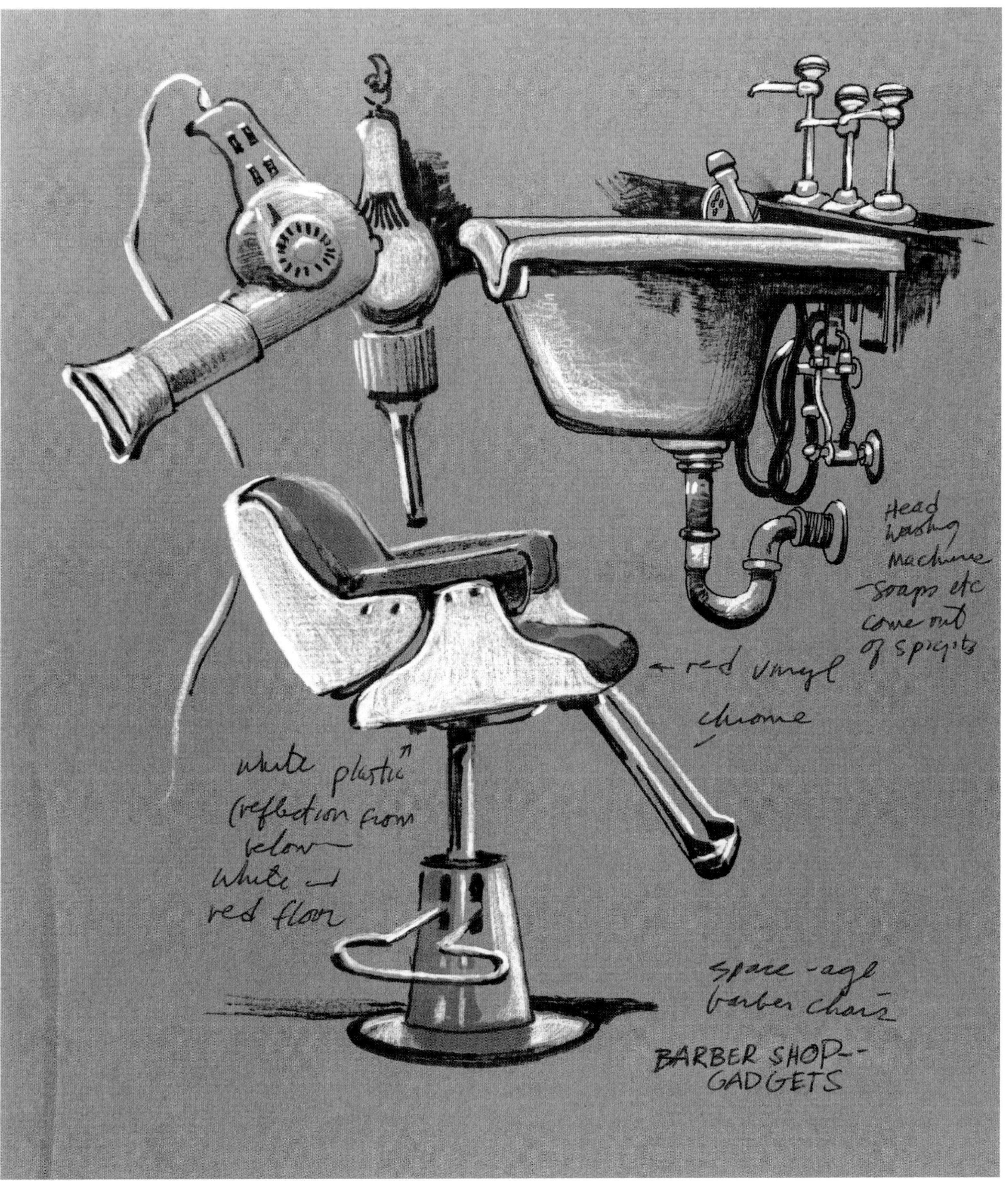
Head washing machine -soaps etc come out of spigots
← red vinyl
chrome
white plastic (reflection from below white and red floor
Space-age barber chair
BARBER SHOP-GADGETS

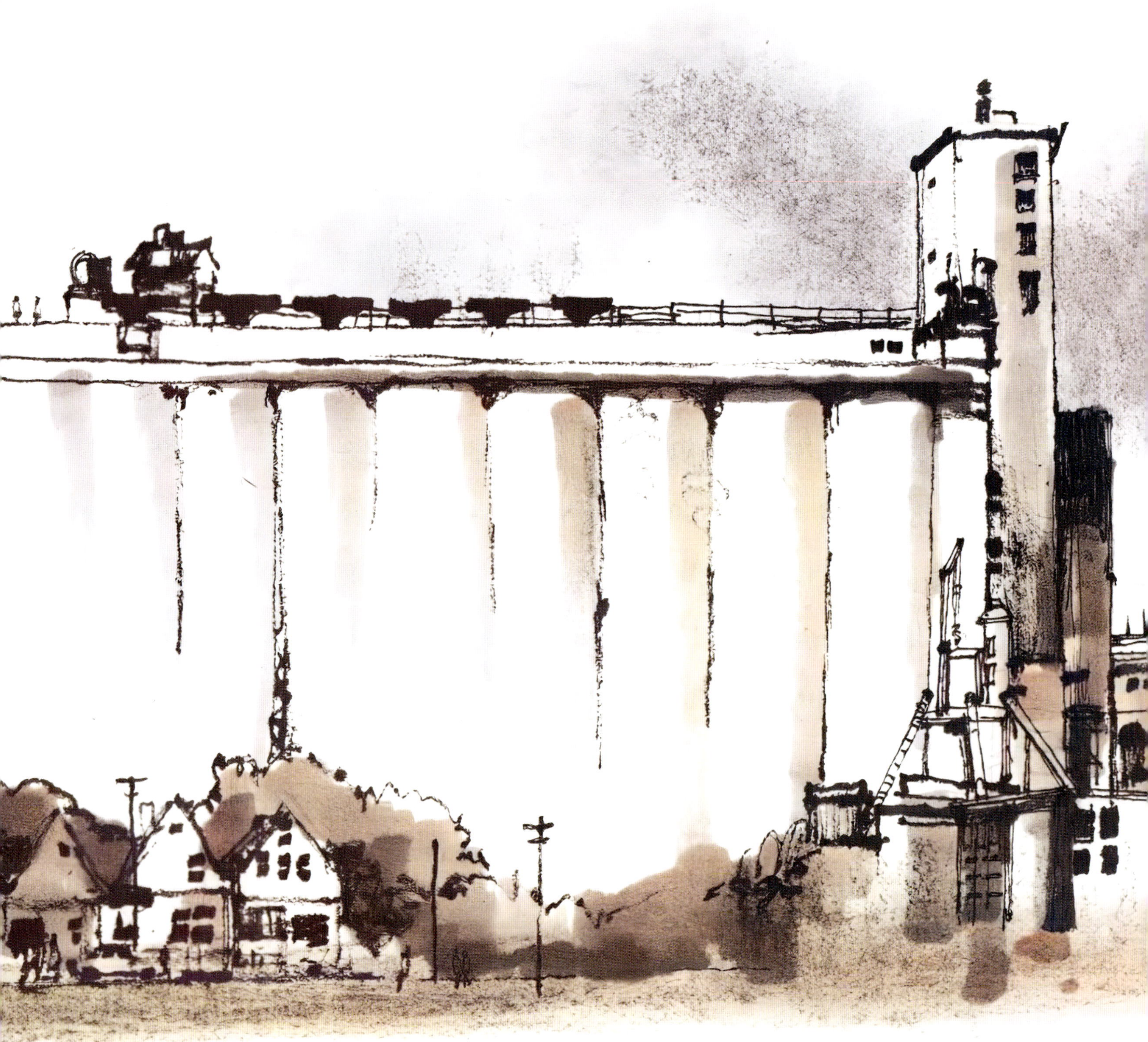

GRAIN SILOS, *calligraphy pens and gray markers and charcoal on sketch paper, 11" x 14". The massiveness of these grain silos juxtaposed with the frail homes beneath suggested to me the power that big industry has over the individual. To express this theme in my sketch, I emphasized the vastness of the silos by simplifying and enlarging their form. In addition, I placed much mechanized detail at the far-right side of the sketch to serve as a foil to the starkness of the silos. The small homes below the silos were kept uniform and rather plain to exaggerate the domination that the silos have over them. —TK*

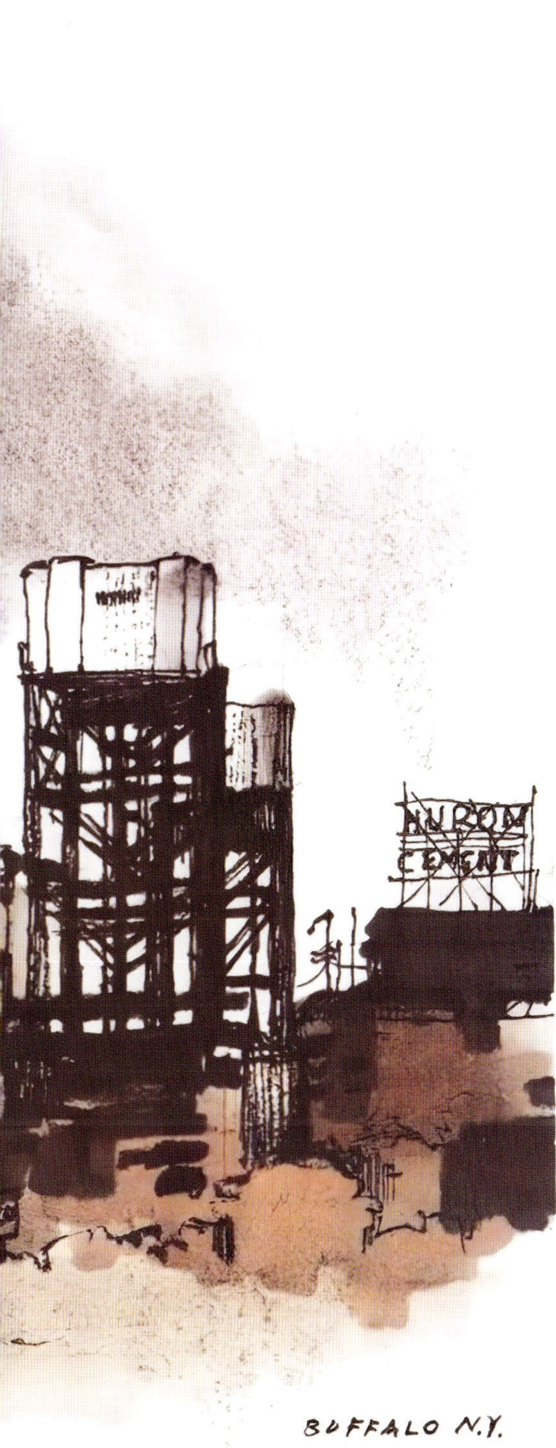

of what can be said in a drawing. You can, for example, record the size, color, texture, and function very easily in words. Also, make a point of writing the place name of where you did the sketch at the bottom of the page.

When you are sketching man-made things—whether they're sailboats or World War II airplanes or cattle feeders—you're likely to be approached by an onlooker who is an expert on the subject. If so, ask them questions and write down what they tell you. They'll not only be delighted to talk about something that they know so much about, but they'll also be touched by the fact that you have taken the time to observe it.

THINKING AS A DOCUMENTARY ARTIST

Sketches of buildings and street scenes can do more than just record mechanical facts. You can also create a provocative combination of elements in a scene to make a specific point about society or culture. For example, imagine this scene: a little cement-statue store with all of the Venus and Cupid birdbaths surrounded by a tall chain-link fence with hubcaps hanging from it. It would be hard to spell out the meaning of a scene like that, but some might say it suggests the way we Americans preserve the image of the classical past in a kind of artificial sanctuary amid the twentieth-century machine culture.

This is tender ground to tread, because meanings in pictures don't translate directly into words, but there's a definite principle at work. Juxtaposition, or the side-by-side placement of two seemingly unrelated elements, can give an otherwise boring sketch an intriguing twist of meaning. Documentary photographers have known this for a long time. For example, those of us who never experienced the Depression of the 1930s have been touched by the poignancy and drama of those years through powerful photographs. The Depression photographers realized that interest and compassion come from juxtaposing the extreme contrasts that surrounded them. A photo of a little girl with a doll is one thing, but a photo of that same girl in a bread line beside many hungry and penniless derelicts has far more power and tells us more about the conditions of that period.

As a sketch artist you have the same opportunity to document the unique features of the age we live in, an age with no less poignancy than the Depression. Yet because you work with a pencil instead of a camera, you have far more freedom to select and compose. By combining all the tools you've been developing in the chapters on mood and people-sketching, as well as the material in this chapter, you can be fully prepared to do documentary art on the spot which will uniquely express your world as you see it.

THE JOY OF EXPLORATION

One of the most important aspects to sketching the man-made world is the fact that it offers you the opportunity to explore aspects of your physical environment that you might otherwise have remained unaware of. More than any other type of subject, man-made objects are often hidden to the public eye. Factories and buildings of all sorts are rich assemblages of mysterious forms waiting to be noticed and recorded. Clockshops, pawnshops, and plumbing shops are examples of the rich variety of specialty stores which all house a wealth of unusual objects. Broken-down relics of other times, other eras, await your scrutiny.

Yet the key to all of this learning and exploration is your sketchbook. A pencil in your hand will directly affect the degree to which you become immersed in the detail of the world you live in.

Sketching in Your Life

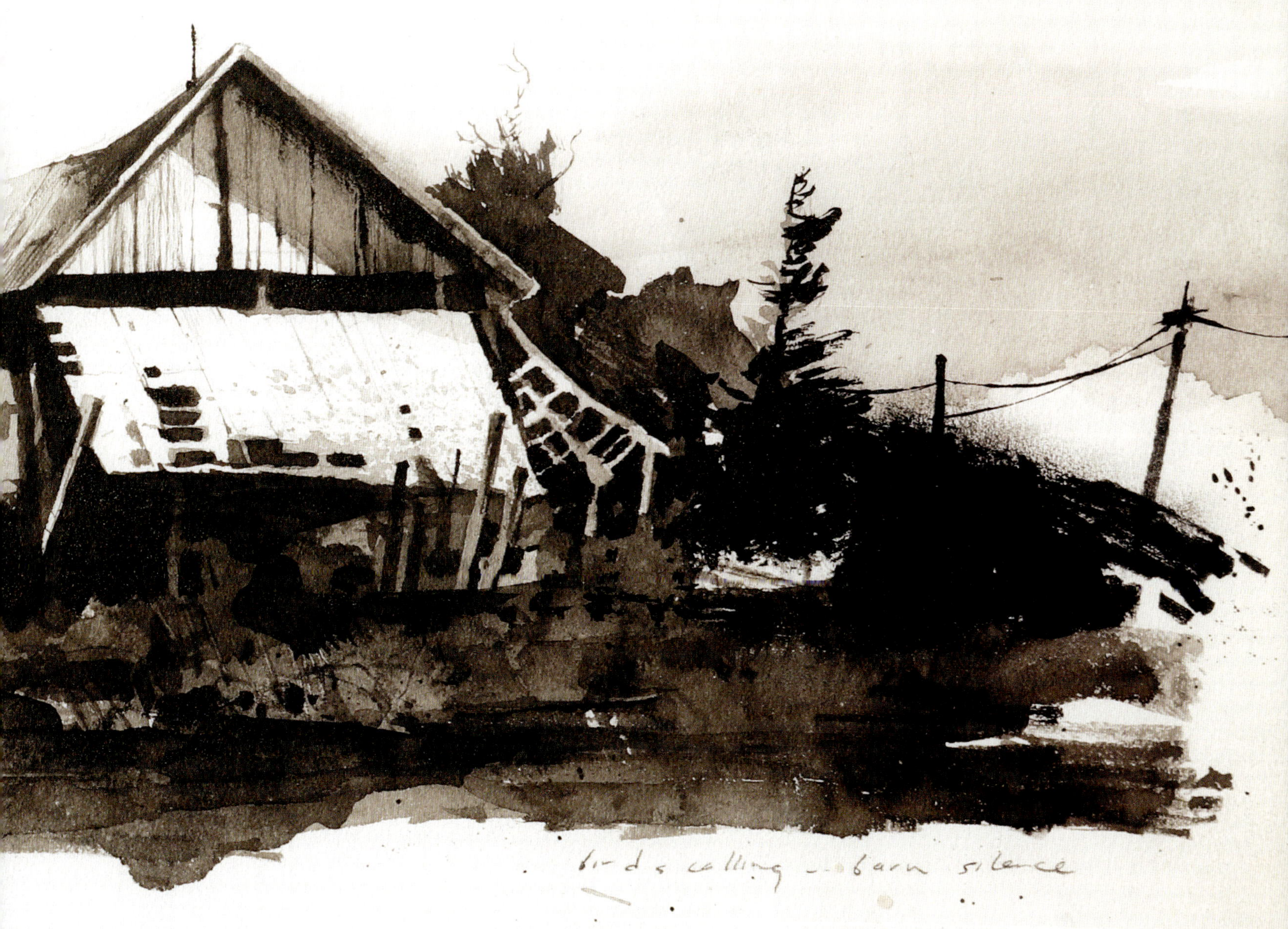
birds calling ... barn silence

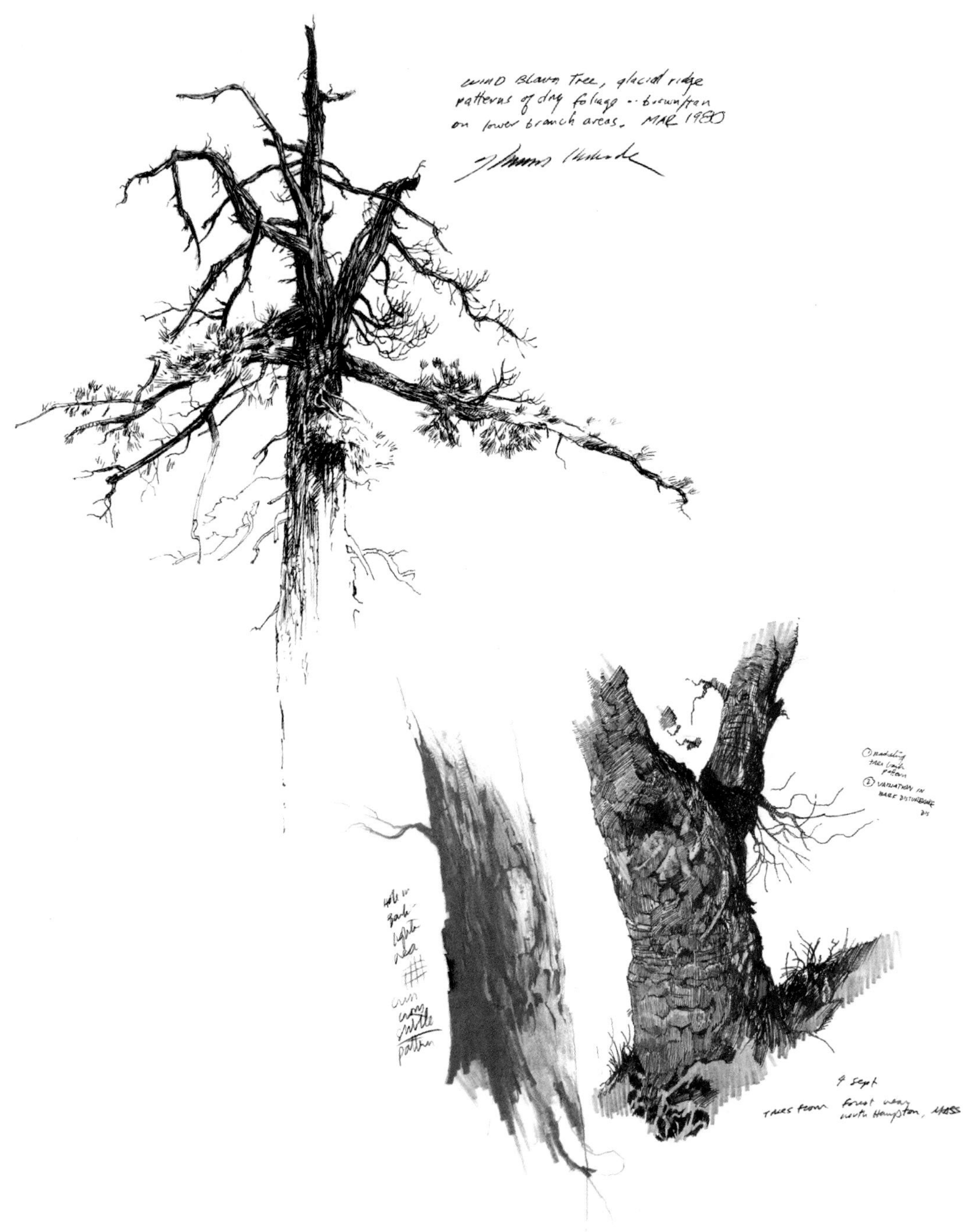

▲ **TREE SKETCHBOOK,** *ballpoint pen, pencil, and pen and ink on smooth paper, 11" x 14". As a landscape painter, trees are more than a personal fascination: they are a part of my profession. To stimulate my study of trees, I have begun a special sketchbook for trees in which I explore bark texture, limb formations, and leaf patterns. To allow the greatest versatility of techniques in these sketches, I custom-bound a sketchbook of smooth two-ply printer's bristol. This paper works well with ballpoint pen, as in the sketch to the left, or with pure pencil as in the sketch in the middle, or fine-point pen and pencil combined, as in the sketch on the right. I find that by keeping a sketchbook devoted to a single type of subject, I motivate myself to explore that subject more fully than I would have otherwise. —TK*

◀◀ **DILAPIDATED BARN,** *wash on illustration board, 10" x 15". With ingenuity, a sketch can be used to enrich your creative and personal life. This sketch of a dilapidated barn in southern California is a good example of the ways that sketching can be put to use. The sketch was initially made as a study for a painting I wanted to do. I returned home intending to put the sketch in my reference file for future use. But at home, when I took a second look at the sketch, I decided that I would rather display it in the studio as a reminder of the sunny picnic that was the occasion for making the sketch. —TK*

So far in this book we've offered a variety of methods designed to make your on-the-spot sketching experience more exciting. If you keep practicing and taking on new challenges, we fully expect you to improve rapidly and accumulate dozens of interesting sketches. But this is only part of the story. The greatest enjoyment comes when you discover how sketching can enrich your entire life. Think of sketching not as an isolated pastime, but as an investment that you make in other areas of your life. For example, if you've always wanted to learn more about a certain area of drawing, such as landscapes, people, or animals, you can motivate yourself by devoting a special sketchbook to that one topic. Or if you are a painter or an illustrator, you can use your sketches to help you develop ideas for finished compositions. Sketches can even be used to brighten the lives of your friends and relatives by means of illustrated letters, travel postcards, and sketching games. What we are offering you in this final chapter are the ways to put sketching to work. Use these in any way that suits your personality.

KEEPING SPECIALIZED SKETCHBOOKS

What do you enjoy sketching the most? People? Plants? Animals? Machines? Whatever it is, you might want to devote a whole sketchbook to that one category of subject matter. Imagine an entire sketchbook devoted to trees—tree silhouettes, light and shade studies, close-up details of bark texture and leaves, and comparative studies of similar species of trees. The biggest advantage to keeping specialized sketchbooks is that they help motivate you to study a topic of interest more fully than you would have otherwise. If you want to try this, devote an empty sketchbook to a topic that you have been wanting to explore. Make the topic broad enough so that the full sketchbook and more is needed to study it. For example, a whole sketchbook devoted to studies of shoes might get tiresome after a while, but if you allowed yourself to study clothes in general, you could fill the book with all kinds of details of shoes, fold patterns, collars, and types of hats that you observe on people you sketch.

Use a sketchbook that is fairly small—5" x 8" is ideal—so that you can conveniently carry it with you any time you go sketching. Start with a thin book, no more than twenty-four or thirty-two pages. In this way, you can have the satisfaction of filling it up soon. Also, make sure the sketchbook you buy for this purpose is sturdy enough to hold up to a lot of wear and tear. We recommend a strong spiral-bound pad. Restrict yourself to just one or two techniques—perhaps just pencil or fountain pen or markers, depending on what you like working with. Using one technique lets you concentrate on exploring the subject, rather than worrying about a lot of styles and media. A whole sketchbook that explores a single category of subject matter with a single technique has a wonderful feeling of continuity and consistency.

The Studio Notebook. Another kind of specialized sketchbook is the studio notebook, an all-purpose study guide that we use in the studio to keep a record of what we have learned. We use the 8" x 10" composition books. The paper quality is not important since most of the notations are in pencil or pen. Every book is numbered and dated, given a table of contents, and placed on a shelf above our desks.

Studio notebooks serve as a record of all the learning and progress we make as artists. Any time we work on a painting, the thumbnails and notes are jotted down. New ideas about composition, technique, and ways of using light and shadow are also recorded. Furthermore, whenever we sit down to study a new book from the library, we take notes of the ideas that come to us as we read. Sometimes we make small copies

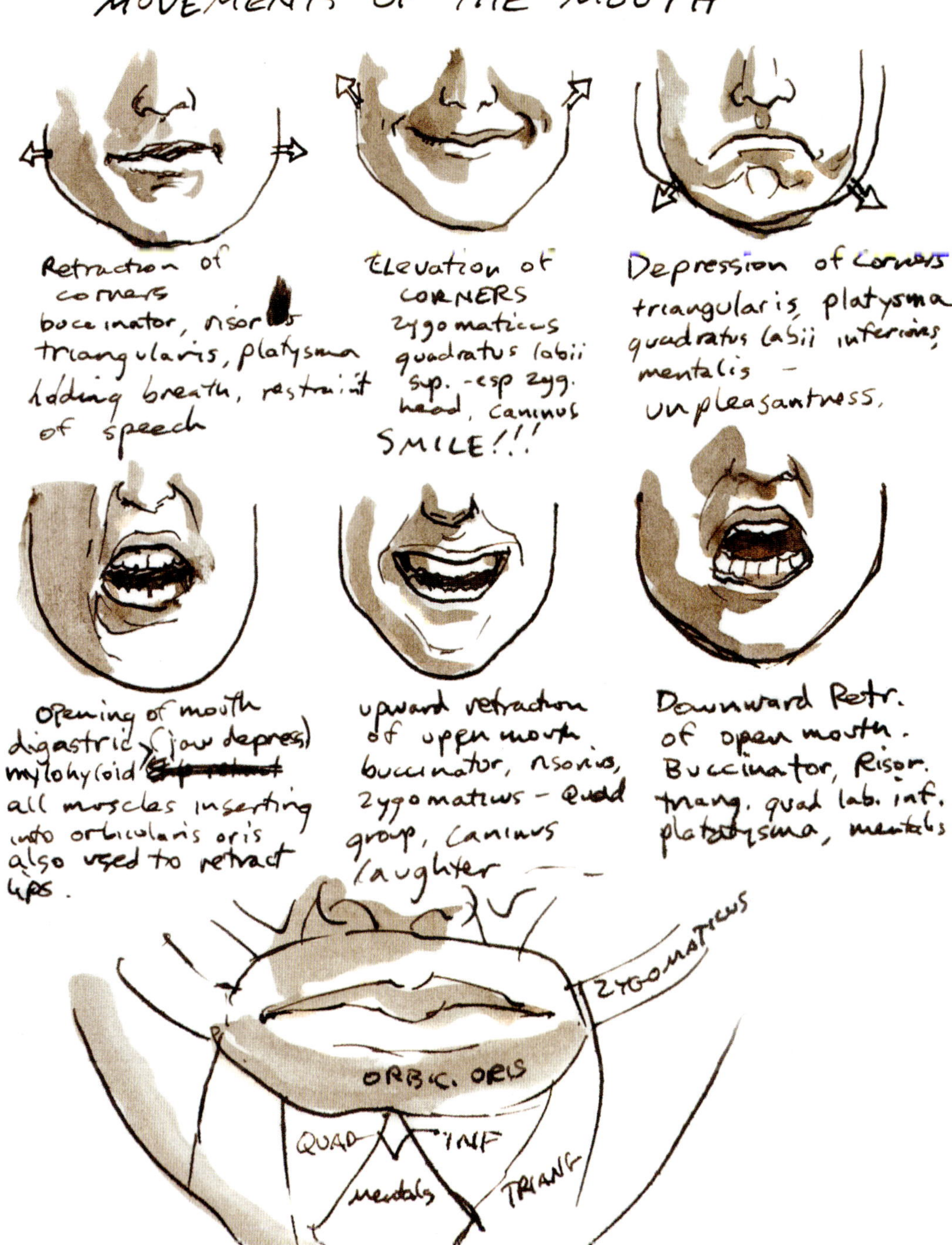

STUDY SKETCHES FROM STUDIO NOTEBOOK, *fountain pen with brown ink and wash, 8" x 10". Whenever I sit down to study from an instructional art book, I find it helpful to keep a pen and a notebook beside me to reinforce what I have learned. In this case, I was studying the facial anatomy section of Stephen Peck's* Atlas of Human Anatomy for the Artist. *But instead of copying the diagrams in the book, I propped up a mirror in front of my drawing table and used myself as a model. Looking back now on these sketches, I realize that though I have forgotten most of the names of the muscles, I remember where the muscles are and what they do, because I took part in the experience of isolating their actions. —JG*

in pencil of other artists' work in order to understand it better.

If you were to browse through our studio notebooks, you would find designs for bicycles and masks and motorized toys, thoughts about nature and the sublime, and ideas for teaching methods. In short, the studio notebook is a storehouse filled with ideas.

No matter what your interests are, you can develop a similar setup for yourself. When you read other instructional art books about anatomy, for example, take out the studio notebook and copy over some of the diagrams. If you are a professional artist, keep a running record of your commissions and assignments, and the flow of ideas that accompanied their creation.

We have a science fiction illustrator friend who says that whenever he needs new ideas for aliens or spacecraft, he glances through his notebook of sketches. Very quickly your studio notebook will become a treasured companion, willingly joining you on voyages of discovery and learning. And once it's filled, a studio notebook is as valuable as anything else you own.

The Idea Notebook. You may want to try yet another form of specialized sketchbook, the idea notebook, which you carry in the form of a 4" x 6" hardbound blank book. To make it always accessible, keep it with you in your pocket, purse, or hiker's belt pouch. What are these small books used for? Ideas—stored in the form of small notations.

As a creative person, you undoubtedly have ideas and inspirations of all sorts throughout your day. We're not necessarily talking about the big, earthshaking, lightning bolt inspirations, but rather the little ones that seem insignificant at the time—an intriguing gesture that sticks in your mind, a striking combination of colors. These can be drawn from observation or purely from your mind. Don't try to be profound—

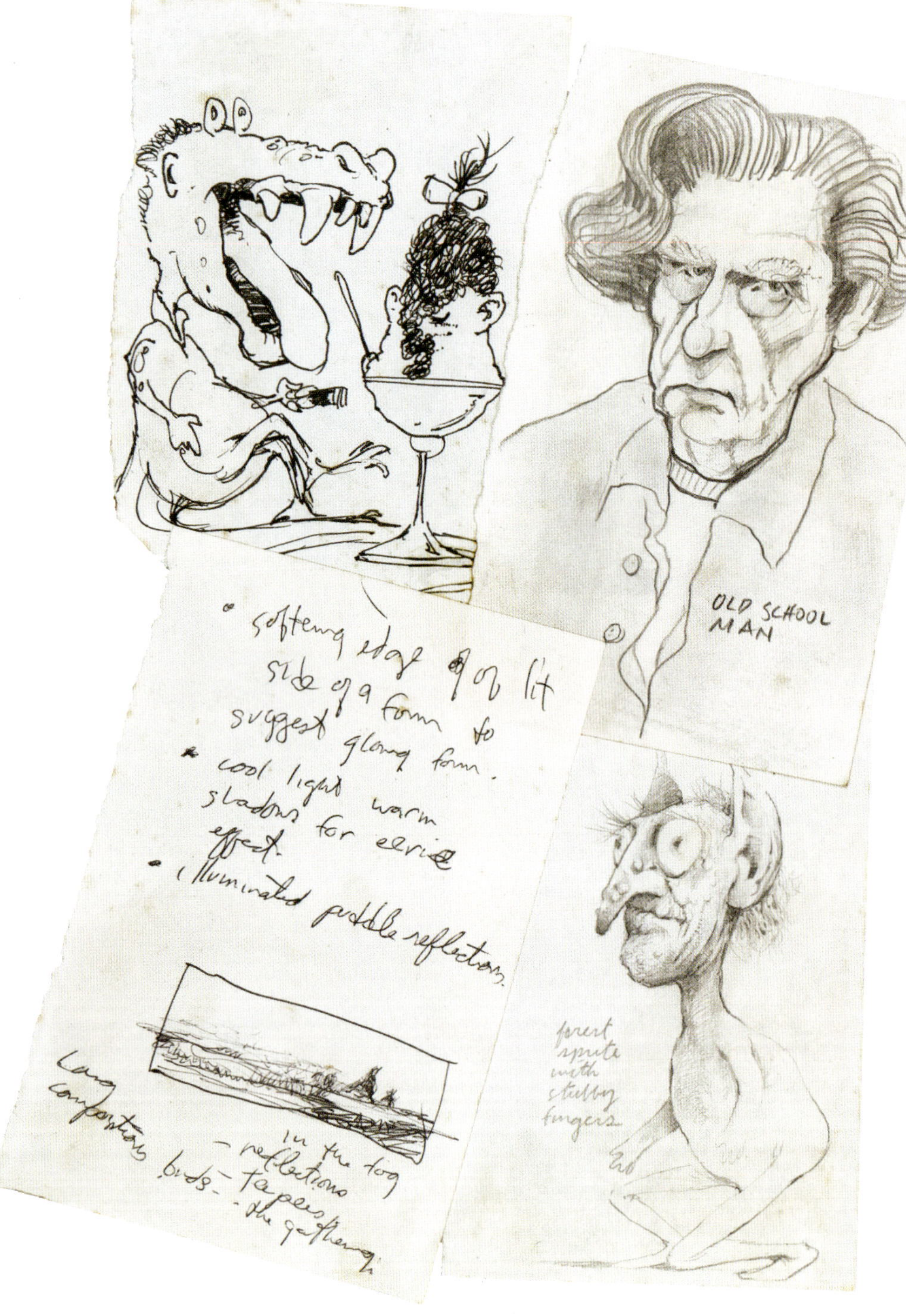

IDEA NOTEBOOK, *pencil and ballpoint pen on smooth paper, 4" x 6" each. Whenever I leave the house, I always carry the essentials: my keys, my wallet, and most importantly, my idea notebook. This 4" x 6" hardbound book fits conveniently into a belt pouch that I consistently wear. I view this rigging as "the tools of the trade" for being an artist. Whenever any small inspiration strikes me, I immediately note it down in my small book. The inspiration might be a quick sketch of someone I observe, as in the sketch in the upper right; or an idea for a future painting, as in the sketch in the lower left; or even absurd creatures doodled while with a friend, as in the sketches at upper left and lower right. In short, my idea notebook is my catchall for anything I happen to take an interest in during the day. —TK and JG*

just try to be sensitive to your ideas. Whether or not you are aware of it, your mind is constantly devising new twists on what you experience. Unfortunately, good ideas always seem to come at the most inopportune times, like when you are standing in the express line at the supermarket. Most of these ideas will go unacknowledged and undeveloped if you don't mark them down.

We have found that the best attitude to have for this kind of sketching is "Note first—analyze later." In other words, when an idea strikes you, no matter how obscure or outlandish, note it down without trying to judge its merits. Use whatever means seem appropriate to convey the idea: pictures, words, numbers, or a combination of all three. Sometimes the entry will consist of nothing more than three words that remind you of your idea. It is meant only for you to understand, so don't worry about legibility or neatness.

What kind of ideas will you note down? That depends on your personality. What interests you might not interest someone else. Our idea books are usually filled with small observational sketches, private speculations about life, and phone numbers of friends. There are no limits on what can be done with an idea book. We've found that it helps to think of idea books as a garden into which you plant seeds of every sort. We find ourselves constantly reaping a rich harvest from this small garden. Many paintings, poems, and projects have their origins in the small idea books we constantly carry.

TRAVEL SKETCHES, TIJUANA, *calligraphy pen on drawing paper, 11" x 14". In foreign countries or unfamiliar cities, I like to head out in a random direction with my travel sketchbook under my arm, collecting little snapshotlike sketches as I ramble along. By putting several little vignettes on the same page, I feel more willing to stop for ordinary scenes that I might have passed up if I were looking for a single monumental subject. The sketches on this page were done in various places of downtown Tijuana, Mexico. The boxing sign and the street-corner scene at the upper right were both sketched from a very crowded section of the sidewalk, and I quickly discovered that the people of Tijuana consider sketching a spectator sport. In the sketch of the small food stand, I used a soft dark tone behind the details of the vegetable crates and bench to tie together all the elements. This tone is made by gently scumbling the flat side of the calligraphy pen on the rough drawing paper. —JG*

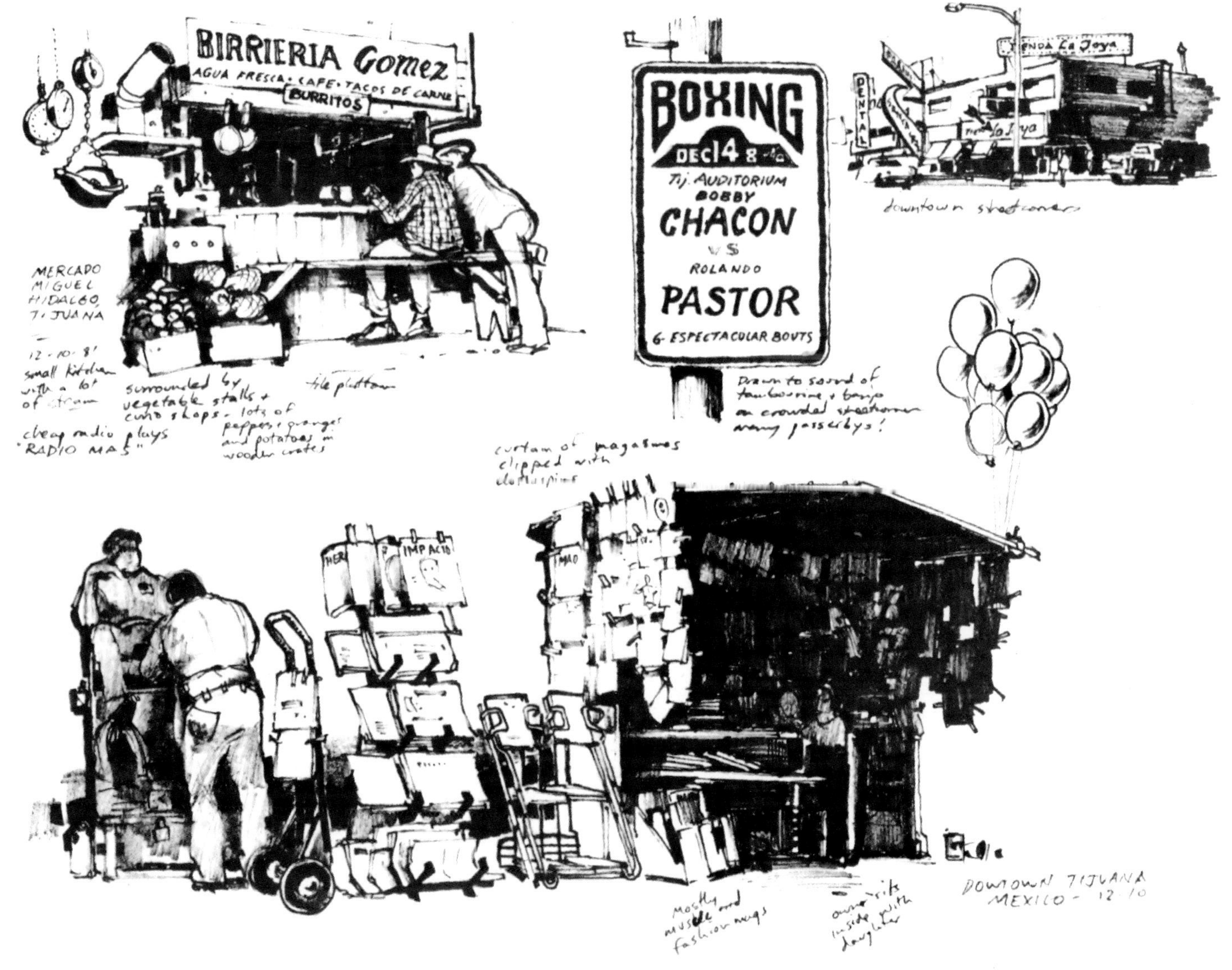

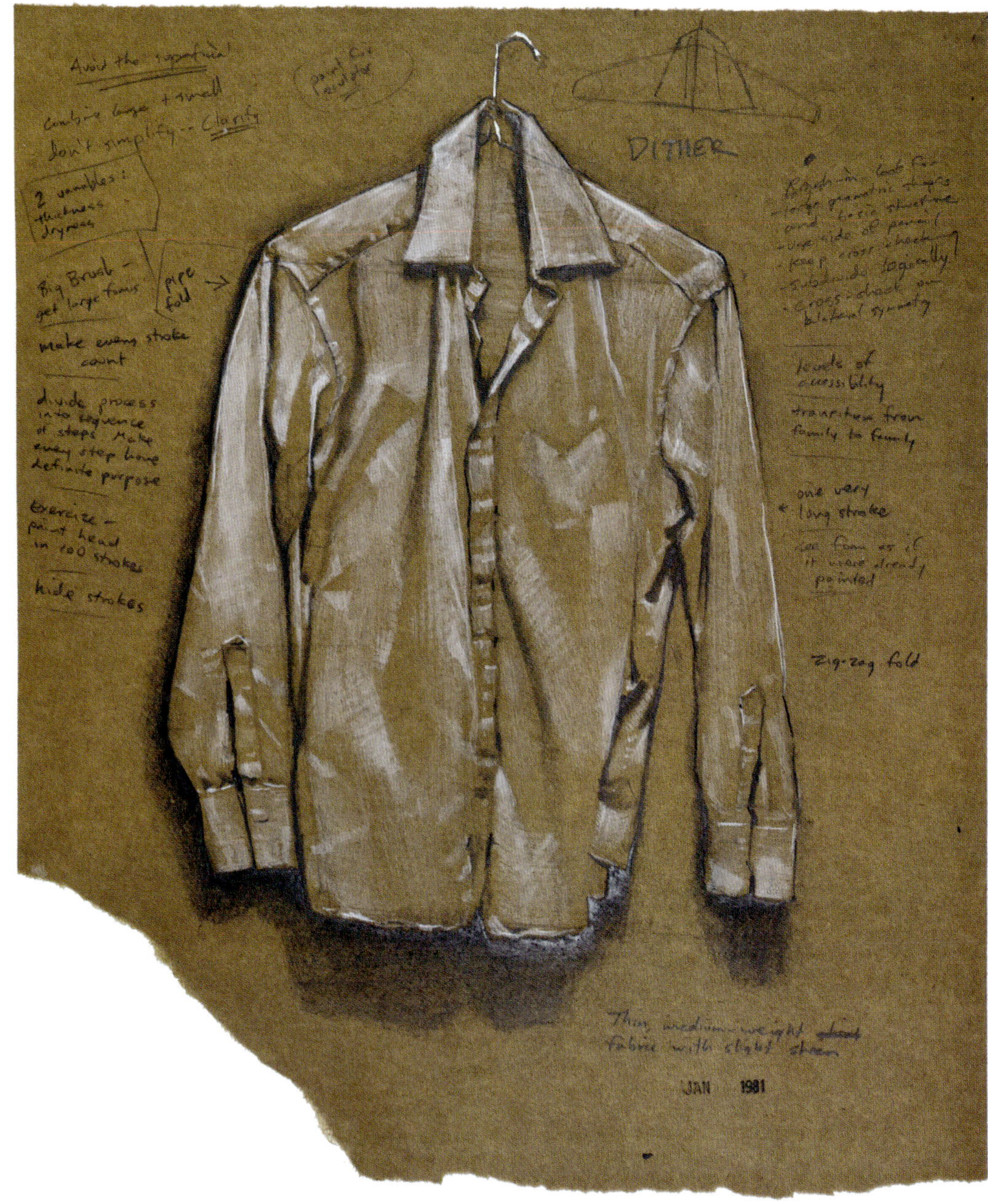

STUDY OF SHIRT, *pencil and white gouache on brown paper, 11" x 14". You can use sketching as a kind of artistic calisthenic warm-up exercise to keep you in shape. I like to keep a large brown paper sketchbook near my easel just for doing analytical still-life studies like this one. An ordinary shirt, lit by a clear light source, provided the subject for this study. As I worked, I noted down in the margins the types of folds I encountered—pipe folds and zig zag folds, for example. I was also thinking about alternating large forms with small forms and large strokes with small strokes. Some of the strokes are miniscule touches with the brush, such as along the front band, although there is one very large stroke running from the right shoulder to the cuff of the sleeve. —JG*

The Travel Sketchbook. Any time you get a chance to travel in an area that is new to you, take along a special sketchbook to record your interpretation of the unique character of that region. Every place has its postcard reputation—San Francisco with the cable cars and bridges, New Orleans with its little jazz clubs, and Maine with its fishing villages. But your sketchbook can help you cut far deeper into the characteristics of a region and go beyond the picturesque.

Here's a good way to get started with regional sketching: bring with you on your vacation a large pad of good drawing paper—about 11" x 14" or 14" x 17"—and also some calligraphy markers, or if you prefer, a fountain pen. When you come to a new area, allow yourself an afternoon to record five or six little impressions on a single page of the sketchbook. Sketch anything that interests you: street scenes, close-ups of people, copies of signs, or details of the local architecture. It's fun to vary the kinds of observations you make. You can have close-ups of small details and grand panoramas on the same page. But try to make each little sketch record a unique aspect of that particular region. The good thing about this approach is that you aren't self-consciously trying to wrap up a whole area in one composition—instead you're making a series of simple "sketch snapshots" that summarizes your experience with an area.

As you become more acquainted with the connection between sketching and traveling, your travel sketchbook can begin to reflect the very personal side of your vacation, just as a scrapbook would. Write down the names of the hotels you stayed at, and perhaps make a little caricature from memory of the desk clerk or bellhop. If you have the travel sketchbook with you at a restaurant, devote a page to a contour drawing of the table setting while you are waiting for the meal to be served. Feel free to paste things into the book. If you see a stage show and do a few sketches of the performers, save

▶ **TRAIL TO THE VALLEY,** *oil on illustration board, 16" x 22". This painting is typical of my recent landscape work. It is included along with the sketches pertaining to it in order to demonstrate the relationship between idea sketches and the final painting. —TK*

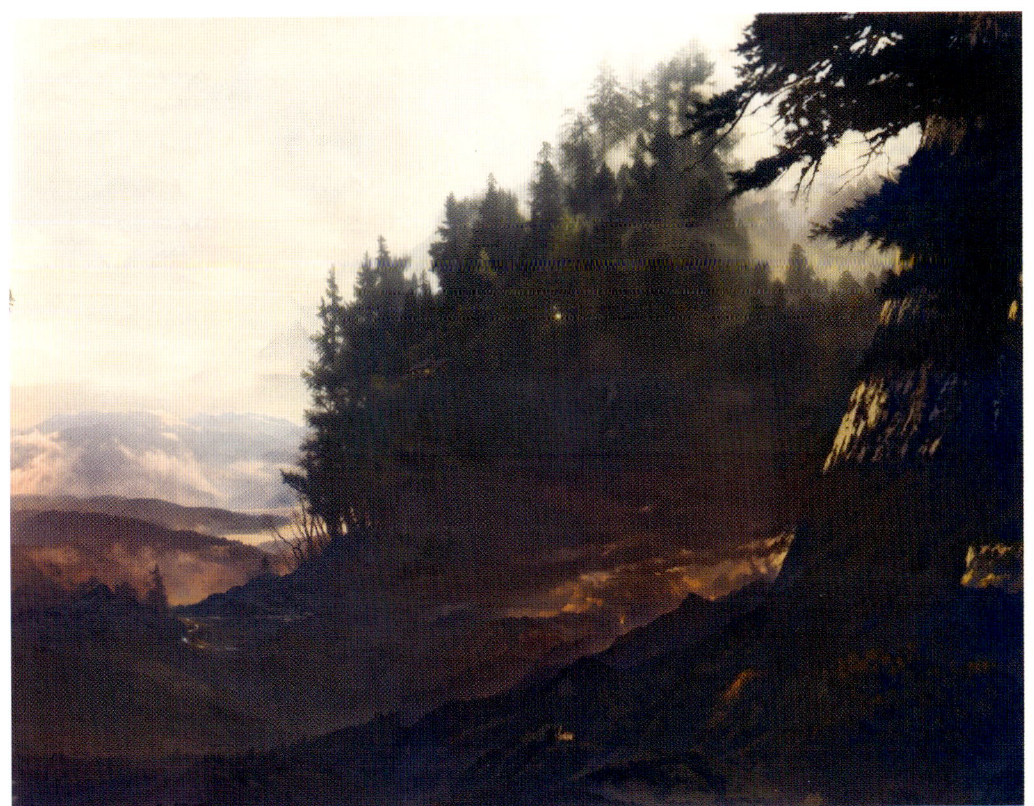

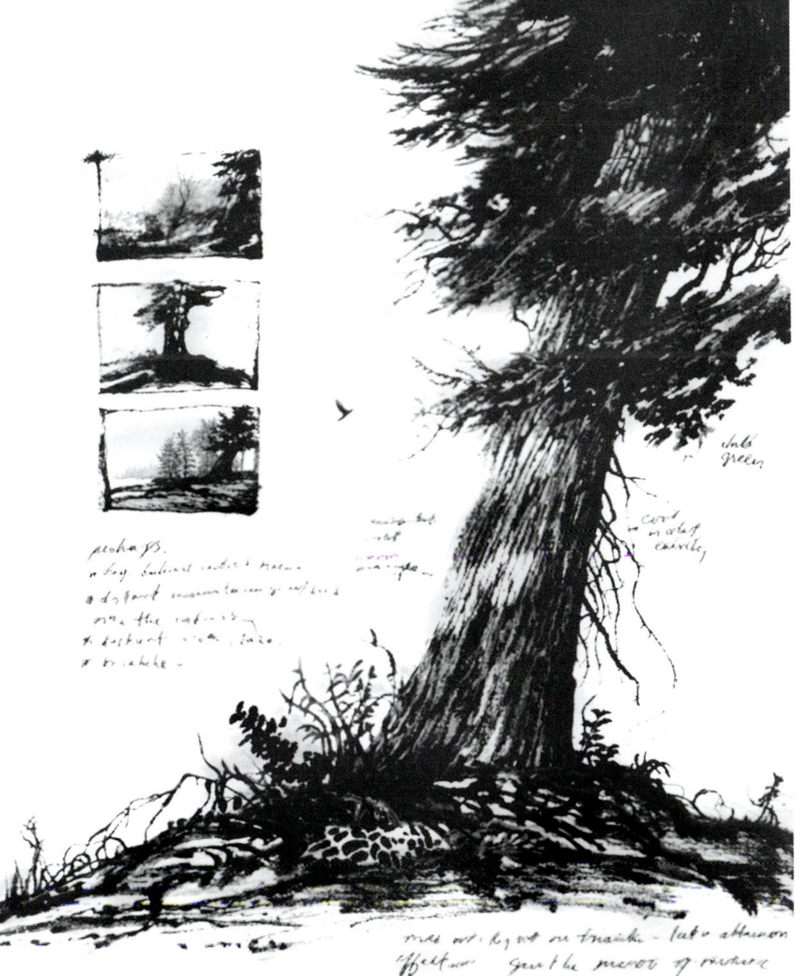

◀ **STUDY FOR TRAIL TO THE VALLEY,** *brush pen on charcoal paper, 9" x 12". Almost every painting that I do either for galleries or just for my own enjoyment has its beginnings in sketches like these. I usually work in either a 9" x 12" hardbound studio sketchbook or a 9" x 12" pad of plain white charcoal paper. I use the bound book when I do my studies in pencil, because it has a smoother tooth that is very receptive to quick pencil work. However, often, as in this sketch, I use brush pen on charcoal paper because of the crispness and detail possible. My procedure for using sketching to develop paintings is simple. I begin by making myself comfortable in my favorite chair, with nothing in my hand but my sketchbook and sketching tool. I draw a few rectangles on a fresh page in order to begin suggesting compositions. To stimulate my imagination, I often leaf through my old sketchbooks or nature magazines as a means of focusing on a particular type of scene. When I have a pretty definite idea of the type of subject I want to tackle, I set all references aside and begin filling small rectangles with ideas about composition. I also do larger detail studies of any object that is crucial to the composition, such as the tree in this case. When it comes time to work on a particular painting, the page relating to the painting is removed from the studio notebook and pinned next to my easel as I work. —TK*

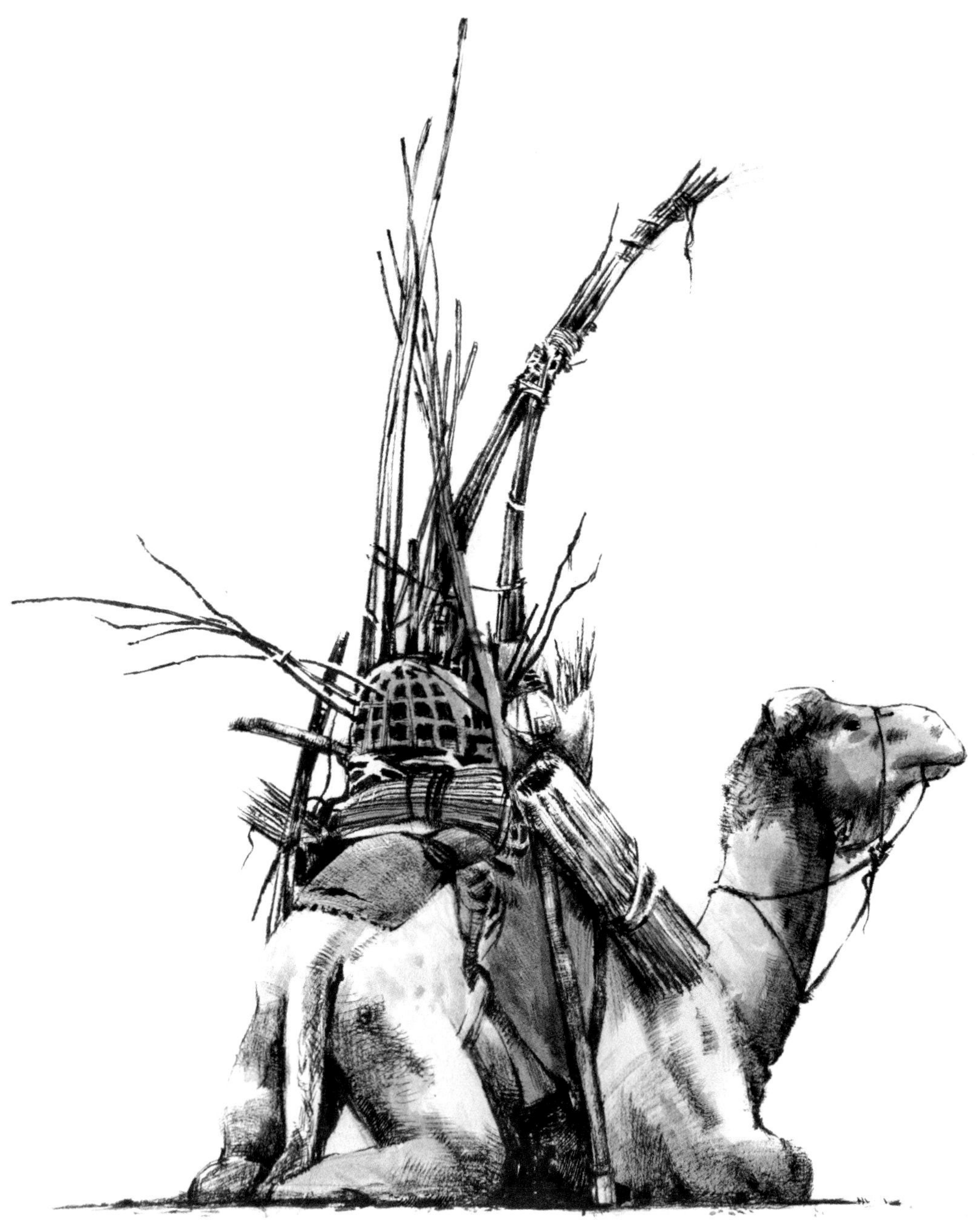

CAMEL WITH PACK, *wash on smooth paper, 8½" x 11". This camel was sketched from an exhibit at a museum. The unusual pack on the back of the camel fascinated me because of the complexity of detail. I paid close attention to the arrangement of reeds, ropes, and baskets that made up the pack, since I knew it would probably be my only chance to sketch such a subject from observation. When I returned home I filed the sketch in my reference file in a folder marked "CAMELS." If I ever need to make an illustration featuring a camel with a pack, I have my sketch to refer to. And, because my sketch is derived from firsthand experience, it is far more useful to me than any number of clipped photos. —TK*

your ticket and glue it to the same page as the sketches.

When you return home, you will have a vivid recollection of your vacation, which you can share with your friends just as you would a slide show.

DEVELOPING SKETCHES INTO PAINTINGS

How does sketching relate to the finished paintings or illustrations that you do completely in the studio? As we've suggested throughout the book, sketches can be the vital link between what you see and experience and how you express yourself in your professional work. In practical terms, that means that your sketches can be used as reference material, just as you might use a photograph. Let's say, for example, that you are working on a painting of a street scene with several figures in front of a shop window and some parked cars on the side of the composition. If you look through your sketchbooks, you may find some studies of window details, awnings, and of course figures in a wide assortment of casual, natural poses. All these can be combined and rearranged into the image you want to paint.

How to Use Sketches as Reference. Most people who work up a painting from on-the-spot sketches for the first time are surprised to discover that even a seemingly fragmentary sketch can help to recall a remarkably vivid memory of the original scene. Having once observed a scene, an artist has tucked away hundreds of impressions, many of which never even make it into the sketch.

A sketch simplifies reality, recording only the essential. Your imagination and memory fill in the rest. Remember that a sketch is actually a great asset as reference for the very fact that it does *not* record literal fact. By the time you have made a sketch, you have probably already made half of the decisions that you will need to organize a subject into a meaningful composition. While you were on the spot, you had a perfect opportunity to readjust the values or the lighting, since you were face-to-face with the real thing.

Now that you are one step removed in the studio, you may feel that more changes are needed to get the effect you want. After the fact, removed from the literal presence of the subject, you will be even freer to make changes to improve on what you have seen. However, at times you will run across a sketch that seems perfectly adaptable to a painting just as it is. If so, you can enlarge the sketch using a squared grid system or a commercial lucigraph machine.

To make your sketches most useful as reference for paintings, keep in mind that your drawings have to be translated into a full range of tones and colors. You will do yourself a favor next time you sketch if you make a special effort to think ahead to how you might use the sketch in a painting. Color notes are a big help of course, but you might also note down in the margin a few thumbnail sketches of other composition possibilities. In general, any sketches that you do on tone paper are easier to paint from at home because the rendering of both lights and darks helps to suggest the whole array of values more economically than a drawing on white paper.

Using Sketches and Photographs as Reference. Some artists work purely from sketches, while others use only photographs as reference. Either way can yield absolutely realistic results. We recommend a sensible combination of both. To say that one kind of reference is "better" than another is to misunderstand both sketching and photography. One is not a replacement for the other. As we've shown in this book, sketching provides a vehicle for closely observing your subject and for beginning the process of deciding how to translate it from three-dimensional reality to a meaningful image. A photograph merely records the scene with all its accidental details, postponing the process of observation and decision-making for later, when you return to the studio.

But keep in mind that the same principles apply when working from photographs as when working on-the-spot. In both, selectivity is necessary to go beyond the available facts into the realm of effective pictures. Never feel that the photograph is more "right" than your own instincts as an artist. If you view the photo as an absolute, you will end up being overwhelmed and it will have a bigger voice in your picture than you do.

When working from photos clipped from magazines, you can avoid this problem by developing the thumbnails for your picture first and then look for photo reference to complete your picture. Let your thumbnail guide all decisions as you develop your painting.

If you are working from a single photo, either one you have taken yourself or a clipped photo, make many thumbnails exploring ways to use the photo in your picture.

It is usually helpful to work from as many photos as possible. For example, when making a studio painting of a landscape subject, we usually pin up a number of photos around the work area that relate to the subject. If the subject is a stream, we pin up a dozen or so photos of streams. That way we can be inspired by the bank in one photo, a rock in another, a ripple in another, and a tree in another. The same applies to human and animal subjects. If you are interested in portraying an elderly gentleman character, find as many photos as possible to work from. One photo may supply the face, another the jacket, a third the trousers, and so on. As your ability to draw improves, you will find it easier to use photo reference in this pick-and-choose method.

Before going on to the final canvas, we do a number of preliminary sketches that serve to organize the reference material into a cohesive single image. These drawings are the most important aspect of working from photos, because by making drawings from your reference before starting your final painting, you allow yourself the opportunity to alter the available reference material to suit the needs of your picture.

These drawings can either be done at the exact size of the final painting and then transferred directly, or else made smaller in size and enlarged with a lucigraph machine or by the grid method.

A final word about photography. Don't feel you have to rely on photos to achieve realism in your work. With enough experience drawing from life, you can translate any sketch into a convincingly realistic painting. Furthermore, incorporating sketches into your working process will yield a personal touch that pictures made purely from photos lack.

Making a Sketch File. If you work professionally as an illustrator or a cartoonist, much of the sketching that you will do will serve as research for assignments that you are doing or that you may have yet to do in the future. A job that you take on may call for a Civil War uniform or a 1920s delivery truck or a spiral staircase. Where do you find reference material? Certainly photographs clipped from magazines and catalogs can be a big help, and most illustrators take advantage of photographic reference by filing it in folders according to subject matter. You might have folders marked: Airplanes; Animals—Domestic; Animals—Wild; Architecture; etc.

What you can do is to either create a similar file for sketches alone, or else mix in sketches with photographs. Once you have sketched regularly for a period of years, you will have accumulated literally thousands of images covering a huge range of subject matter, and almost any assignment you get can draw upon actual observation that you have done. It seems

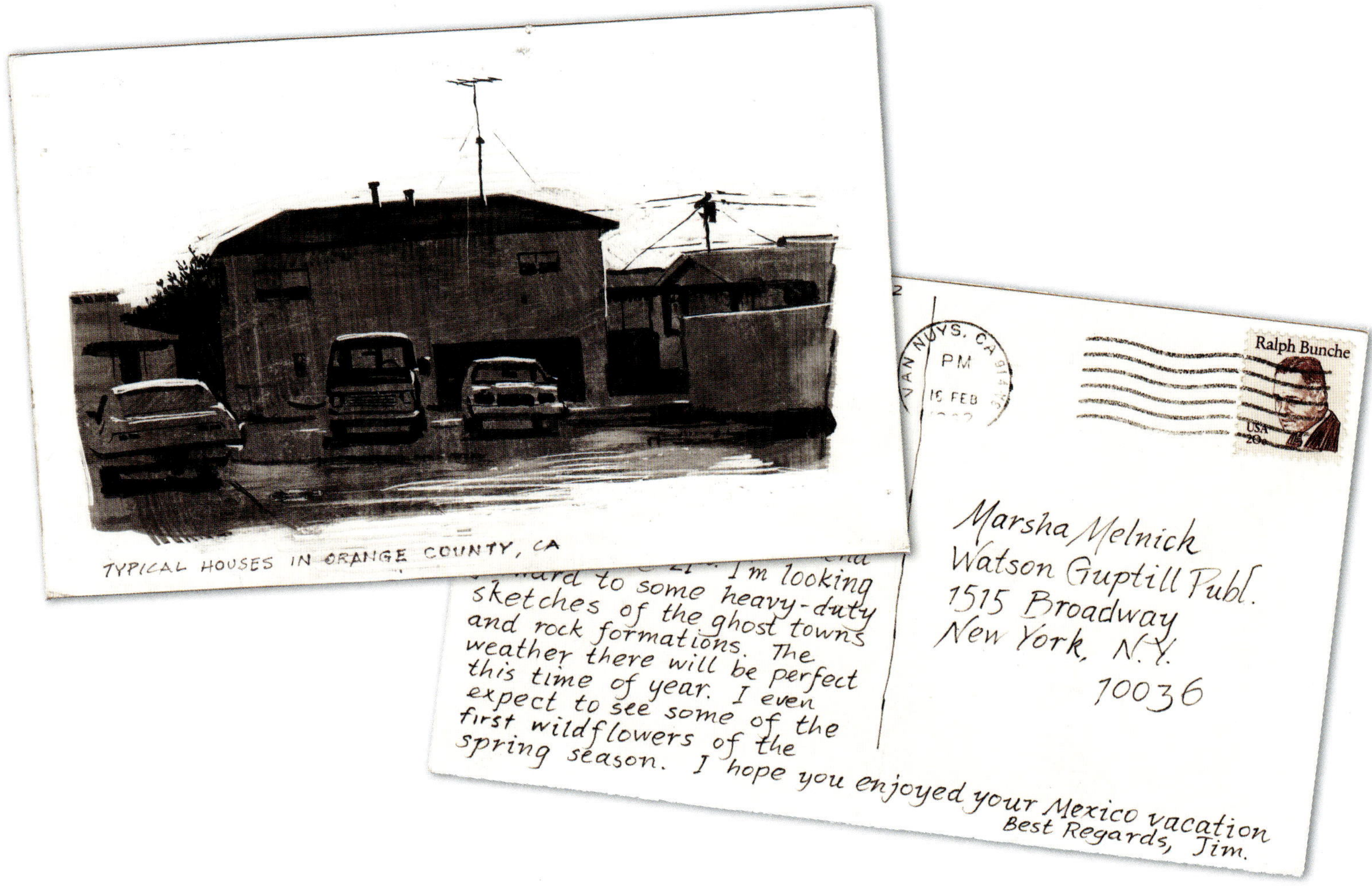

TRAVEL POSTCARD, *brush and ink on scratchboard, 4½" x 7". Some of the smaller sketches that I have accumulated from various sojourns away from home make perfect images for postcards. I especially enjoy using very ordinary, everyday subject matter in my postcards, rather than the picturesque scenes that are commercially available. Usually I will use a standard blank postcard, purchased from the post office. In this case I just made a sketch into a postcard after the fact. The surface is scratchboard, a smooth surface with a special coating that allows white lines to be cut through areas of dark. The forms are stated in just three values—white, black, and a dark gray. —JG*

as though every sketch somehow makes its way into an illustration at some point. The work that you do in museums and foreign countries will extend your range so broadly that art directors can count on you to be incredibly versatile in what you can draw or paint.

SHARING SKETCHES WITH OTHERS

You can use sketching as a way of benefiting not only yourself, but also those around you. Here are a few of the ways that we often use to let others in on the joy of sketching:

Illustrated Letters. We often use small and cartoonlike sketches in our letters as a means of adding interest. It takes only a moment or two to draw, but nothing prevents you from spending a few more minutes to make a more finished drawing in your letter. If you want to get even a little more elaborate, you can add some washes of watercolor or pastel or markers to give a note of color to the letter. Anything goes—the point is to have fun and enliven your page.

Try making the illustration the keynote to the content of the letter. We have a friend whose mother loves to tell about the latest antics of her two pet cats. Though she is not an artist, she enjoys beginning each letter with a small doodle illustrating the latest hiding place or acrobatic maneuver of her cats. This makes her written descriptions much more vivid as well as giving her a starting place for leading into other news. When you want to relate a sketch to the written content of the letter, it is best to draw right on the same page.

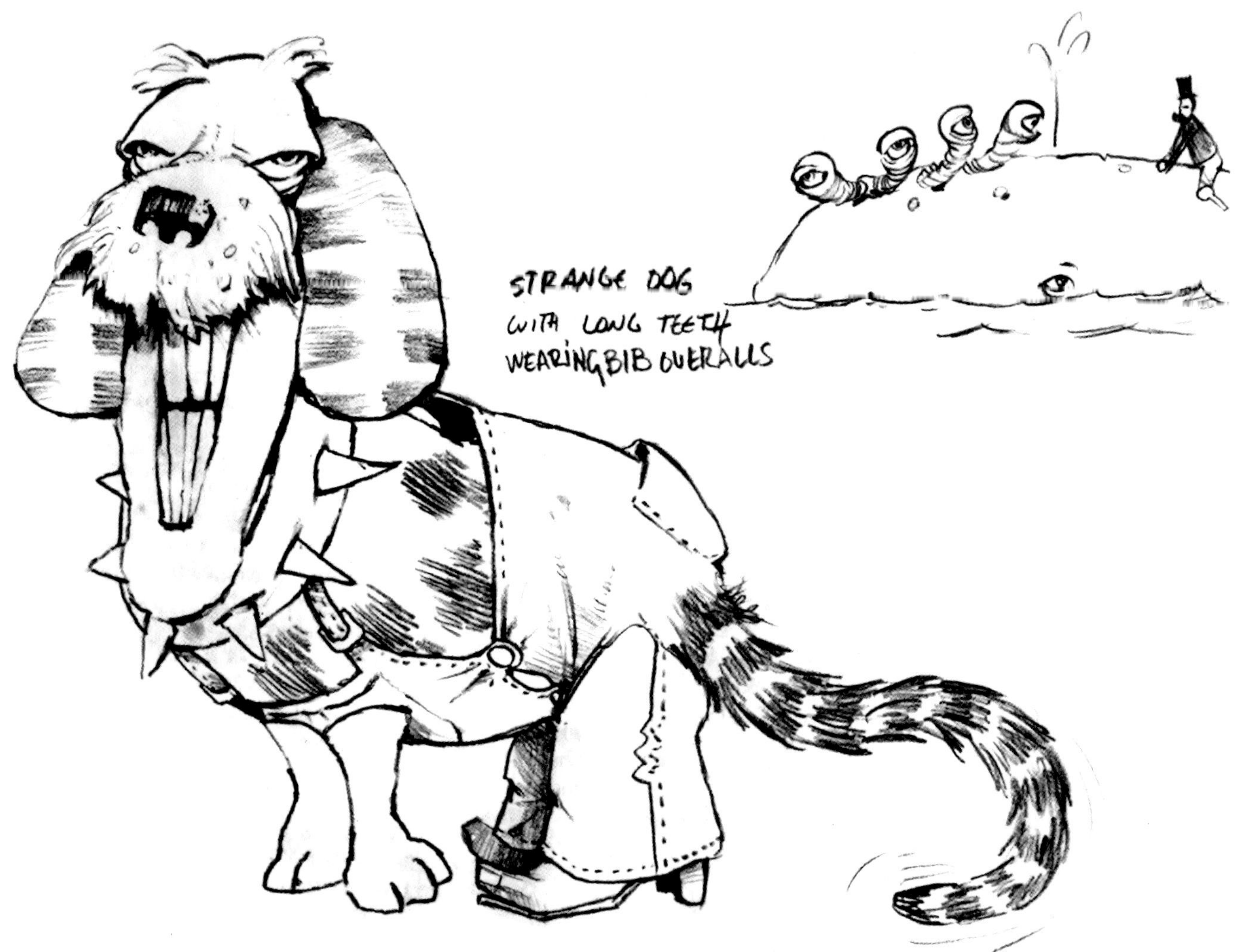

STRANGE DOG WITH LONG TEETH WEARING BIB OVERALLS, *pencil on sketch paper, 9" x 12". Art by committee produces curious results. This sketch was created in collaboration with a group of animators who joined me for lunch. One person drew the eyes, nose, and whiskers. He then passed it on to the next person, who spontaneously drew in the mouth and the spiky collar. A third person indicated the ears and tail, leaving the fourth person to come up with the wonderful idea of the overalls and boots. It's great fun to be passed a half-finished drawing by someone else and use their ideas as a springboard for your own. —JG*

If you want to type the letter first, allow a few blocks of empty space to be filled in later with a sketch. The finished letter will have a handsome, engaging appearance that will be as fun to read as it was to write. If you want to spend some extra time and make a really careful sketch to send to your friend, do so on a separate page. Your friend then owns an original picture that he or she can clip on the outside of the refrigerator or perhaps even protect in a picture frame. We have more than once visited people to whom we had sent sketches and been flattered to find the sketch behind glass and hanging on the wall in their home. Do you need ideas for what to sketch? Simple—just look through some of your recent sketchbooks and make a copy of a sketch that you think might have special meaning to your friend. Copying the sketch not only has the advantage of allowing you to keep your own originals, but it also gives you, as an artist, the benefit of reinterpreting and improving upon your first impression of the subject. Like a good ghost story, a sketch will get better with each retelling.

As an alternative, you can make inexpensive photocopies of your best black-and-white sketches to use as stationery. If you make enough copies at one time, you will have plenty of pictures to choose from when you sit down to write a letter. Remember to select sketches that have some reference to your personal life, to give them more meaning in the context of a personal letter.

Travel Postcards. When you travel, carry along a bundle of blank postcards, which can be purchased inexpensively at any post office. These can become your travel postcards in place of the commercial scenic postcards, which lack handmade charm. Use the back side for the sketch, which you can do from life or copy from your sketchbook, and then write your message on the reverse side. Using a calligraphy marker or a ballpoint pen, you can make a quick drawing that won't be damaged or smudged in the mail. Whenever we travel, we make a point of spending an evening now and then making postcards in coffee shops.

Sketching Games. Next time you are at a restaurant with friends, draw an unusual head from your imagination. Pass the sketchbook to the person next to you and say, "Would you mind giving this person a body?" More often than not, you will arouse the imagination of your friend, who will eagerly continue the sketch, following the daring example that you set. Creativity will build as the sketch is passed around, and soon you will have a number of interesting and humorous sketches to serve as your memory of the evening.

Any time a group of friends gathers around a table is your opportunity to initiate a sketching game. A recent dinner party of ours featured a huge stack of paper and a bucket full of pencils. Everyone grabbed a few sheets of paper and a pencil and began. We gave out suggestions for the group—easy things: "Everyone draw a person wearing a strange hat" or "Draw your favorite gym teacher." The latter is particularly effective because it suggests vivid memories to most people which they then translate humorously on paper. Once we got the momentum going, people were coming up with suggestions for sketching games that we had never anticipated. In one game we began by inventing a simple limerick and passing it on to the next person to illustrate. In another we had one person suggest four arbitrary adjectives, such as gnarled, gruesome, giddy, and overstuffed, which we then used as inspiration for four character faces.

You can probably come up with even wilder ideas for sketching games with your friends. To keep everyone involved, take turns coming up with the suggestions. You'll find that the product of the group creative mind will far surpass the imagination of any single individual, and yet, will clearly reflect the input of each individual.

SKETCHING ALONE OR WITH OTHERS

Having read through this book and seen the range of exciting options open to you through sketching, the next step for you to take is to think about what types of sketching you want to experiment with, given the time you can realistically take from your other pursuits. Many of the sketches that you will do will be spontaneous, taking place on a whim. But you can't always rely on spontaneity to motivate you to sketch as much as you'd like to. It often helps to plan ahead and make a definite commitment to a time for sketching each week.

A good way to do this is to organize a sketch group from your friends or art school classmates. Together you can decide on a schedule of sketching outings that accommodates everyone's needs and interests. Five or six people make an ideal number for a sketching group; it's easily manageable, and if one or two people don't show up one week, you still have a large enough group. We recommend going to places that guarantee plenty of good subject matter—such as the botanical gardens, the zoo, a boatyard, or a farm. Having a group of people all pursuing similar problems as yourself provides a network of support and encouragement that can make the sketching process much more enjoyable.

Sketching with just a single friend has its own special rewards. If your friend is also an artist, you can make informal plans each Saturday for lunch on the town and an afternoon of sketching. With just two people, you can get into the public scene of sidewalks and restaurants more comfortably than you could with a group. People-sketching with a companion is especially exciting, because you can share your observations and compare your different interpretations of the same character.

However, at times, all of us need to be alone, and sketching is a perfect vehicle for doing so. It is relaxing, meditative, and requires you to concentrate very deeply on what you see. Sketching may be one of the few excuses you have to leave behind all the worries of home or work or relationships. Being alone allows you to be freer in your choices of places to sketch, as well as allowing you to explore the subject at your own pace. Sometimes you will use sketching just to escape and relax; other times you will want to use it to challenge yourself and concentrate.

Whether you sketch alone or with others, just remember that the opportunity to sketch is always there, but only when you set your mind to sketching will it actually happen. If you are like virtually every other artist we've met, you can be sure that once you make that commitment, sketching will become a self-sustaining habit that will enliven your life and the lives of others around you.

Summing Up

THE WORD *SKETCHING*, we hope, has a different sound to your ear now than it did when you first picked up this book. Sure, it can mean the carefree scribbling that we all do during our idle moments. But it also can be a deeply involving way to experience life, one that calls upon every resource that you have to offer, from your ability to be patient and observant when studying nature to your ability to disregard the facts and draw from your imagination. Contradictions? Certainly. But that's what keeps all of us alive as artists, the pull that we feel from so many different directions when we sit down face-to-face with life.

And yet, beyond all the variety of styles and approaches to sketching that we've shown you in this book, we want to stress some of the recurring themes that apply universally to everything you do. For example, the idea of enjoyment: what makes sketching, or any kind of art for that matter, enjoyable? We have always worked from the assumption that an artist is happiest when he or she is completely immersed in a new challenge and when that experience leads to rapid improvements in competence. It's at the opposite end of the spectrum from boredom, which comes from the feeling of being in a rut and repeating the same safe methods time after time. If anything, enjoyment is more closely tied in with the feeling that you have stretched yourself just a little beyond your limitations. This attitude is just as important to the people who make sketching a hobby as it is for the professional artist who makes it a big part of his life. If you stretch your limits as an artist now and then, be assured that you are experiencing growth. Your enjoyment will then be guaranteed by the rapid improvements you will make.

Another thing that comes through in every chapter of this book is the vital importance of direct contact. The best way to understand a plant or a machine or a human being is to look with your own eyes and record your observation with your own hand. And there is no substitute for sketching when it comes to recording the outside world. But sketching also gives you direct contact with another world—that of your own inner self, your emotions, your imagination, your personal experiences, and your relationships with those you love. When we wrote this book, we decided from the start that these seemingly nebulous areas of art making deserve every bit as much attention, with just as much practical advice as any of the other topics.

And even though this book has given you a lot of useful methods and techniques, the bottom line is that you are on your own when you begin to sketch. There are hundreds of approaches that could be taken; we offer only a few to get you well on your way. Friends of ours, using our ideas as their starting point, have taken sketching all the way from the weeds on the back doorstep to the jungles of Malaysia, and we expect that if one of you ever packs a suitcase for a spaceflight, your sketchbook will be tucked in there.

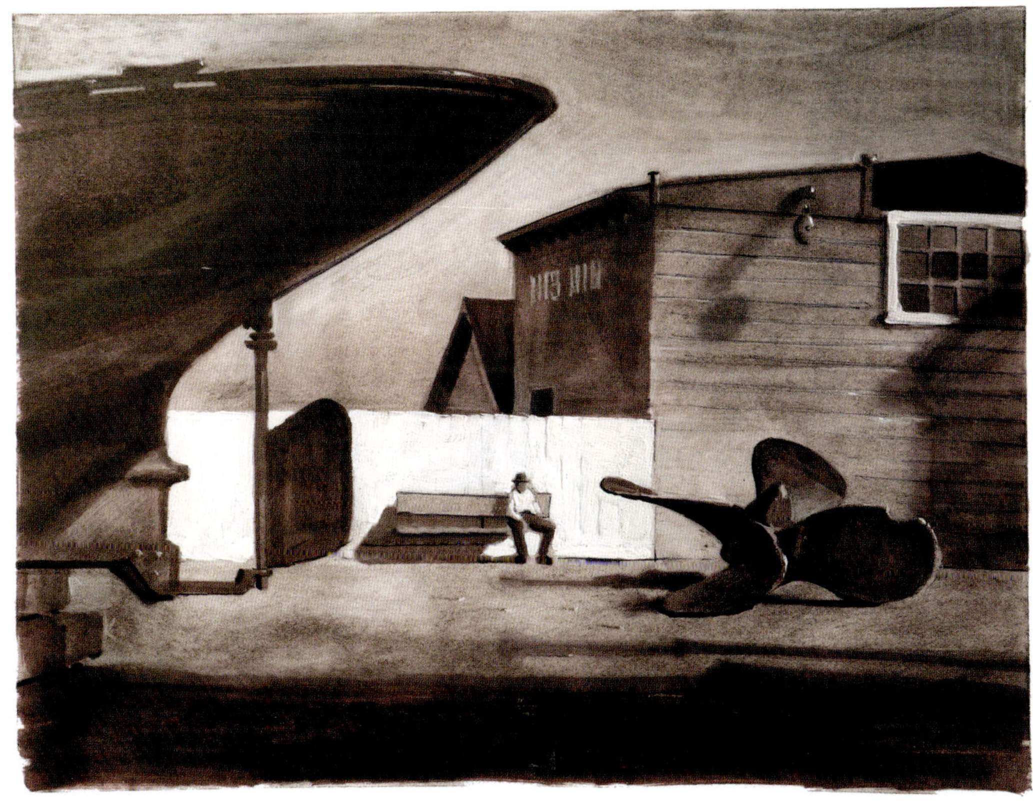

PROPELLER, *charcoal, markers, and gouache, 9" x 12". This boatyard offered all the raw materials I needed to create an almost abstract composition, where surreal juxtapositions create a strange mood. —JG*

Bibliography

Baskett, John. *Constable Oil Sketches*. New York: Watson-Guptill Publications, 1966.

Borgman, Harry. *Landscape Painting with Markers*. New York: Watson Guptill Publications, 1977.

Bridgman, George B. *Bridgman's Complete Guide to Drawing from Life*. New York: Weathervane Books, 1952.

Calderon, Frank W. *Animal Painting and Anatomy*. New York: Dover Publications, Inc., 1975.

Carlson, John F. *Elementary Principles of Landscape Painting*. New York: Bridgman Publishers Inc., 1929.

Edwards, Betty. *Drawing on the Right Side of the Brain*. Los Angeles: J. P. Tarcher, 1979.

Guptill, Arthur L. *Freehand Drawing Self-Taught*. New York: Watson Guptill Publications, 1933.

———. *Rendering in Pen and Ink*. New York: Watson-Guptill Publications, 1976.

Henri, Robert. *The Art Spirit*. Philadelphia: J. B. Lippincott Company, 1960.

Hill, Adrian. *Sketching and Painting Out-of-Doors*. London: Blandford Press, 1961.

Hogarth, Paul. *Creative Pencil Drawing*. New York: Watson-Guptill Publications, 1964.

Kautzky, Theodore. *Pencil Broadsides*. New York: Reinhold Publishing Corporation, 1940.

Kley, Heinrich. *The Drawings of Heinrich Kley*. New York: Dover Publications, Inc., 1961.

Leslie, Clare Walker. *Nature Drawing: A Tool for Learning*. New Jersey: Prentice Hall, Inc., 1980.

Loomis, Andrew. *Creative Illustration*. New York: Bonanza Books, 1947.

Meglin, Nick. *The Art of Humorous Illustration*. New York: Watson-Guptill Publications, 1973.

———. *On-The-Spot Drawing*. New York: Watson- Guptill Publications, 1976.

Peck, Stephen Rogers. *Atlas of Human Anatomy for the Artist*. New York: Oxford University Press, 1951.

Searle, Ronald and Webb, Kaye. *Paris Sketchbook*. New York: George Braziller, Inc., 1958.

Stebbins, Theodore E. *American Master Drawings and Watercolors*. New York: Harper and Row, 1976.

———. Close Observation: *Selected Oil Sketches by Frederick E. Church*. Washington, DC: Smithsonian Institution Press, 1978.

Vernam, Roger. *Drawing People for Fun*. New York: Harper & Brothers Publishers, 1943.

Watson, Ernest W. *Course in Pencil Sketching*. New York: Van Nostrand Reinhold Company, 1964.

Wilkinson, Gerald. *Turner's Early Sketchbooks*. New York: Watson-Guptill Publications, 1972.

Wyeth, Andrew. *Dry Brush and Pencil Drawings*. Greenwich, CT: New York Graphic Society Ltd., 1963.

Index

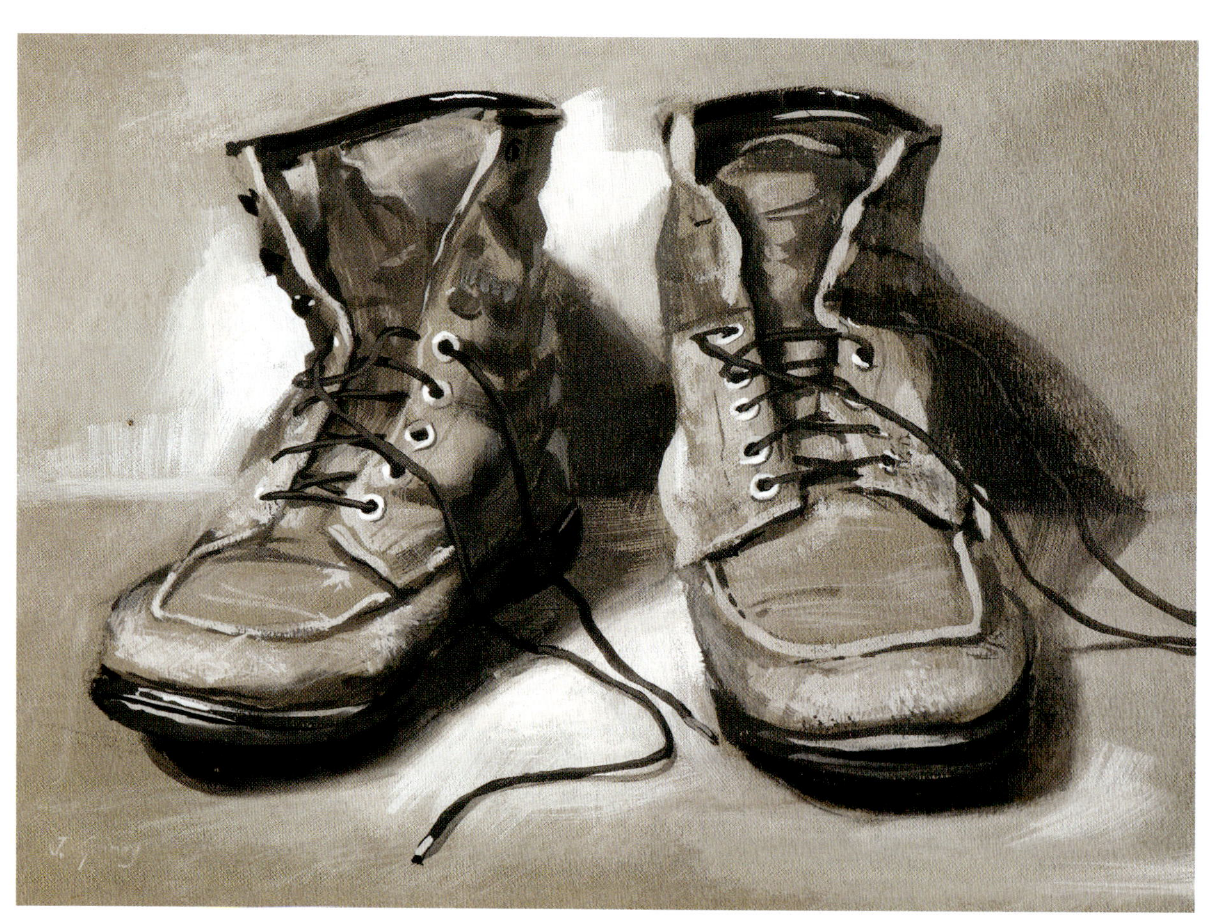